Ranma 1/2

VOL. 21
Action Edition

Story and Art by
RUMIKO TAKAHASHI

English Adaptation/Gerard Jones
Translation/Kaori Inoue
Touch-Up Art & Lettering/Wayne Truman
Cover and Interior Design & Graphics/Yuki Ameda
Editor (1st Edition)/Julie Davis
Editor (Action Edition)/Urian Brown

Managing Editor/Annette Roman
Director of Production/Noboru Watanabe
VP of Publishing/Alvin Lu
Sr. Director of Acquisitions/Rika Inouye
VP of Sales and Marketing/Liza Coppola
Publisher/Hyoe Narita

Printed in Canada.

Published by VIZ Media, LLC
P.O. Box 77010
San Francisco, CA 94107

1st Edition Published 2003

Action Edition
10 9 8 7 6 5 4 3 2 1
First Printing, October 2005

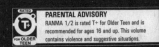

PARENTAL ADVISORY
RANMA 1/2 is rated T+ for Older Teen and is
recommended for ages 16 and up. This volume
contains violence and suggestive situations.

www.viz.com

Ranma ½

VOL. 21   Action Edition

STORY & ART BY
RUMIKO TAKAHASHI

STORY THUS FAR

The Tendos are an average, run-of-the-mill Japanese family—on the surface, that is. Soun Tendo is the owner and proprietor of the Tendo Dojo, where "Anything Goes Martial Arts" is practiced. Like the name says, anything goes, and usually does.

When Soun's old friend Genma Saotome comes to visit, Soun's three lovely young daughters—Akane, Nabiki and Kasumi—are told that it's time for one of them to become the fiancée of Genma's teenage son, as per an agreement made between the two fathers years ago. Youngest daughter Akane—who says she hates boys—is quickly nominated for bridal duty by her sisters.

Unfortunately, Ranma and his father have suffered a strange accident. While training in China, both plunged into one of many "cursed" springs at the legendary martial arts training ground of Jusenkyo. These springs transform the unlucky dunkee into whomever—or whatever—drowned there hundreds of years ago.

From then on, a splash of cold water turns Ranma's father into a giant panda, and Ranma becomes a beautiful, busty young woman. Hot water reverses the effect...but only until next time. As it turns out, Ranma and Genma aren't the only ones who have taken the Jusenkyo plunge—and it isn't long before they meet several other members of the Jusenkyo "cursed."

Although their parents are still determined to see Ranma and Akane marry and assume ownership of the training hall, Ranma seems to have a strange talent for accumulating surplus fiancées...and Akane has a few stubbornly determined suitors of her own. Will the two ever work out their differences and get rid of all these "extra" people, or will they just call the whole thing off? What's a half-boy, half-girl (not to mention all-girl, *angry* girl) to do...?

CAST OF CHARACTERS

THE SAOTOMES

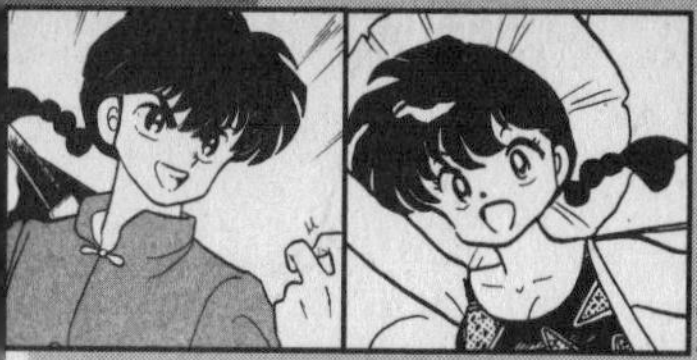

RANMA SAOTOME
Martial artist with far too many fiancées, and an ego that won't let him take defeat. Changes into a girl when splashed with cold water.

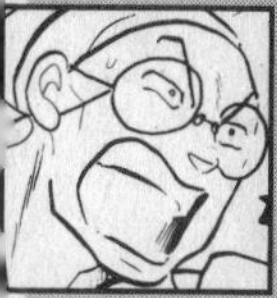

GENMA SAOTOME
Genma's father. Changes into a roly-poly, sign-talkin' panda when wet.

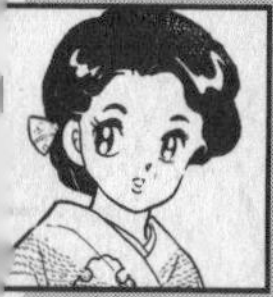

NODOKA SAOTOME
Genma's oh-so-traditional wife and Ranma's oh-so-deadly mom, Nodoka has taken an oath to eliminate *both* her dearly beloveds should her boy grow up to be less than manly. Um....

THE MASTER

HAPPOSAI and COLOGNE
One's a pint-sized pervert and the other's the pint-sized proprietor of the Cat Cafe. Your guess as to who's who.

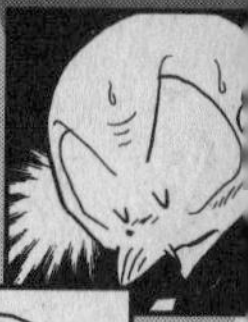

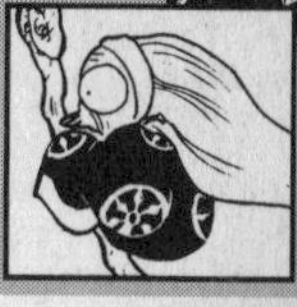

THE TENDOS

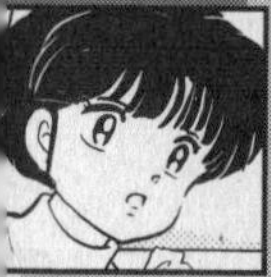

AKANE TENDO
Martial artist, tomboy, and Ranma's reluctant fiancée. Still totally in the dark about the "Ryoga/P-chan" thing.

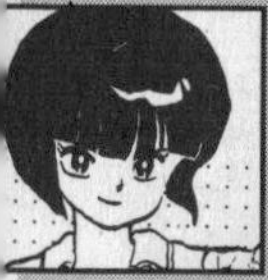

NABIKI TENDO
Middle Tendo daughter. Nothing comes close to her love of money.

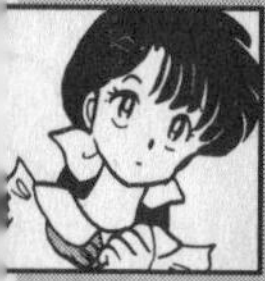

KASUMI TENDO
Eldest Tendo daughter who's the sweet-natured, stay-at-home type.

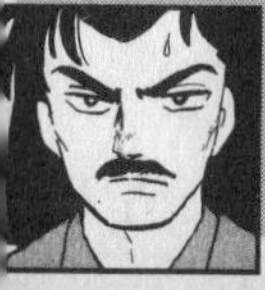

SOUN TENDO
Tendo family patriarch and former Happosai disciple. Easily excitable.

THE SUITORS

SHAMPOO
Chinese-Amazon great-granddaughter to Cologne. Has come all the way from China to either kill Ranma...or marry him.

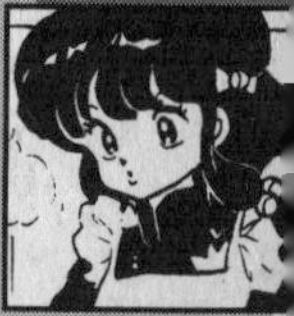

MOUSSE
Myopic master of hidden weapons. Continually thwarted (however inadvertently) in his pursuit of Shampoo by Ranma.

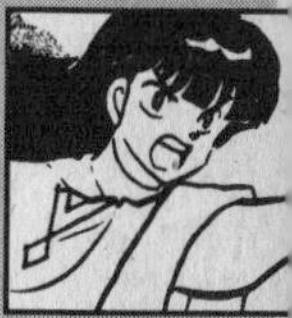

UKYO KUONJI
Spatula-wielding, childhood-betrothed, would-be sweetheart of Ranma's.

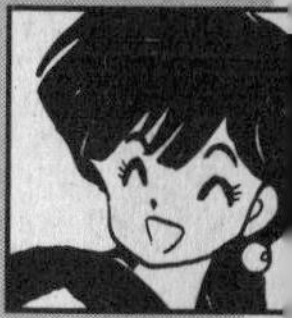

AND IN THIS CORNER...

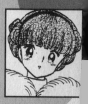

MARIKO KONJO
Cheerleading champion of Seishun ("Seisyun") High who, heaven knows why, falls in love with Kuno and enters a "cheer-off" against Ranma to prove it.

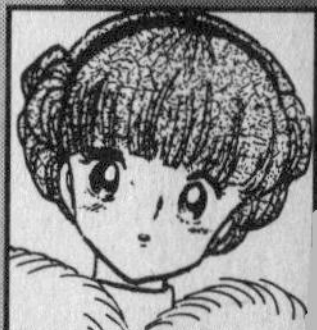

CONTENTS

Part 1

PANTYHOSE TARO RETURNS!

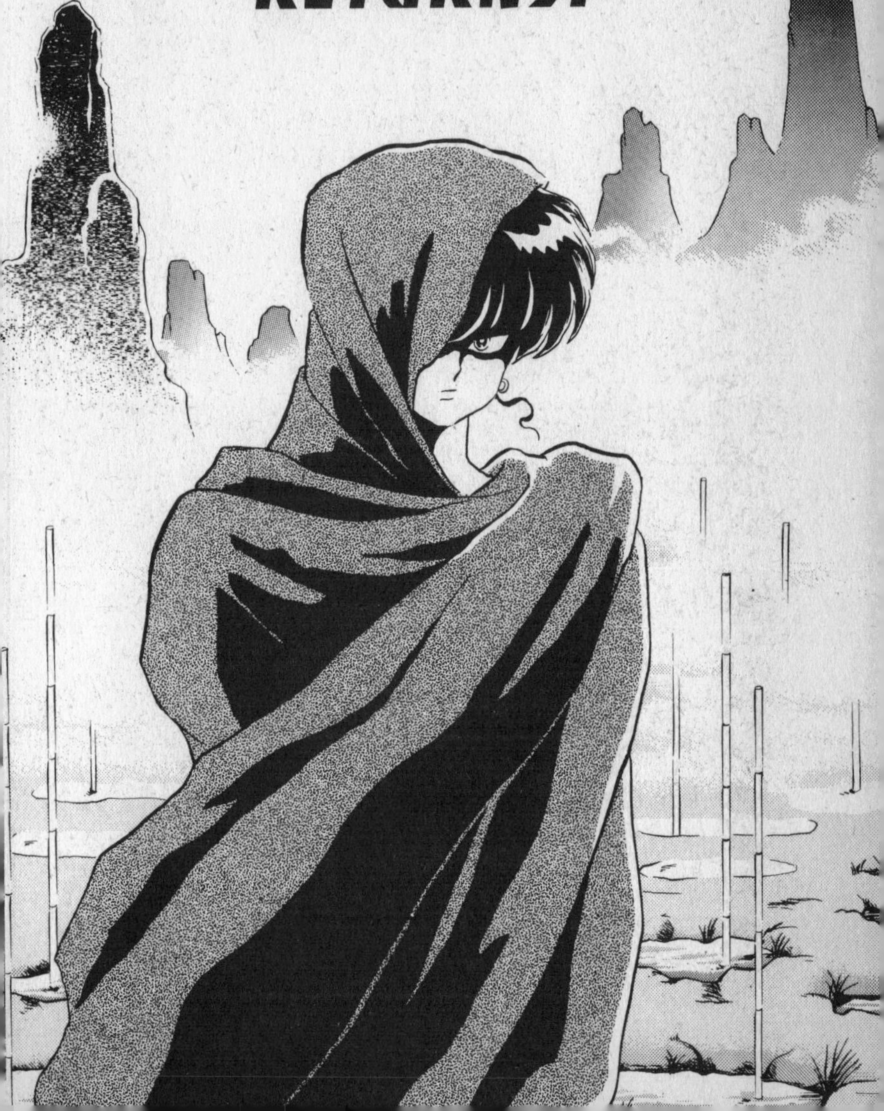

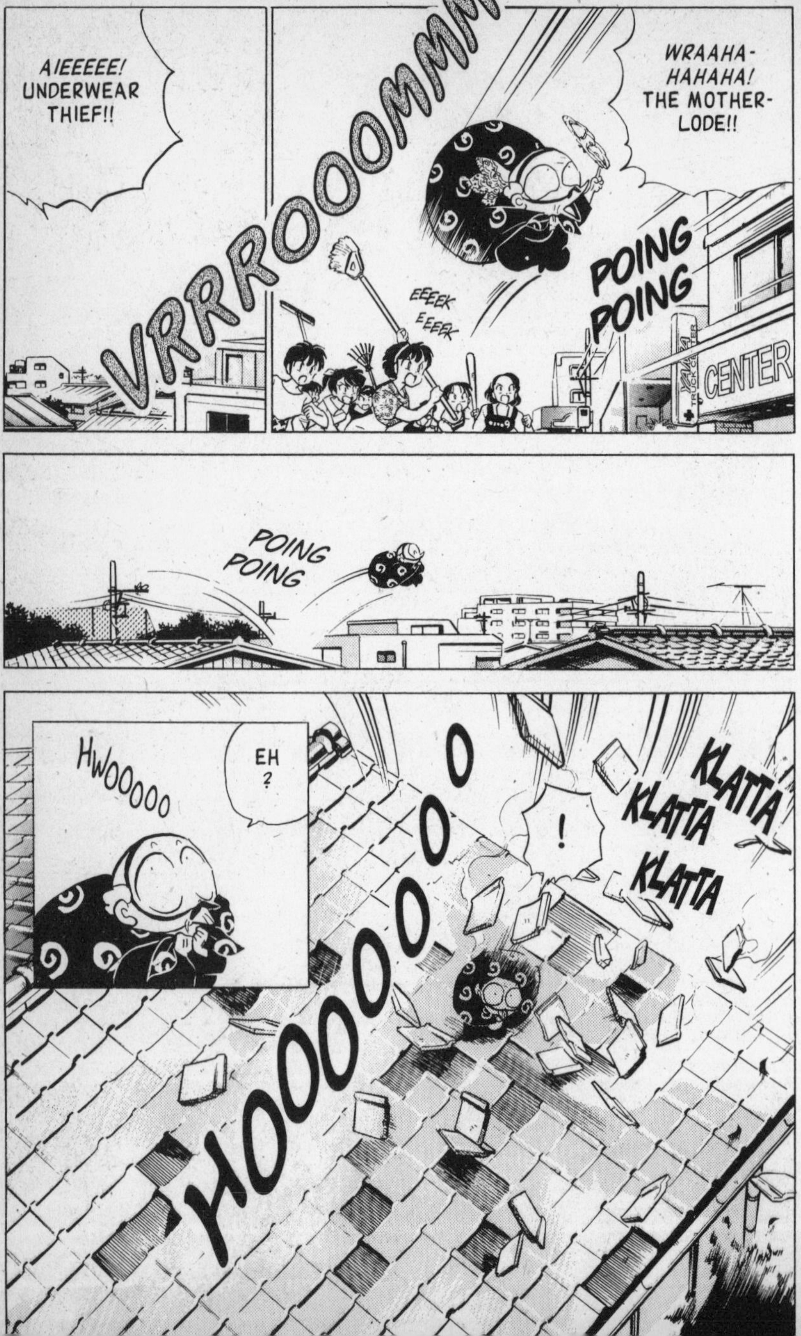
AIEEEEE! UNDERWEAR THIEF!!
VRRROOOMMM
WRAAHA-HAHAHA! THE MOTHER-LODE!!
EEEEK EEEEK
POING POING
CENTER
POING POING
HWOOOOO
EH?
HOOOOOOOO
!
KLATTA KLATTA KLATTA

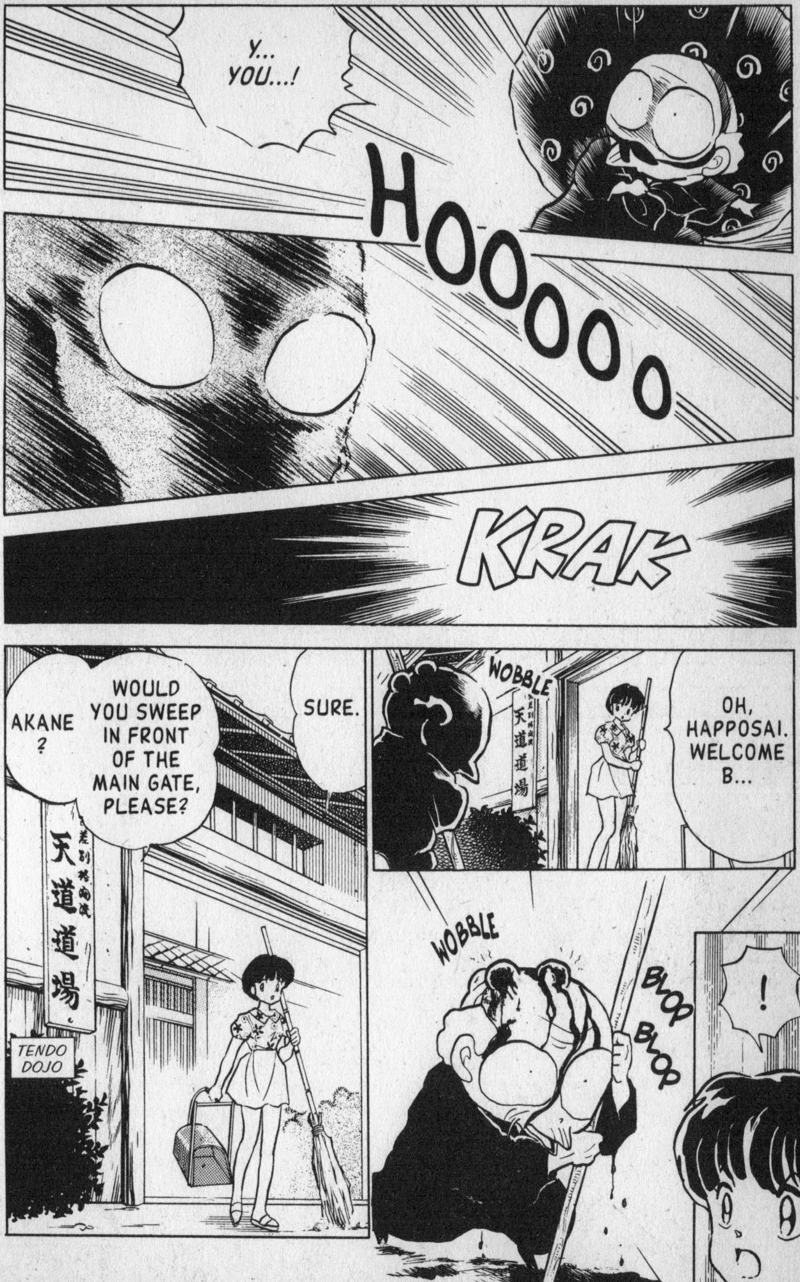
Y... YOU...!
HOOOOOO
KRAK
AKANE?
WOULD YOU SWEEP IN FRONT OF THE MAIN GATE, PLEASE?
SURE.
天道道場
TENDO DOJO
WOBBLE
OH, HAPPOSAI. WELCOME B...
WOBBLE
BLOOP BLOOP
!

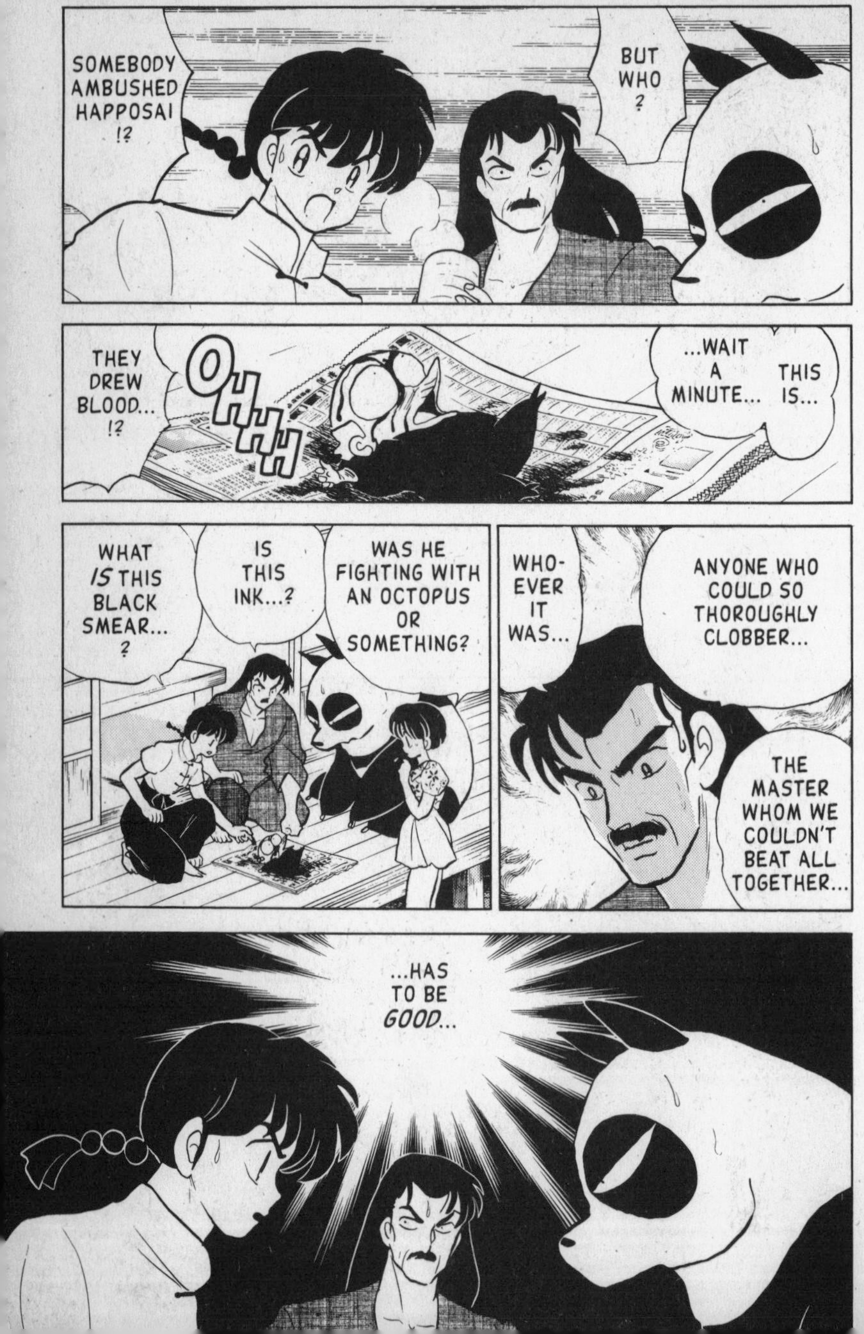
SOMEBODY AMBUSHED HAPPOSAI !?
BUT WHO ?
THEY DREW BLOOD... !?
OHHH
...WAIT A MINUTE... THIS IS...
WHAT IS THIS BLACK SMEAR... ?
IS THIS INK...?
WAS HE FIGHTING WITH AN OCTOPUS OR SOMETHING?
WHO-EVER IT WAS...
ANYONE WHO COULD SO THOROUGHLY CLOBBER...
THE MASTER WHOM WE COULDN'T BEAT ALL TOGETHER...
...HAS TO BE GOOD...

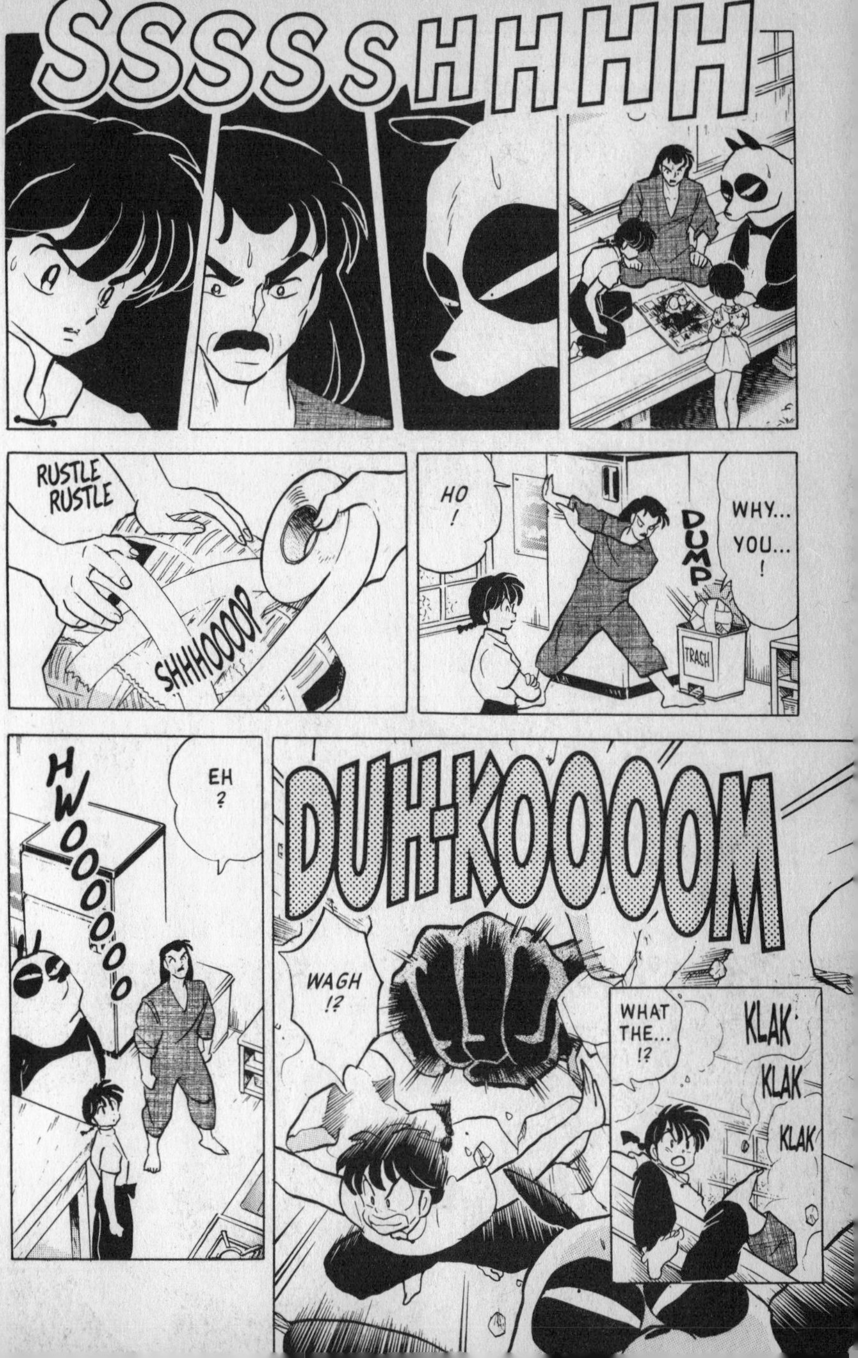
SSSSSHHHHH
RUSTLE RUSTLE
SHHOOOOP
HO!
WHY... YOU...!
DUMP
TRASH
HWOOOOOOOO
EH?
DUH-KOOOOM
WAGH!?
WHAT THE...!?
KLAK
KLAK
KLAK

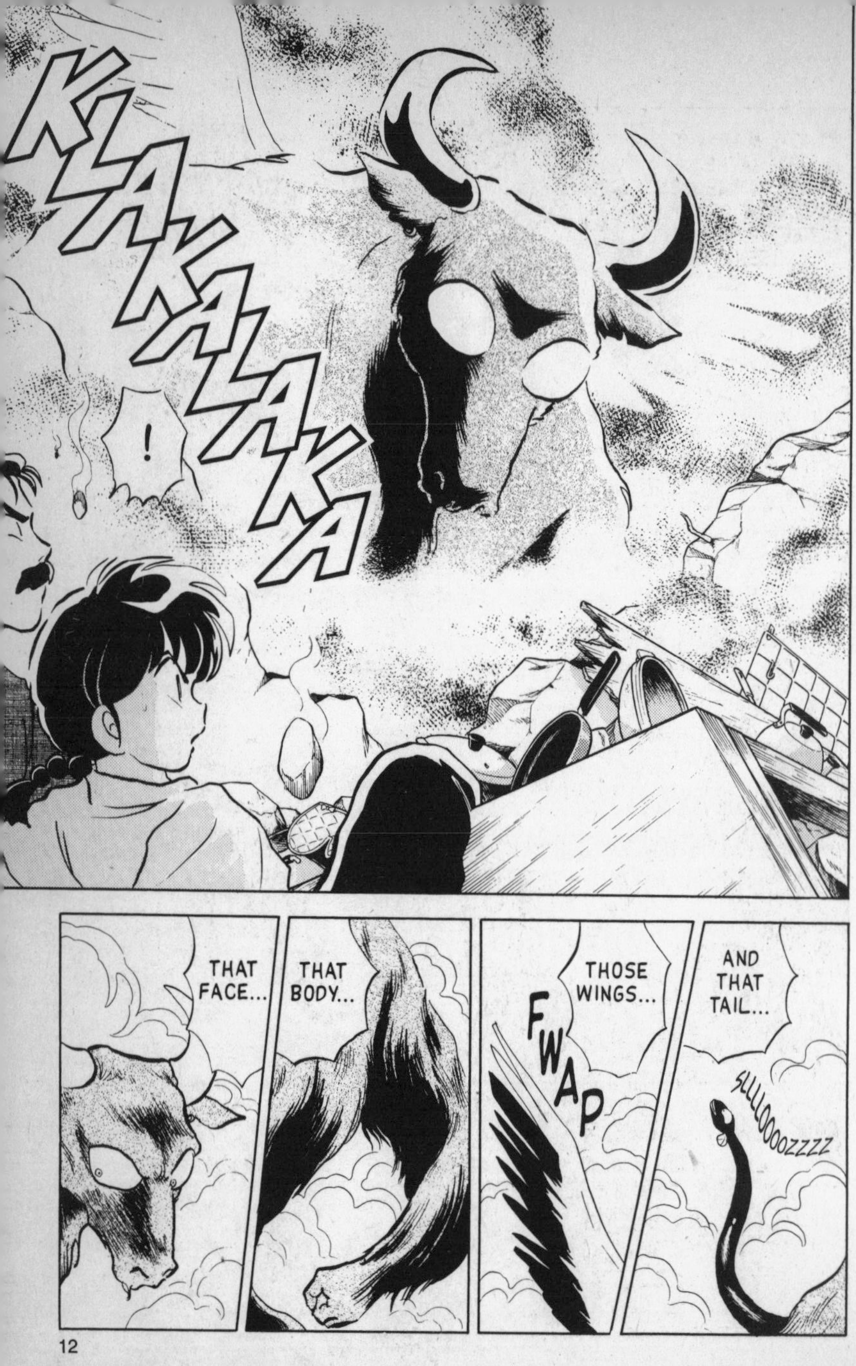
KLAKALAKA
!
THAT FACE...
THAT BODY...
THOSE WINGS...
FWAP
AND THAT TAIL...
SLLLLOOOOZZZZ

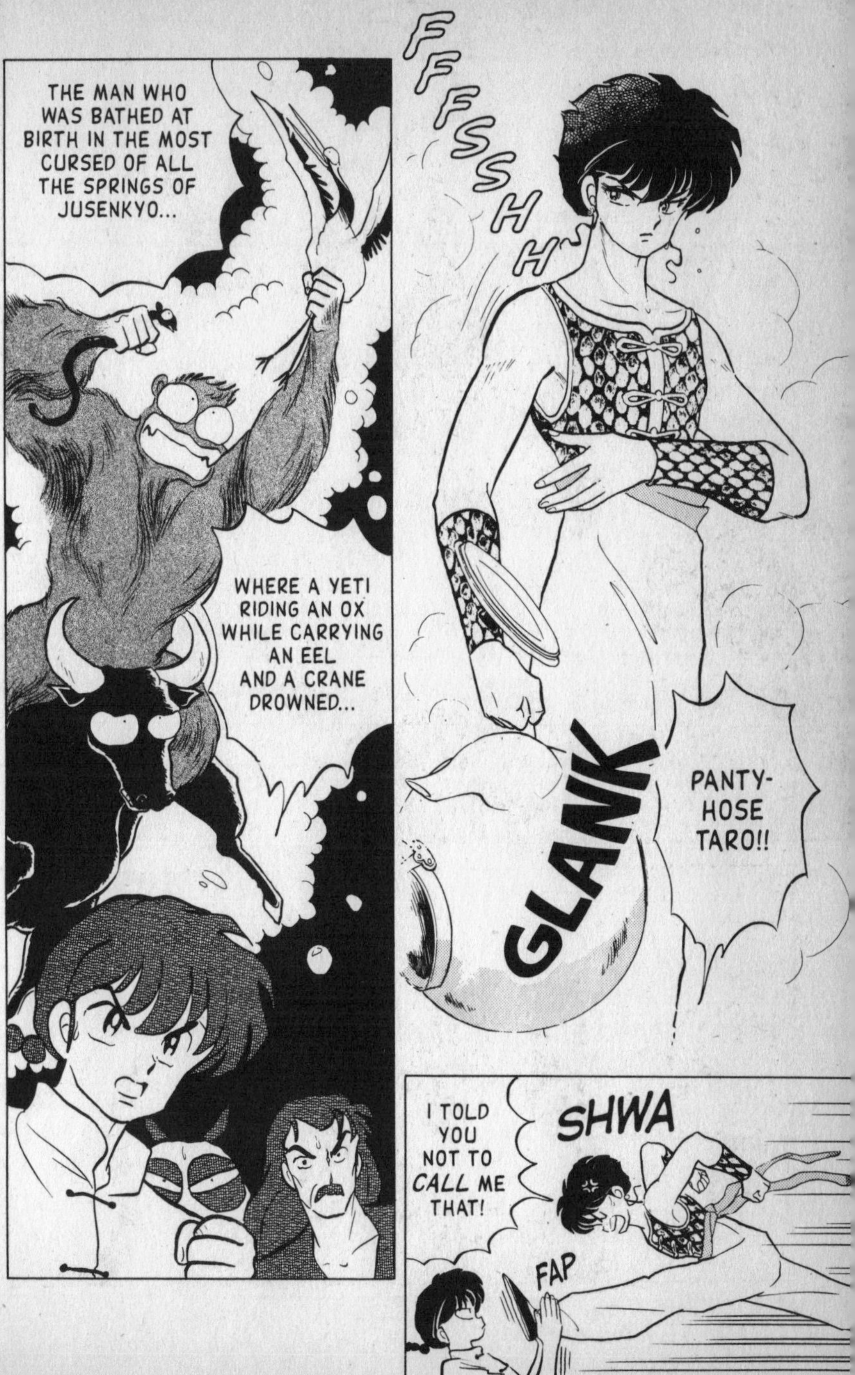
THE MAN WHO WAS BATHED AT BIRTH IN THE MOST CURSED OF ALL THE SPRINGS OF JUSENKYO...
WHERE A YETI RIDING AN OX WHILE CARRYING AN EEL AND A CRANE DROWNED...
FFFSSHH
GLANK
PANTY-HOSE TARO!!
I TOLD YOU NOT TO *CALL* ME THAT!
SHWA
FAP

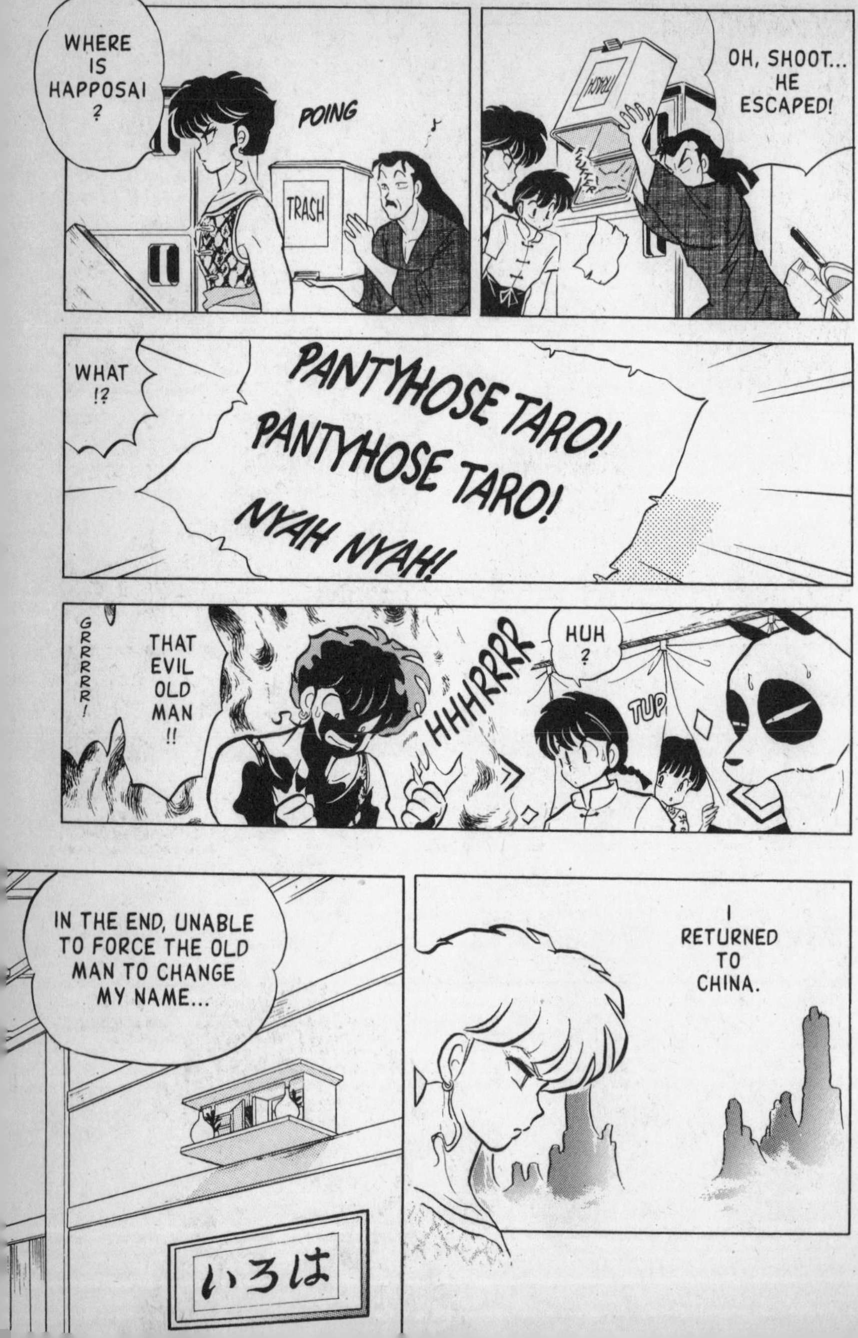
WHERE IS HAPPOSAI?
POING
TRASH
TRASH
OH, SHOOT... HE ESCAPED!
FLUTTER
WHAT!?
PANTYHOSE TARO! PANTYHOSE TARO! NYAH NYAH!
GRRRRR!
THAT EVIL OLD MAN!!
HHHRRRR
HUH?
TUP
IN THE END, UNABLE TO FORCE THE OLD MAN TO CHANGE MY NAME...
いろは
I RETURNED TO CHINA.

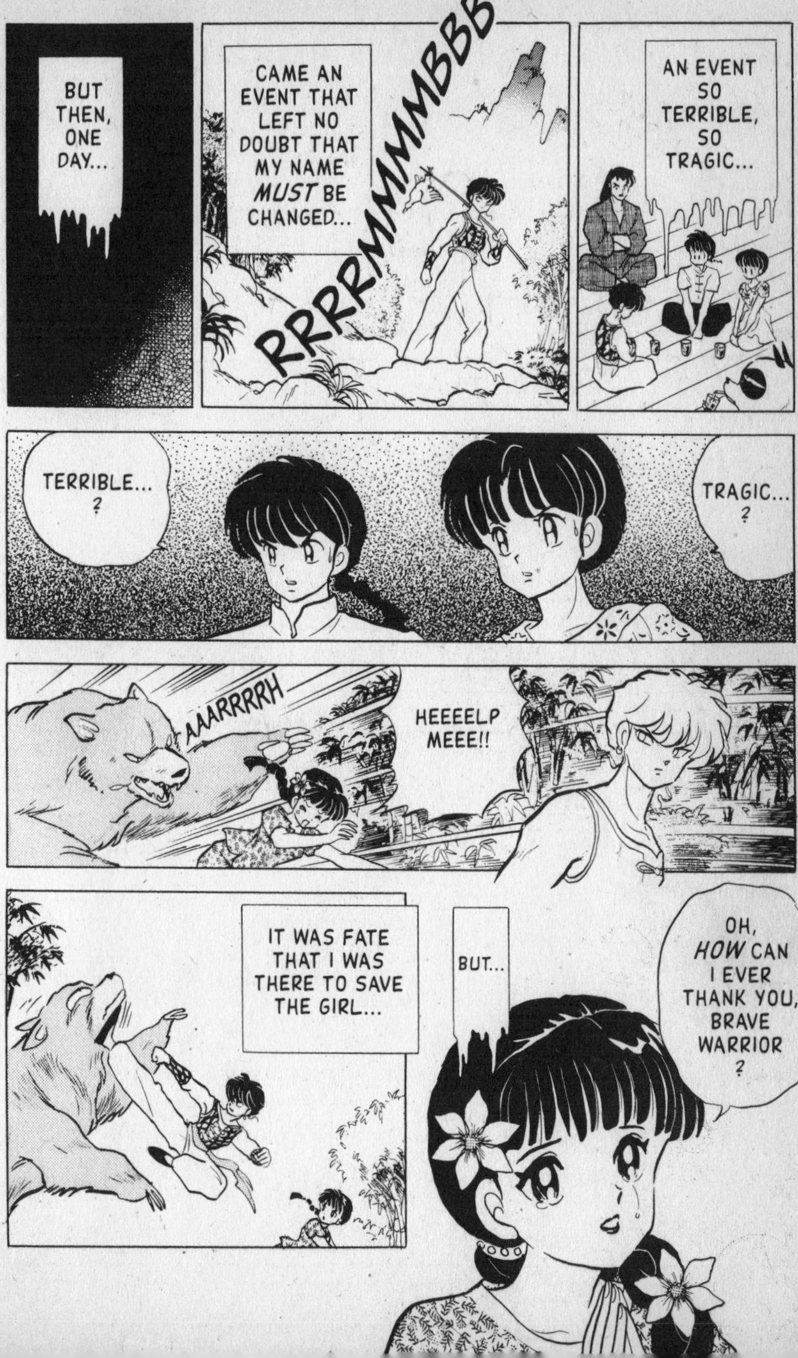
BUT THEN, ONE DAY...
CAME AN EVENT THAT LEFT NO DOUBT THAT MY NAME *MUST* BE CHANGED...
RRRRMMMMBBB
AN EVENT SO TERRIBLE, SO TRAGIC...
TERRIBLE...?
TRAGIC...?
AAARRRRH
HEEEELP MEEE!!
IT WAS FATE THAT I WAS THERE TO SAVE THE GIRL...
BUT...
OH, *HOW* CAN I EVER THANK YOU, BRAVE WARRIOR?

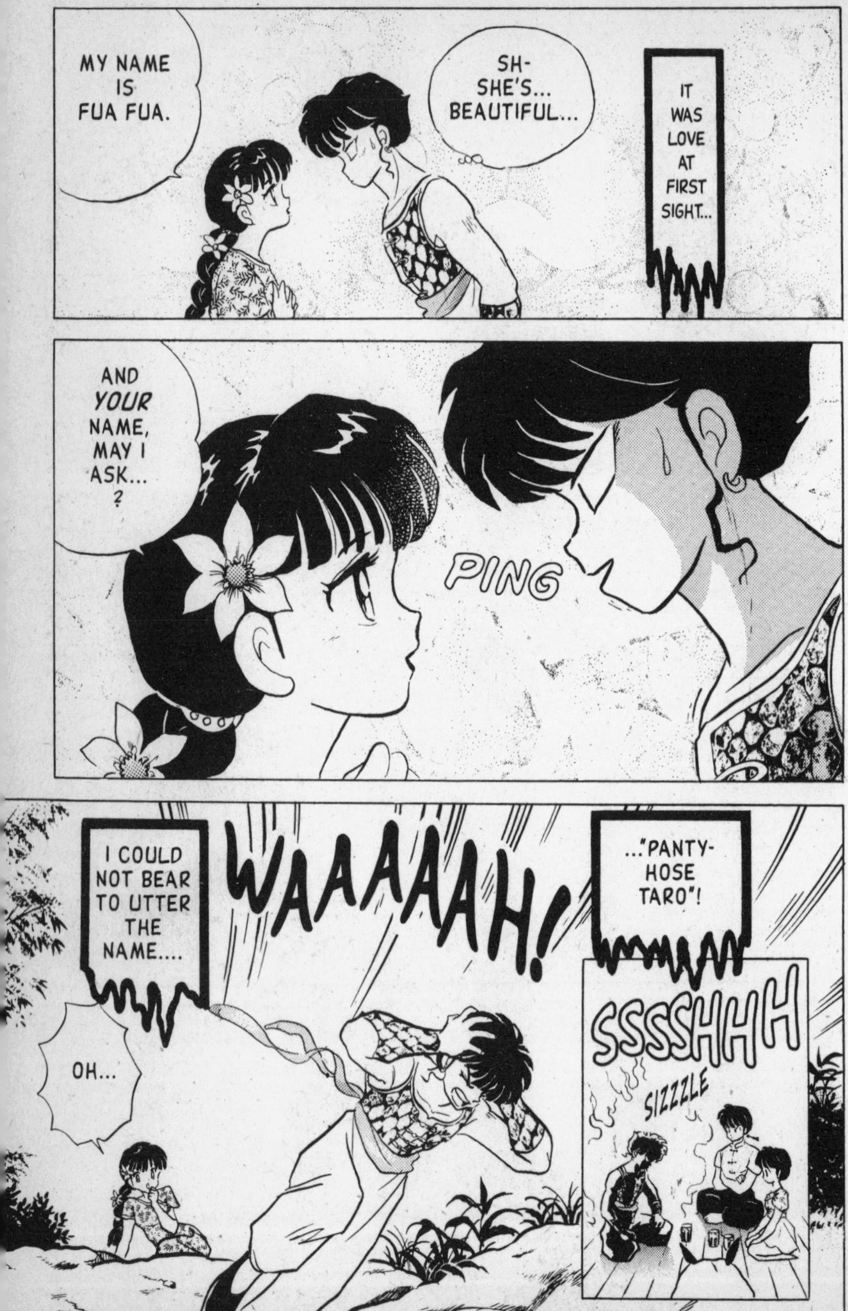
MY NAME IS FUA FUA.
SH- SHE'S... BEAUTIFUL...
IT WAS LOVE AT FIRST SIGHT...
AND YOUR NAME, MAY I ASK... ?
PING
I COULD NOT BEAR TO UTTER THE NAME....
WAAAAAAH!
..."PANTY-HOSE TARO"!
OH...
SSSSHHH
SIZZZLE

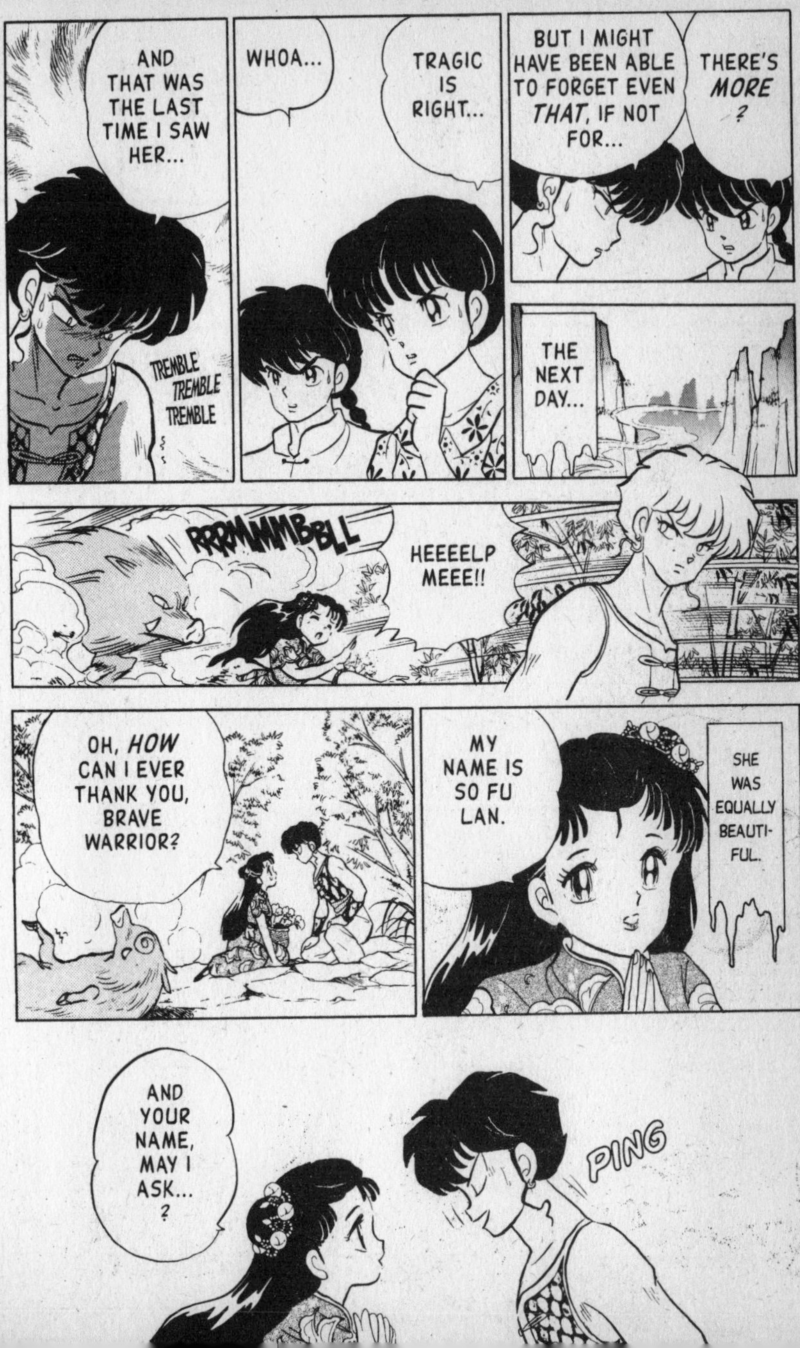
AND THAT WAS THE LAST TIME I SAW HER...
TREMBLE TREMBLE TREMBLE
WHOA...
TRAGIC IS RIGHT...
BUT I MIGHT HAVE BEEN ABLE TO FORGET EVEN *THAT*, IF NOT FOR...
THERE'S *MORE*?
THE NEXT DAY...
RRRMMMBBLL
HEEEELP MEEE!!
OH, *HOW* CAN I EVER THANK YOU, BRAVE WARRIOR?
MY NAME IS SO FU LAN.
SHE WAS EQUALLY BEAUTI-FUL.
AND YOUR NAME, MAY I ASK...?
PING

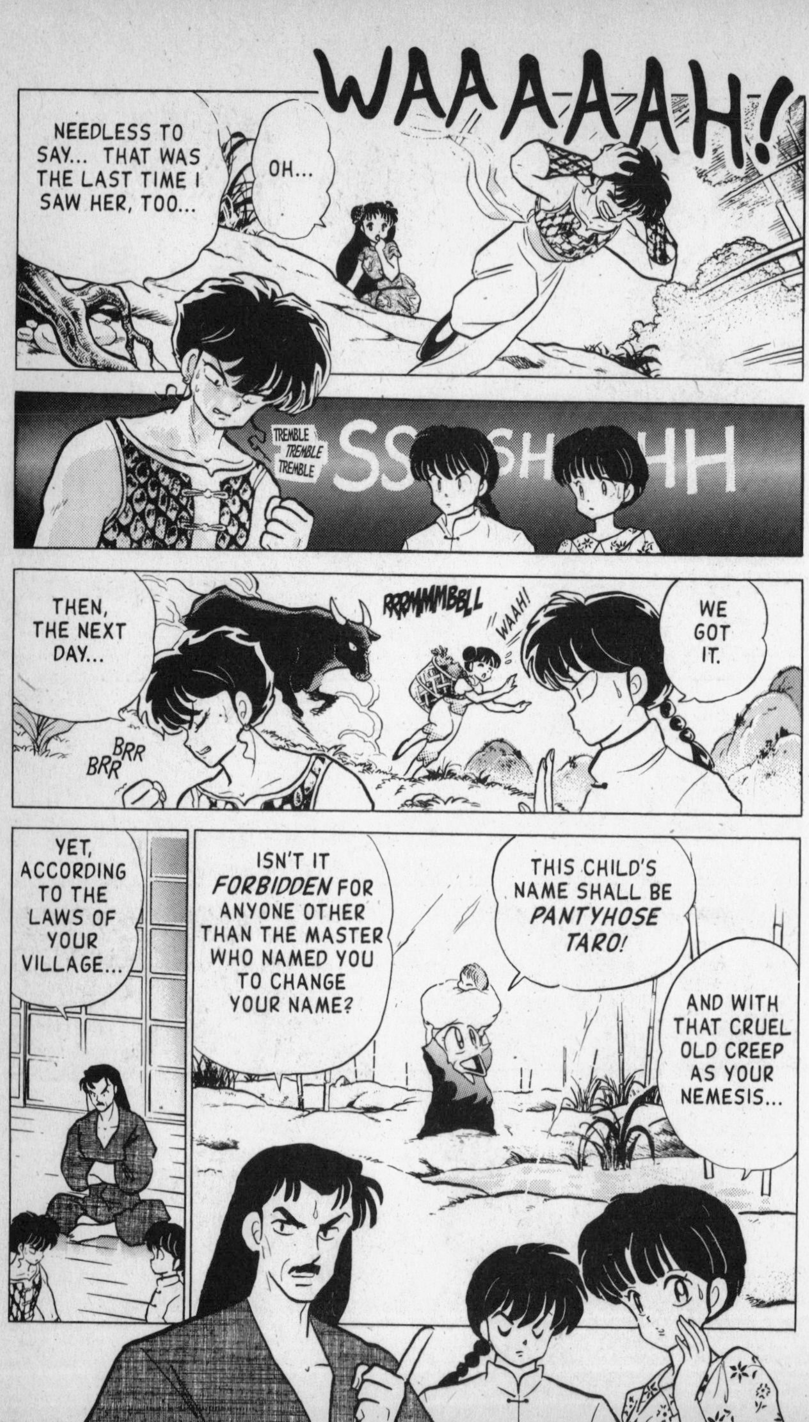
WAAAAAH!!
NEEDLESS TO SAY... THAT WAS THE LAST TIME I SAW HER, TOO...
OH...
TREMBLE TREMBLE TREMBLE
SSSHHHH
THEN, THE NEXT DAY...
BRR BRR
RRRMMMBBLL
WAAH!
WE GOT IT.
YET, ACCORDING TO THE LAWS OF YOUR VILLAGE...
ISN'T IT FORBIDDEN FOR ANYONE OTHER THAN THE MASTER WHO NAMED YOU TO CHANGE YOUR NAME?
THIS CHILD'S NAME SHALL BE PANTYHOSE TARO!
AND WITH THAT CRUEL OLD CREEP AS YOUR NEMESIS...

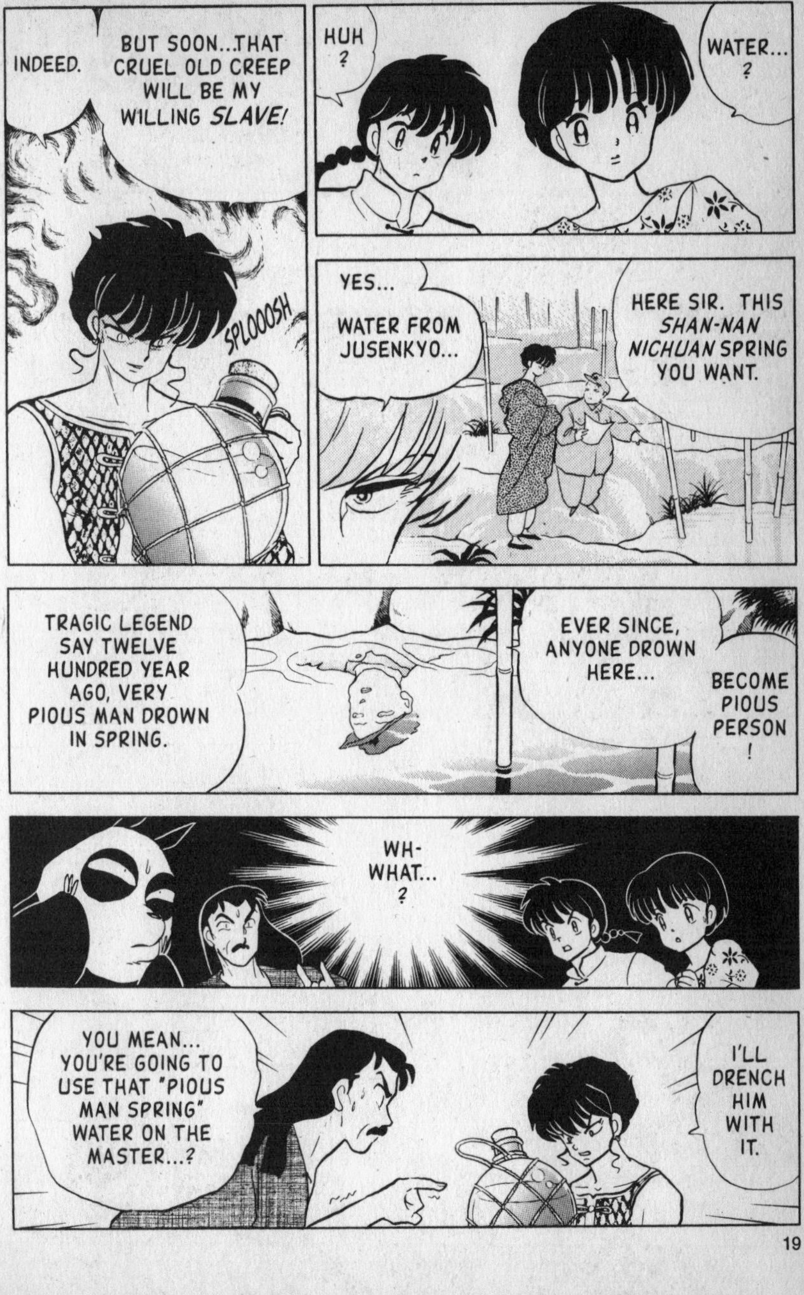
INDEED.
BUT SOON...THAT CRUEL OLD CREEP WILL BE MY WILLING *SLAVE!*
SPLOOOSH
HUH ?
WATER... ?
YES...
WATER FROM JUSENKYO...
HERE SIR. THIS *SHAN-NAN NICHUAN* SPRING YOU WANT.
TRAGIC LEGEND SAY TWELVE HUNDRED YEAR AGO, VERY PIOUS MAN DROWN IN SPRING.
EVER SINCE, ANYONE DROWN HERE...
BECOME PIOUS PERSON !
WH-WHAT... ?
YOU MEAN... YOU'RE GOING TO USE THAT "PIOUS MAN SPRING" WATER ON THE MASTER...?
I'LL DRENCH HIM WITH IT.

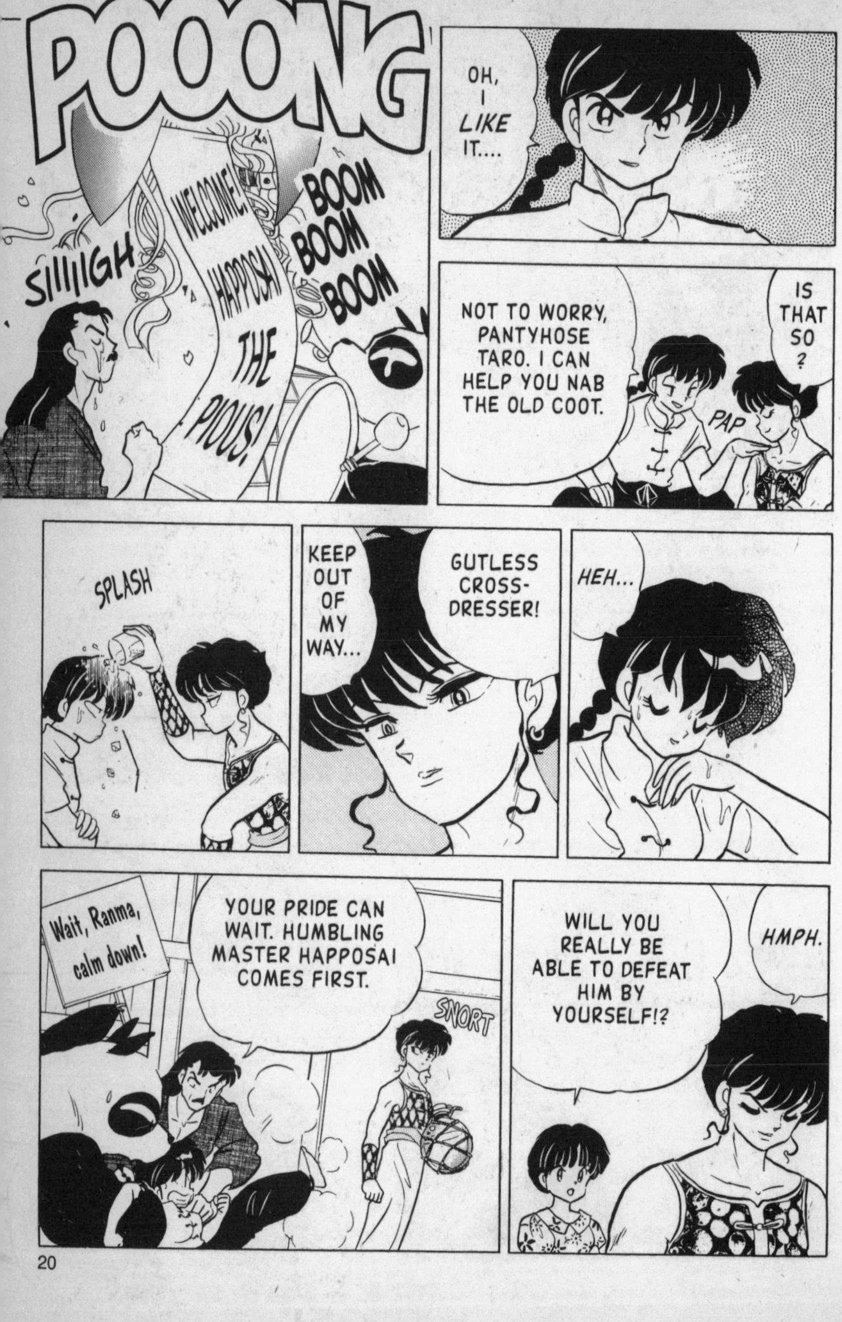
POOONG
WELCOME! HAPPOSAI THE PIOUS!
BOOM BOOM BOOM
SIIIIIGH
OH, I LIKE IT....
NOT TO WORRY, PANTYHOSE TARO. I CAN HELP YOU NAB THE OLD COOT.
IS THAT SO?
PAP
SPLASH
KEEP OUT OF MY WAY...
GUTLESS CROSS-DRESSER!
HEH...
Wait, Ranma, calm down!
YOUR PRIDE CAN WAIT. HUMBLING MASTER HAPPOSAI COMES FIRST.
SNORT
WILL YOU REALLY BE ABLE TO DEFEAT HIM BY YOURSELF!?
HMPH.

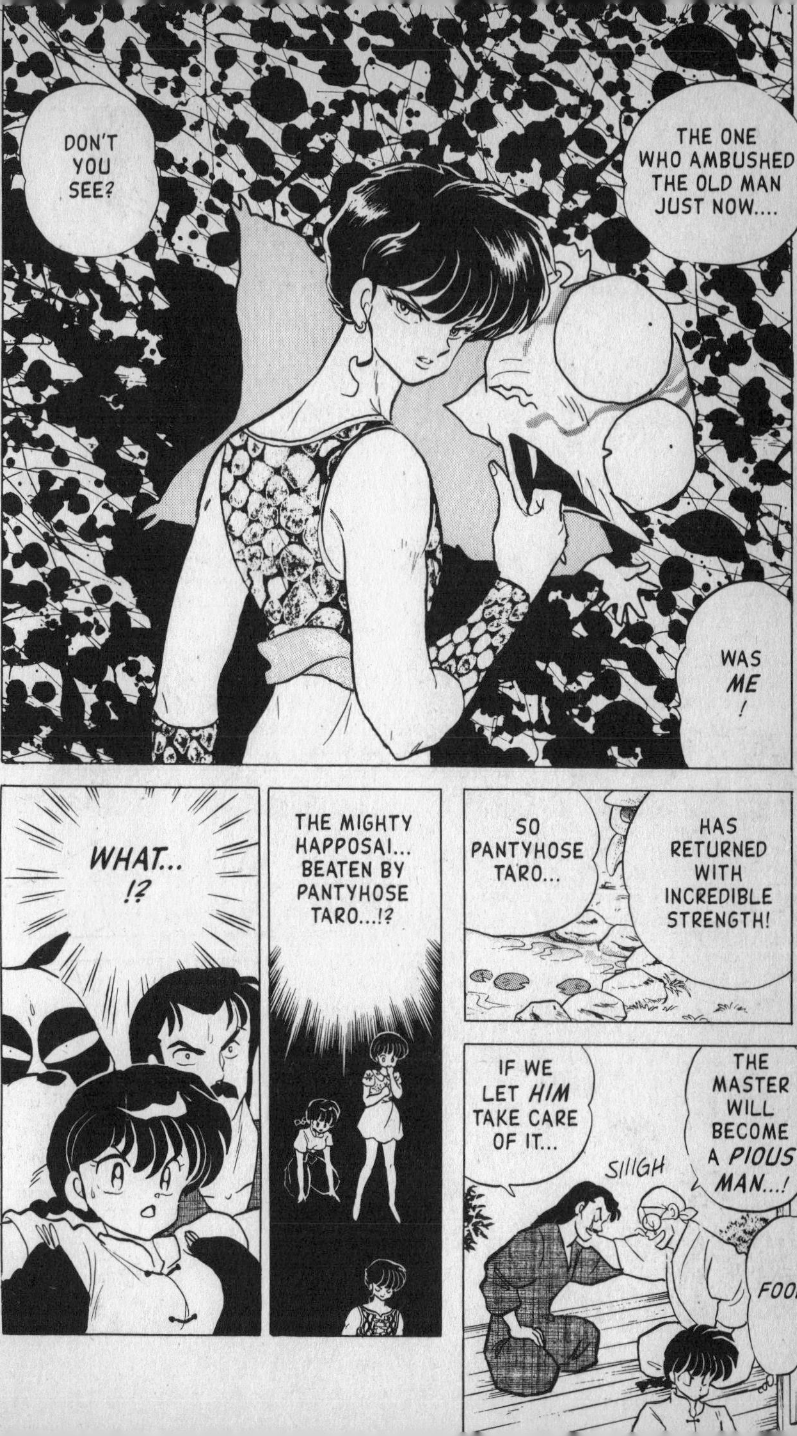
DON'T YOU SEE?
THE ONE WHO AMBUSHED THE OLD MAN JUST NOW....
WAS *ME*!
WHAT...!?
THE MIGHTY HAPPOSAI... BEATEN BY PANTYHOSE TARO...!?
SO PANTYHOSE TARO...
HAS RETURNED WITH INCREDIBLE STRENGTH!
IF WE LET *HIM* TAKE CARE OF IT...
THE MASTER WILL BECOME A *PIOUS MAN*...!
SIIIGH
FOOEY.

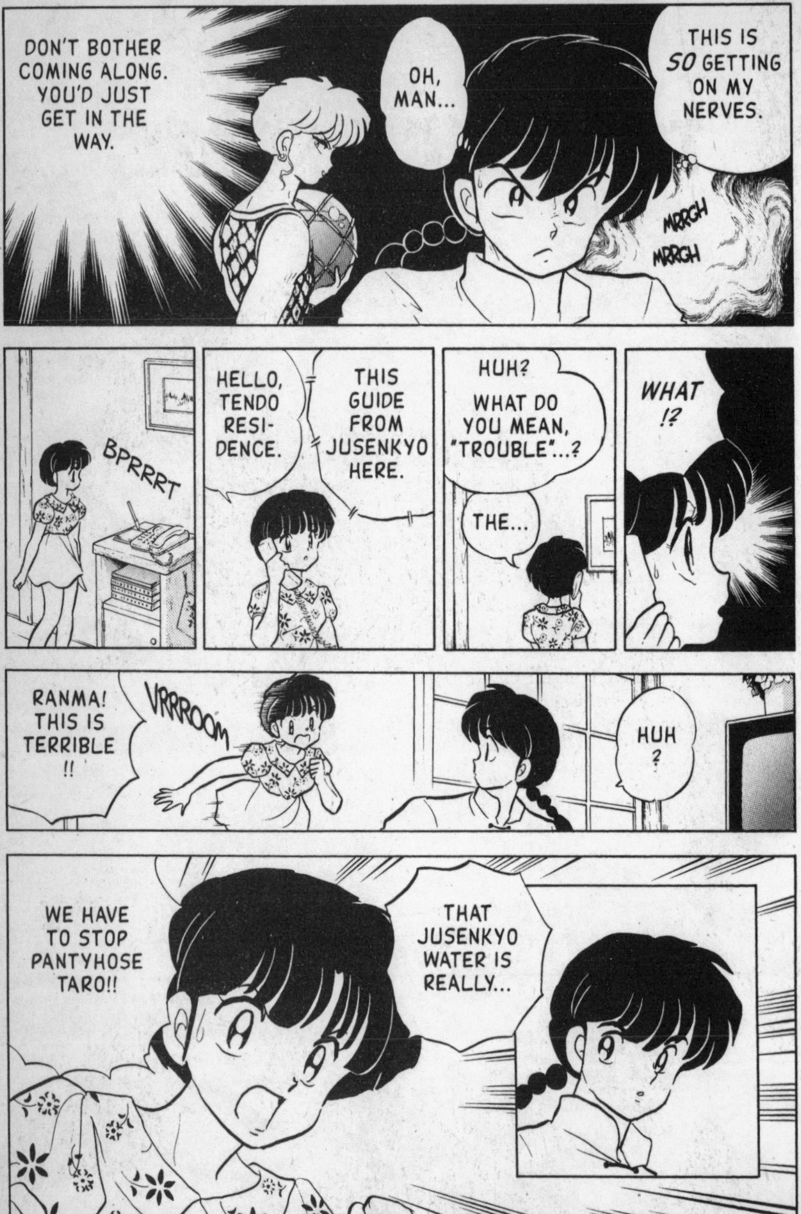
DON'T BOTHER COMING ALONG. YOU'D JUST GET IN THE WAY.
OH, MAN...
THIS IS SO GETTING ON MY NERVES.
MRRGH MRRGH
BPRRRT
HELLO, TENDO RESI-DENCE.
THIS GUIDE FROM JUSENKYO HERE.
HUH?
WHAT DO YOU MEAN, "TROUBLE"...?
THE...
WHAT !?
RANMA! THIS IS TERRIBLE !!
VRRROOM
HUH ?
WE HAVE TO STOP PANTYHOSE TARO!!
THAT JUSENKYO WATER IS REALLY...

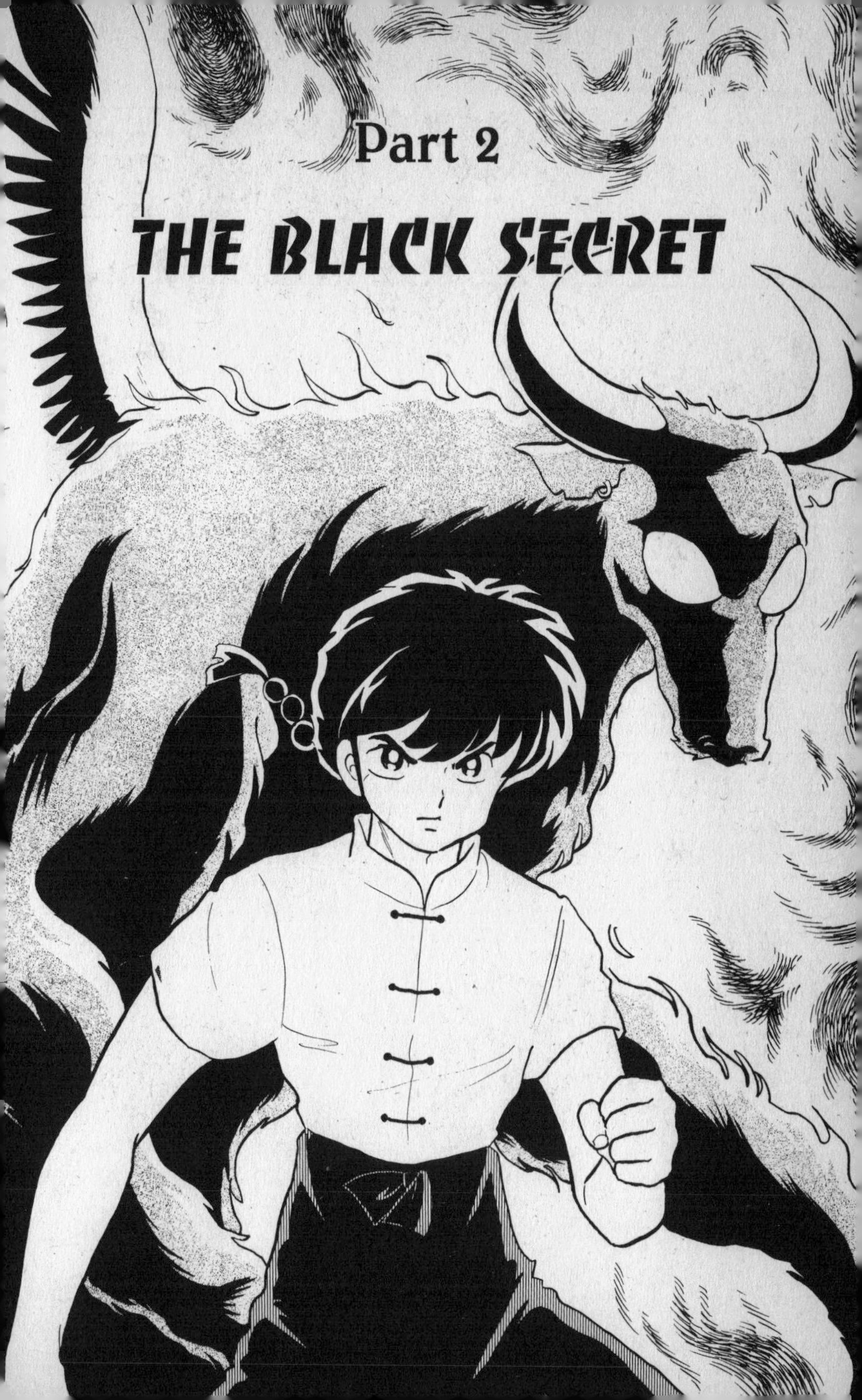
Part 2
THE BLACK SECRET

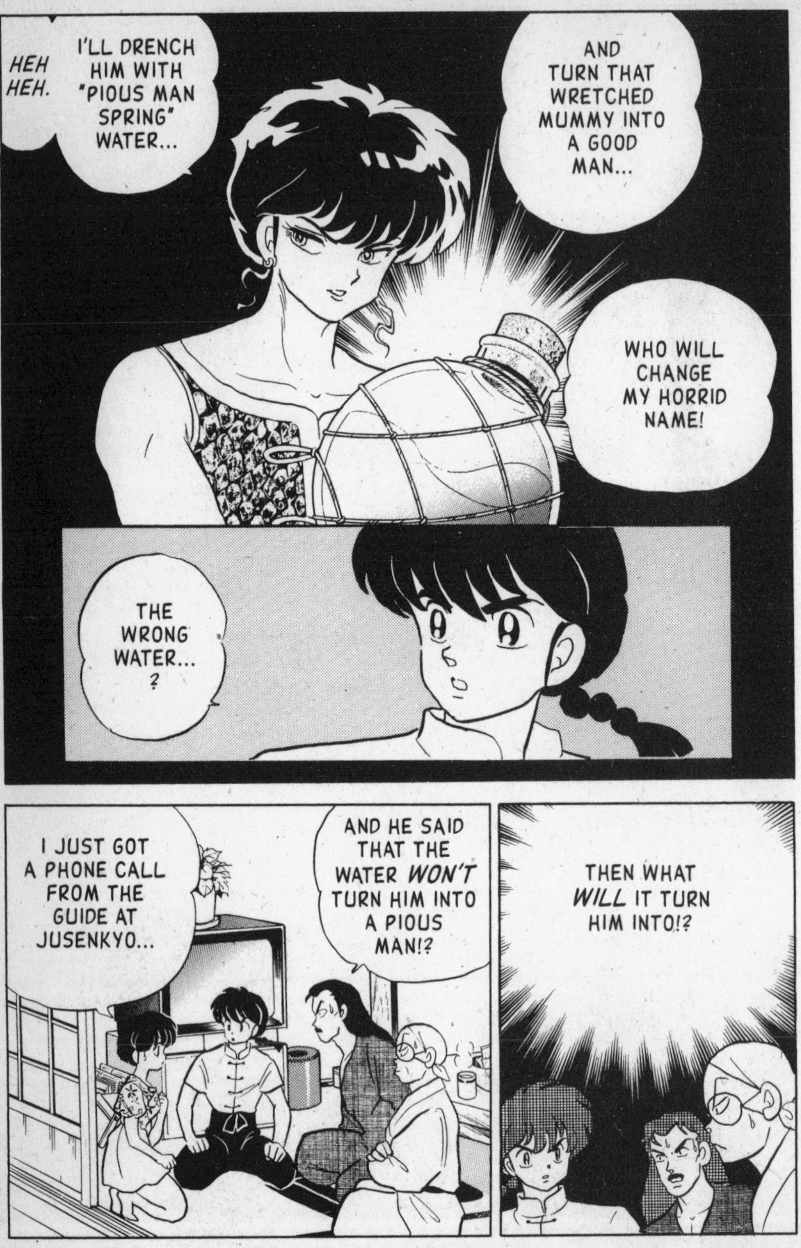
HEH HEH.
I'LL DRENCH HIM WITH "PIOUS MAN SPRING" WATER...
AND TURN THAT WRETCHED MUMMY INTO A GOOD MAN...
WHO WILL CHANGE MY HORRID NAME!
THE WRONG WATER...?
I JUST GOT A PHONE CALL FROM THE GUIDE AT JUSENKYO...
AND HE SAID THAT THE WATER WON'T TURN HIM INTO A PIOUS MAN!?
THEN WHAT WILL IT TURN HIM INTO!?

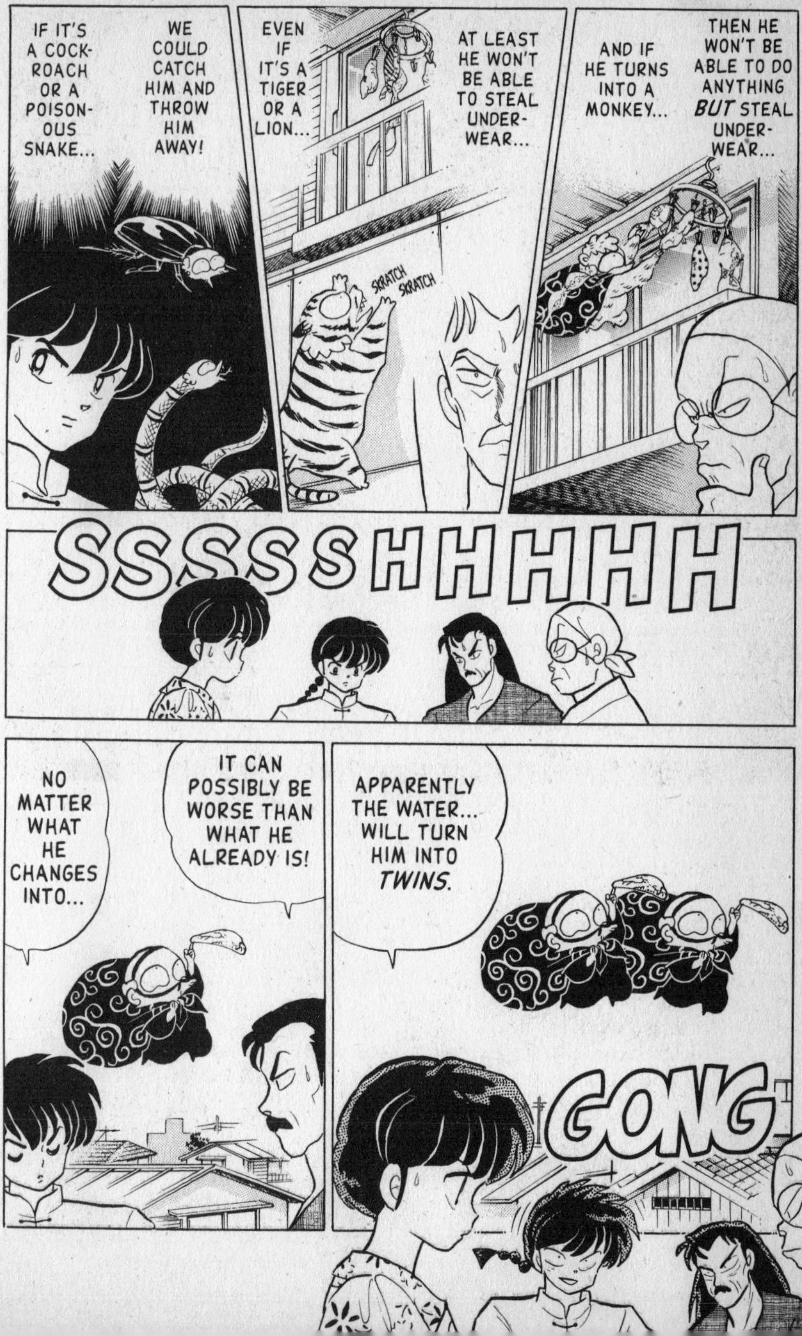
IF IT'S A COCK-ROACH OR A POISON-OUS SNAKE...
WE COULD CATCH HIM AND THROW HIM AWAY!
EVEN IF IT'S A TIGER OR A LION...
SKRATCH SKRATCH
AT LEAST HE WON'T BE ABLE TO STEAL UNDER-WEAR...
AND IF HE TURNS INTO A MONKEY...
THEN HE WON'T BE ABLE TO DO ANYTHING *BUT* STEAL UNDER-WEAR...
SSSSSHHHHHH
NO MATTER WHAT HE CHANGES INTO...
IT CAN POSSIBLY BE WORSE THAN WHAT HE ALREADY IS!
APPARENTLY THE WATER... WILL TURN HIM INTO *TWINS*.
GONG

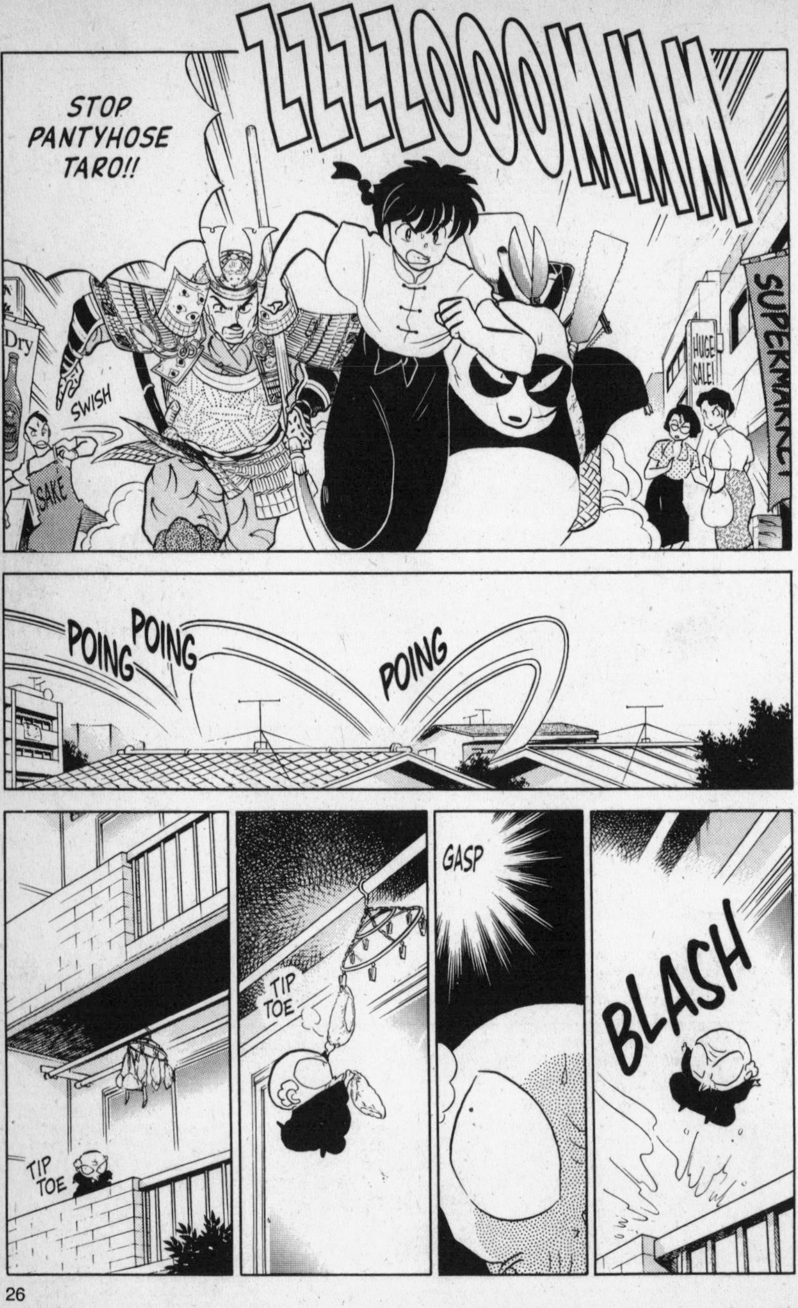
ZZZZZOOOOMMMM
STOP PANTYHOSE TARO!!
Dry
SWISH
SAKE
HUGE SALE!
SUPERMARKET
POING
POING
POING
TIP TOE
TIP TOE
GASP
BLASH

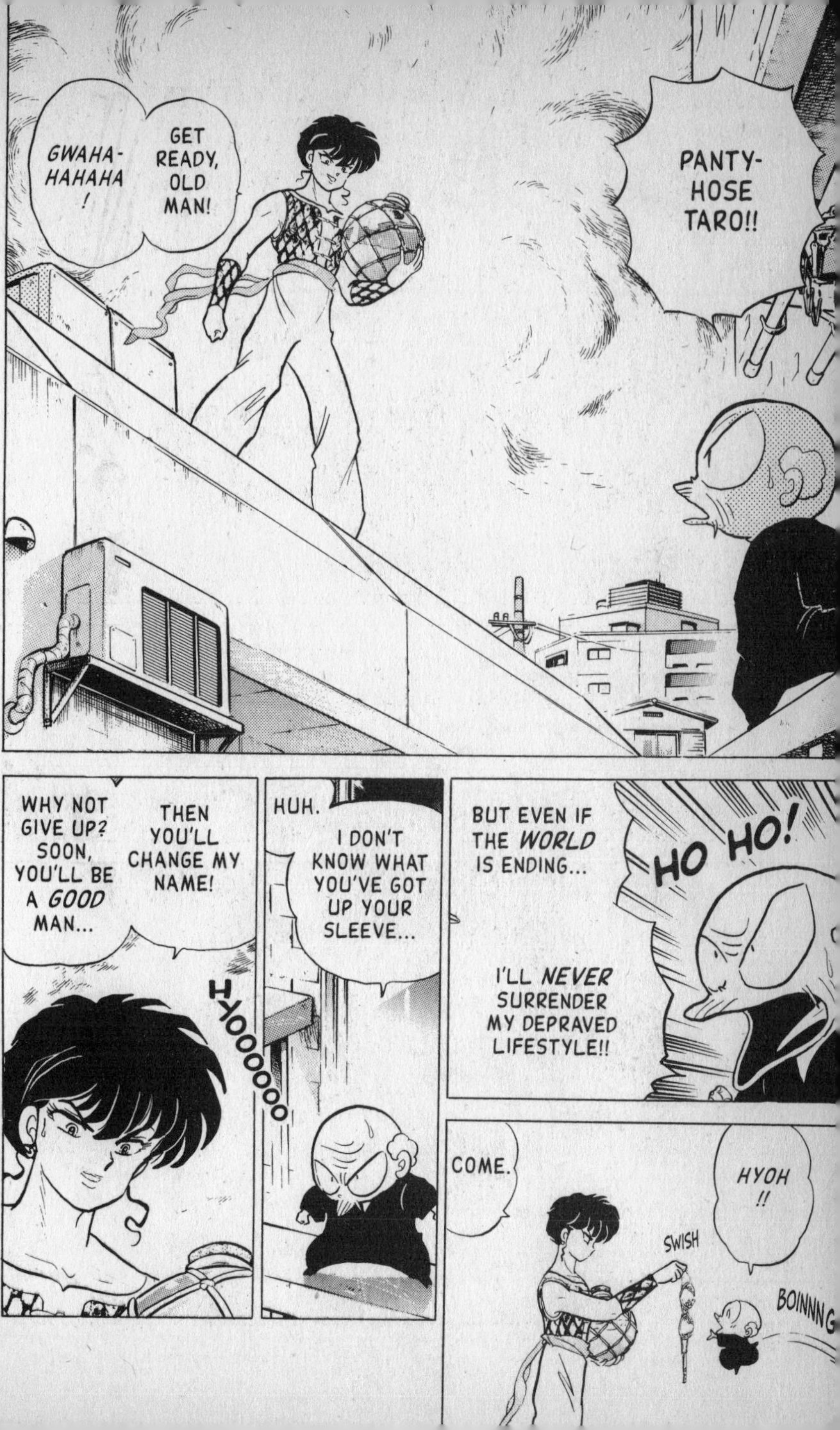
GWAHA-HAHAHA!
GET READY, OLD MAN!
PANTY-HOSE TARO!!
WHY NOT GIVE UP? SOON, YOU'LL BE A GOOD MAN...
THEN YOU'LL CHANGE MY NAME!
HYOOOOOOO
HUH.
I DON'T KNOW WHAT YOU'VE GOT UP YOUR SLEEVE...
BUT EVEN IF THE WORLD IS ENDING...
HO HO!
I'LL NEVER SURRENDER MY DEPRAVED LIFESTYLE!!
COME.
HYOH!!
SWISH
BOINNNG

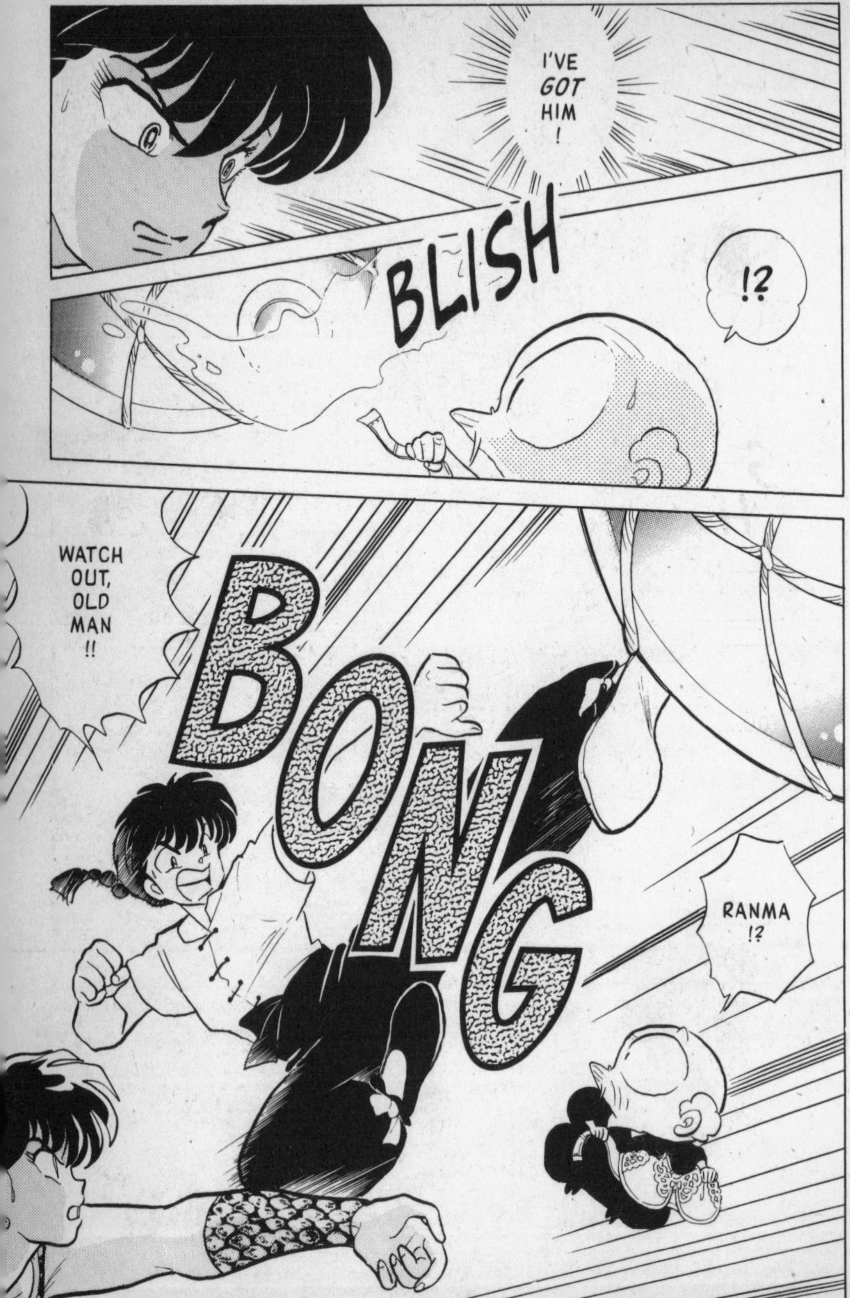
I'VE *GOT* HIM !
BLISH
!?
WATCH OUT, OLD MAN !!
BONG
RANMA !?

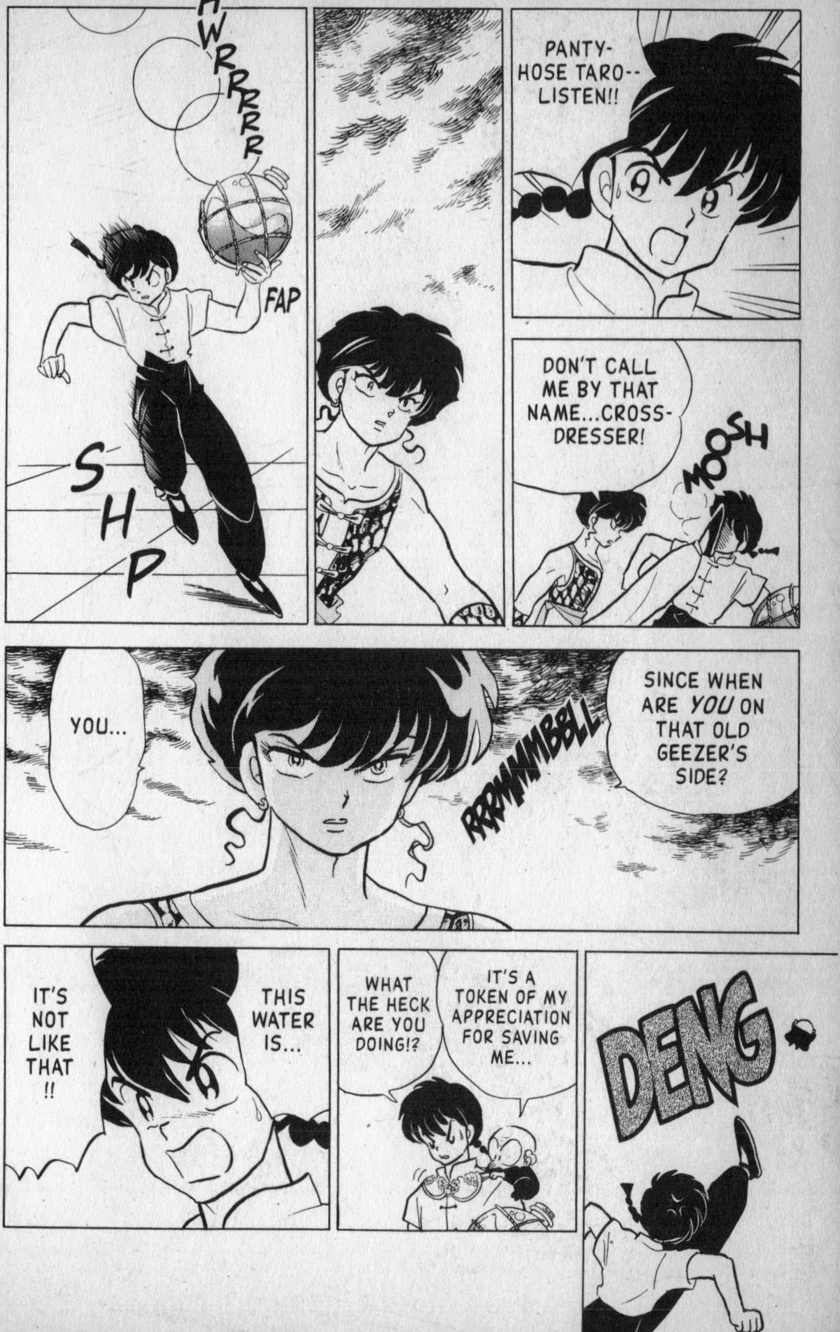
HWRRRRRR
FAP
SHP
PANTY-HOSE TARO--LISTEN!!
DON'T CALL ME BY THAT NAME...CROSS-DRESSER!
MOOSH
YOU...
RRRMMMBBLL
SINCE WHEN ARE YOU ON THAT OLD GEEZER'S SIDE?
IT'S NOT LIKE THAT!!
THIS WATER IS...
WHAT THE HECK ARE YOU DOING!?
IT'S A TOKEN OF MY APPRECIATION FOR SAVING ME...
DENG

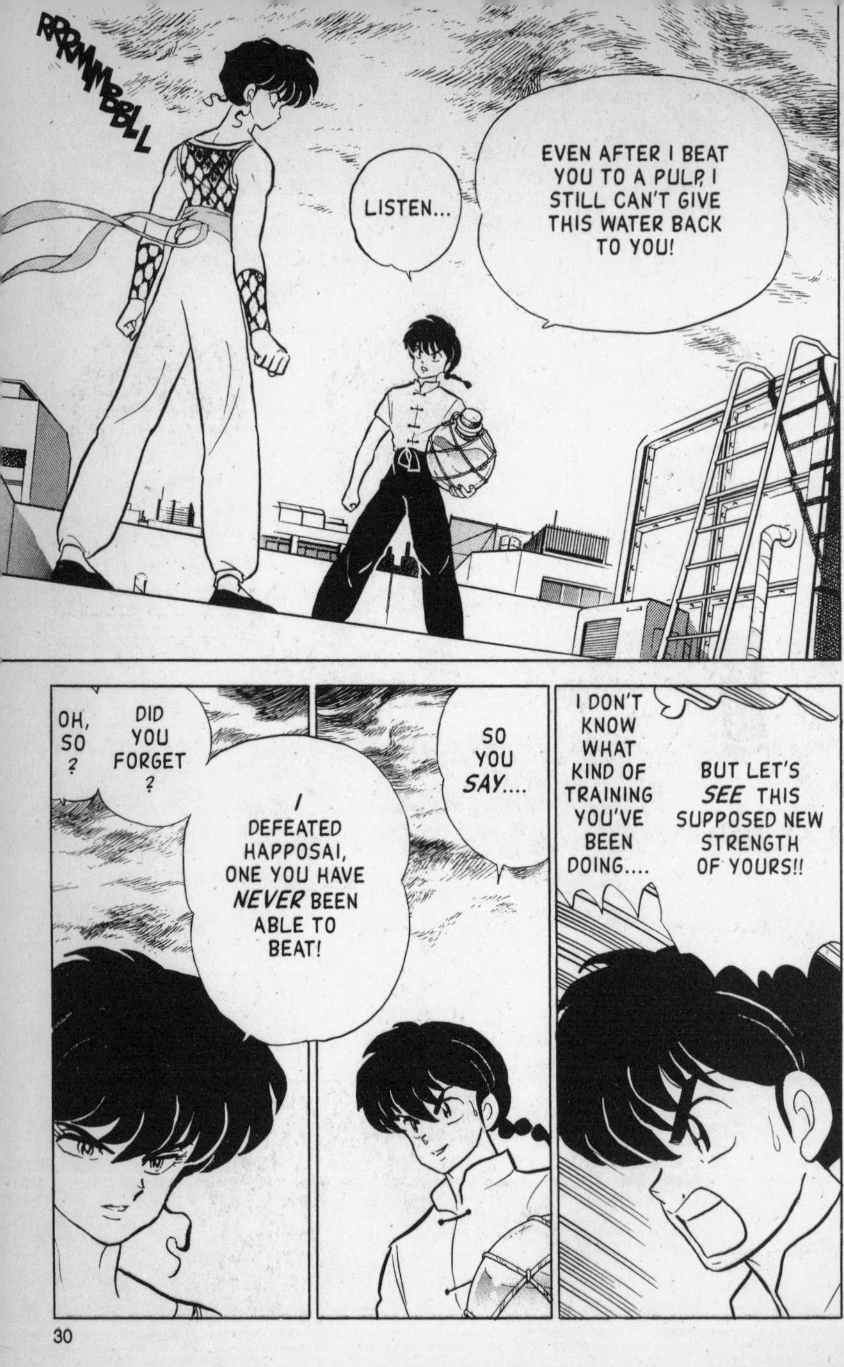

RRRMMBBLL
LISTEN...
EVEN AFTER I BEAT YOU TO A PULP, I STILL CAN'T GIVE THIS WATER BACK TO YOU!
OH, SO?
DID YOU FORGET?
I DEFEATED HAPPOSAI, ONE YOU HAVE NEVER BEEN ABLE TO BEAT!
SO YOU SAY....
I DON'T KNOW WHAT KIND OF TRAINING YOU'VE BEEN DOING....
BUT LET'S SEE THIS SUPPOSED NEW STRENGTH OF YOURS!!

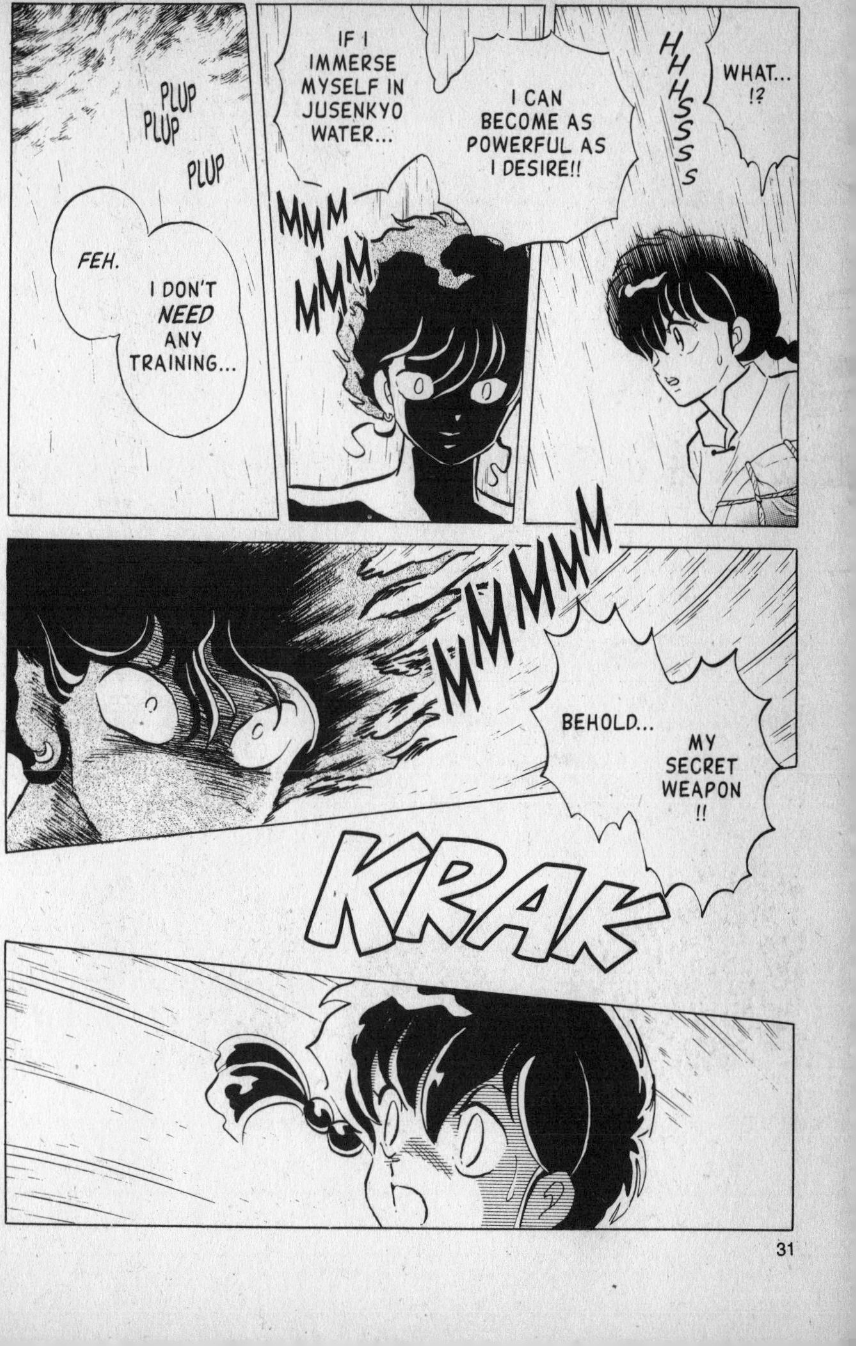
PLUP
PLUP
PLUP
FEH.
I DON'T *NEED* ANY TRAINING...
IF I IMMERSE MYSELF IN JUSENKYO WATER...
I CAN BECOME AS POWERFUL AS I DESIRE!!
MMM
MMM
HHHSSSS
WHAT... !?
MMMMMMM
BEHOLD...
MY SECRET WEAPON !!
KRAK

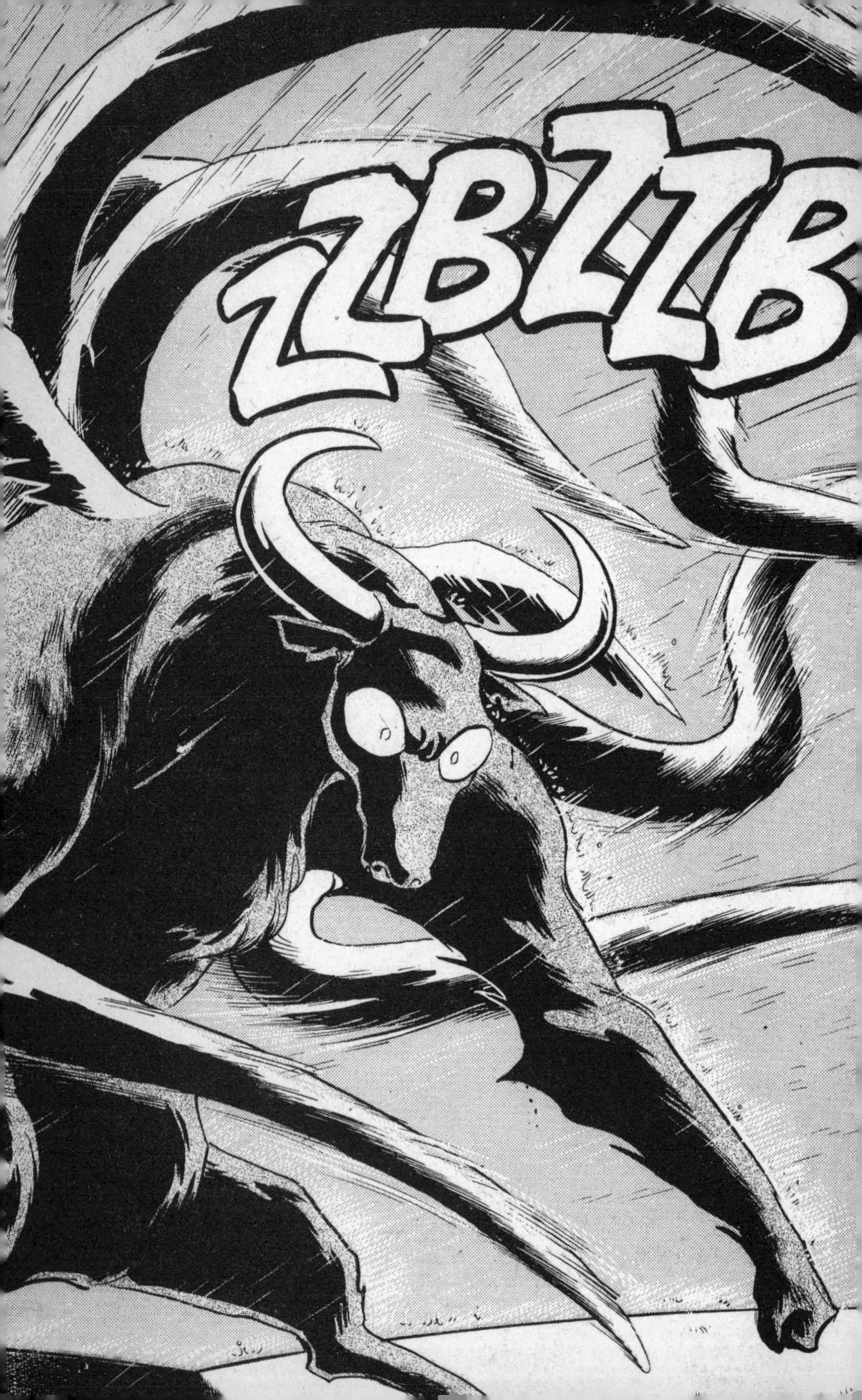
ZBLB

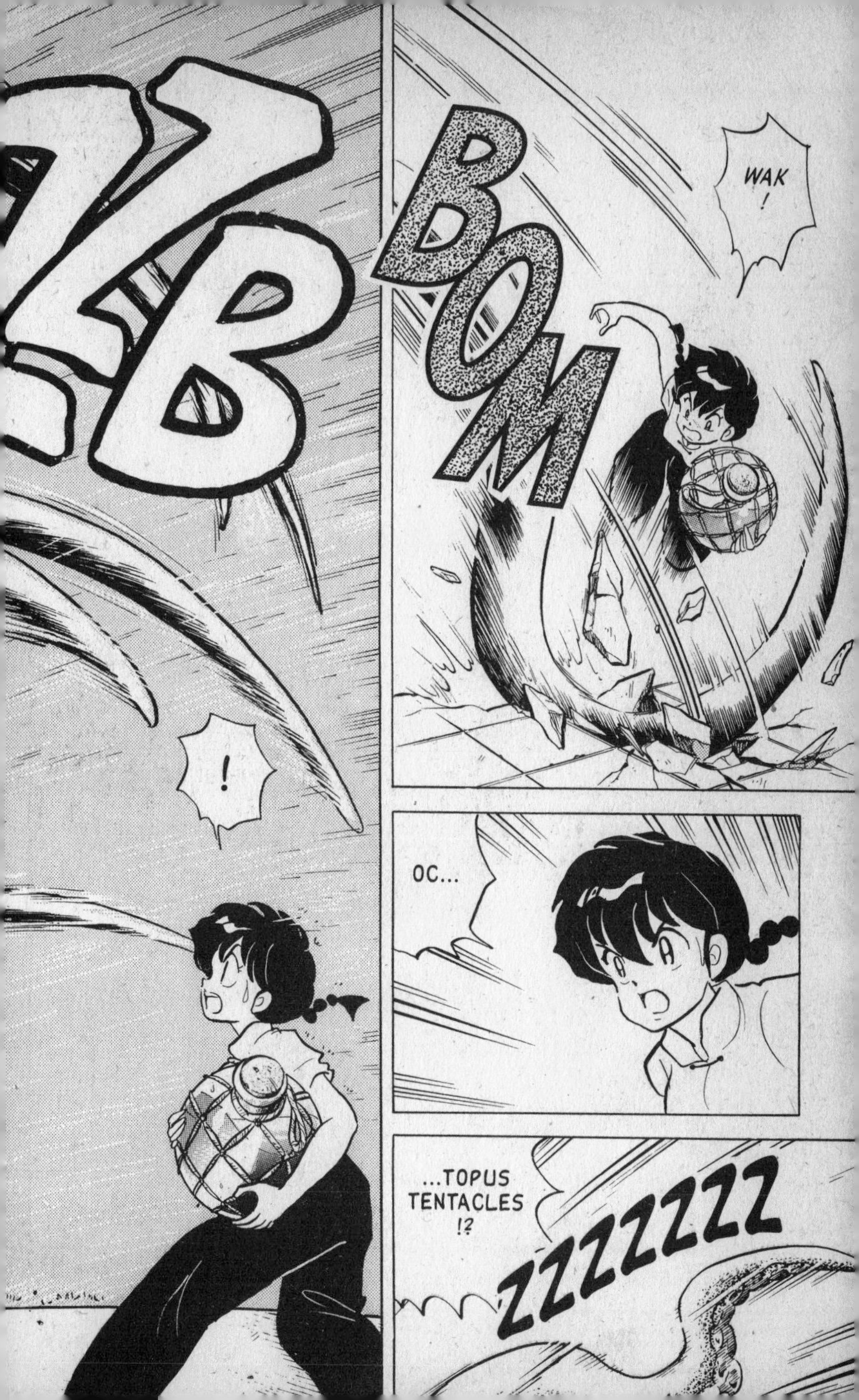
ZZB
!
BOOM
WAK
!
OC...
...TOPUS
TENTACLES
!?
ZZZZZZZ

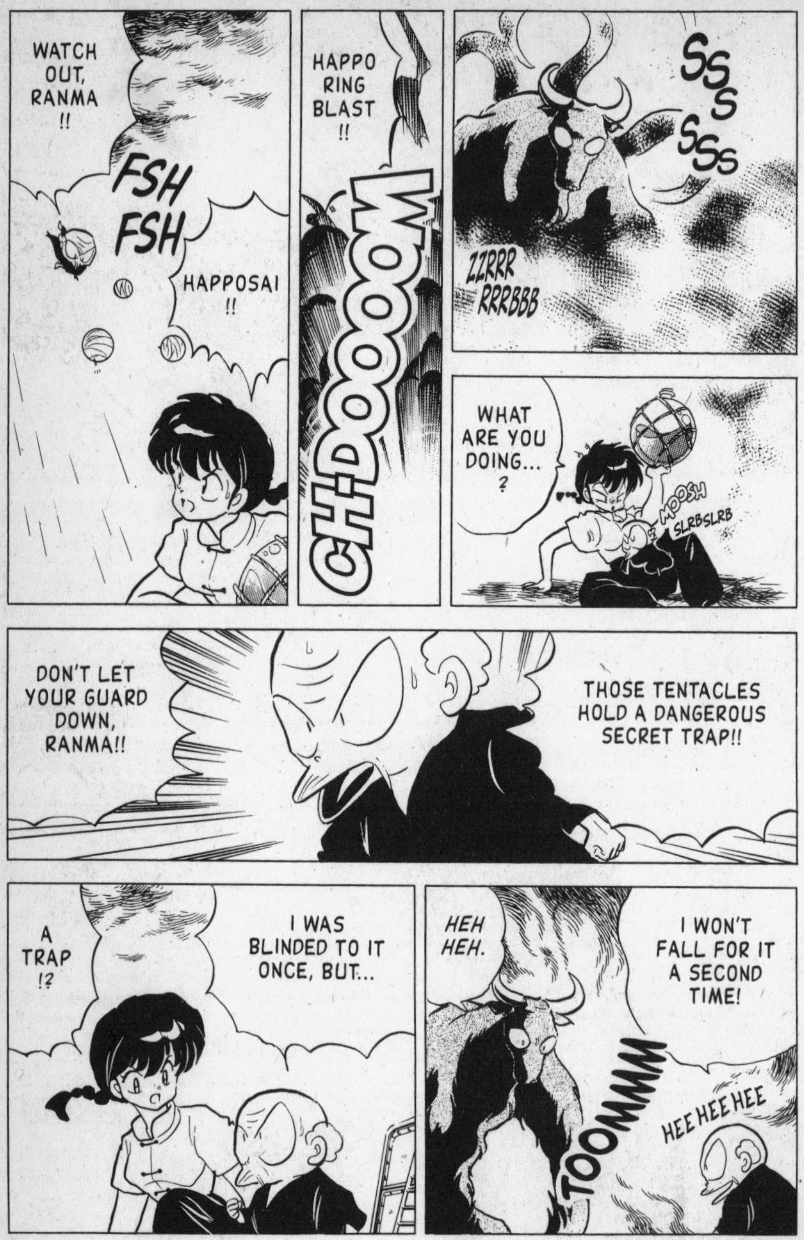
WATCH OUT, RANMA !!
FSH FSH
HAPPOSAI !!
HAPPO RING BLAST !!
CH-DOOOOOM
SSS SSS
ZZRRR RRRBBB
WHAT ARE YOU DOING... ?
MOOSH
SLRBSLRB
DON'T LET YOUR GUARD DOWN, RANMA!!
THOSE TENTACLES HOLD A DANGEROUS SECRET TRAP!!
A TRAP !?
I WAS BLINDED TO IT ONCE, BUT...
HEH HEH.
I WON'T FALL FOR IT A SECOND TIME!
TOOMMM
HEE HEE HEE

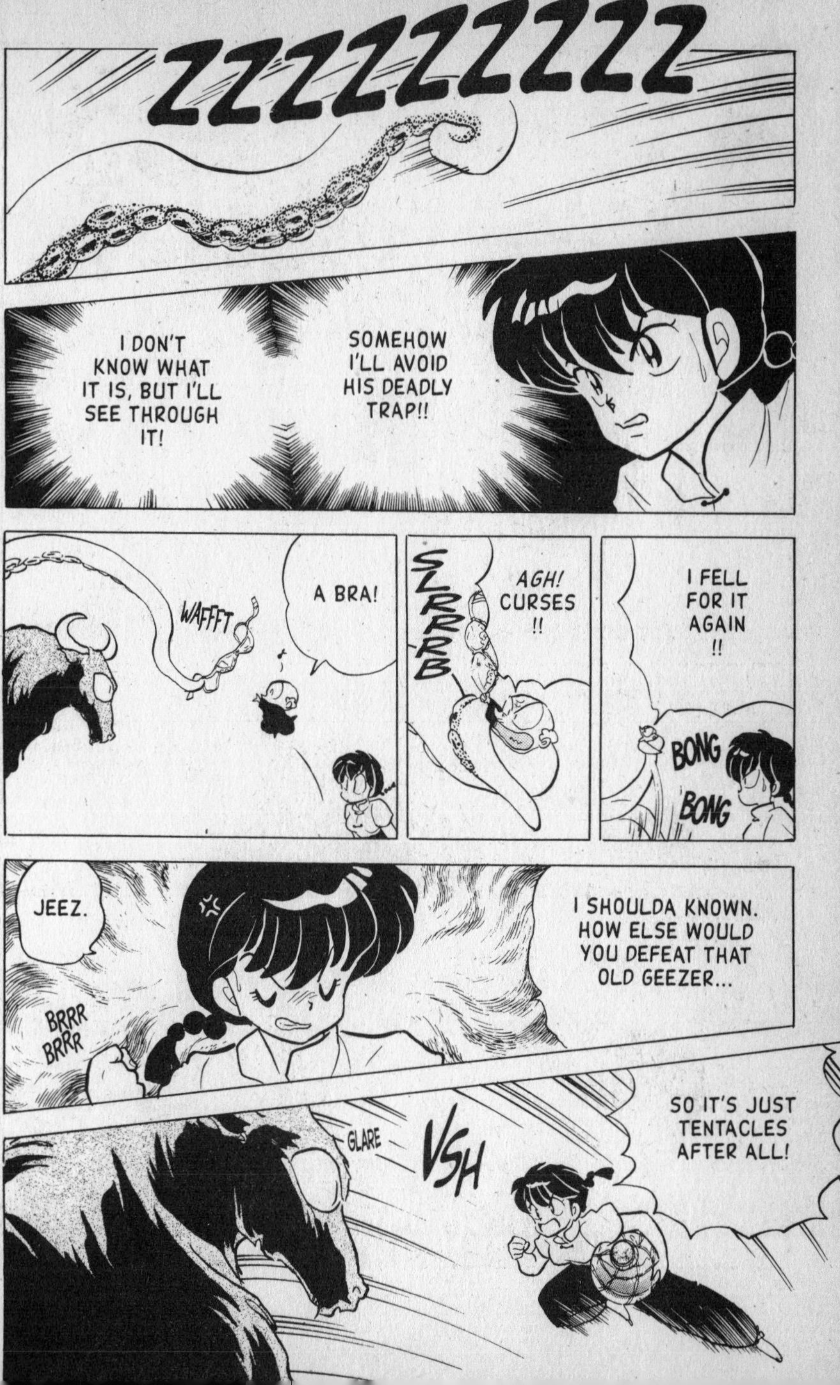
ZZZZZZZZZZ
I DON'T KNOW WHAT IT IS, BUT I'LL SEE THROUGH IT!
SOMEHOW I'LL AVOID HIS DEADLY TRAP!!
WAFFFT
A BRA!
SLRRRB
AGH! CURSES !!
I FELL FOR IT AGAIN !!
BONG
BONG
JEEZ.
I SHOULDA KNOWN. HOW ELSE WOULD YOU DEFEAT THAT OLD GEEZER...
BRRR BRRR
GLARE
VSH
SO IT'S JUST TENTACLES AFTER ALL!

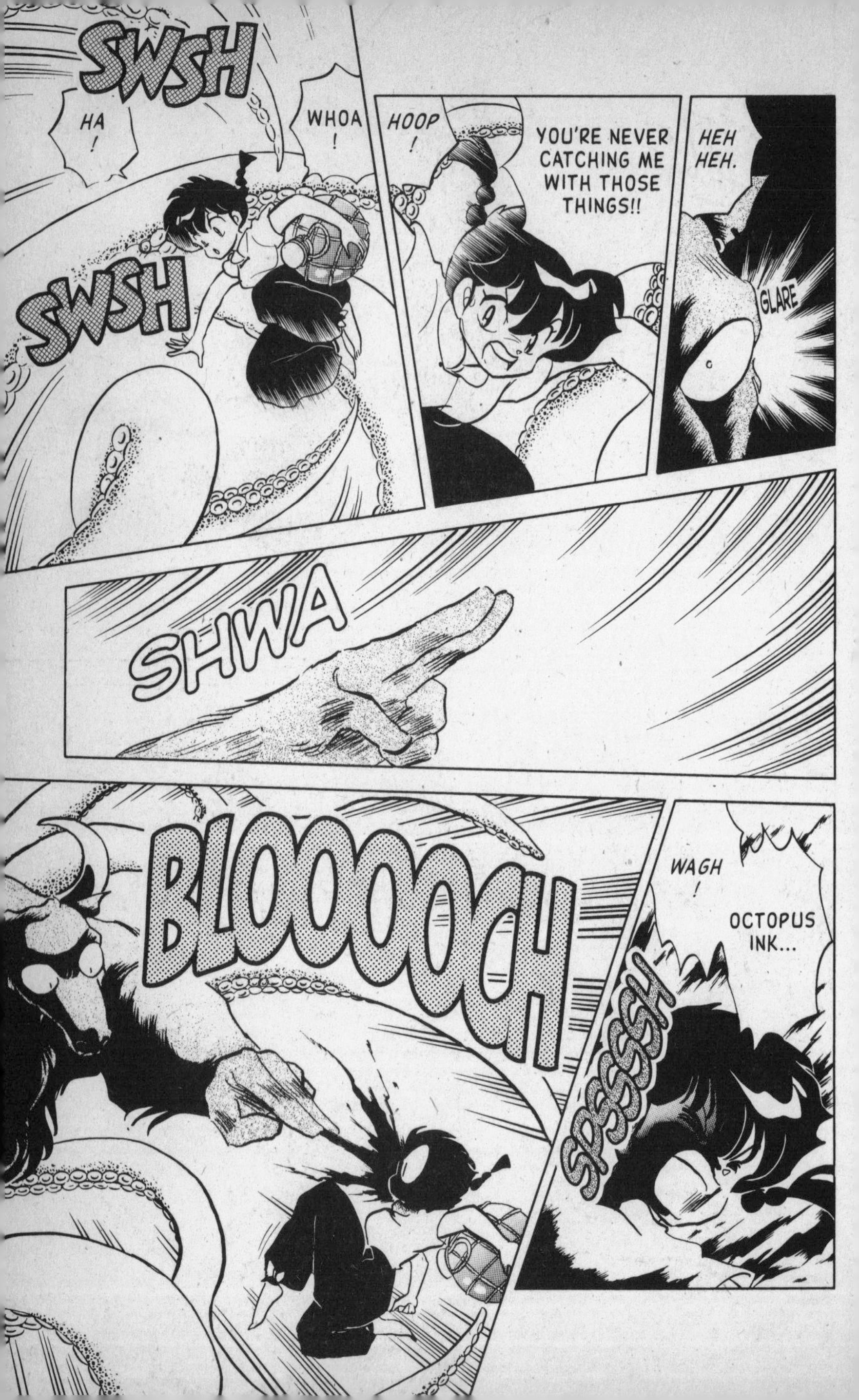
SWSH
HA!
WHOA!
SWSH
HOOP!
YOU'RE NEVER CATCHING ME WITH THOSE THINGS!!
HEH HEH.
GLARE
SHWA
BLOOOOCH
WAGH!
OCTOPUS INK...
SPSSSSH

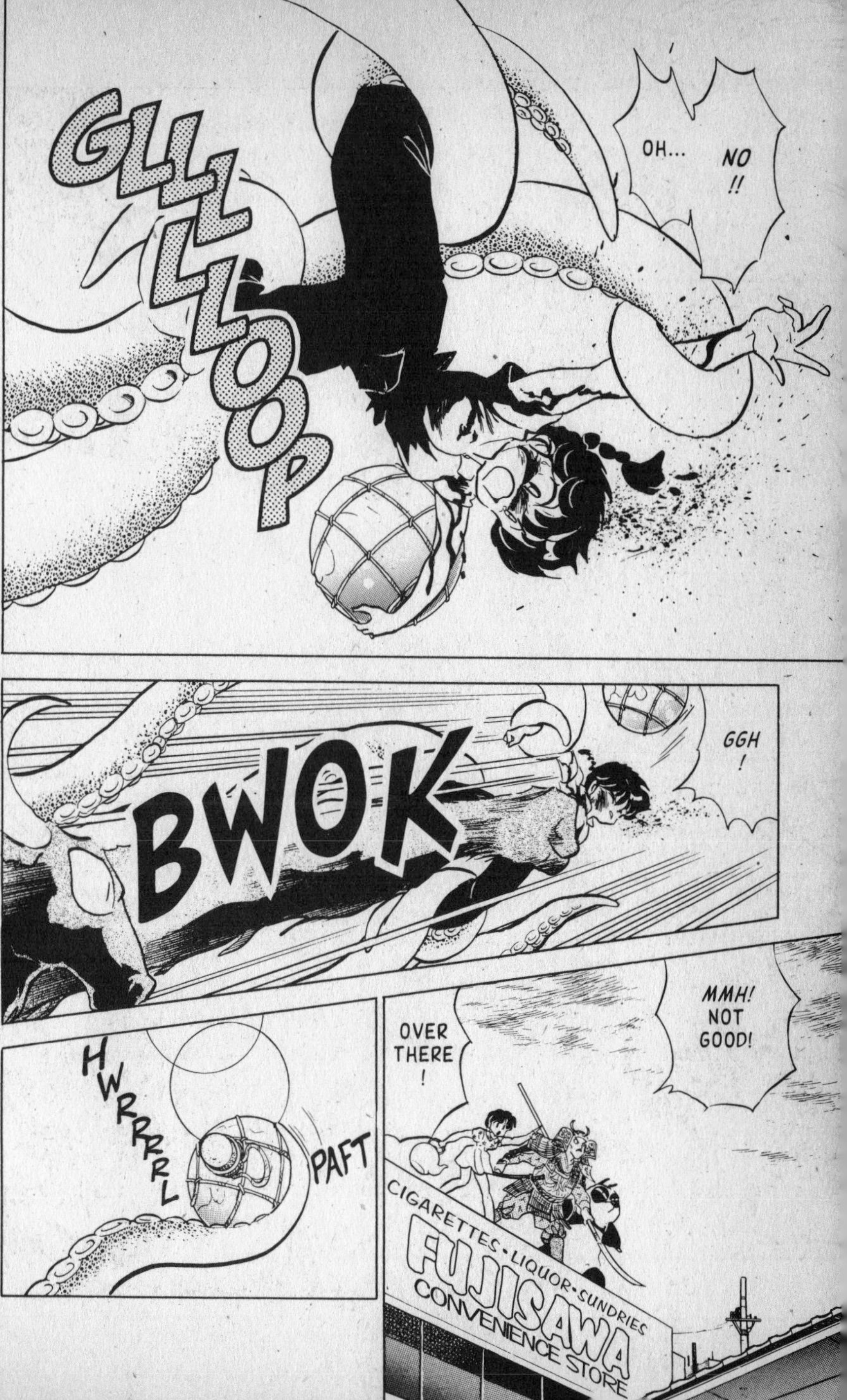
GLLLLOOP
OH... NO !!
BWOK
GGH !
HWRRRRL
PAFT
OVER THERE !
MMH! NOT GOOD!
CIGARETTES • LIQUOR • SUNDRIES
FUJISAWA
CONVENIENCE STORE

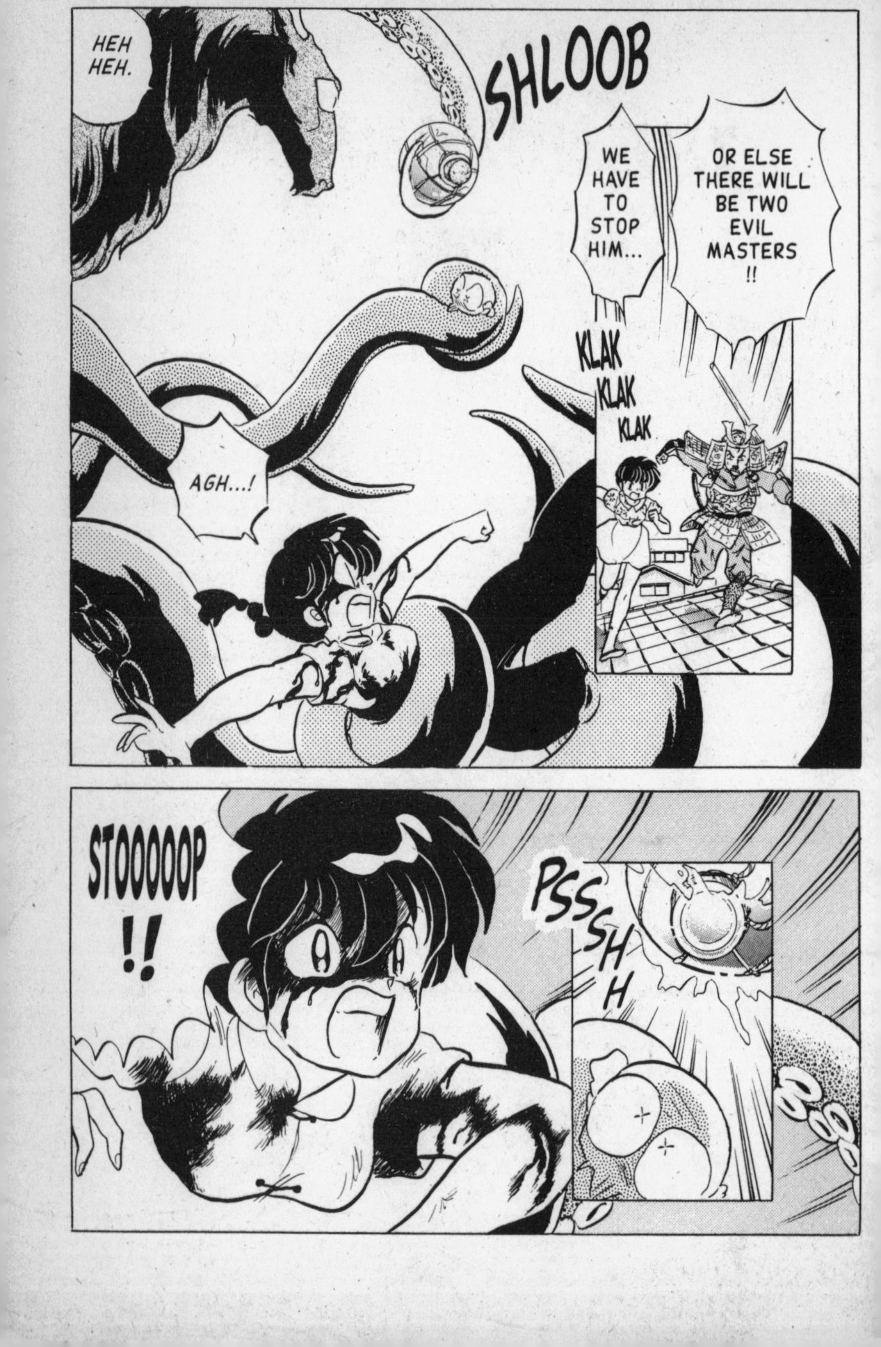
HEH HEH.
SHLOOB
AGH...!
WE HAVE TO STOP HIM...
OR ELSE THERE WILL BE TWO EVIL MASTERS !!
KLAK KLAK KLAK
STOOOOOP !!
PSSSHH

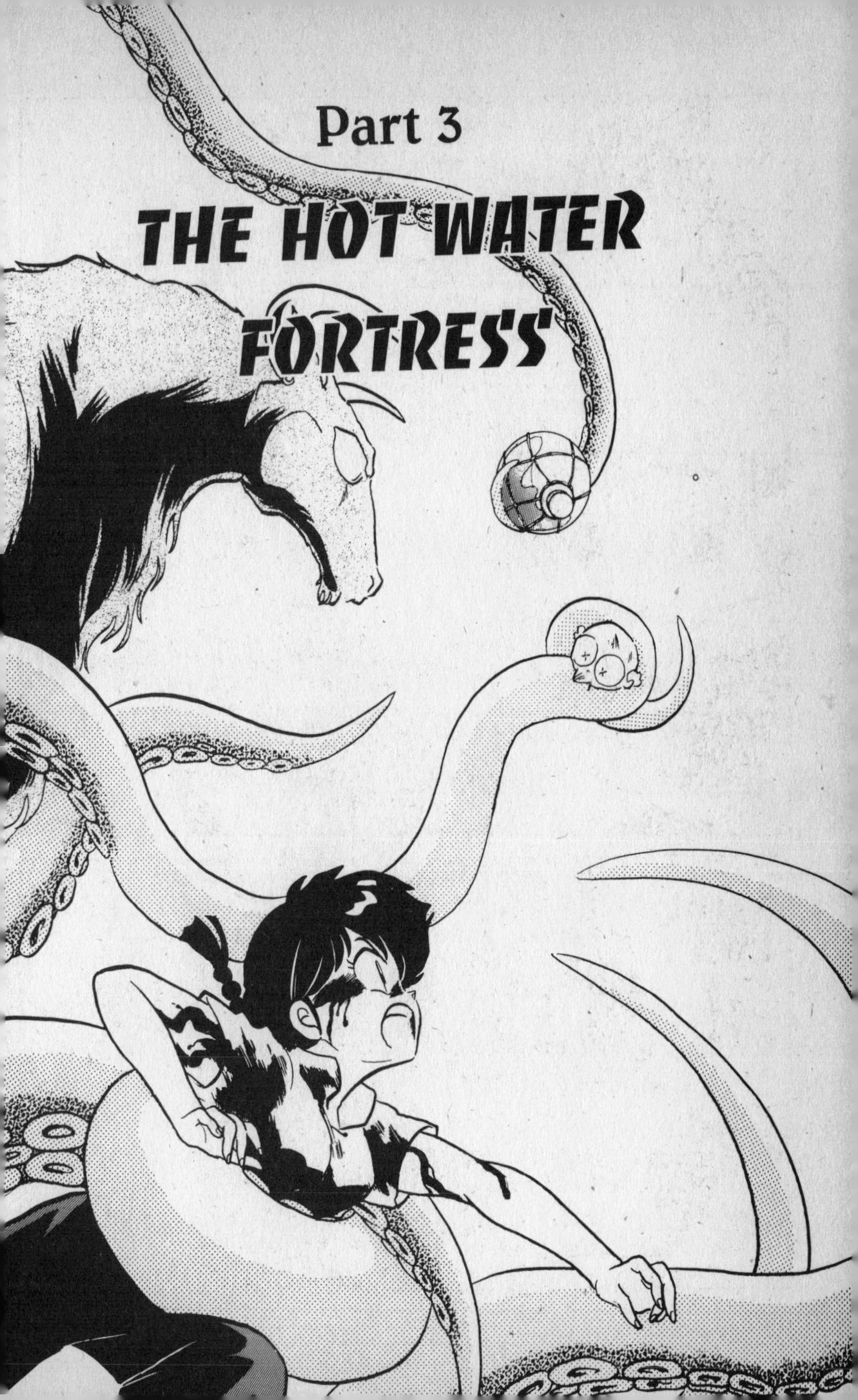
Part 3
THE HOT WATER FORTRESS

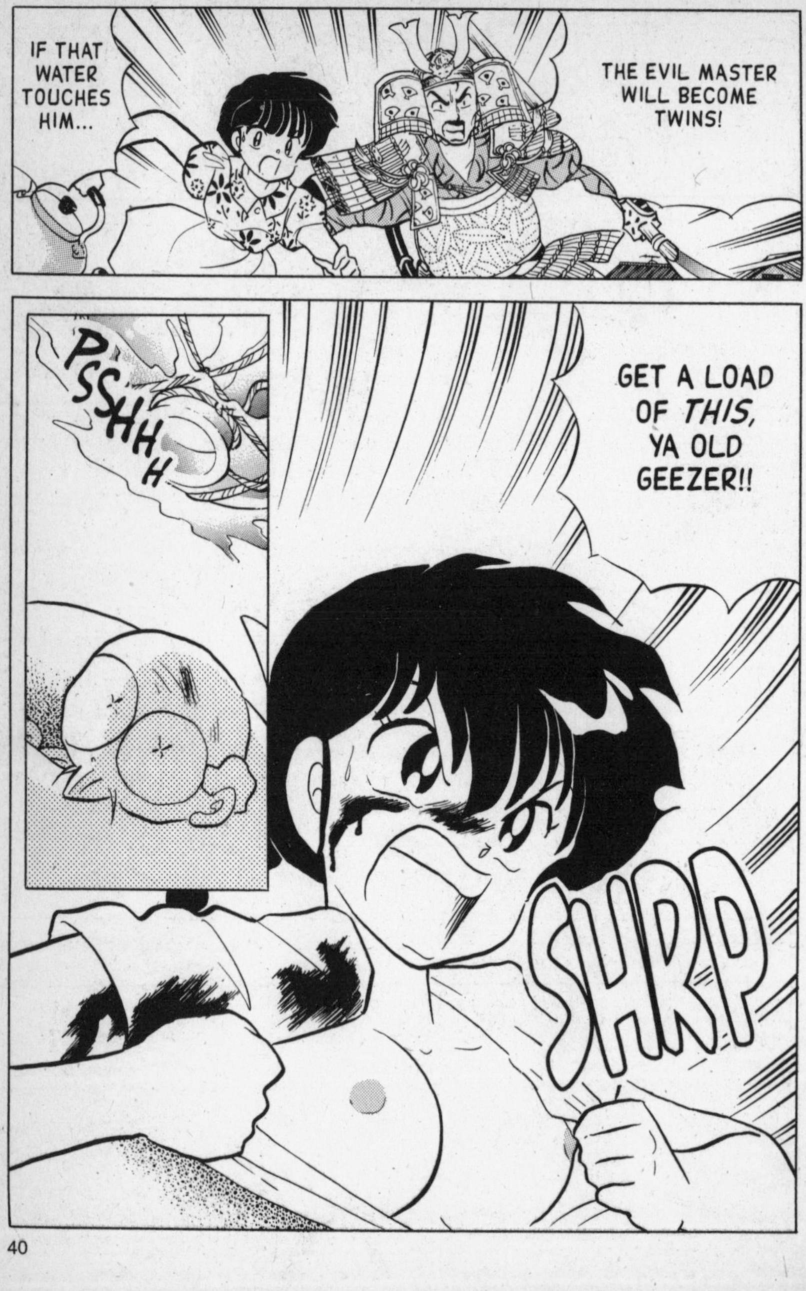
IF THAT WATER TOUCHES HIM...
THE EVIL MASTER WILL BECOME TWINS!
PSSHHH
GET A LOAD OF *THIS*, YA OLD GEEZER!!
SHRP

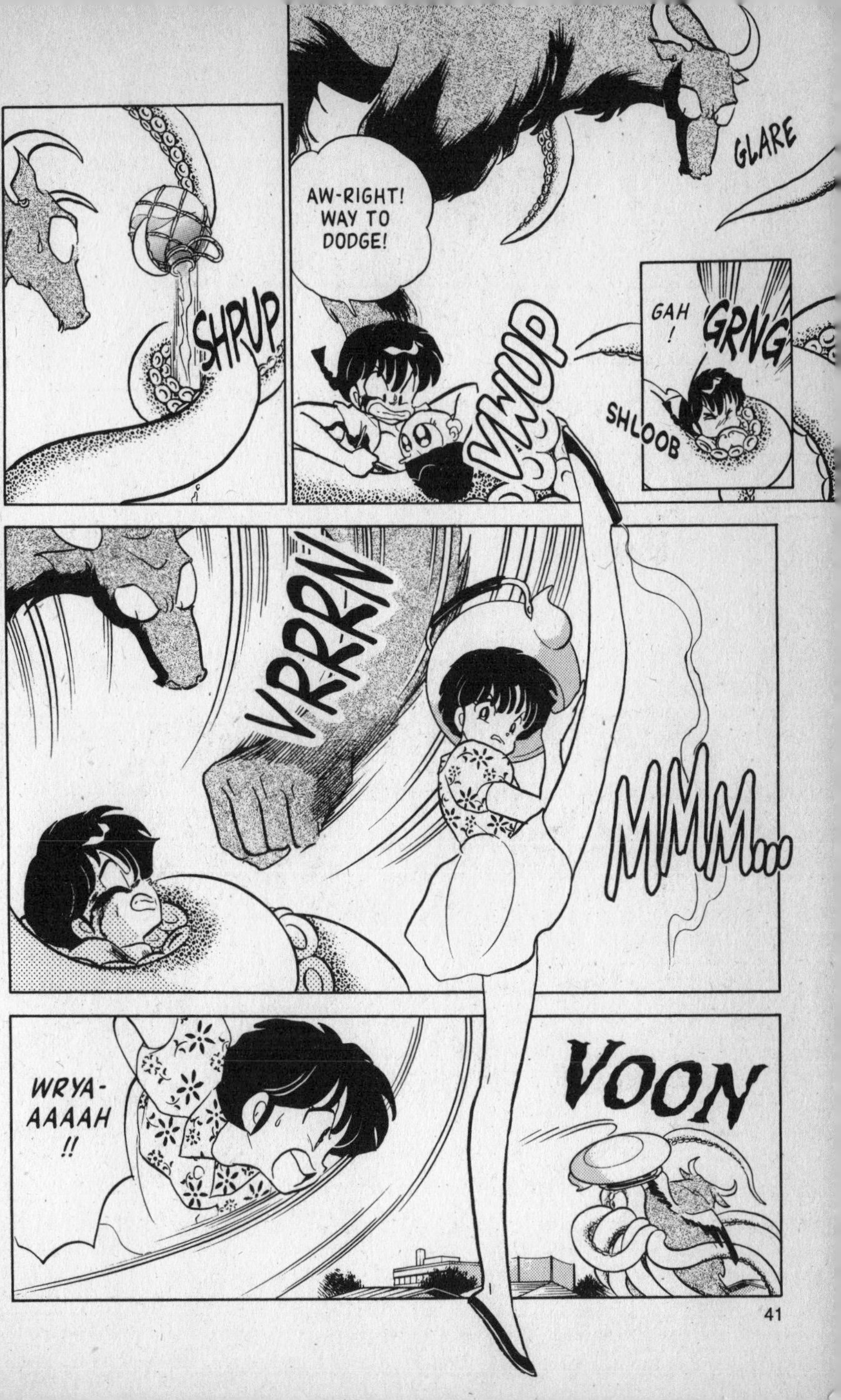
SHRUP
AW-RIGHT! WAY TO DODGE!
GLARE
WWUP
GAH !
GRNG
SHLOOB
VRRRN
MMM...
WRYA-AAAAH !!
VOON

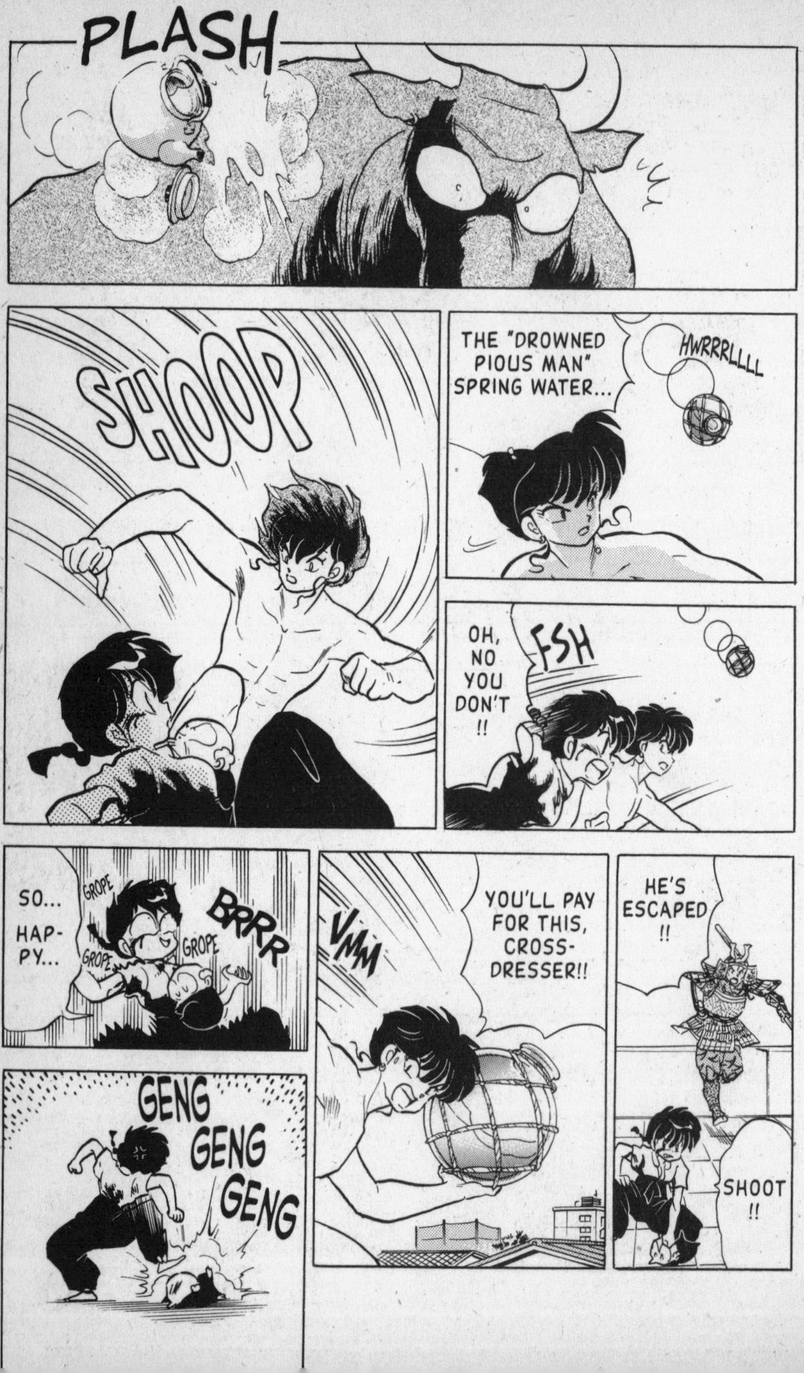
PLASH
SHOOP
THE "DROWNED PIOUS MAN" SPRING WATER...
HWRRRLLLL
OH, NO YOU DON'T !!
FSH
SO... HAP-PY...
GROPE
GROPE
GROPE
BRRRR
VMM
YOU'LL PAY FOR THIS, CROSS-DRESSER!!
HE'S ESCAPED !!
SHOOT !!
GENG
GENG
GENG

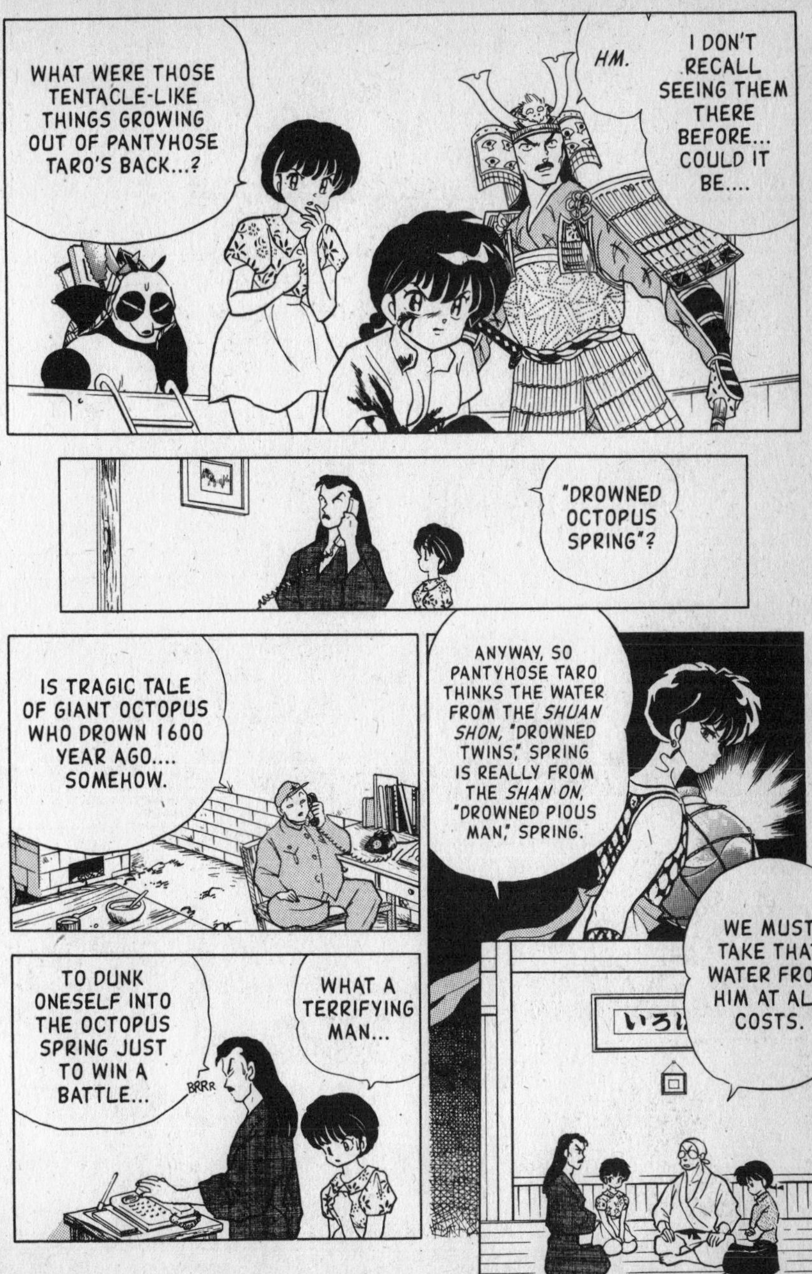

WHAT WERE THOSE TENTACLE-LIKE THINGS GROWING OUT OF PANTYHOSE TARO'S BACK...?
HM.
I DON'T RECALL SEEING THEM THERE BEFORE... COULD IT BE....
"DROWNED OCTOPUS SPRING"?
IS TRAGIC TALE OF GIANT OCTOPUS WHO DROWN 1600 YEAR AGO.... SOMEHOW.
TO DUNK ONESELF INTO THE OCTOPUS SPRING JUST TO WIN A BATTLE...
BRRR
WHAT A TERRIFYING MAN...
ANYWAY, SO PANTYHOSE TARO THINKS THE WATER FROM THE *SHUAN SHON*, "DROWNED TWINS," SPRING IS REALLY FROM THE *SHAN ON*, "DROWNED PIOUS MAN," SPRING.
WE MUST TAKE THAT WATER FROM HIM AT ALL COSTS.
いろは

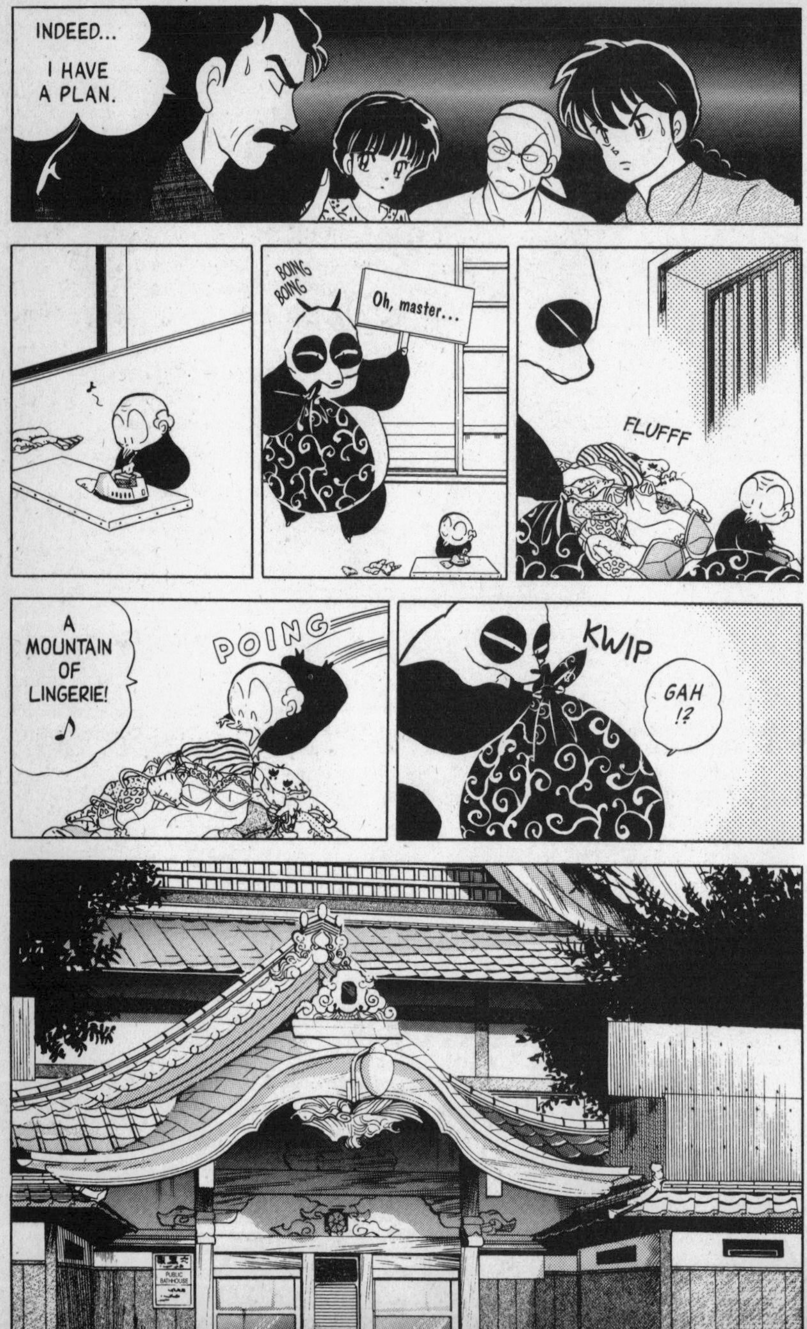
INDEED...
I HAVE A PLAN.
BOING BOING
Oh, master...
FLUFFF
A MOUNTAIN OF LINGERIE! ♪
POING
KWIP
GAH !?
PUBLIC BATHHOUSE

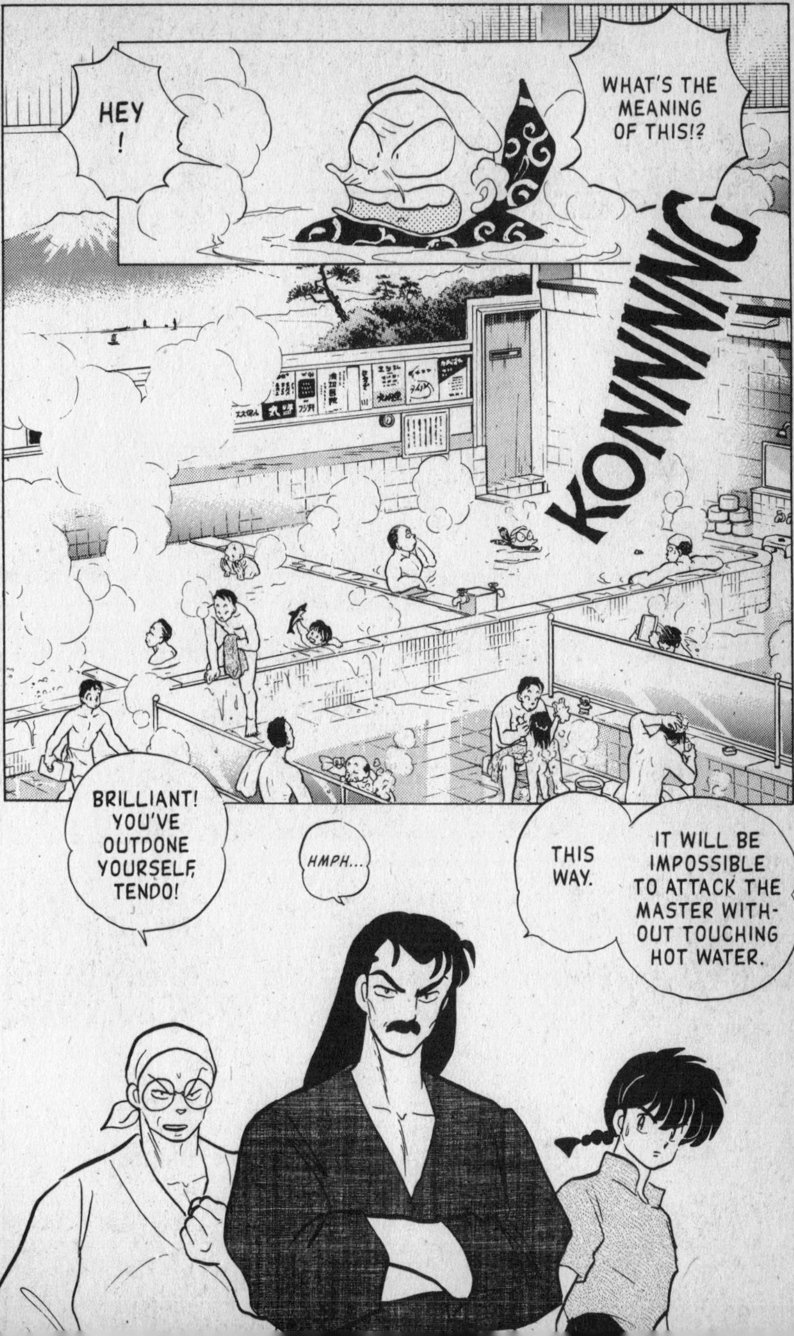
HEY!
WHAT'S THE MEANING OF THIS!?
KONNNG
BRILLIANT! YOU'VE OUTDONE YOURSELF, TENDO!
HMPH...
THIS WAY.
IT WILL BE IMPOSSIBLE TO ATTACK THE MASTER WITH-OUT TOUCHING HOT WATER.

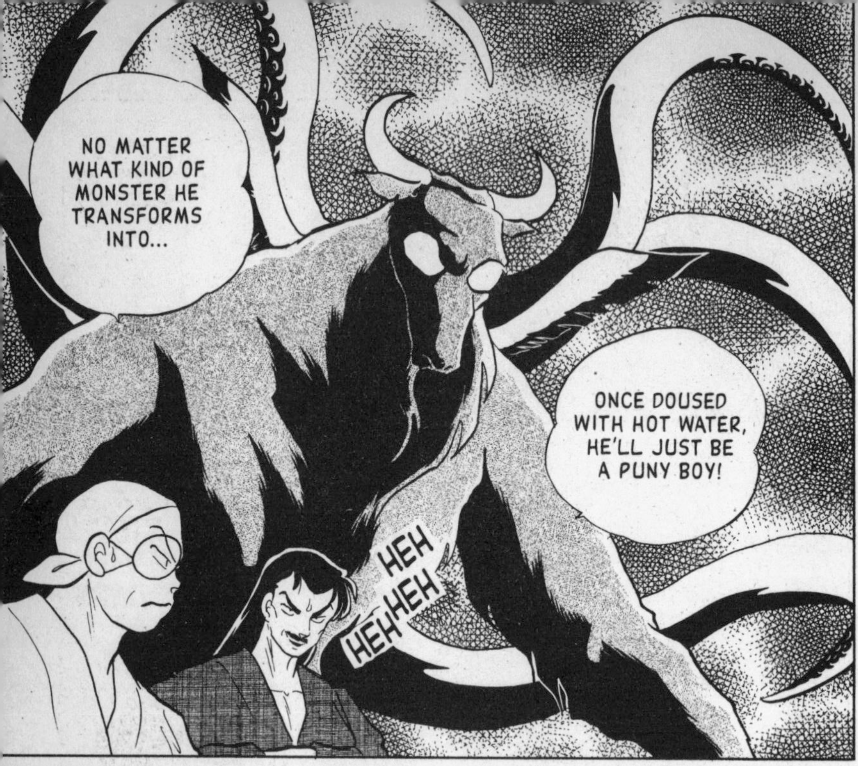
NO MATTER WHAT KIND OF MONSTER HE TRANSFORMS INTO...
ONCE DOUSED WITH HOT WATER, HE'LL JUST BE A PUNY BOY!
HEH HEH HEH
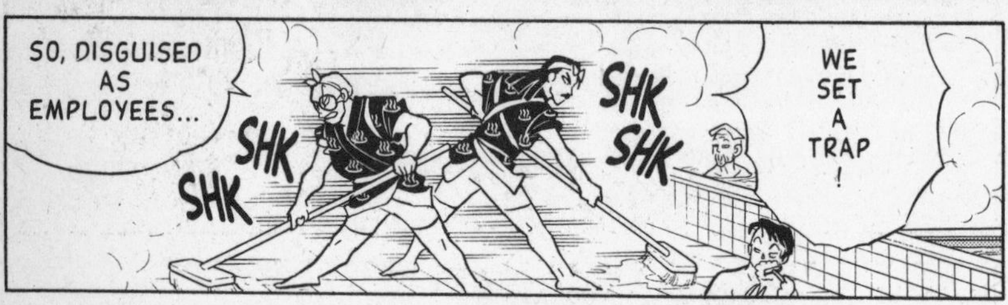
SO, DISGUISED AS EMPLOYEES...
SHK SHK
SHK SHK
WE SET A TRAP!
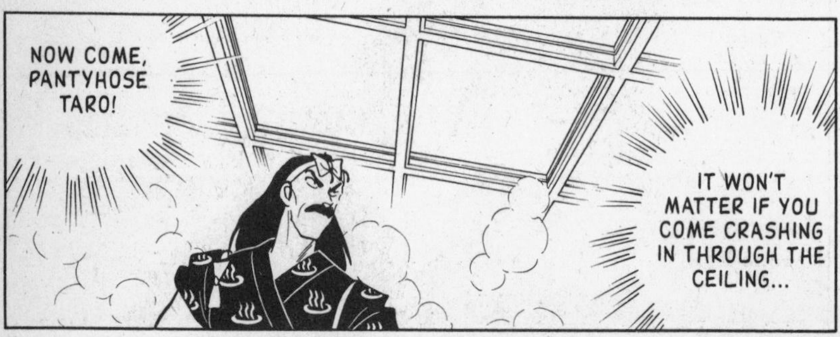
NOW COME, PANTYHOSE TARO!
IT WON'T MATTER IF YOU COME CRASHING IN THROUGH THE CEILING...

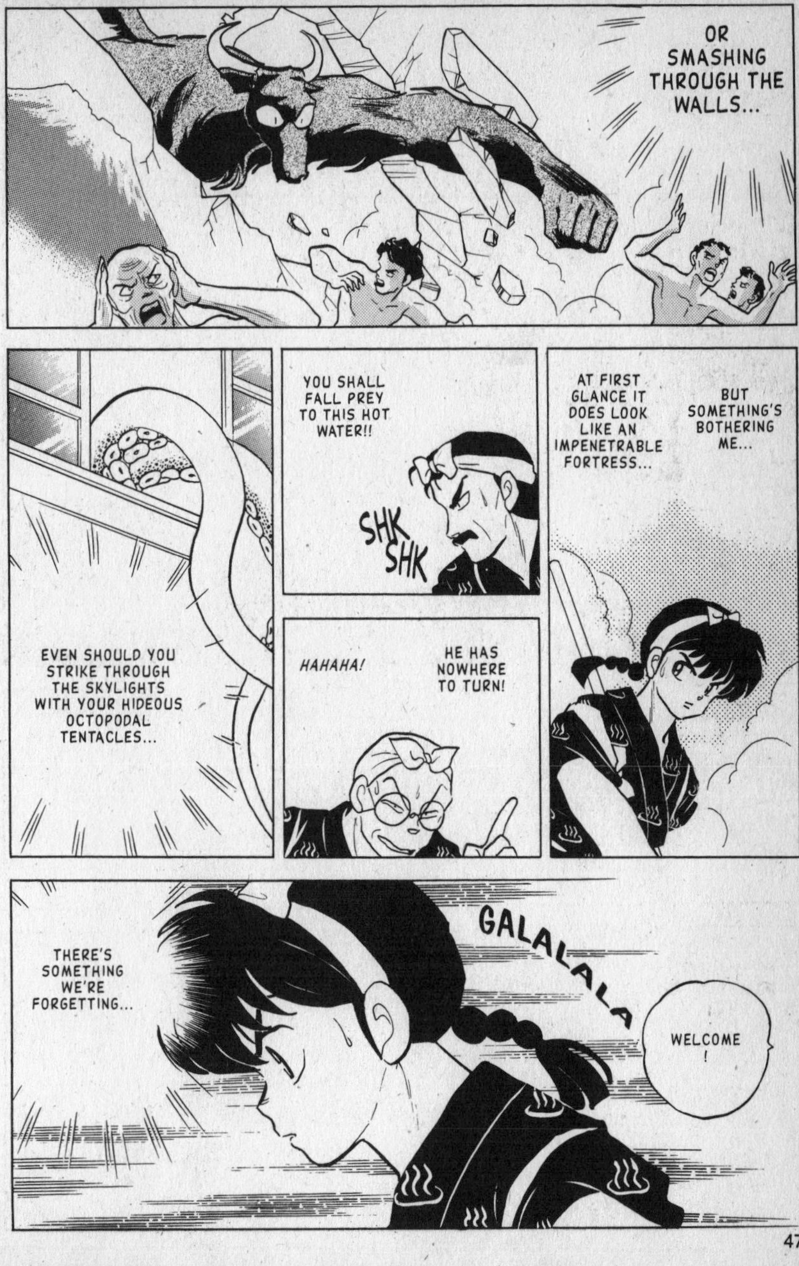
OR SMASHING THROUGH THE WALLS...
EVEN SHOULD YOU STRIKE THROUGH THE SKYLIGHTS WITH YOUR HIDEOUS OCTOPODAL TENTACLES...
YOU SHALL FALL PREY TO THIS HOT WATER!!
SHK SHK
HAHAHA!
HE HAS NOWHERE TO TURN!
AT FIRST GLANCE IT DOES LOOK LIKE AN IMPENETRABLE FORTRESS...
BUT SOMETHING'S BOTHERING ME...
THERE'S SOMETHING WE'RE FORGETTING...
GALALALALA
WELCOME!

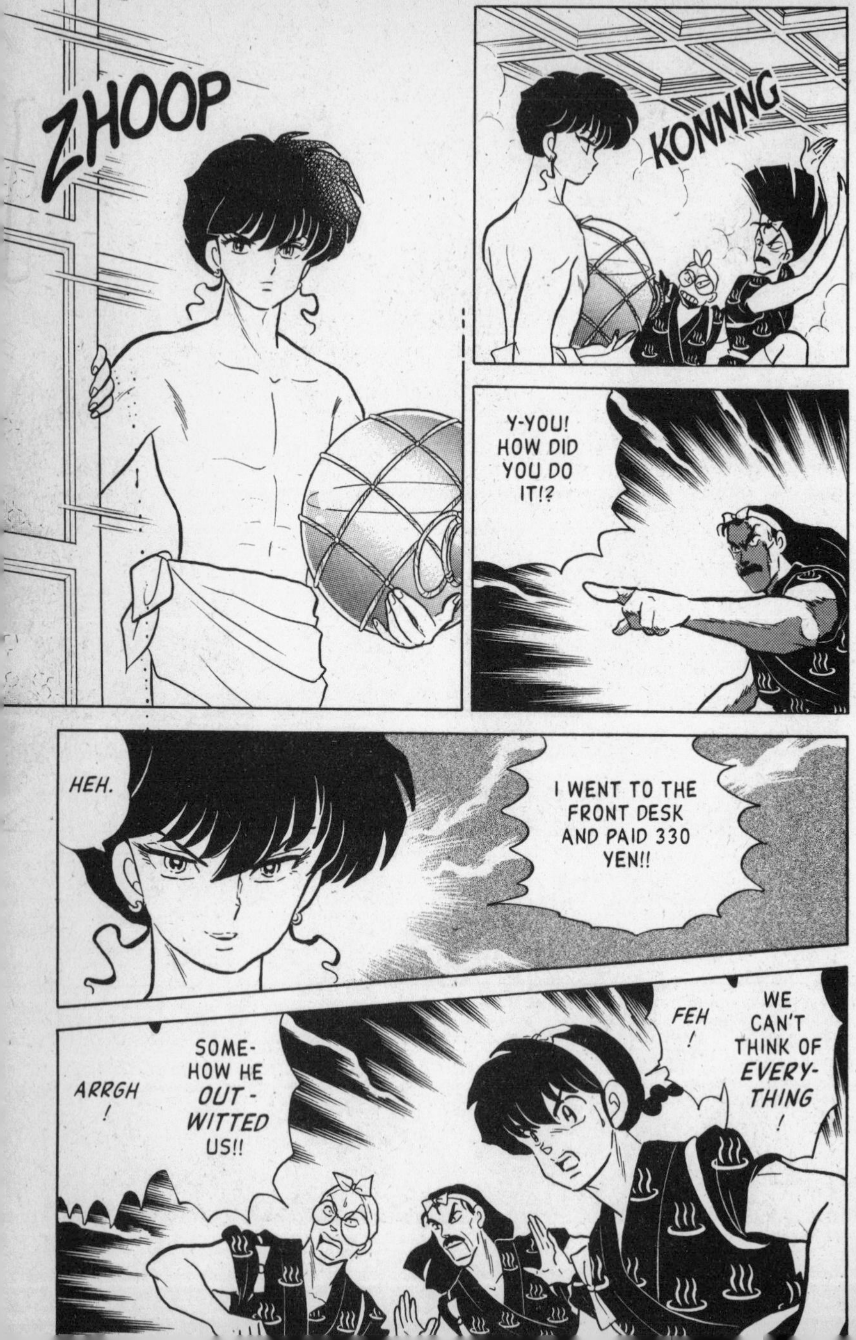
ZHOOP
KONNNG
Y-YOU! HOW DID YOU DO IT!?
HEH.
I WENT TO THE FRONT DESK AND PAID 330 YEN!!
ARRGH!
SOME-HOW HE OUT-WITTED US!!
FEH!
WE CAN'T THINK OF EVERY-THING!

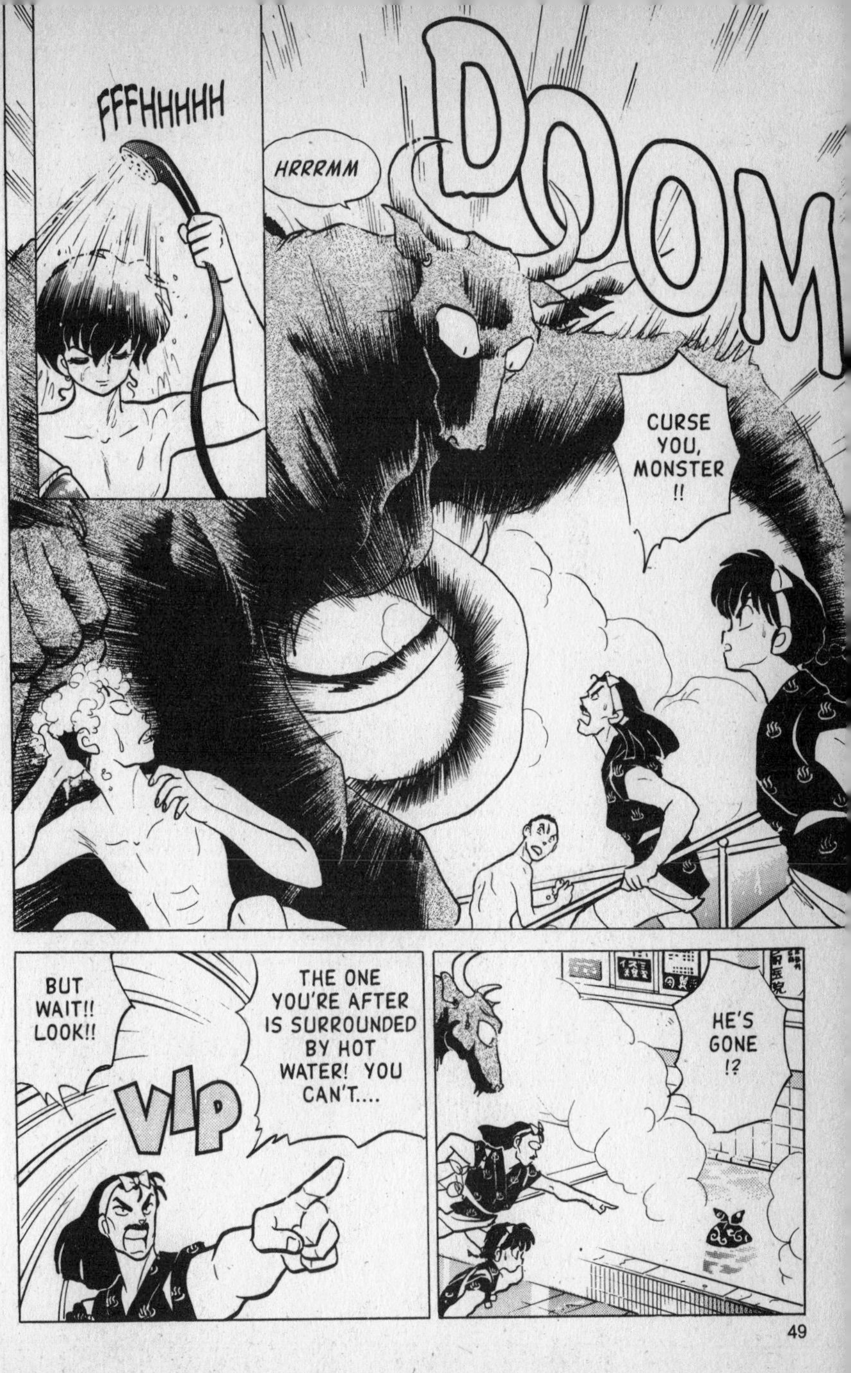
FFFHHHHH
HRRRMM
DOOOM
CURSE YOU, MONSTER !!
BUT WAIT!! LOOK!!
THE ONE YOU'RE AFTER IS SURROUNDED BY HOT WATER! YOU CAN'T....
VIP
HE'S GONE !?

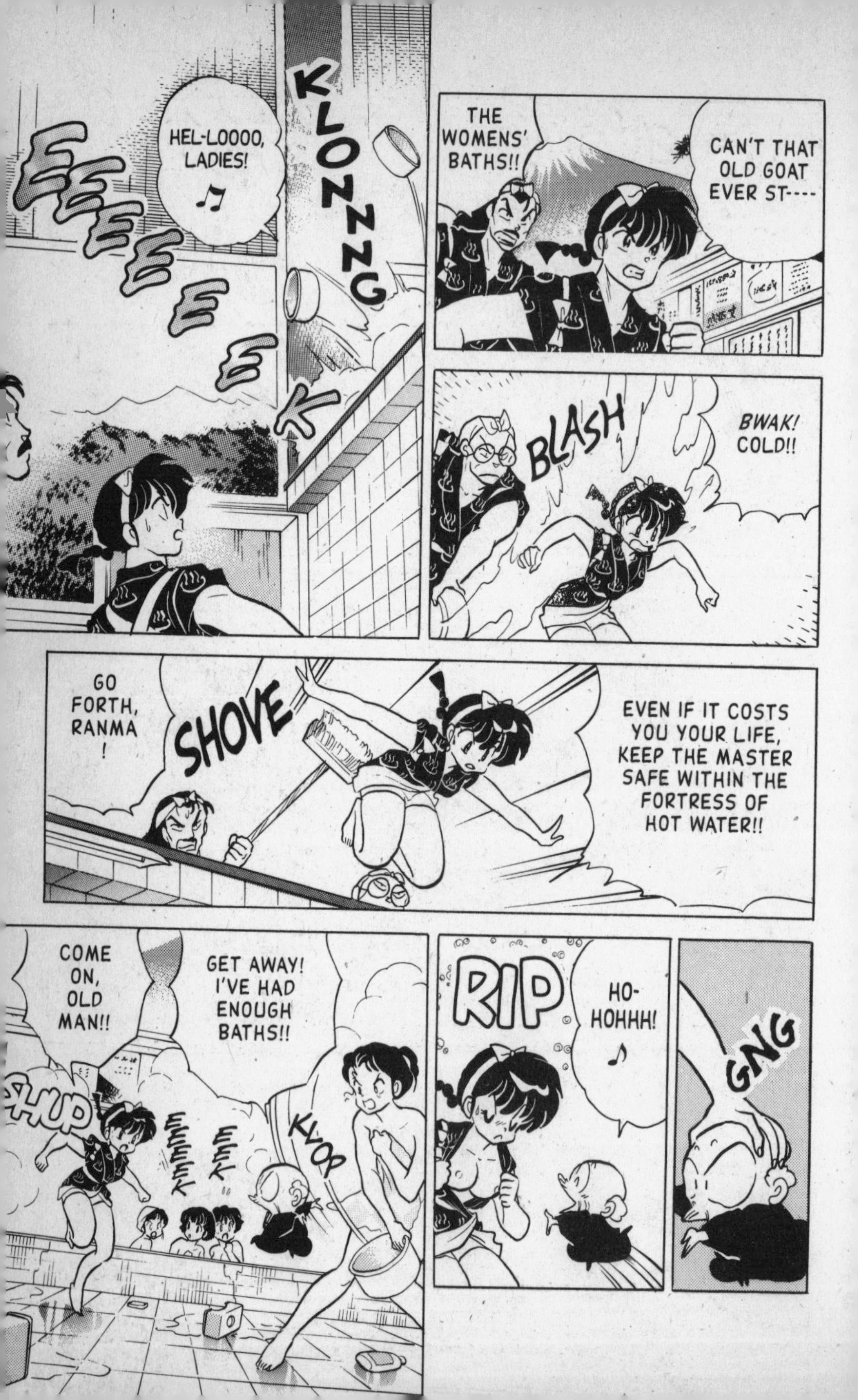
EEEEEEEK
HEL-LOOOO, LADIES! ♪
KLONNNG
THE WOMENS' BATHS!!
CAN'T THAT OLD GOAT EVER ST----
BLASH
BWAK! COLD!!
GO FORTH, RANMA!
SHOVE
EVEN IF IT COSTS YOU YOUR LIFE, KEEP THE MASTER SAFE WITHIN THE FORTRESS OF HOT WATER!!
COME ON, OLD MAN!!
GET AWAY! I'VE HAD ENOUGH BATHS!!
EEEEK
EEEK
KLOP
RIP
HO-HOHHH! ♪
GNG

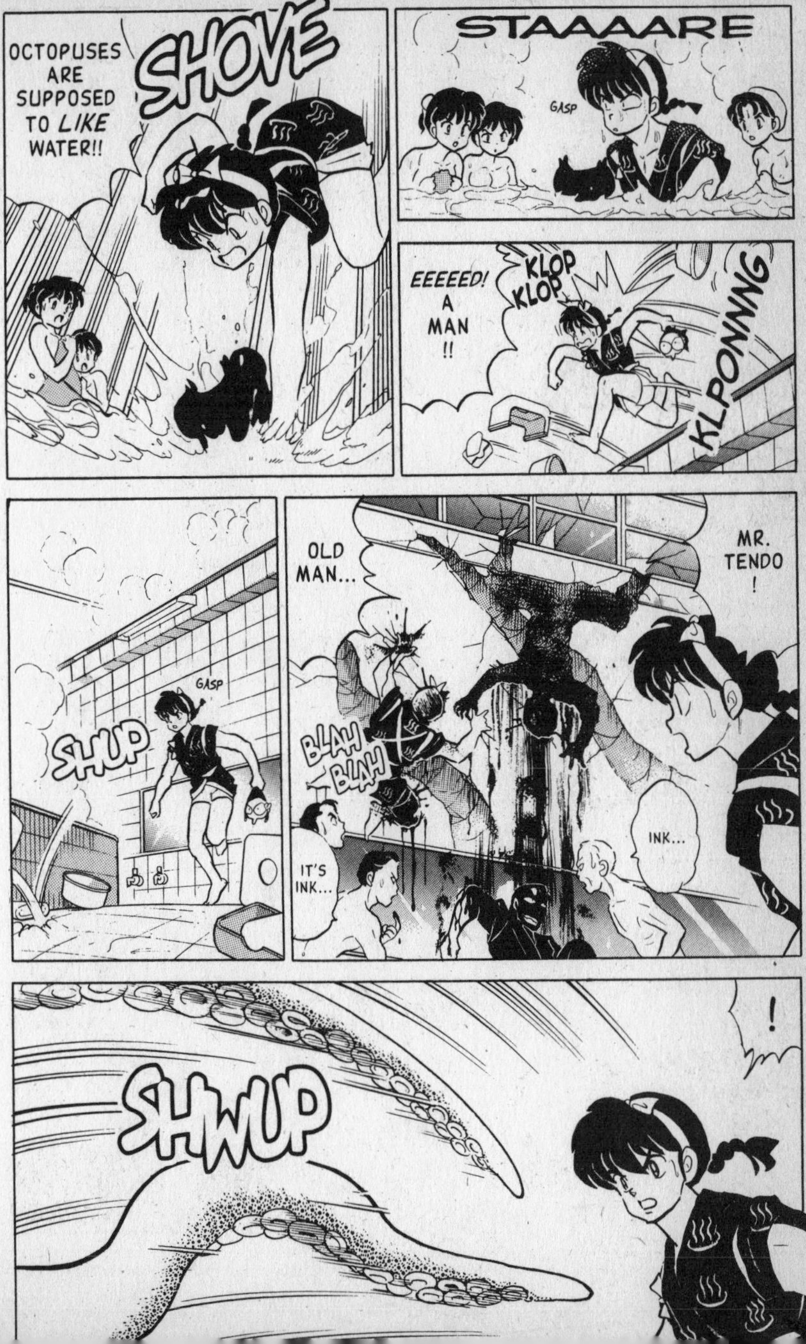
OCTOPUSES ARE SUPPOSED TO LIKE WATER!!
SHOVE
STAAAAARE
GASP
EEEEED! A MAN !!
KLOP KLOP
KLPONNNG
GASP
SHUP
OLD MAN...
MR. TENDO !
BLAH BLAH
IT'S INK...
INK...
!
SHWUP

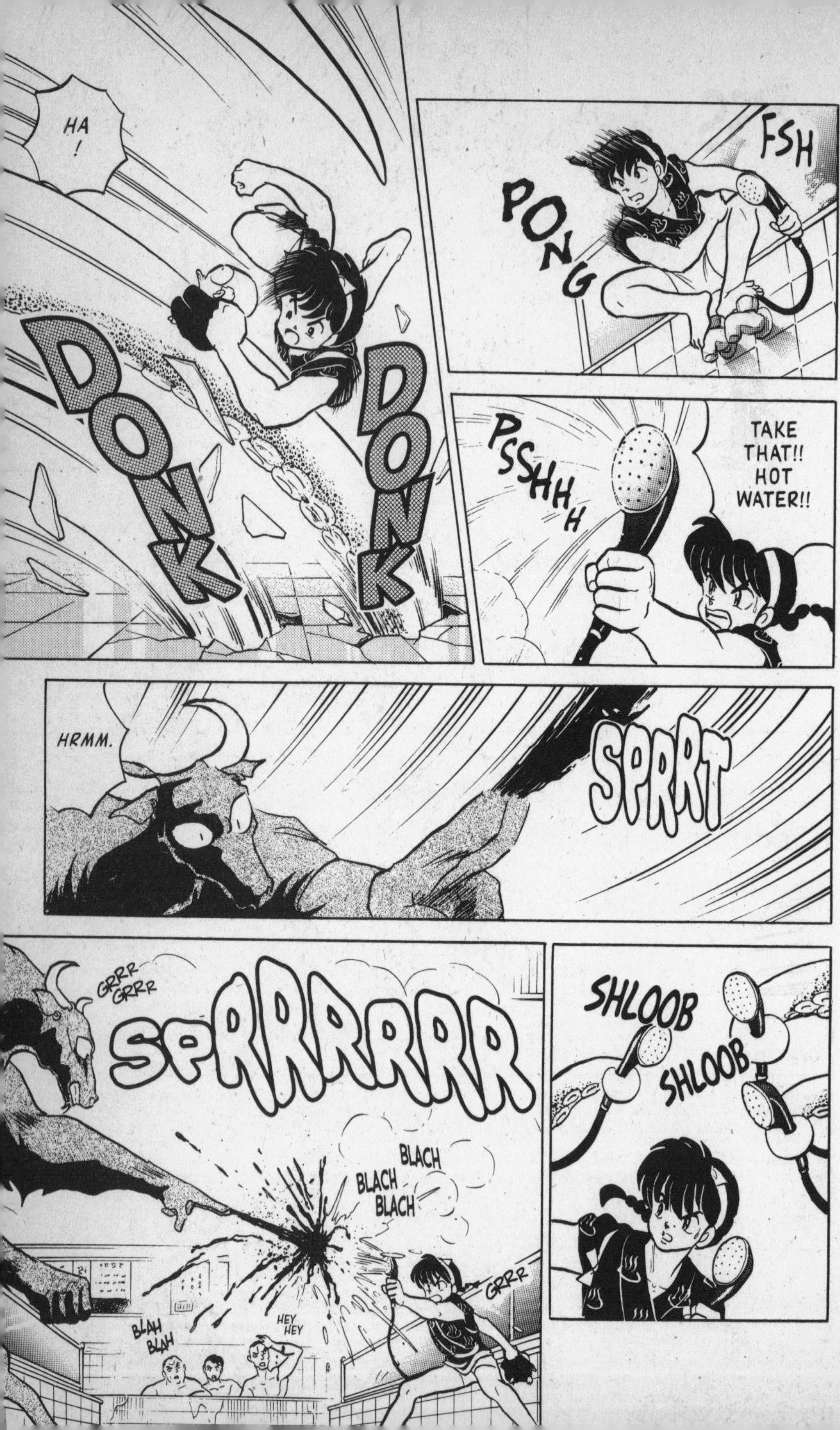
HA!
DONK
DONK
PONG
FSH
PSSHHHH
TAKE THAT!! HOT WATER!!
HRMM.
SPRRT
GRRR GRRR
SPRRRRRRR
BLACH
BLACH
BLACH
BLACH
GRRR
BLAH BLAH
HEY HEY
SHLOOB
SHLOOB

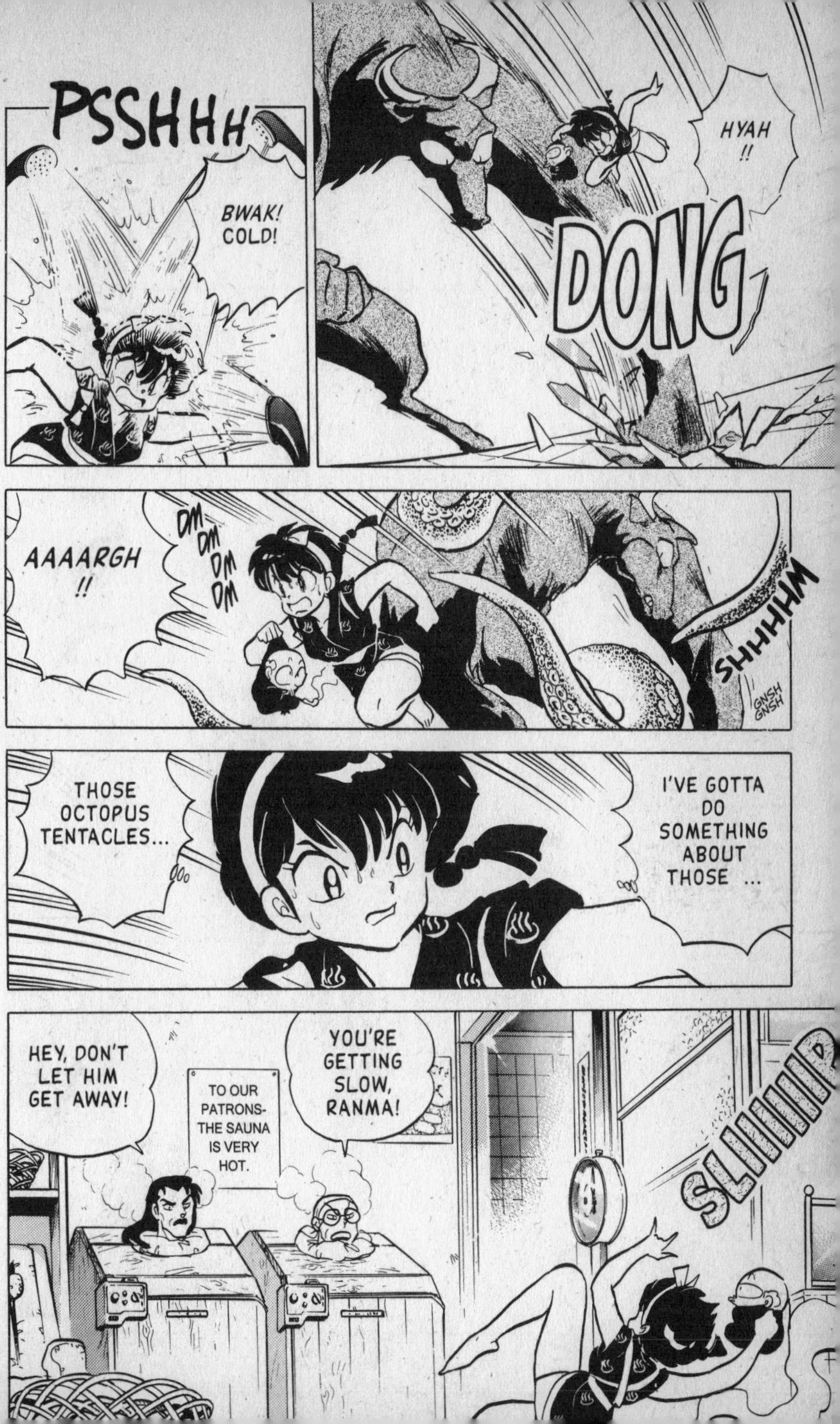
PSSHHH
BWAK! COLD!
HYAH !!
DONG
AAAARGH !!
DM DM DM DM
SHHHHM
GNSH GNSH
THOSE OCTOPUS TENTACLES...
I'VE GOTTA DO SOMETHING ABOUT THOSE ...
HEY, DON'T LET HIM GET AWAY!
TO OUR PATRONS- THE SAUNA IS VERY HOT.
YOU'RE GETTING SLOW, RANMA!
SLIIIIIP

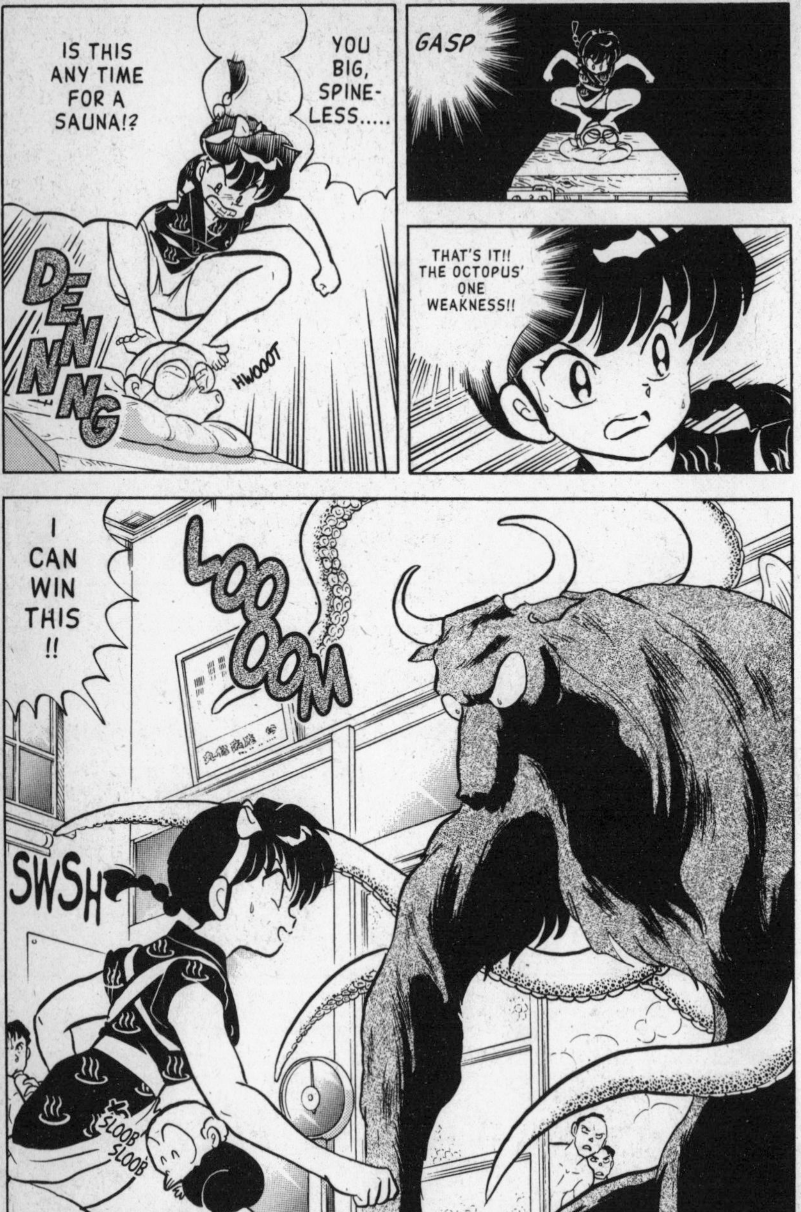
IS THIS ANY TIME FOR A SAUNA!?
YOU BIG, SPINE-LESS.....
DENNNG
HWOOOT
GASP
THAT'S IT!! THE OCTOPUS' ONE WEAKNESS!!
I CAN WIN THIS !!
LOOOOOM
SWSH
SLOOB SLOOB

Part 4
TENTACULAR SPECTACULAR

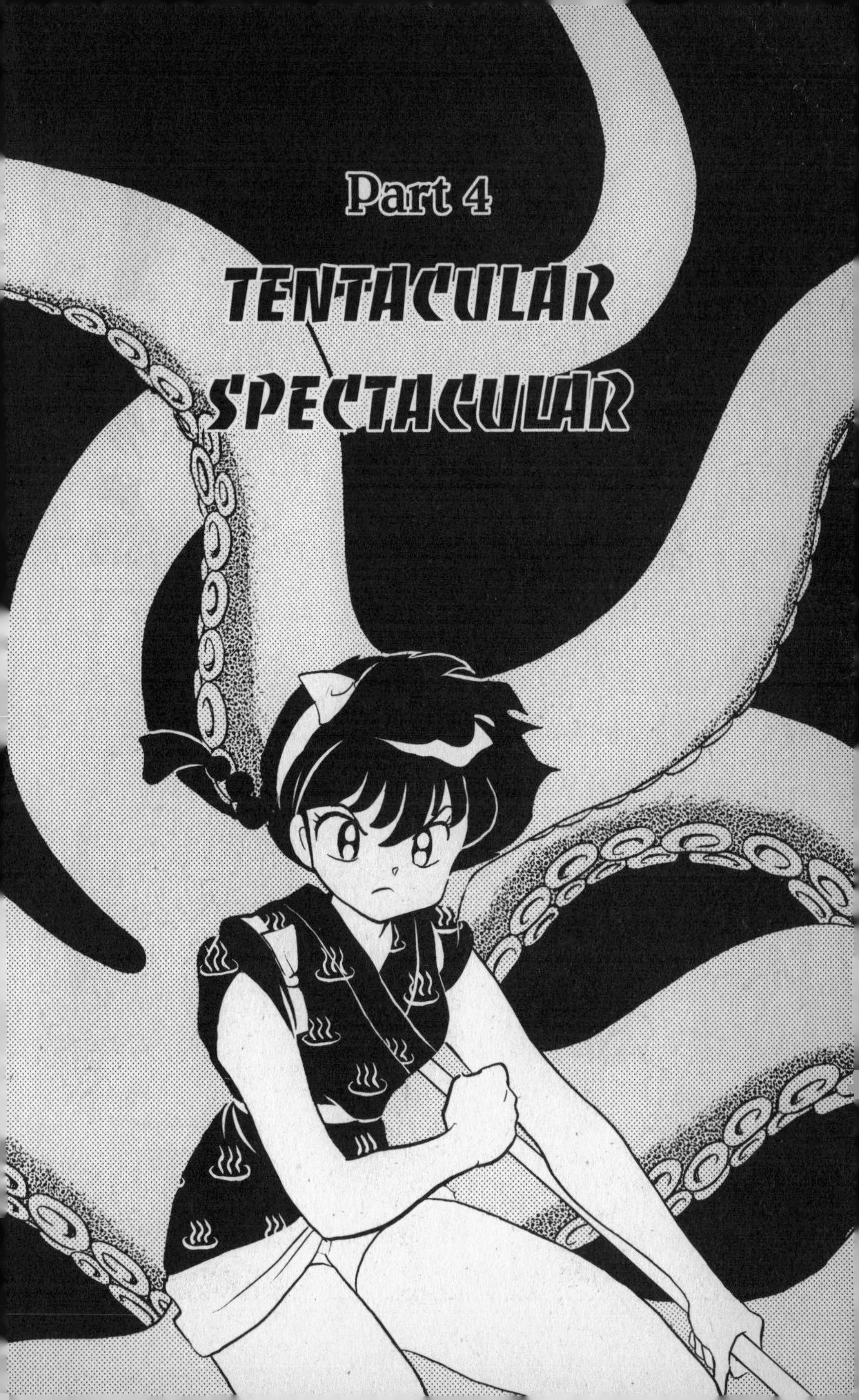

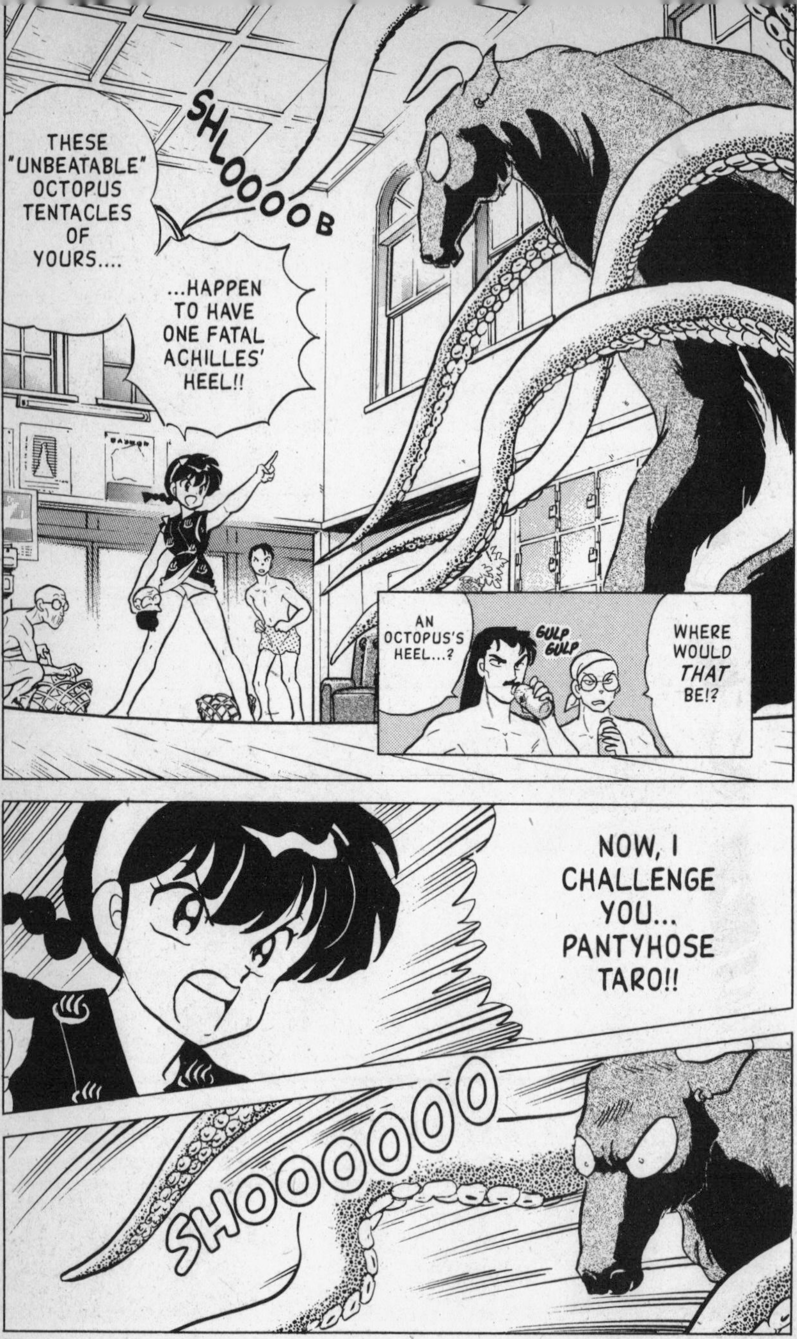
THESE "UNBEATABLE" OCTOPUS TENTACLES OF YOURS....
SHLOOOOOB
...HAPPEN TO HAVE ONE FATAL ACHILLES' HEEL!!
AN OCTOPUS'S HEEL...?
GULP GULP
WHERE WOULD THAT BE!?
NOW, I CHALLENGE YOU... PANTYHOSE TARO!!
SHOOOOOO

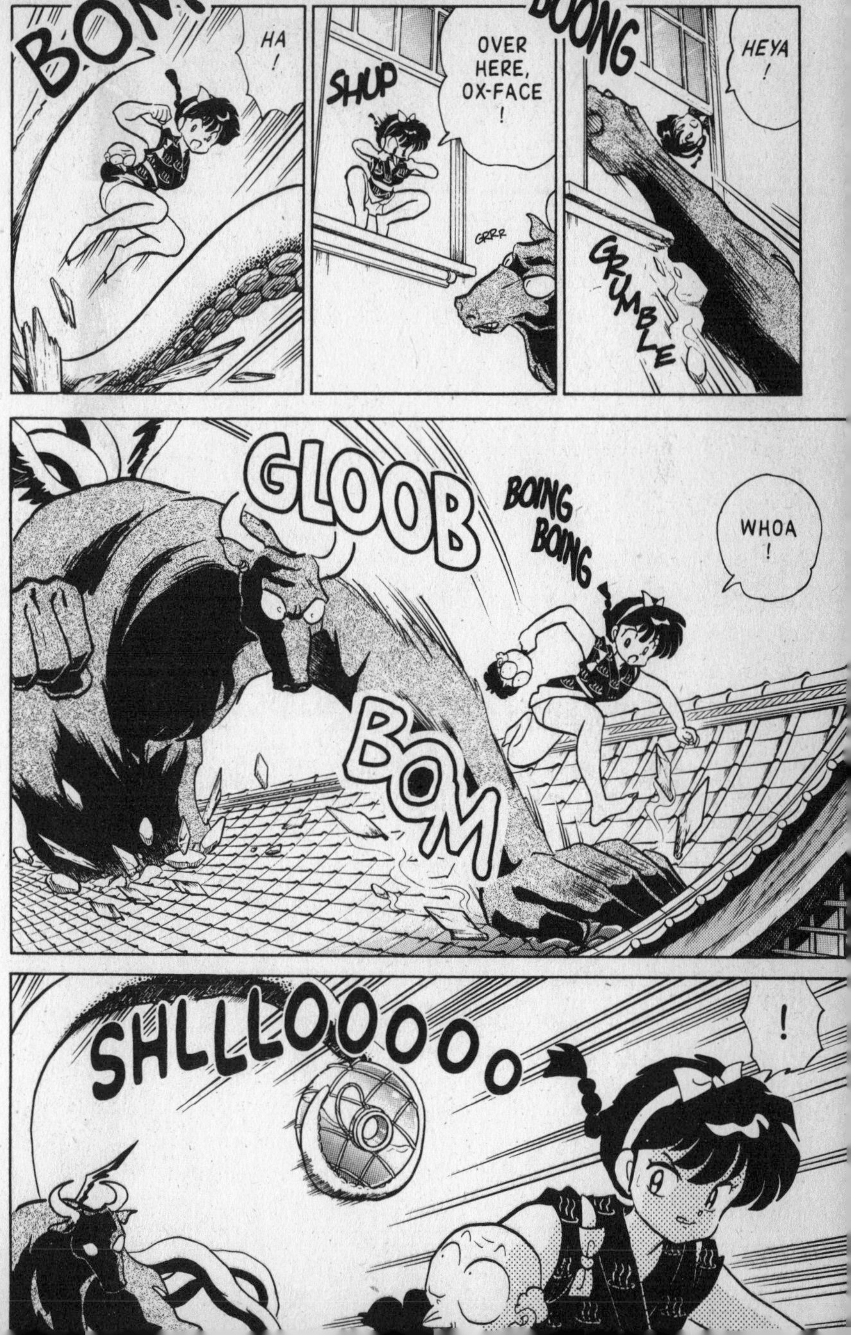
BOM
HA!
SHUP
OVER HERE, OX-FACE!
GRRR
BOONG
HEYA!
GRUMBLE
GLOOB
BOING BOING
WHOA!
BOM
SHLLOOOOOO
!

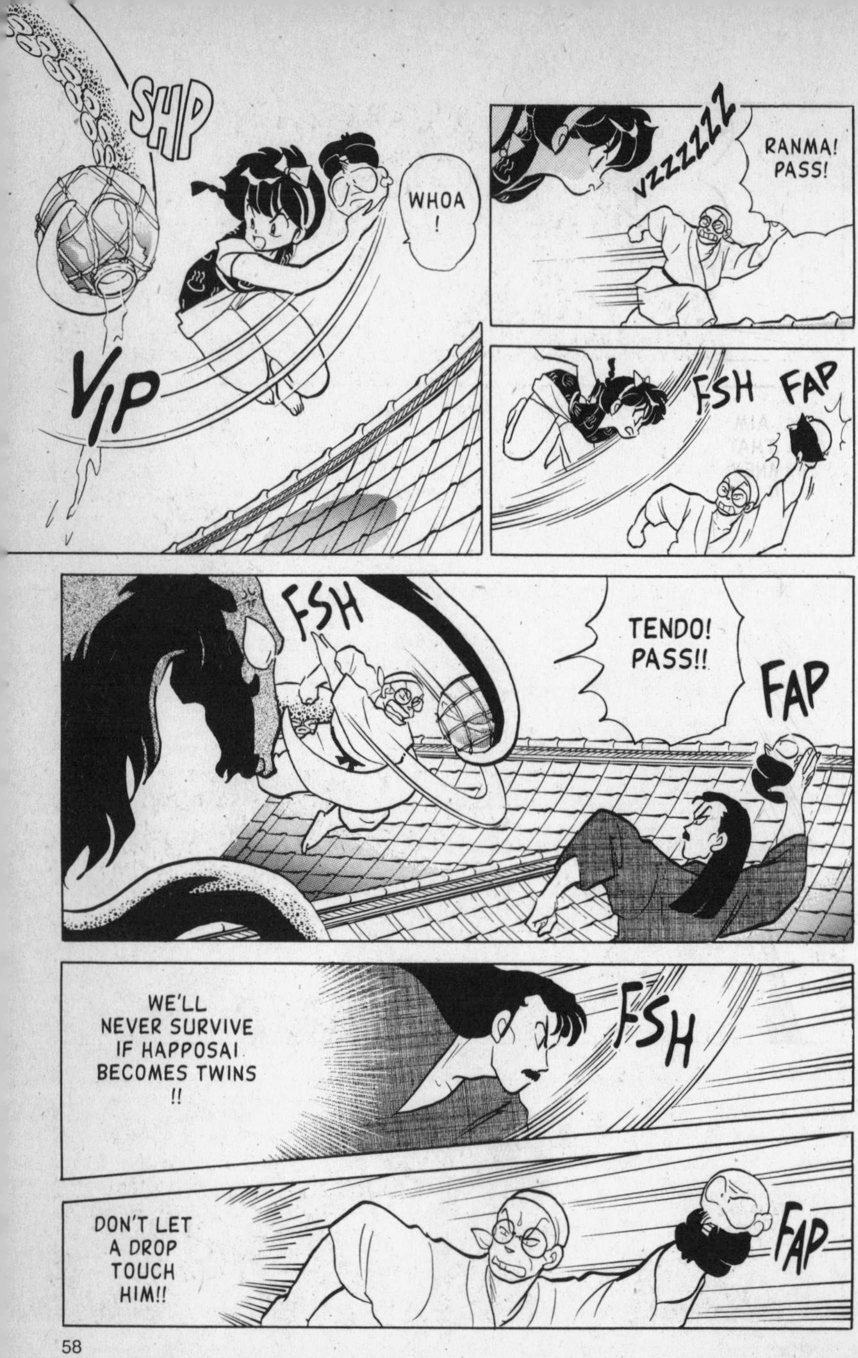
SHP
WHOA!
VIP
VZZZZZZ
RANMA! PASS!
FSH
FAP
FSH
TENDO! PASS!!
FAP
WE'LL NEVER SURVIVE IF HAPPOSAI BECOMES TWINS!!
FSH
DON'T LET A DROP TOUCH HIM!!
FAP

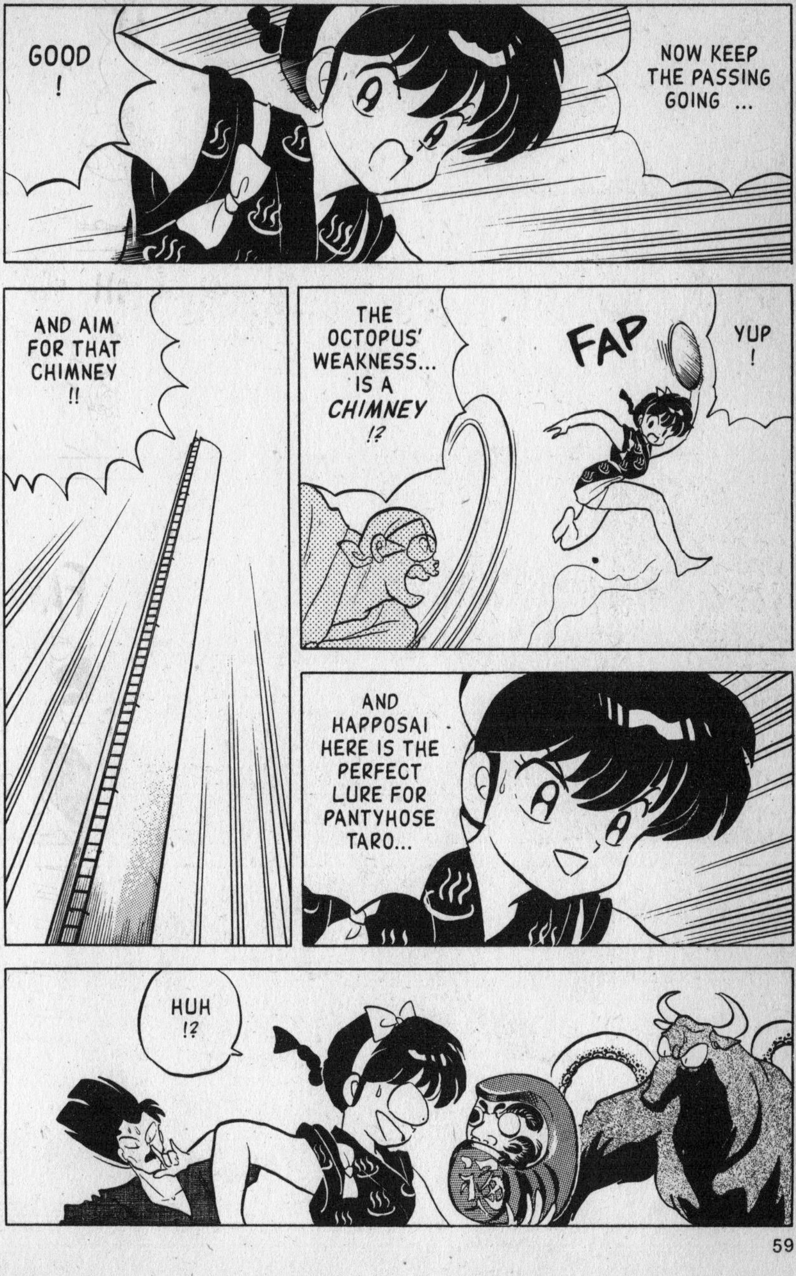
GOOD
!
NOW KEEP THE PASSING GOING ...
AND AIM FOR THAT CHIMNEY
!!
THE OCTOPUS' WEAKNESS... IS A *CHIMNEY*
!?
FAP
YUP
!
AND HAPPOSAI HERE IS THE PERFECT LURE FOR PANTYHOSE TARO...
HUH
!?

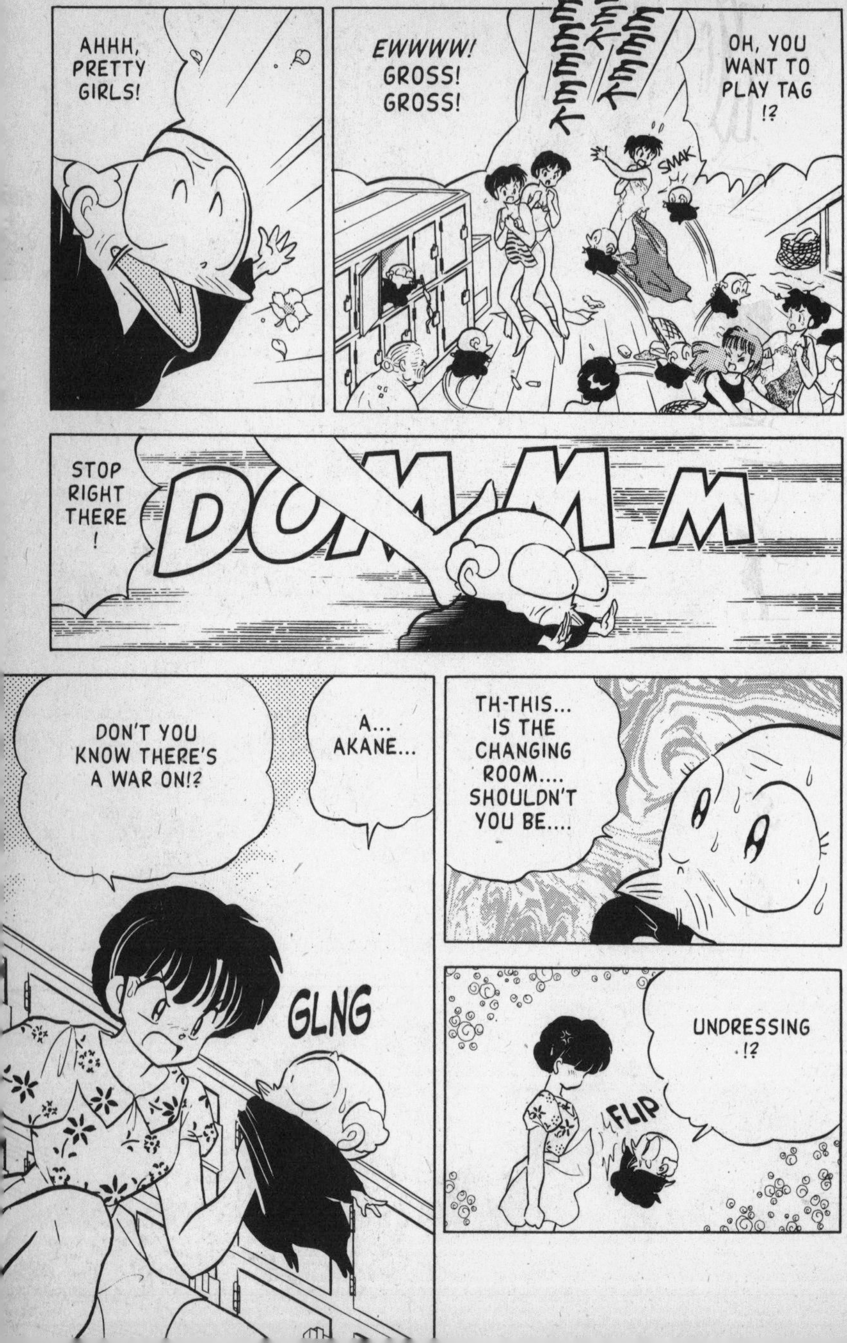
AHHH, PRETTY GIRLS!
EWWWW! GROSS! GROSS!
EEEEEEK
EEEEEEK
EEEEEEK
OH, YOU WANT TO PLAY TAG !?
SMAK
STOP RIGHT THERE !
DOMMM M
DON'T YOU KNOW THERE'S A WAR ON!?
A... AKANE...
GLNG
TH-THIS... IS THE CHANGING ROOM.... SHOULDN'T YOU BE....
UNDRESSING !?
FLIP

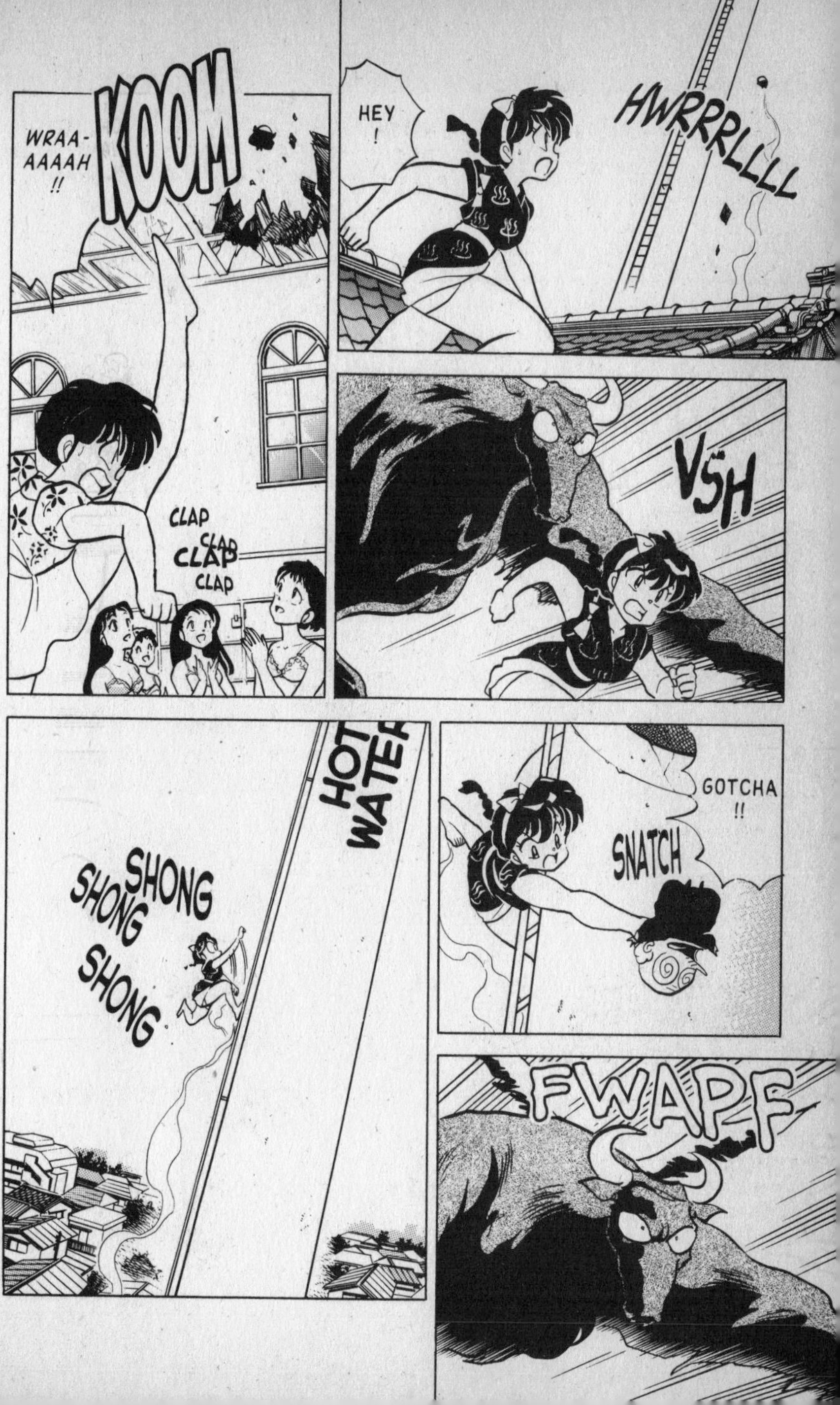
KOOM
WRAA-AAAAH !!
CLAP
CLAP
CLAP
CLAP
HEY !
HWRRRLLLL
VSH
SHONG
SHONG
SHONG
HOT WATER
GOTCHA !!
SNATCH
FWAPF

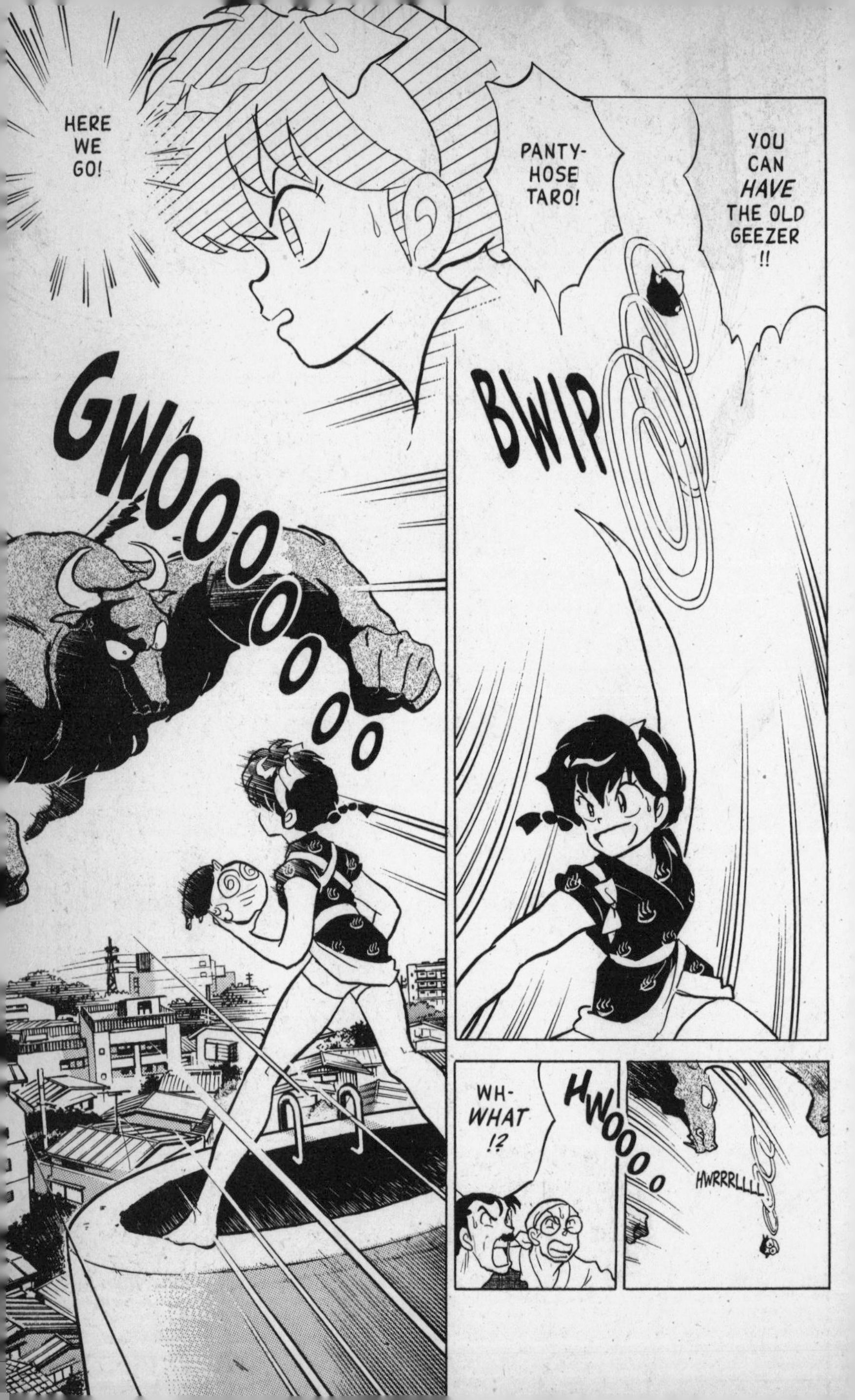
HERE WE GO!
GWOOOOOOOOO
PANTY-HOSE TARO!
YOU CAN *HAVE* THE OLD GEEZER !!
BWIP
WH-*WHAT* !?
HWOOOOo
HWRRRLLLL

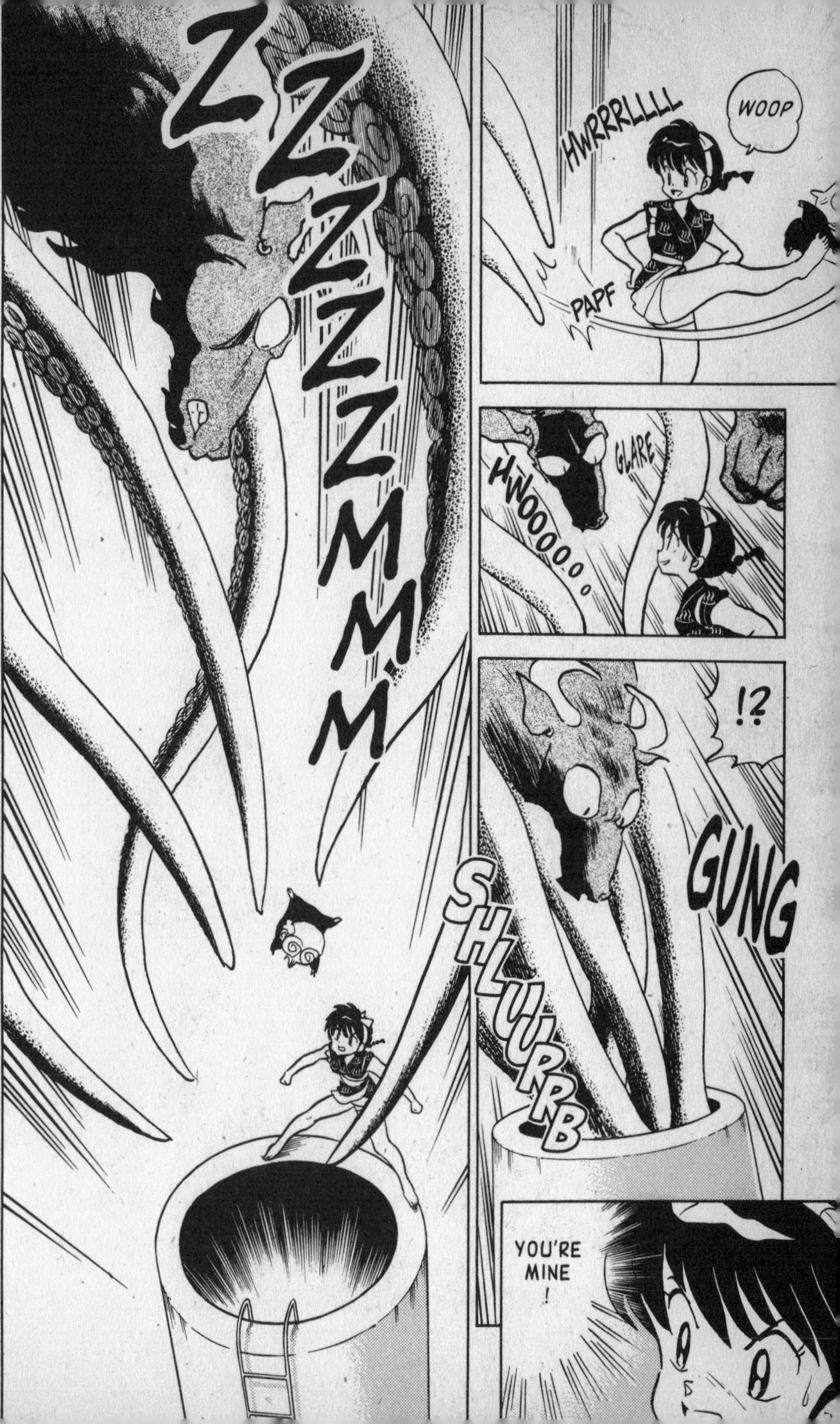
ZZZZZZMMMM
HWRRRLLLL
WOOP
PAPF
HWOOOO.O.O
GLARE
!?
GUNG
SHLUURB
YOU'RE MINE !

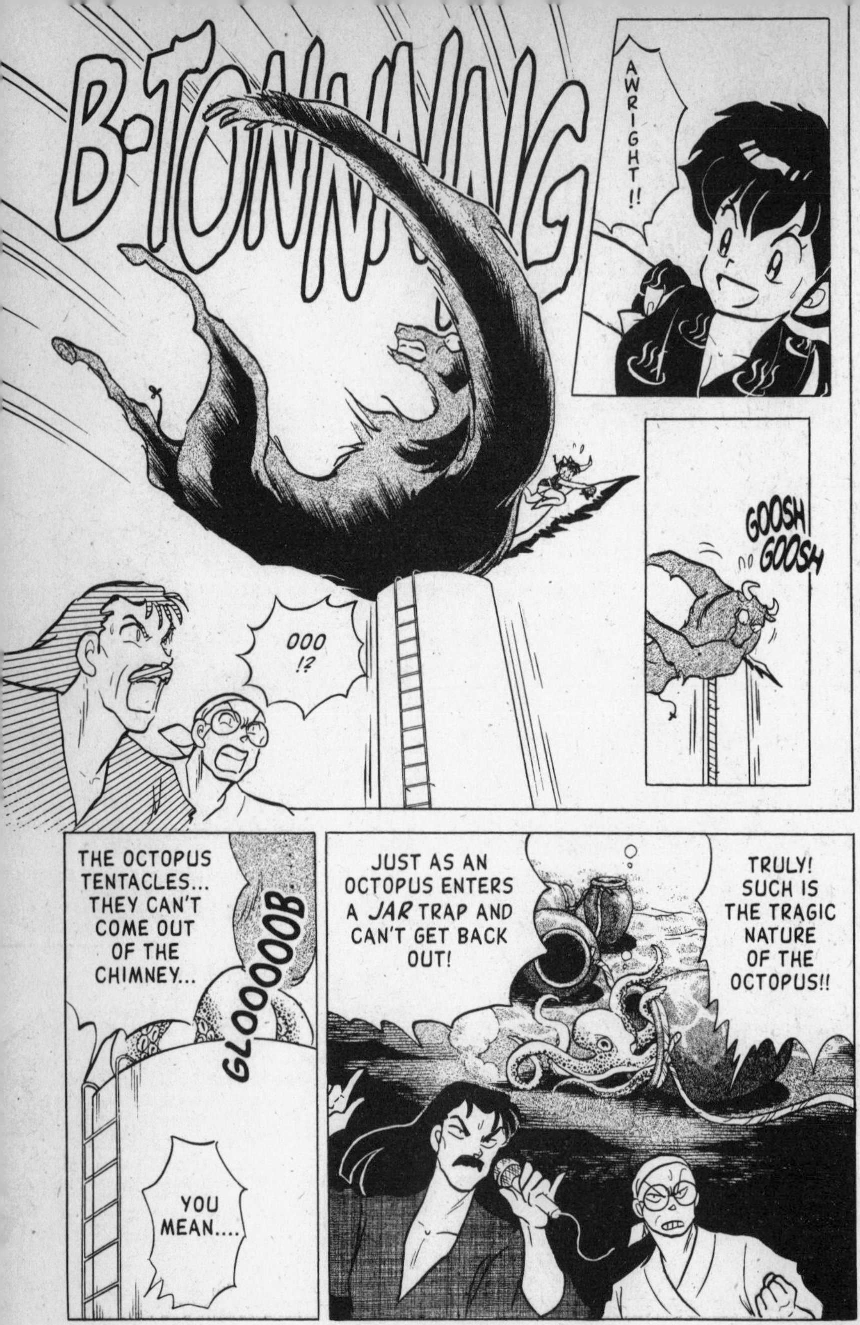
B-TONNNNG
OOO !?
AWRIGHT!!
GOOSH GOOSH
THE OCTOPUS TENTACLES... THEY CAN'T COME OUT OF THE CHIMNEY...
GLOOOOOOB
YOU MEAN....
JUST AS AN OCTOPUS ENTERS A *JAR* TRAP AND CAN'T GET BACK OUT!
TRULY! SUCH IS THE TRAGIC NATURE OF THE OCTOPUS!!

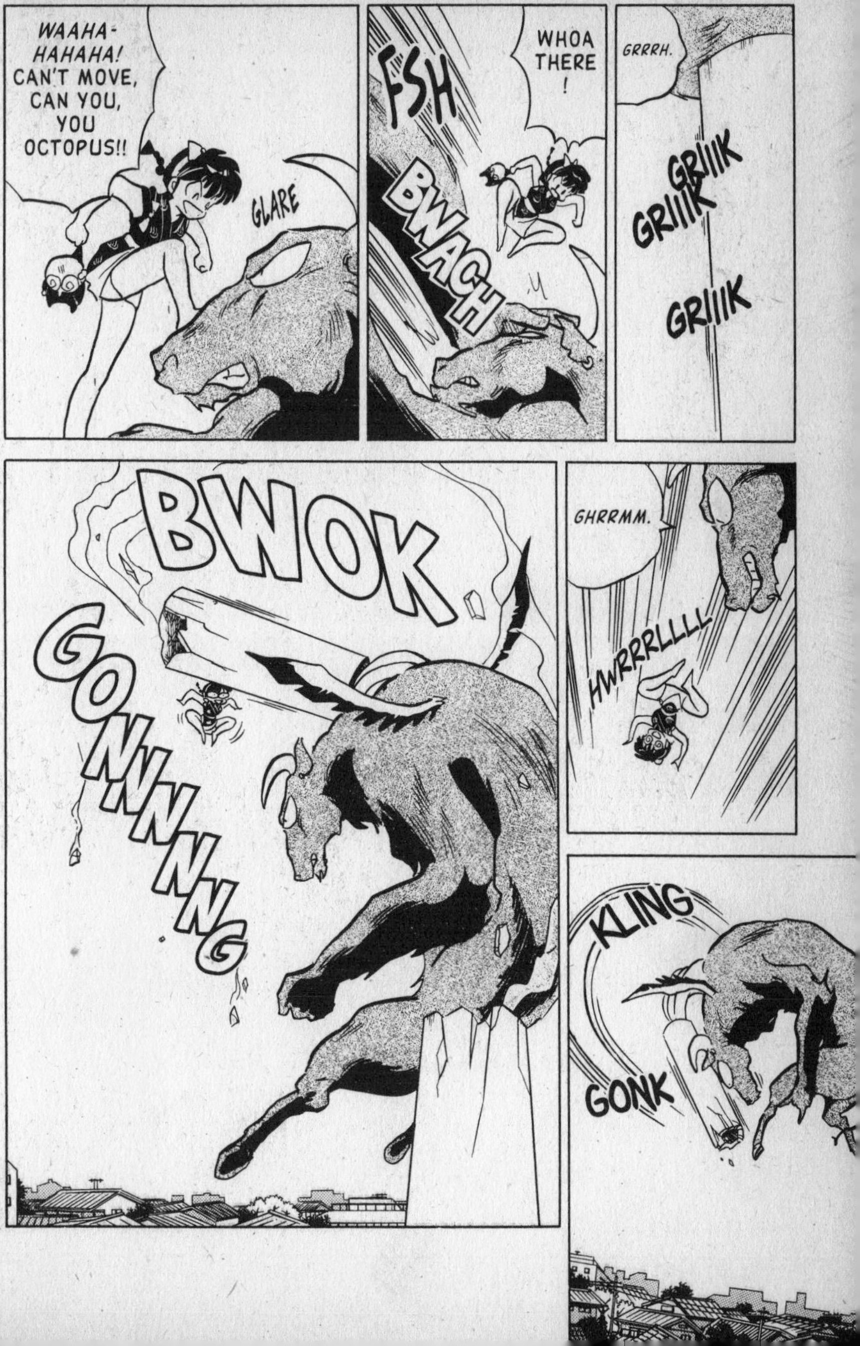
WAAHA-HAHAHA! CAN'T MOVE, CAN YOU, YOU OCTOPUS!!
GLARE
FSH
WHOA THERE!
BWACH
GRRRH.
GRIIIK
GRIIIK
GRIIIK
BWOK
GONNNNNG
GHRRMM.
HWRRRLLLL
KLING
GONK

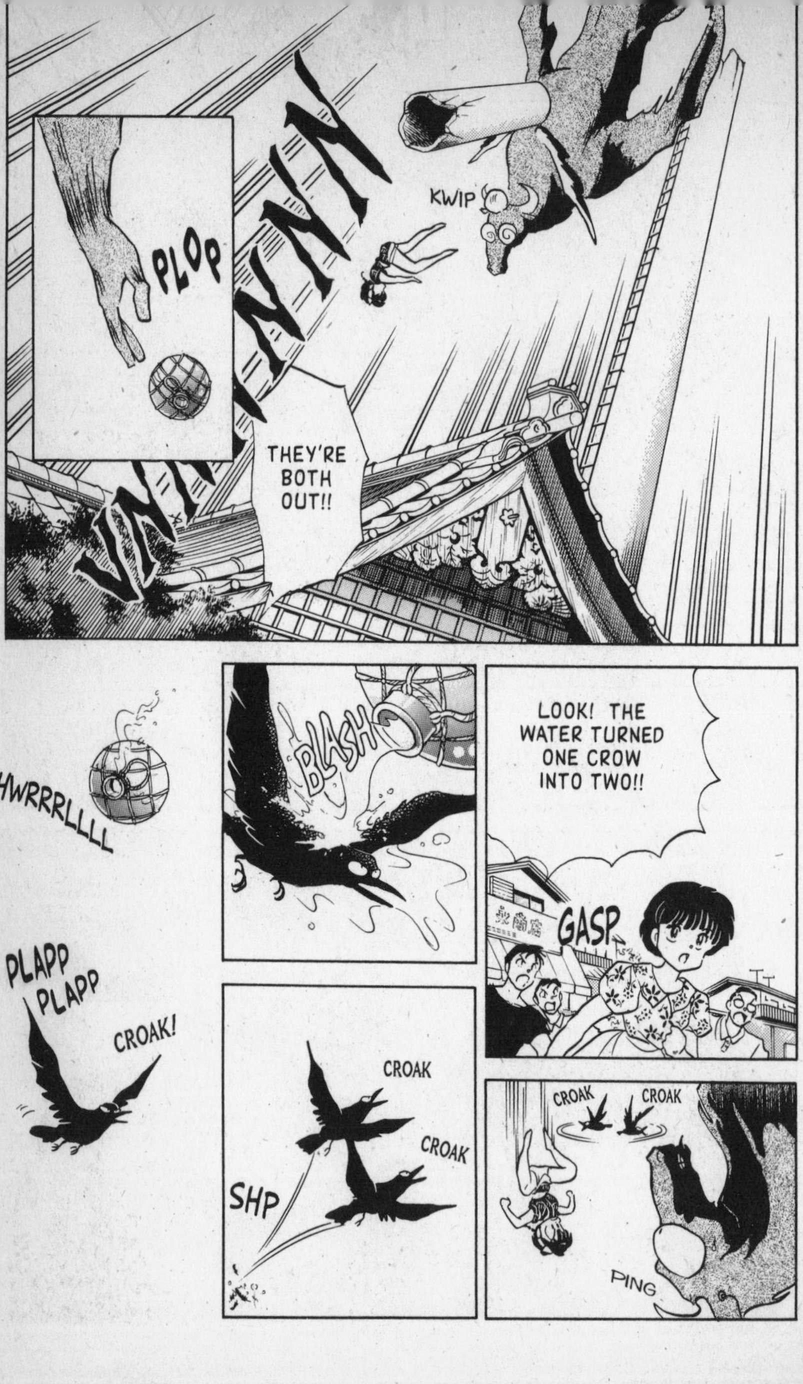

PLOP
KWIP
THEY'RE BOTH OUT!!
HWRRRLLLL
BLASH
LOOK! THE WATER TURNED ONE CROW INTO TWO!!
GASP
PLAPP PLAPP
CROAK!
CROAK
CROAK
SHP
CROAK
CROAK
PING

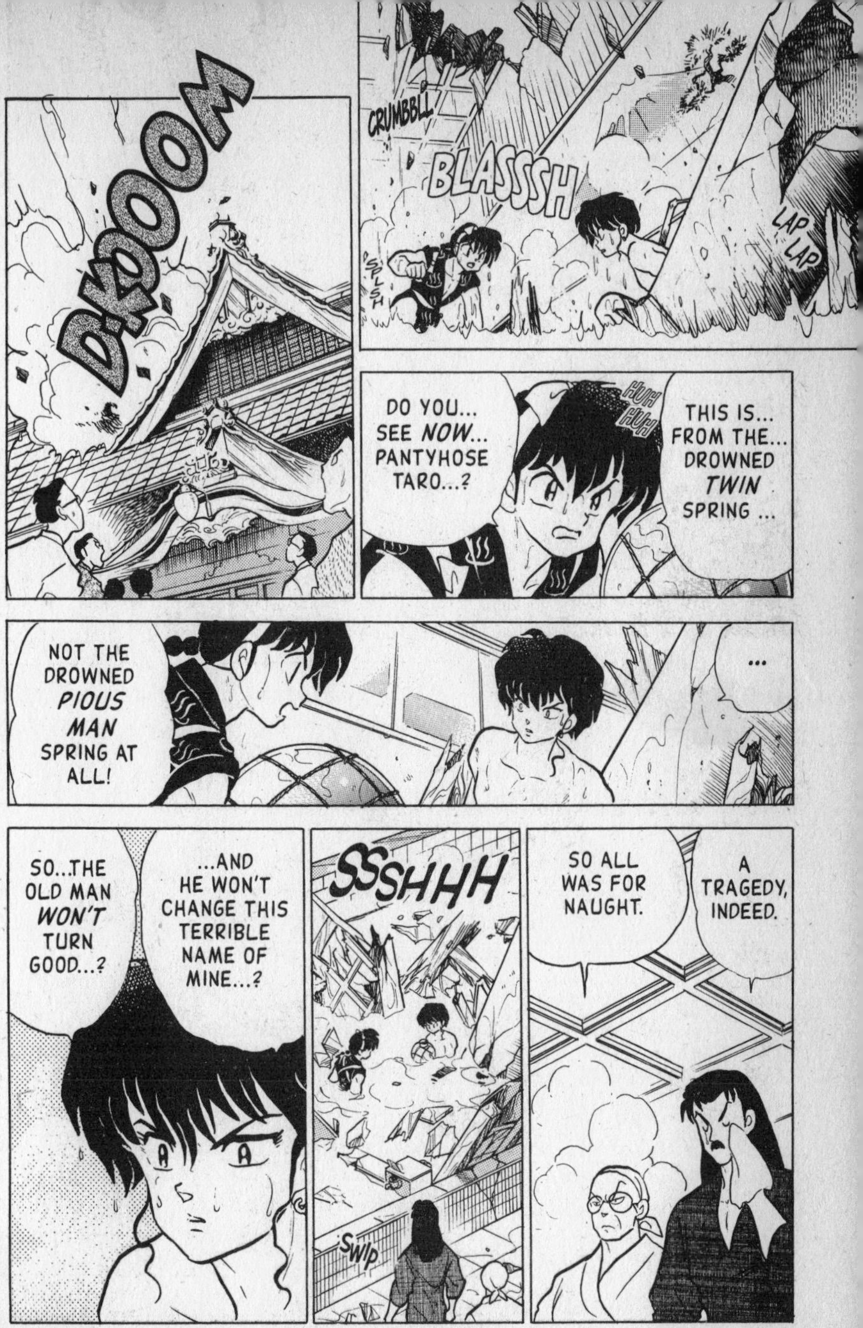
D-DOOM
CRUMBBLL
BLASSSH
SPLSH
LAP LAP
DO YOU... SEE *NOW*... PANTYHOSE TARO...?
HUH HUH
THIS IS... FROM THE... DROWNED *TWIN* SPRING ...
NOT THE DROWNED *PIOUS MAN* SPRING AT ALL!
...
SO...THE OLD MAN *WON'T* TURN GOOD...?
...AND HE WON'T CHANGE THIS TERRIBLE NAME OF MINE...?
SSSHHH
SWIP
SO ALL WAS FOR NAUGHT.
A TRAGEDY, INDEED.

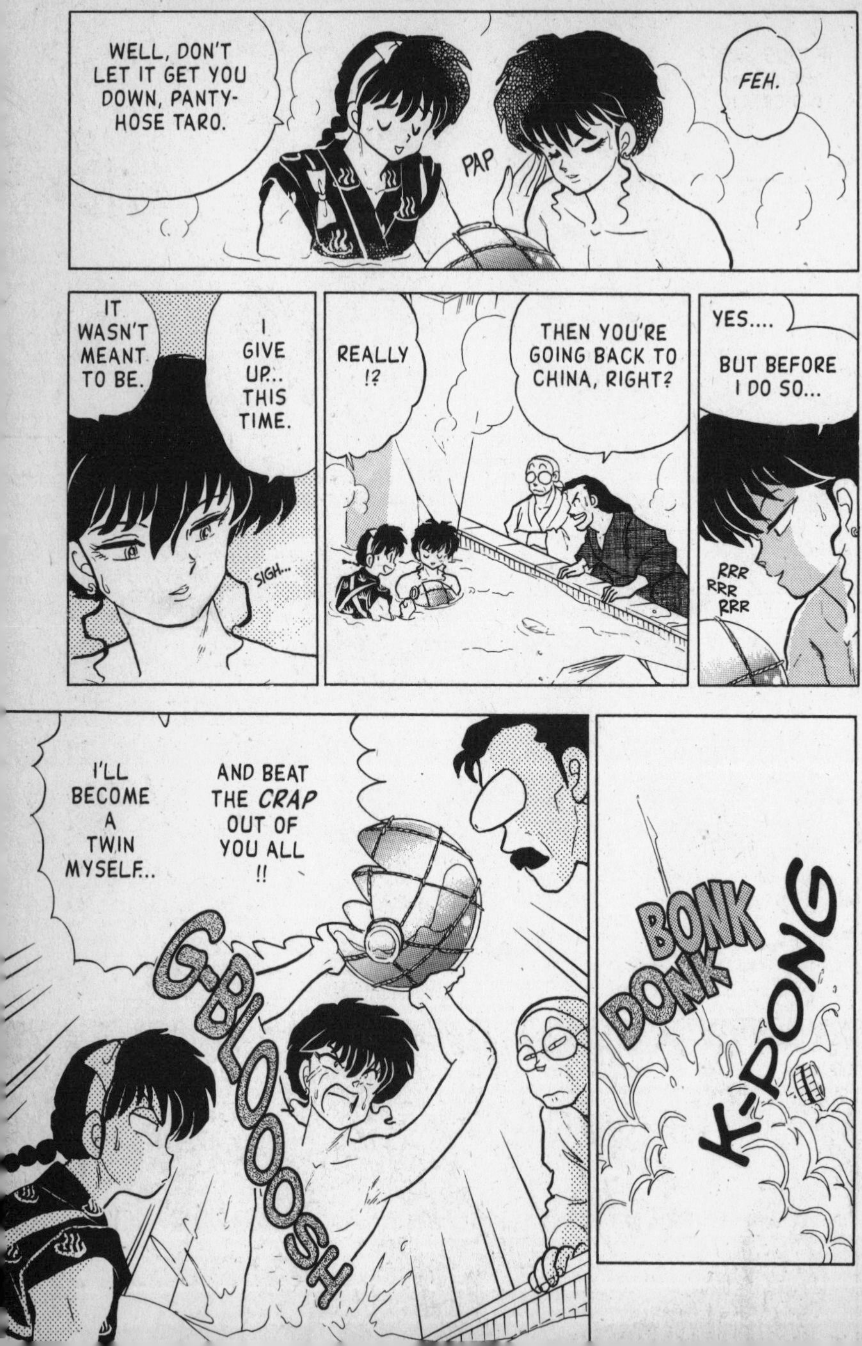
WELL, DON'T LET IT GET YOU DOWN, PANTY-HOSE TARO.
PAP
FEH.
IT WASN'T MEANT TO BE.
I GIVE UP... THIS TIME.
SIGH...
REALLY !?
THEN YOU'RE GOING BACK TO CHINA, RIGHT?
YES....
BUT BEFORE I DO SO...
RRR RRR RRR
I'LL BECOME A TWIN MYSELF...
AND BEAT THE *CRAP* OUT OF YOU ALL !!
G-BLOOOSH
BONK
DONK
K-PONG

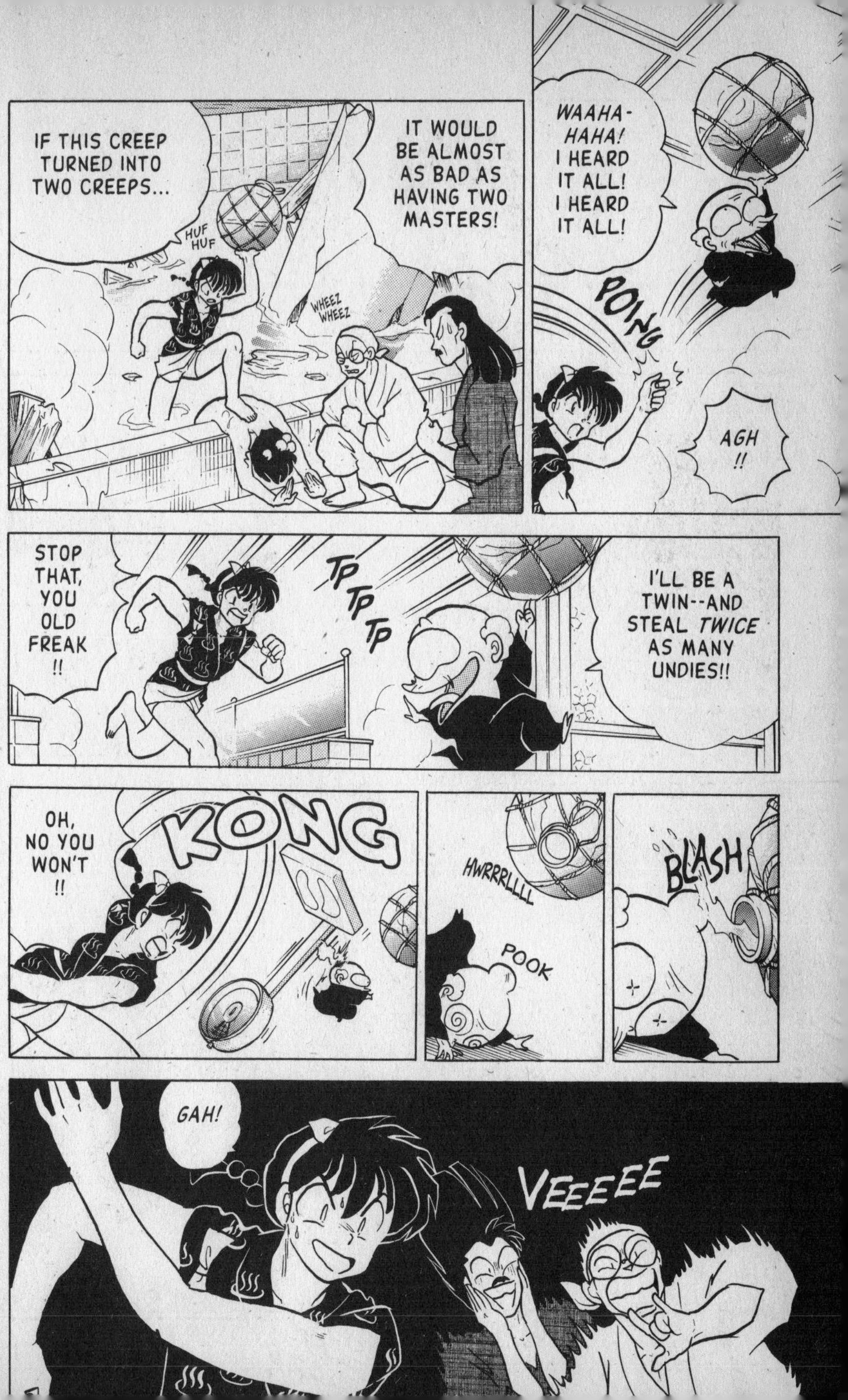
IF THIS CREEP TURNED INTO TWO CREEPS...
HUF HUF
IT WOULD BE ALMOST AS BAD AS HAVING TWO MASTERS!
WHEEZ WHEEZ
WAAHA-HAHA! I HEARD IT ALL! I HEARD IT ALL!
POING
AGH !!
STOP THAT, YOU OLD FREAK !!
TP TP TP
I'LL BE A TWIN--AND STEAL TWICE AS MANY UNDIES!!
OH, NO YOU WON'T !!
KONG
HWRRRLLLL
POOK
BLASH
GAH!
VEEEEE

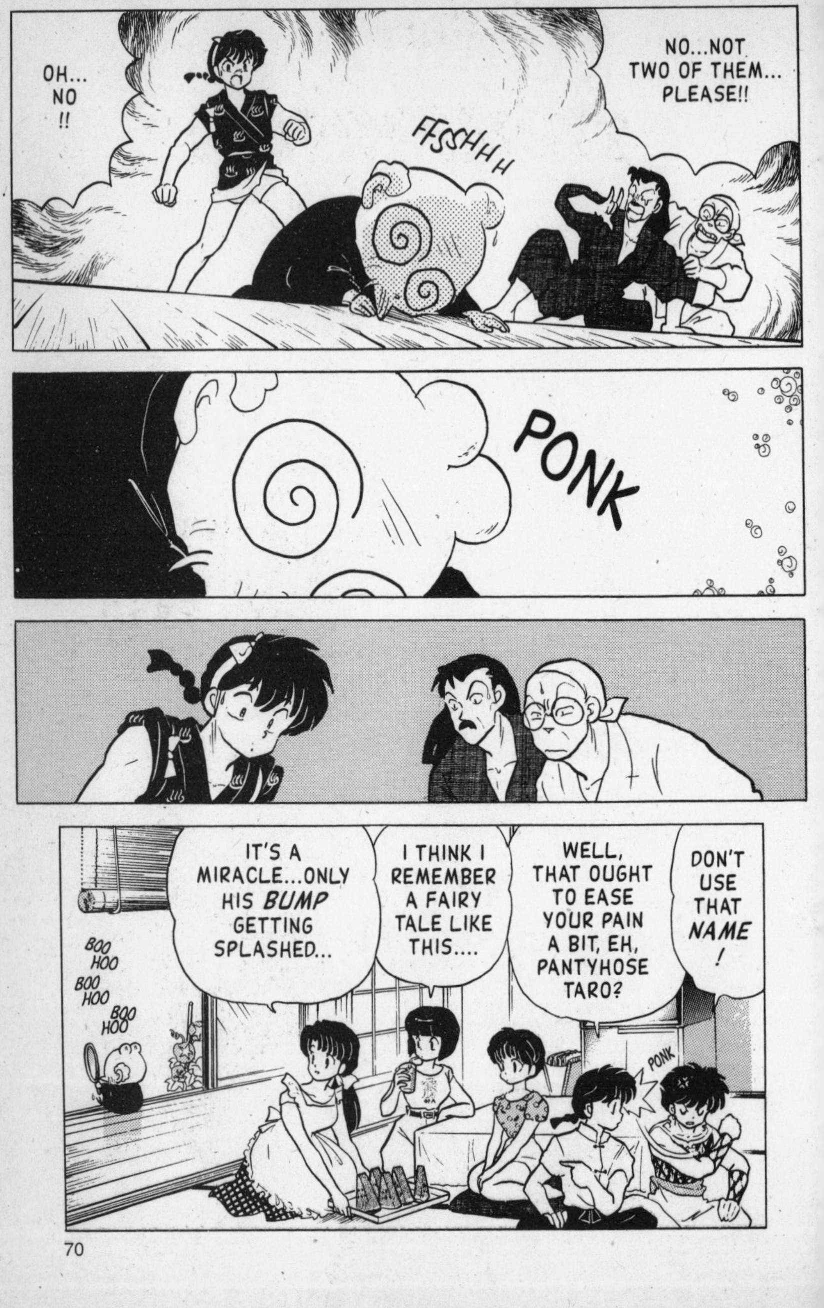
OH... NO !!
FFSSHHH
NO...NOT TWO OF THEM... PLEASE!!
PONK
BOO HOO
BOO HOO
BOO HOO
IT'S A MIRACLE...ONLY HIS *BUMP* GETTING SPLASHED...
I THINK I REMEMBER A FAIRY TALE LIKE THIS....
WELL, THAT OUGHT TO EASE YOUR PAIN A BIT, EH, PANTYHOSE TARO?
DON'T USE THAT *NAME* !
PONK

Part 5

STOMPERELLA

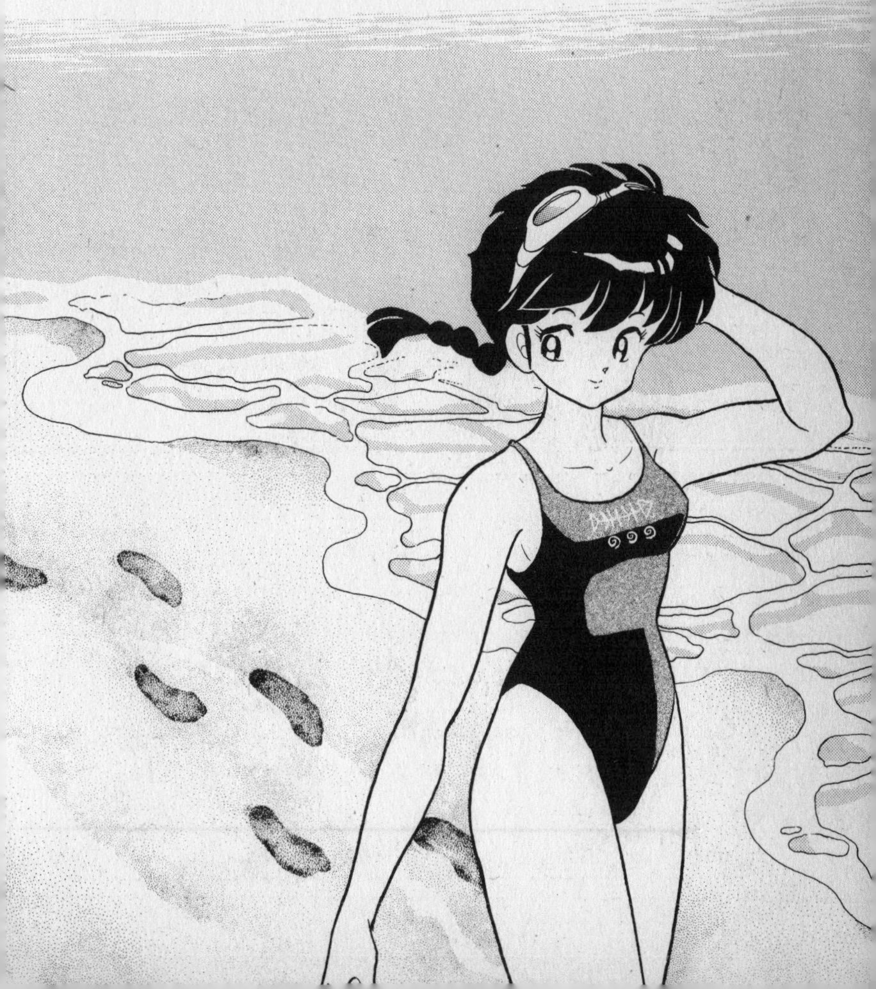

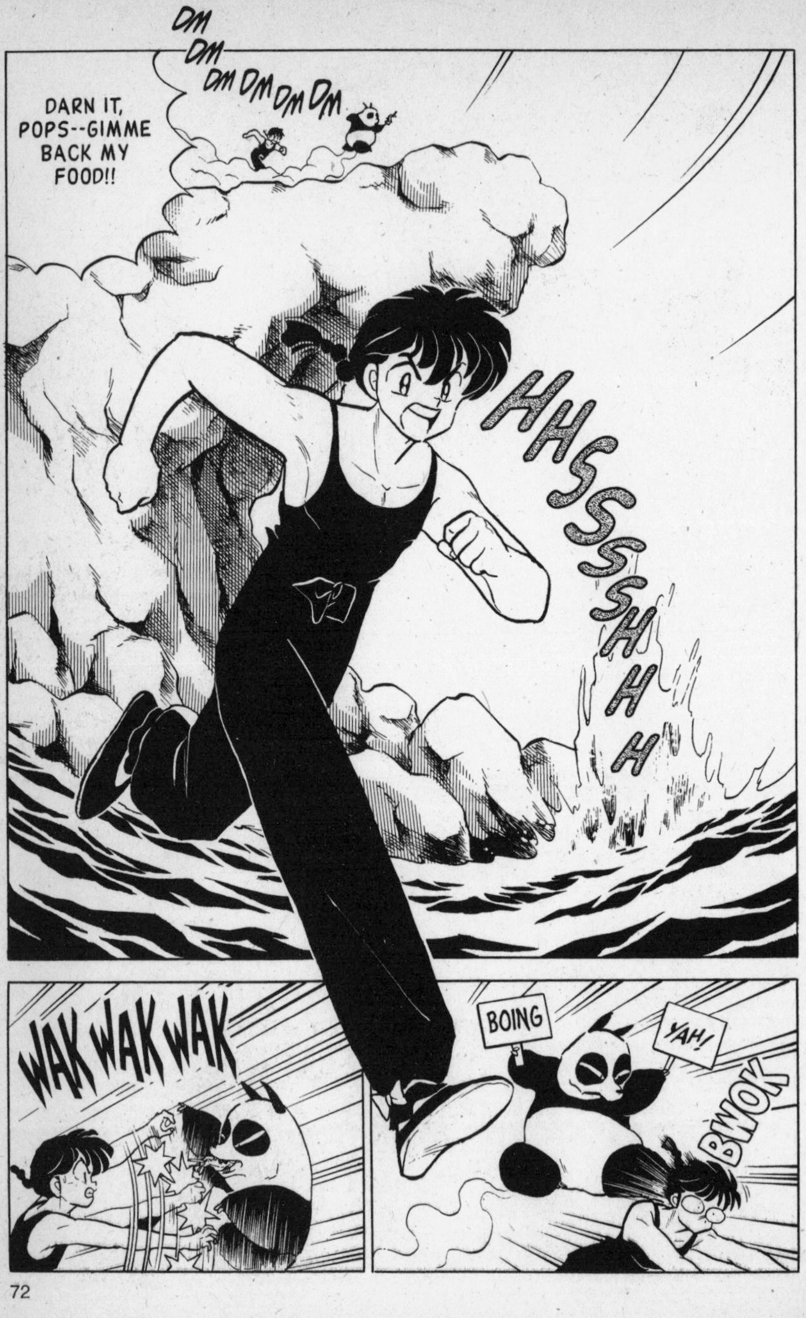
DM DM DM DM DM DM DM
DARN IT, POPS--GIMME BACK MY FOOD!!
HHSSSSSHHHH
WAK WAK WAK
BOING
YAH!
BWOK

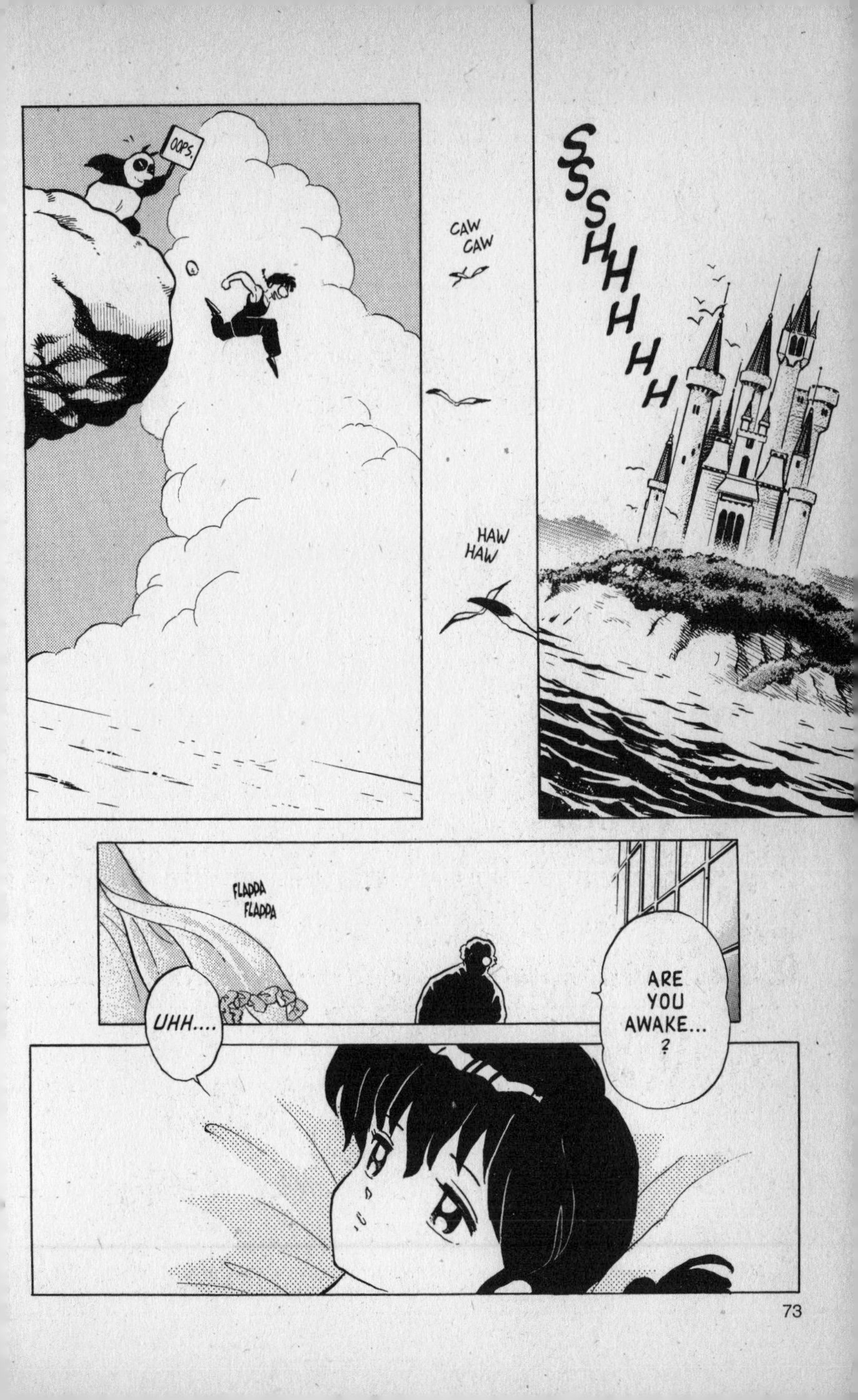
OOPS.
CAW CAW
HAW HAW
SSSHHHHH
FLAPPA FLAPPA
ARE YOU AWAKE... ?
UHH....

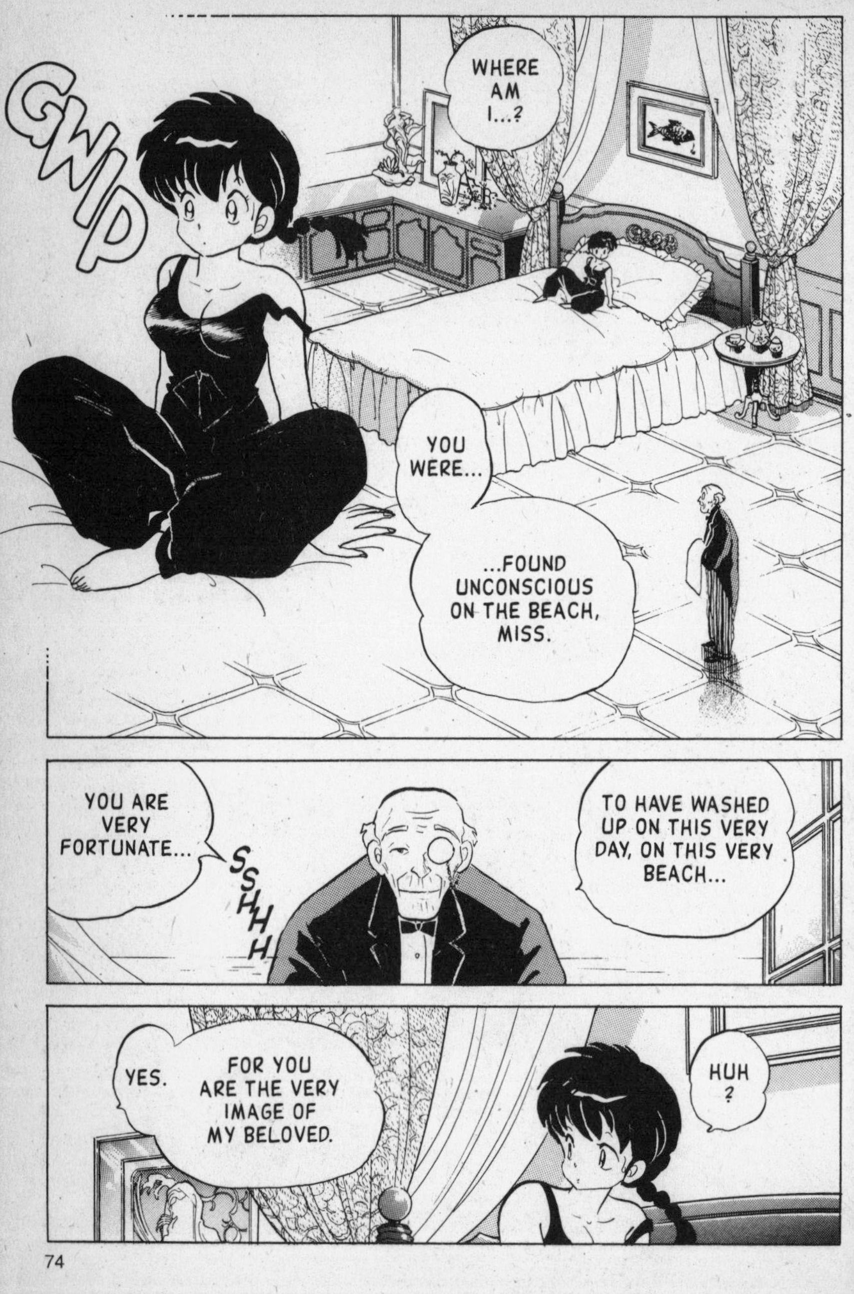
GWIP
WHERE AM I...?
YOU WERE...
...FOUND UNCONSCIOUS ON THE BEACH, MISS.
YOU ARE VERY FORTUNATE...
SSHHH
TO HAVE WASHED UP ON THIS VERY DAY, ON THIS VERY BEACH...
YES.
FOR YOU ARE THE VERY IMAGE OF MY BELOVED.
HUH?

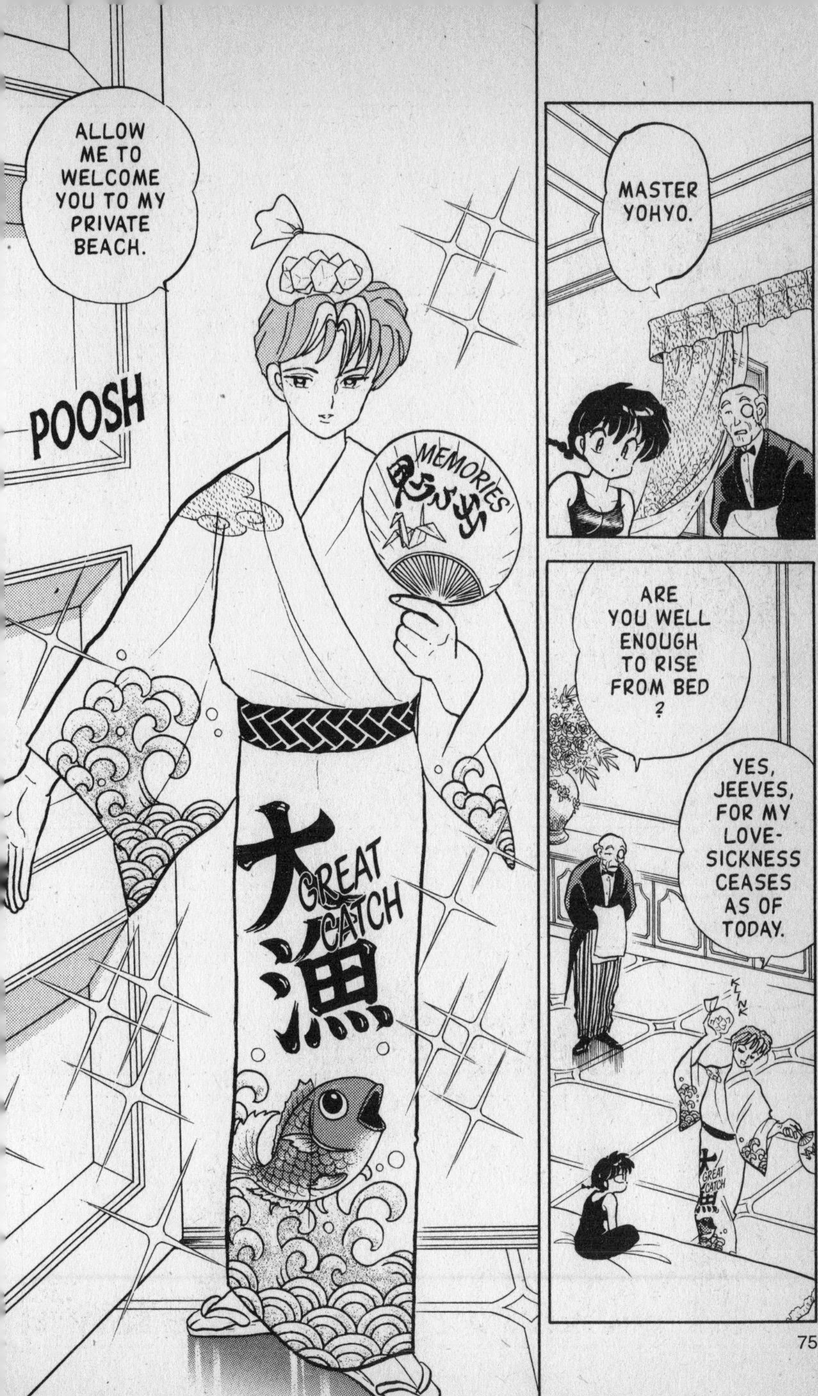
ALLOW ME TO WELCOME YOU TO MY PRIVATE BEACH.
POOSH
MEMORIES
GREAT CATCH
MASTER YOHYO.
ARE YOU WELL ENOUGH TO RISE FROM BED?
YES, JEEVES, FOR MY LOVE-SICKNESS CEASES AS OF TODAY.
KLINK

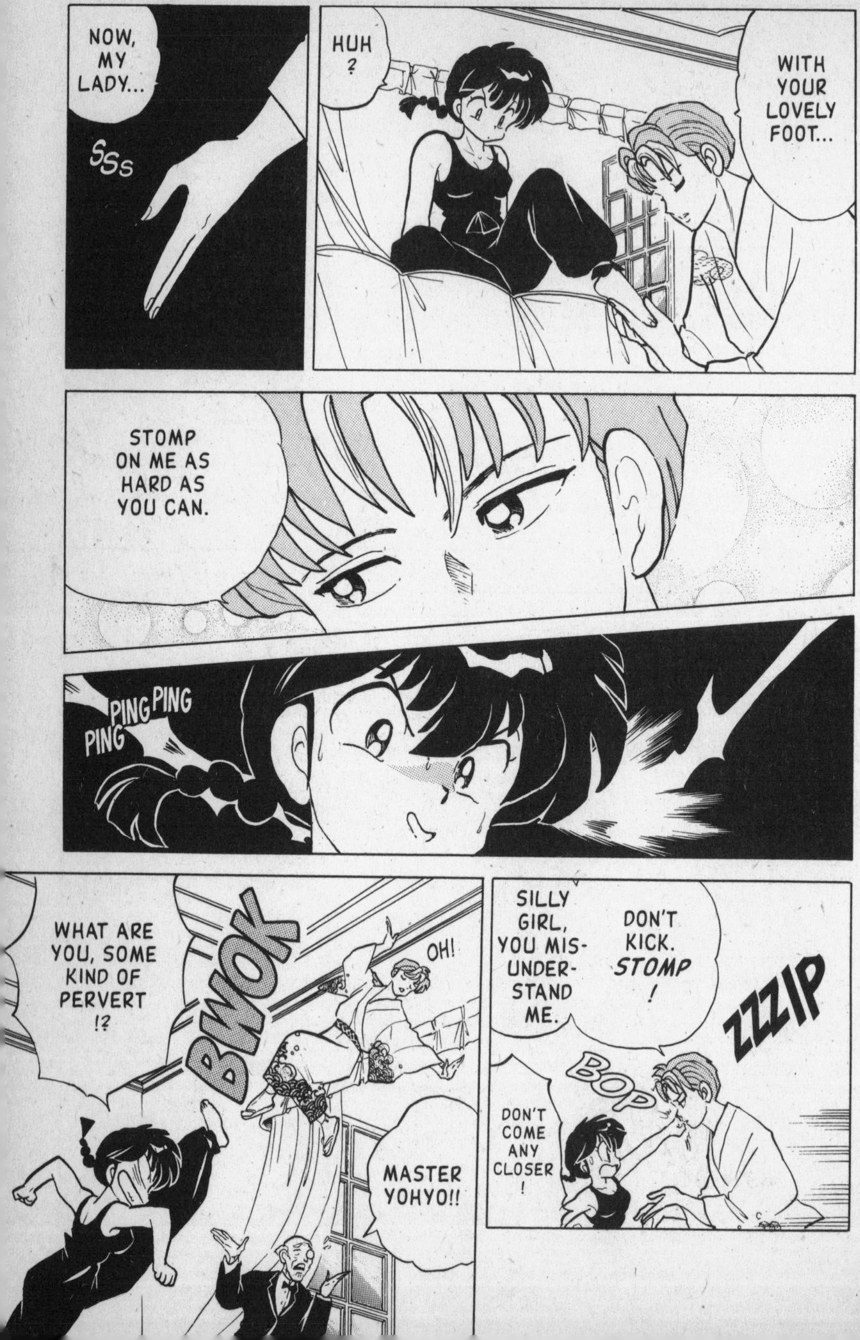
NOW, MY LADY...
SSS
HUH?
WITH YOUR LOVELY FOOT...
STOMP ON ME AS HARD AS YOU CAN.
PING PING PING
WHAT ARE YOU, SOME KIND OF PERVERT!?
BWOK
OH!
MASTER YOHYO!!
SILLY GIRL, YOU MISUNDERSTAND ME.
DON'T KICK. STOMP!
ZZZIP
BOP
DON'T COME ANY CLOSER!

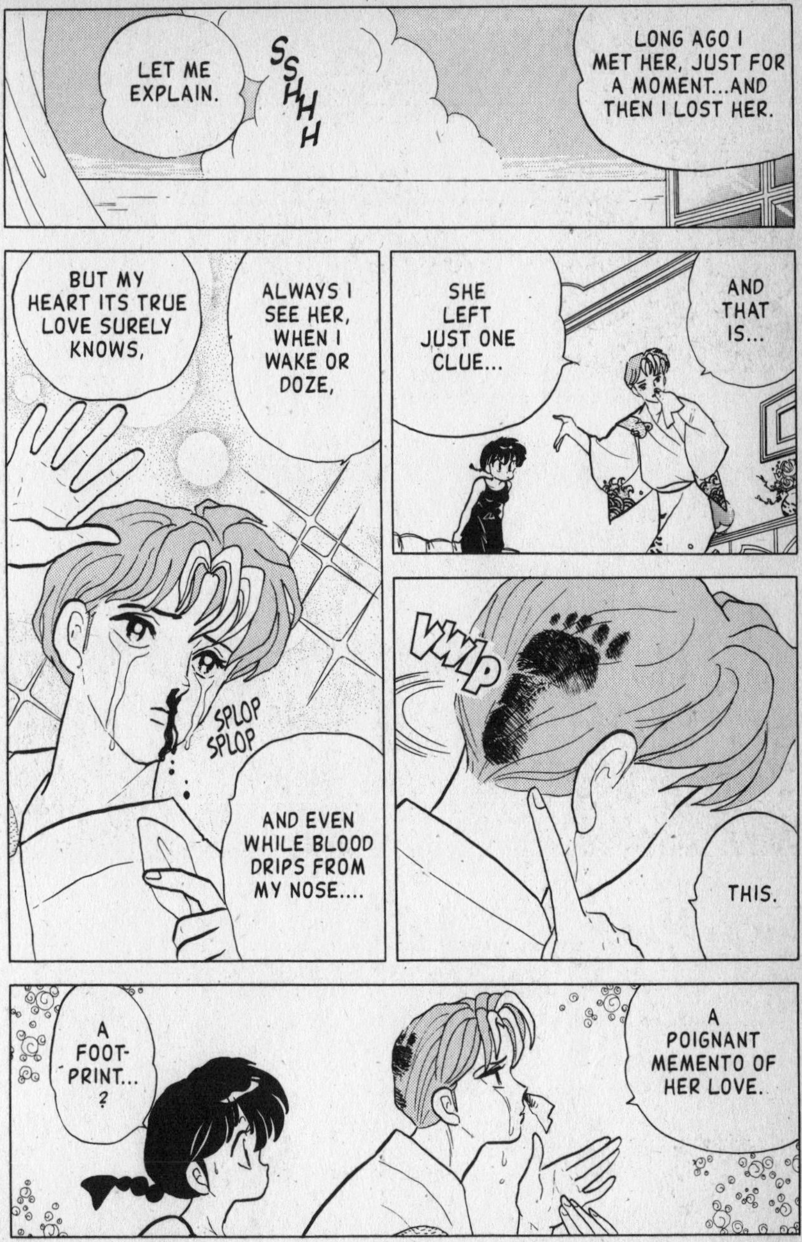
LET ME EXPLAIN.
SSHHH
LONG AGO I MET HER, JUST FOR A MOMENT...AND THEN I LOST HER.
ALWAYS I SEE HER, WHEN I WAKE OR DOZE,
BUT MY HEART ITS TRUE LOVE SURELY KNOWS,
SPLOP SPLOP
AND EVEN WHILE BLOOD DRIPS FROM MY NOSE....
SHE LEFT JUST ONE CLUE...
AND THAT IS...
VWIP
THIS.
A FOOT-PRINT...?
A POIGNANT MEMENTO OF HER LOVE.

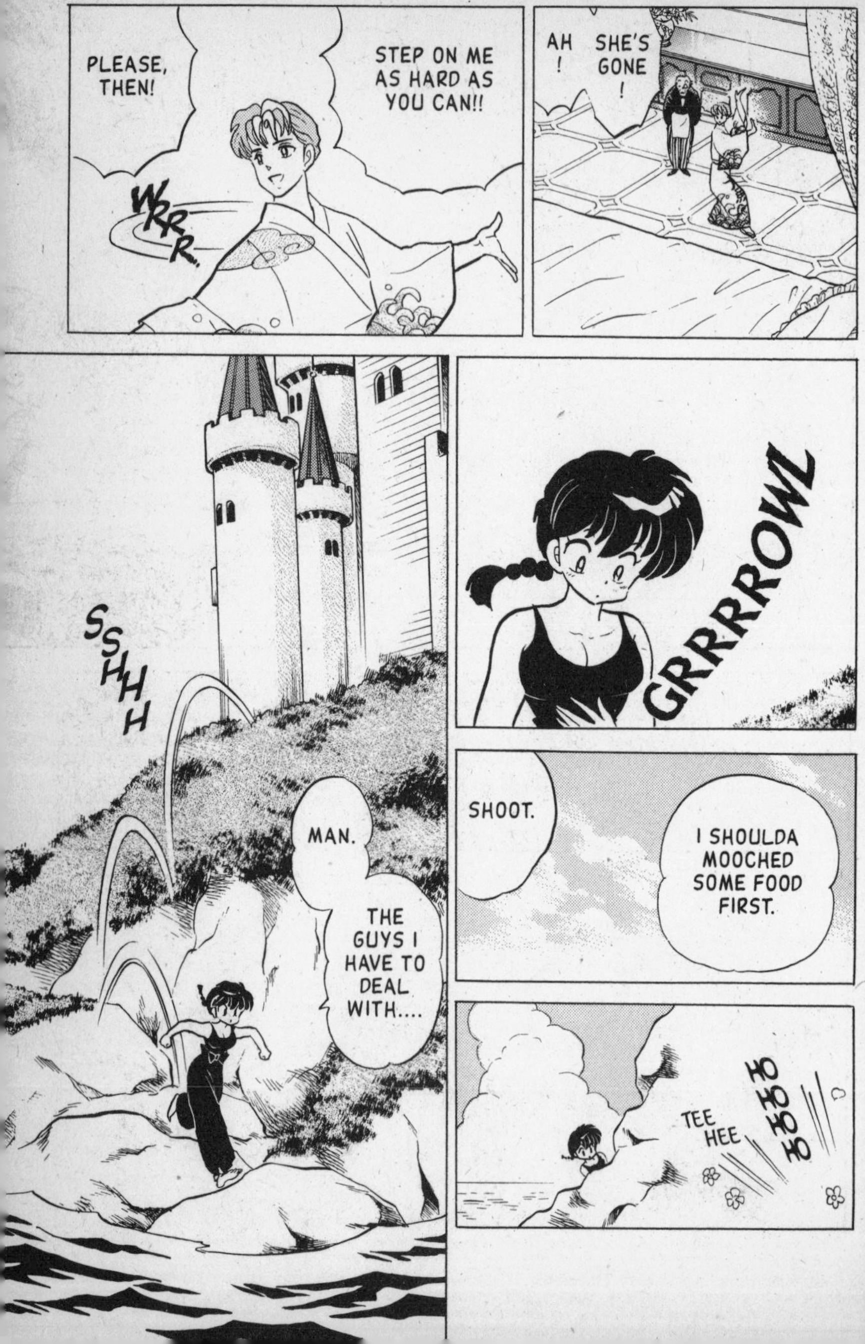
PLEASE, THEN!
STEP ON ME AS HARD AS YOU CAN!!
WRRR.
AH!
SHE'S GONE!
SSHHH
MAN.
THE GUYS I HAVE TO DEAL WITH....
GRRRROWL
SHOOT.
I SHOULDA MOOCHED SOME FOOD FIRST.
TEE HEE
HO HO HO HO

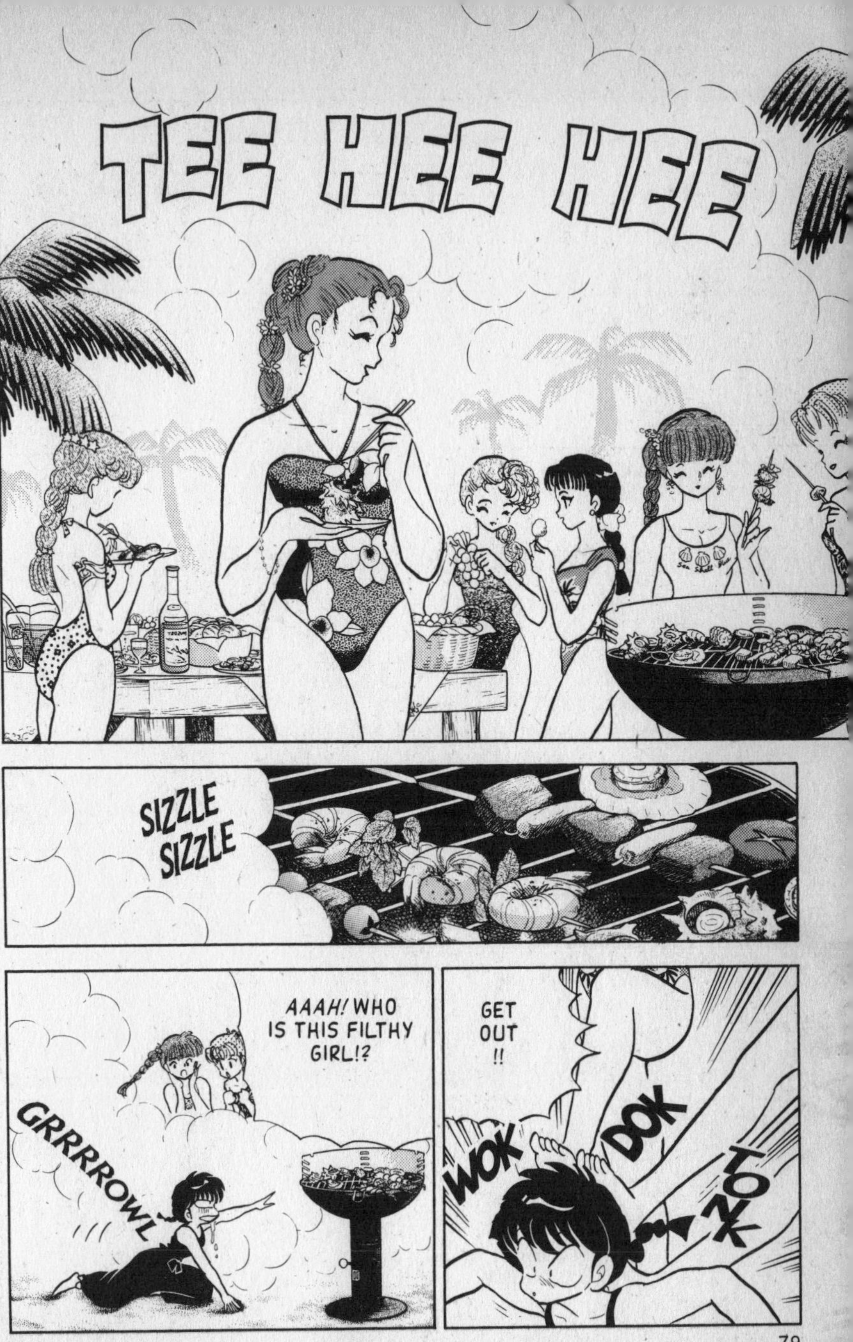
TEE HEE HEE
SIZZLE SIZZLE
AAAH! WHO IS THIS FILTHY GIRL!?
GRRRROWL
GET OUT !!
WOK
DOK
TONK

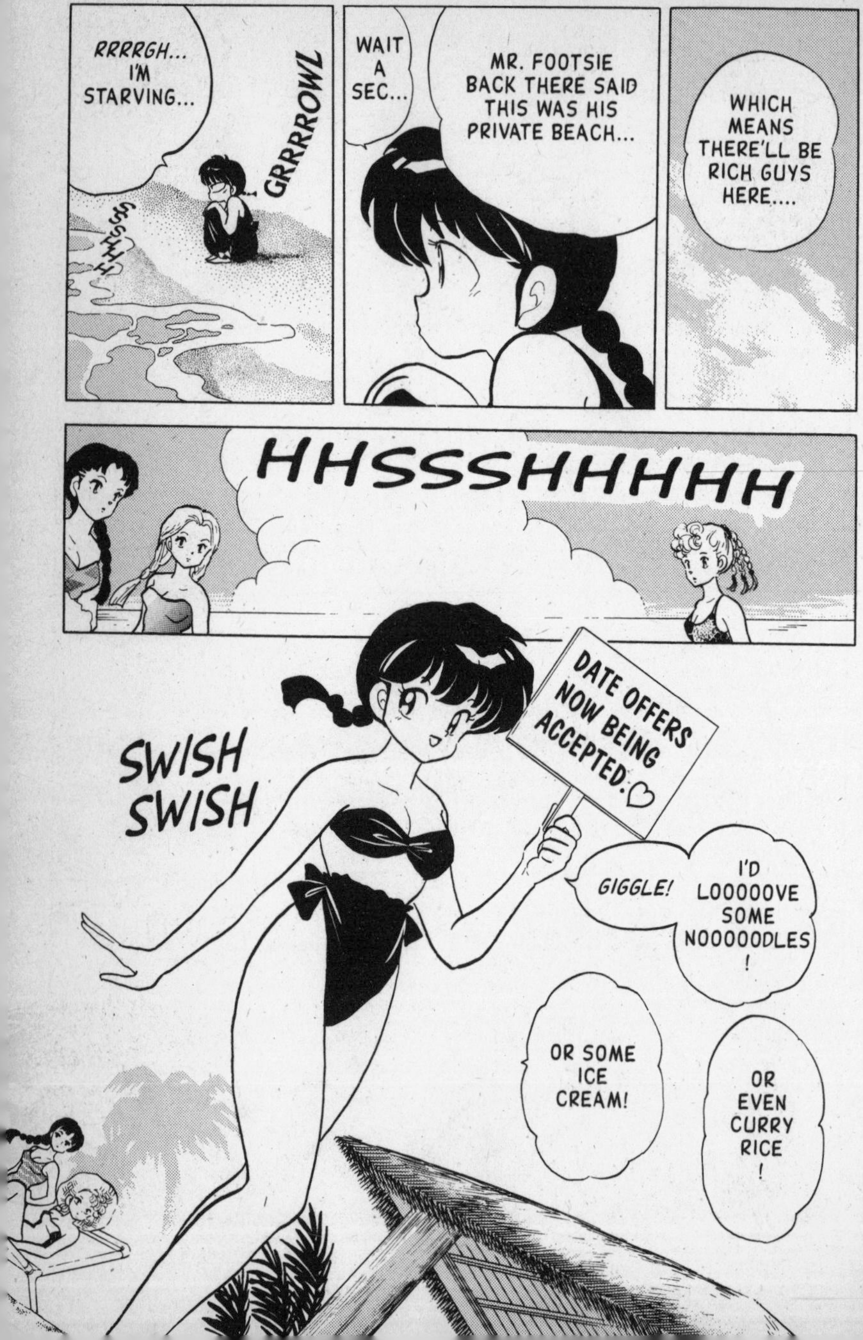
RRRRGH... I'M STARVING...
GRRRROWL
HHSSSS
WAIT A SEC...
MR. FOOTSIE BACK THERE SAID THIS WAS HIS PRIVATE BEACH...
WHICH MEANS THERE'LL BE RICH GUYS HERE....
HHSSSHHHHHH
DATE OFFERS NOW BEING ACCEPTED.♡
SWISH SWISH
GIGGLE!
I'D LOOOOOVE SOME NOOOOODLES!
OR SOME ICE CREAM!
OR EVEN CURRY RICE!

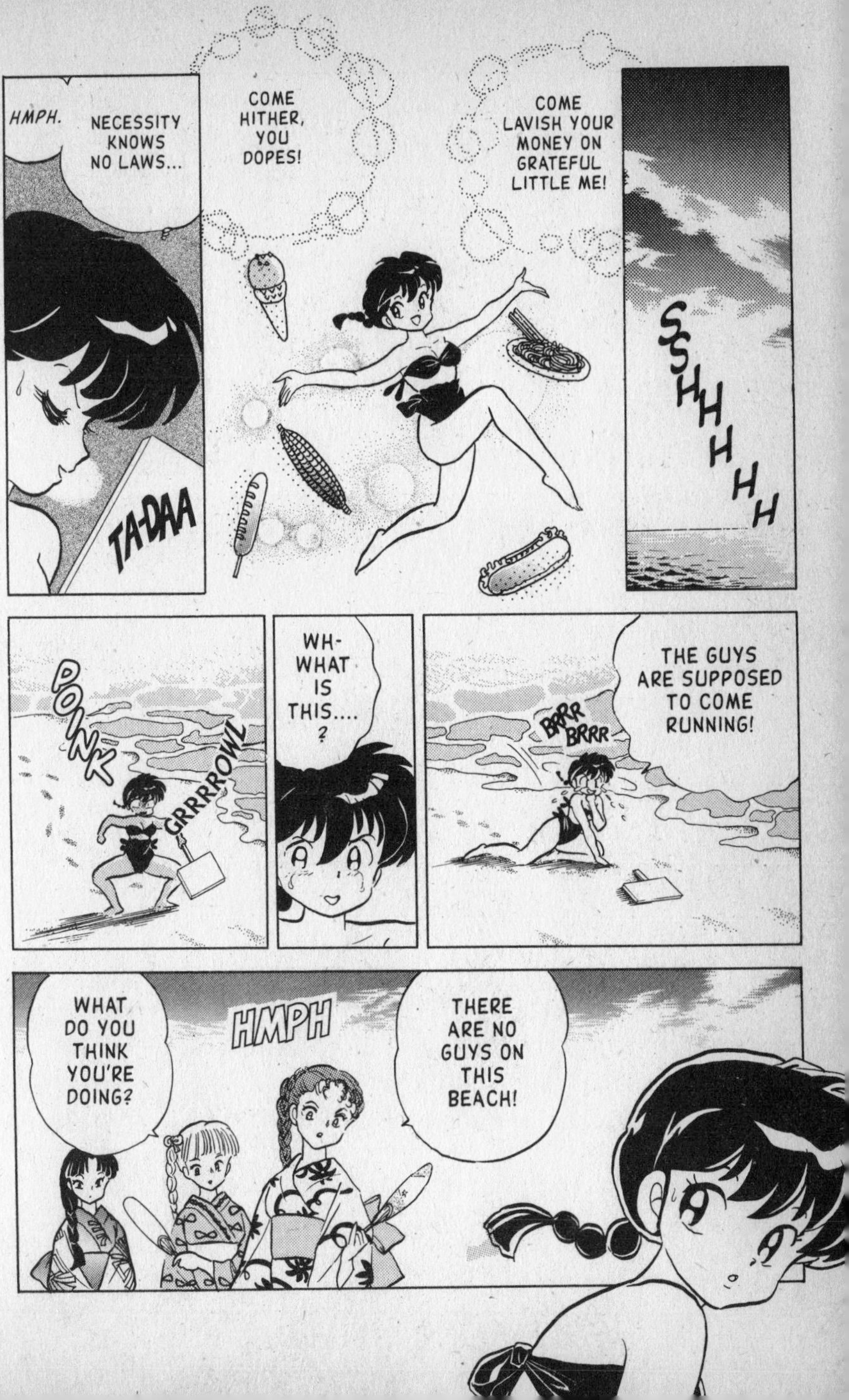
HMPH.
NECESSITY KNOWS NO LAWS...
TA-DAA
COME HITHER, YOU DOPES!
COME LAVISH YOUR MONEY ON GRATEFUL LITTLE ME!
SSHHHHHH
POINK
GRRRROWL
WH-WHAT IS THIS....?
THE GUYS ARE SUPPOSED TO COME RUNNING!
BRRR BRRR
WHAT DO YOU THINK YOU'RE DOING?
HMPH
THERE ARE NO GUYS ON THIS BEACH!

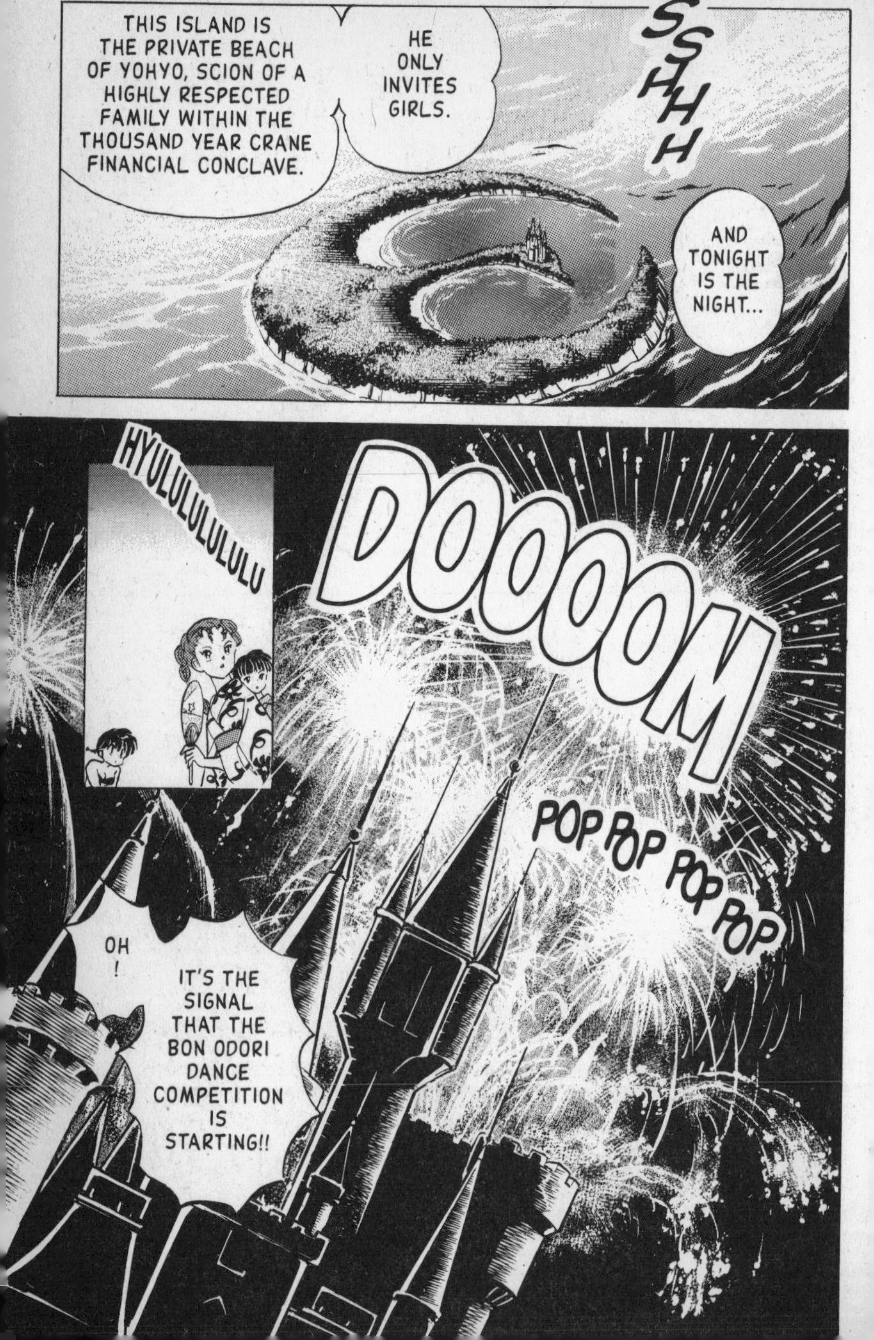
THIS ISLAND IS THE PRIVATE BEACH OF YOHYO, SCION OF A HIGHLY RESPECTED FAMILY WITHIN THE THOUSAND YEAR CRANE FINANCIAL CONCLAVE.
HE ONLY INVITES GIRLS.
SSHHH
AND TONIGHT IS THE NIGHT...
HYULULULULULU
DOOOOOM
POP POP POP POP POP
OH!
IT'S THE SIGNAL THAT THE BON ODORI DANCE COMPETITION IS STARTING!!

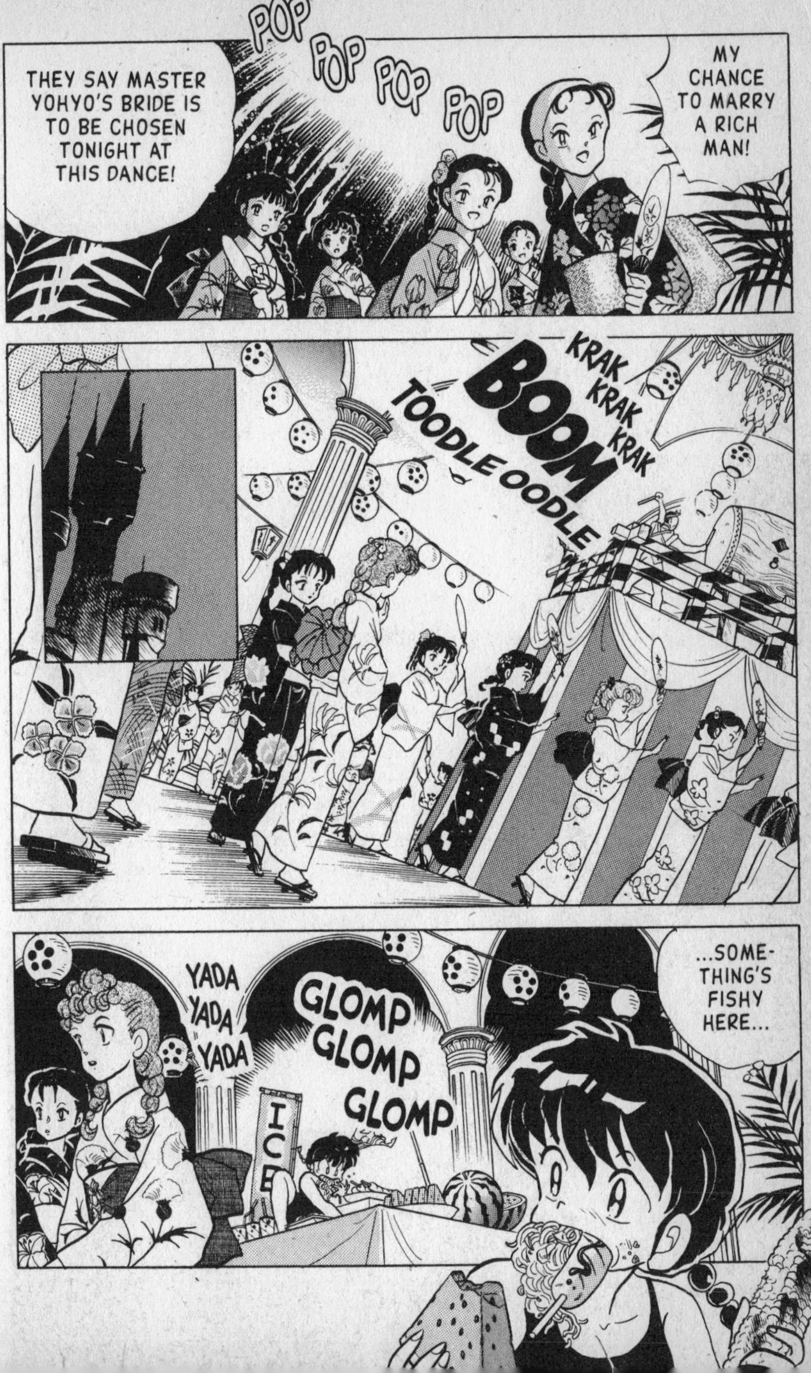
THEY SAY MASTER YOHYO'S BRIDE IS TO BE CHOSEN TONIGHT AT THIS DANCE!
POP POP POP POP
MY CHANCE TO MARRY A RICH MAN!
KRAK KRAK KRAK KRAK
BOOM
TOODLE OODLE
YADA YADA YADA
GLOMP GLOMP GLOMP
ICE
...SOME-THING'S FISHY HERE...

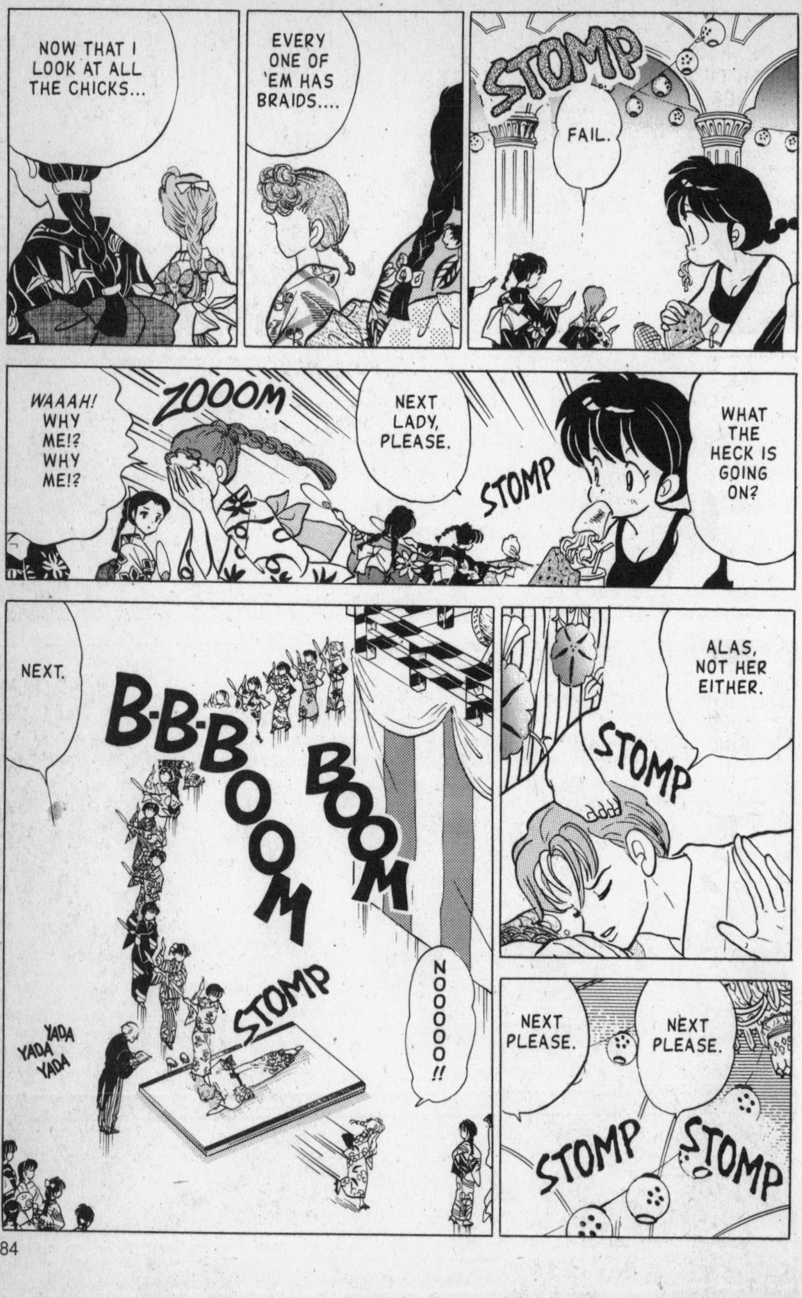
NOW THAT I LOOK AT ALL THE CHICKS...
EVERY ONE OF 'EM HAS BRAIDS....
STOMP
FAIL.
WAAAH! WHY ME!? WHY ME!?
ZOOOM
NEXT LADY, PLEASE.
STOMP
WHAT THE HECK IS GOING ON?
NEXT.
B-B-BOOOM
BOOM
STOMP
YADA YADA YADA
NOOOOOO!!
ALAS, NOT HER EITHER.
STOMP
NEXT PLEASE.
NEXT PLEASE.
STOMP
STOMP

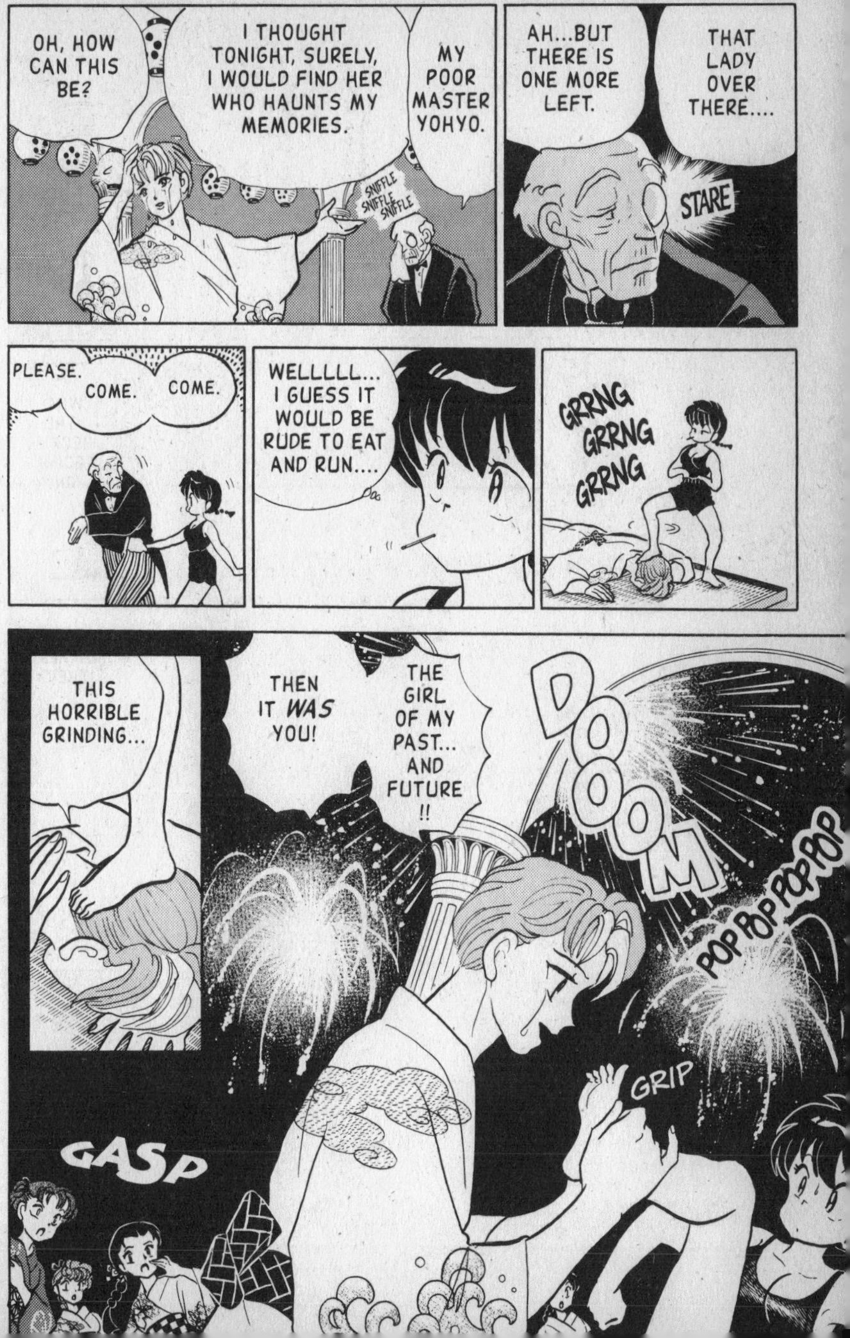
OH, HOW CAN THIS BE?
I THOUGHT TONIGHT, SURELY, I WOULD FIND HER WHO HAUNTS MY MEMORIES.
SNIFFLE SNIFFLE SNIFFLE
MY POOR MASTER YOHYO.
AH...BUT THERE IS ONE MORE LEFT.
THAT LADY OVER THERE....
STARE
PLEASE. COME. COME.
WELLLLL... I GUESS IT WOULD BE RUDE TO EAT AND RUN....
GRRNG GRRNG GRRNG
THIS HORRIBLE GRINDING...
THEN IT *WAS* YOU!
THE GIRL OF MY PAST... AND FUTURE !!
DOOOOM
POP POP POP POP
GRIP
GASP

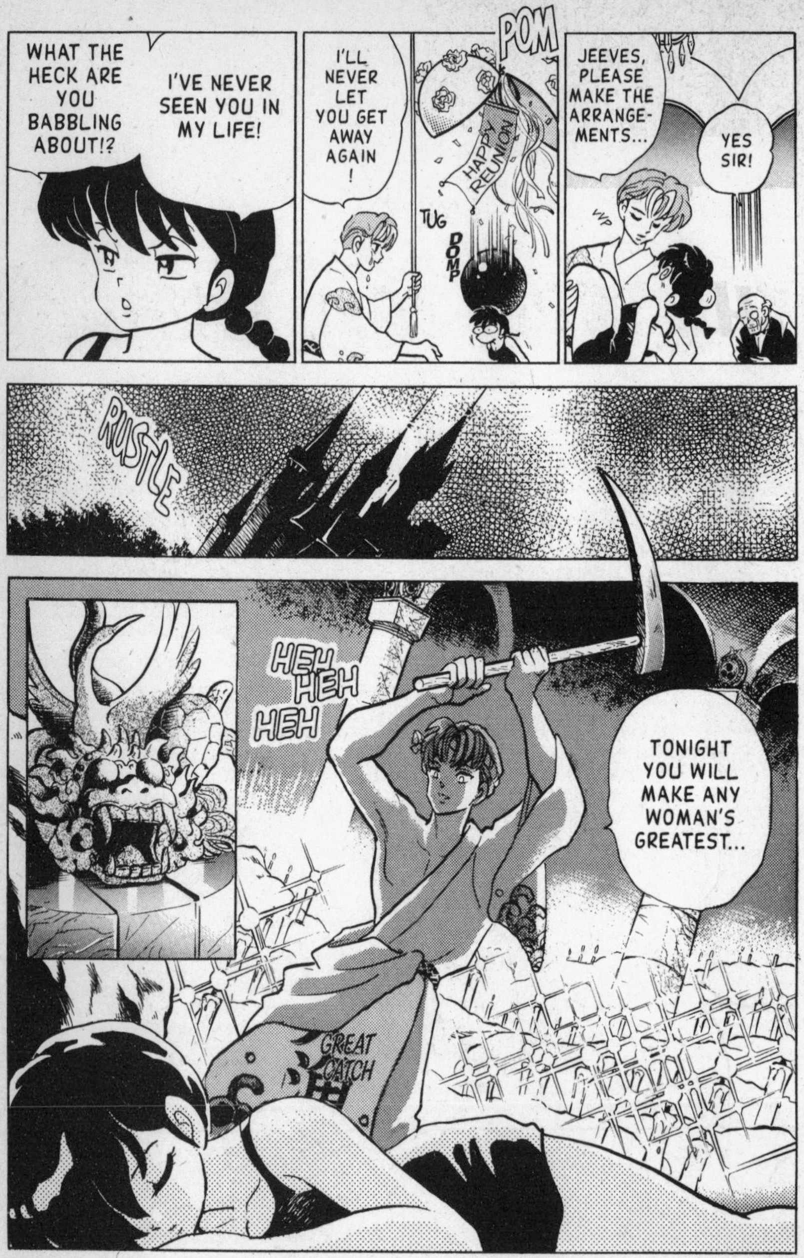

WHAT THE HECK ARE YOU BABBLING ABOUT!?
I'VE NEVER SEEN YOU IN MY LIFE!
I'LL NEVER LET YOU GET AWAY AGAIN !
POM
HAPPY REUNION
TUG
DOMP
JEEVES, PLEASE MAKE THE ARRANGE-MENTS...
YES SIR!
RUSTLE
HEH HEH HEH
TONIGHT YOU WILL MAKE ANY WOMAN'S GREATEST...
GREAT CATCH

Part 6
THE FAIRY TALE ENDING

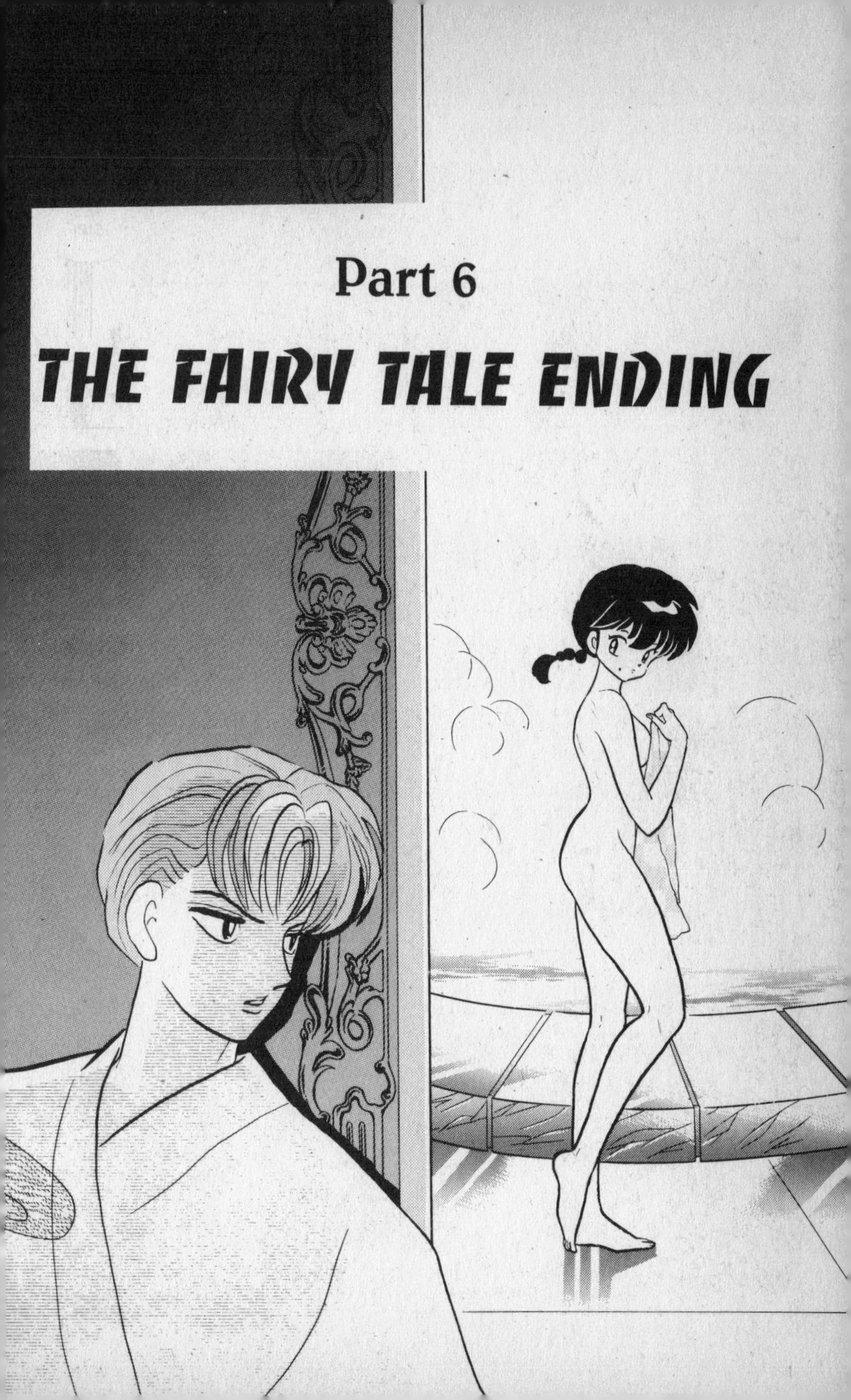

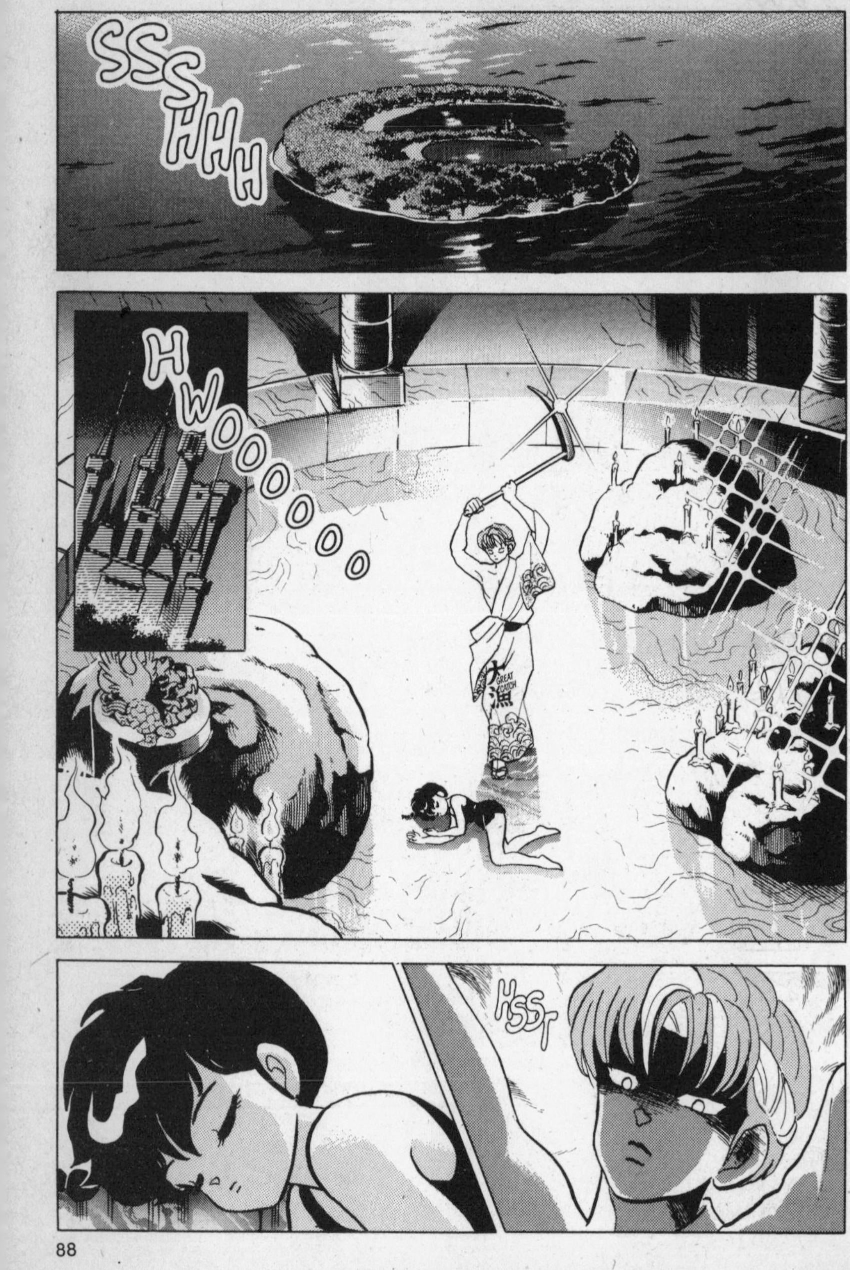
SSSHHH
HWOOOOOOO
大 GREAT CATCH 漁
HSST

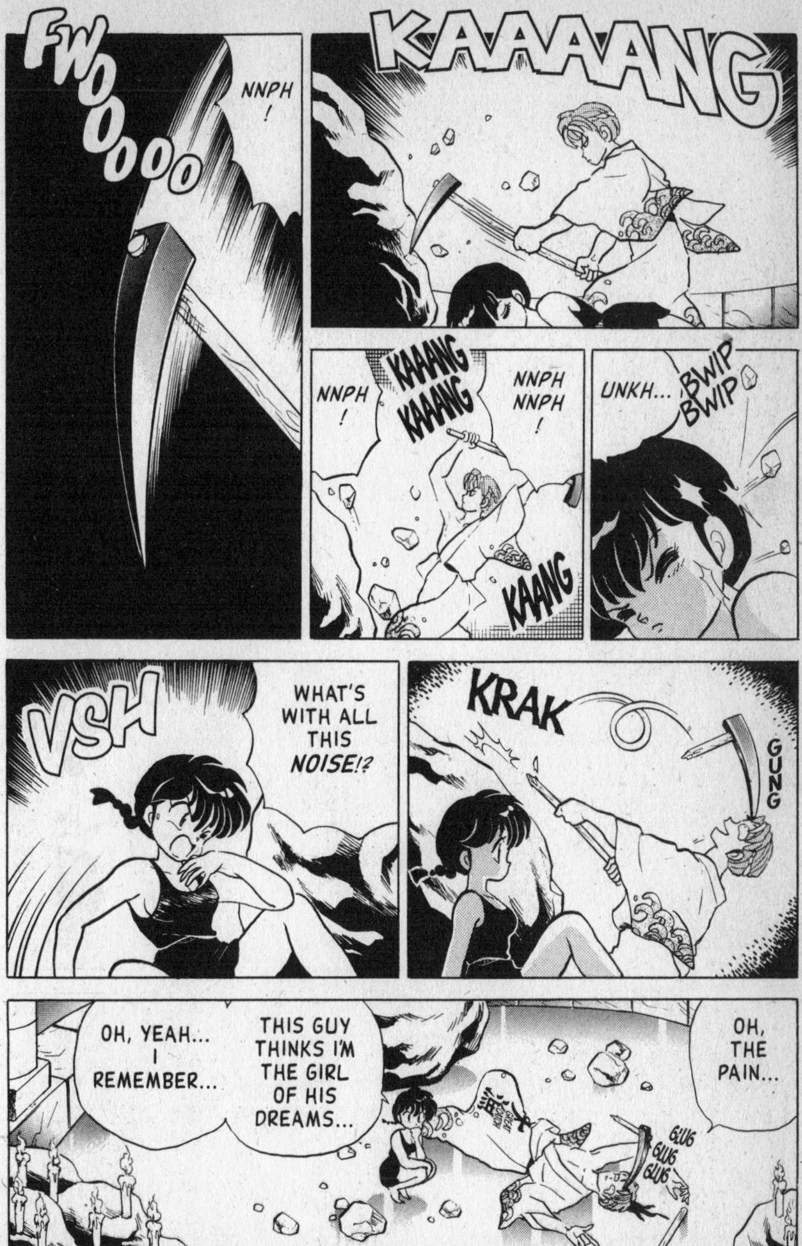
FWOOOOO
NNPH!
KAAAAANG
NNPH!
KAAANG KAAANG
NNPH NNPH!
KAANG
UNKH...
BWIP BWIP
VSH
WHAT'S WITH ALL THIS NOISE!?
KRAK
GUNG
OH, YEAH... I REMEMBER...
THIS GUY THINKS I'M THE GIRL OF HIS DREAMS...
GLUG GLUG GLUG
OH, THE PAIN...

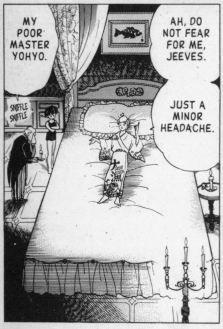

MY POOR MASTER YOHYO.

AH, DO NOT FEAR FOR ME, JEEVES.

JUST A MINOR HEADACHE.

SNIFFLE SNIFFLE

AND JUST WHEN YOU'VE BEEN REUNITED WITH THE LADY YOU LOVE...

LOOK.

SNIFFLE SNIFFLE

THIS HAS GOTTA BE A MISTAKE.

I SWEAR. I'VE NEVER MET YOU BEFORE.

IT HAPPENED WHILE I WAS ON A JOURNEY TO TRAIN FOR A HOT SPRING EXCAVATION.

MEMORIES

HOT SPRING EXCAVATION...?

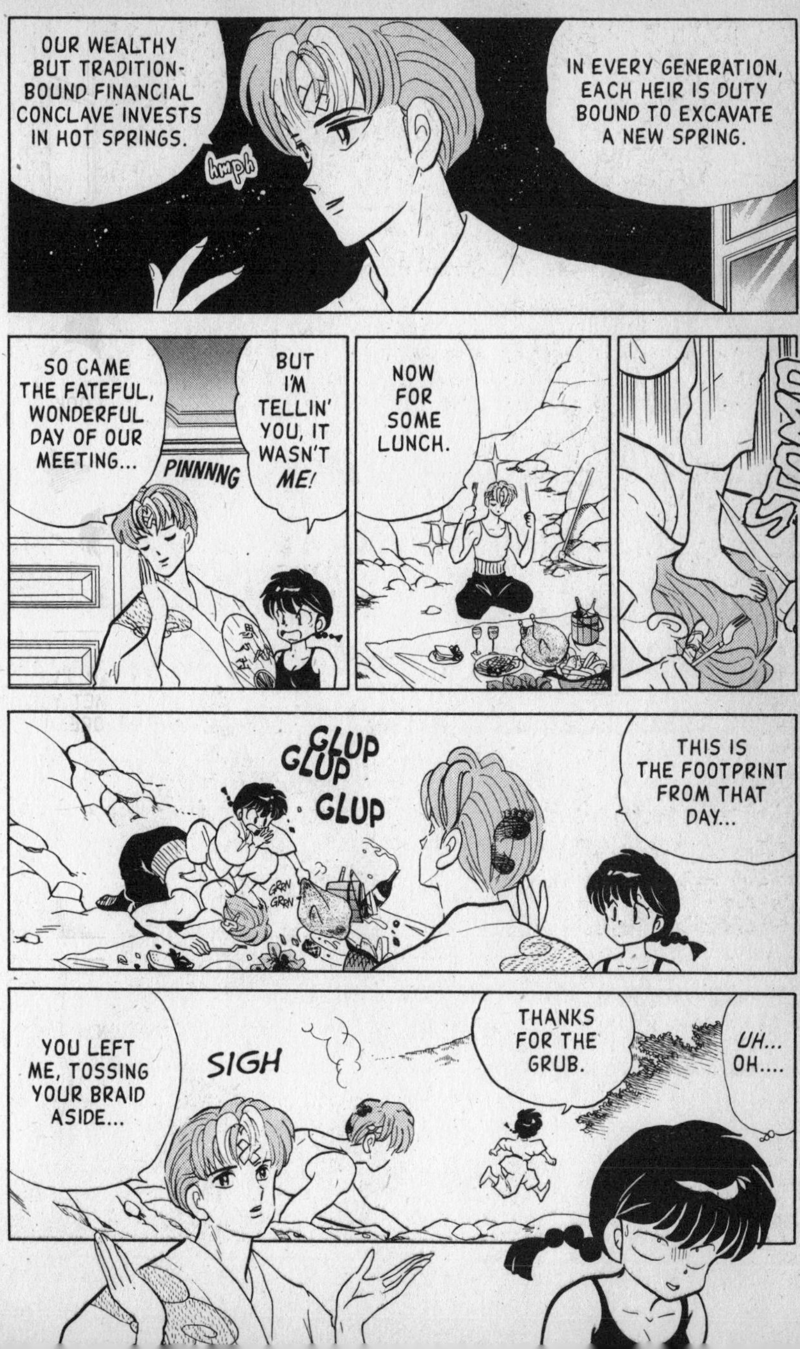
OUR WEALTHY BUT TRADITION-BOUND FINANCIAL CONCLAVE INVESTS IN HOT SPRINGS.
hmph
IN EVERY GENERATION, EACH HEIR IS DUTY BOUND TO EXCAVATE A NEW SPRING.
SO CAME THE FATEFUL, WONDERFUL DAY OF OUR MEETING...
BUT I'M TELLIN' YOU, IT WASN'T ME!
PINNNNG
NOW FOR SOME LUNCH.
STOMP
GLUP GLUP GLUP
GRRN GRRN
THIS IS THE FOOTPRINT FROM THAT DAY...
YOU LEFT ME, TOSSING YOUR BRAID ASIDE...
SIGH
THANKS FOR THE GRUB.
UH... OH....

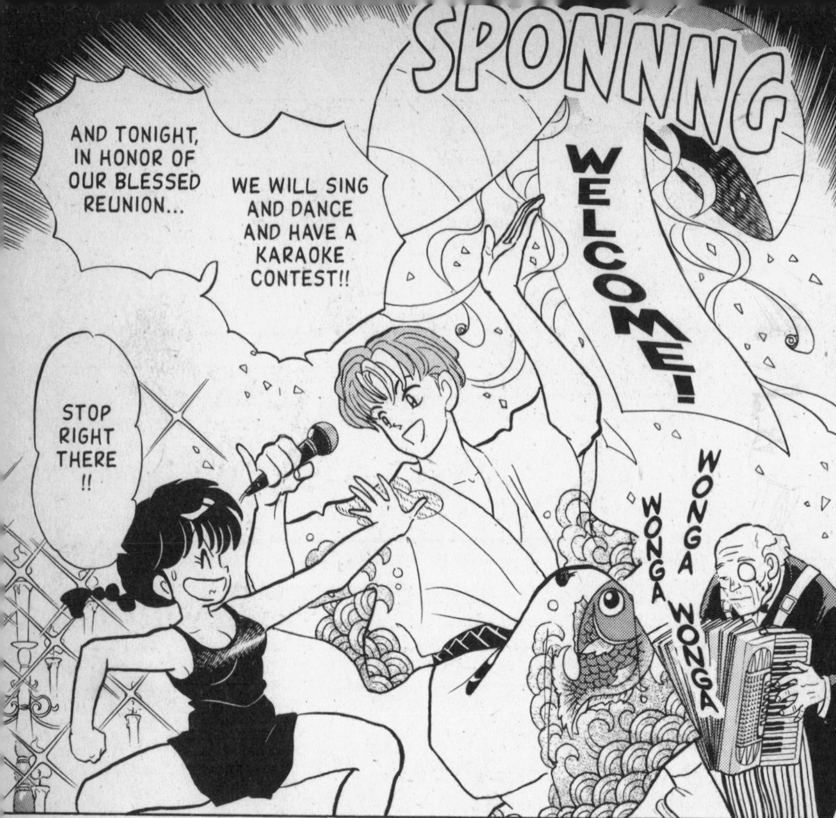
SPONNNG
AND TONIGHT, IN HONOR OF OUR BLESSED REUNION...
WE WILL SING AND DANCE AND HAVE A KARAOKE CONTEST!!
WELCOME!
STOP RIGHT THERE !!
WONGA WONGA
WONGA WONGA
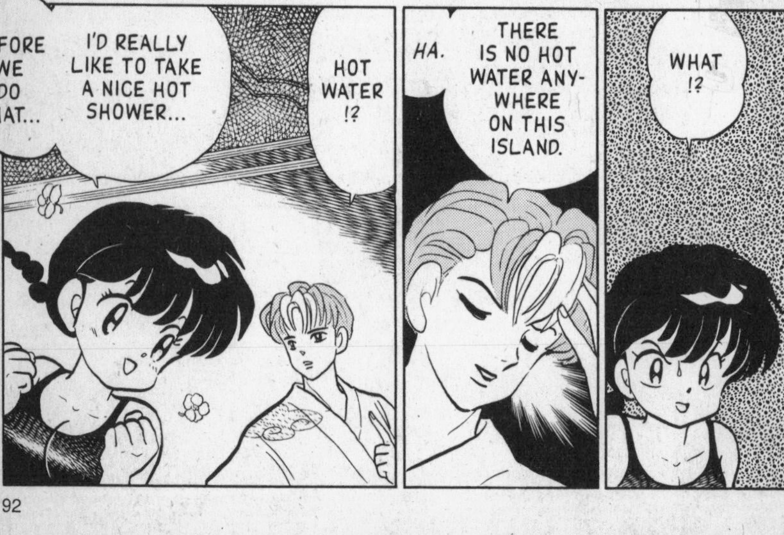
BEFORE WE DO THAT...
I'D REALLY LIKE TO TAKE A NICE HOT SHOWER...
HOT WATER !?
HA.
THERE IS NO HOT WATER ANY-WHERE ON THIS ISLAND.
WHAT !?

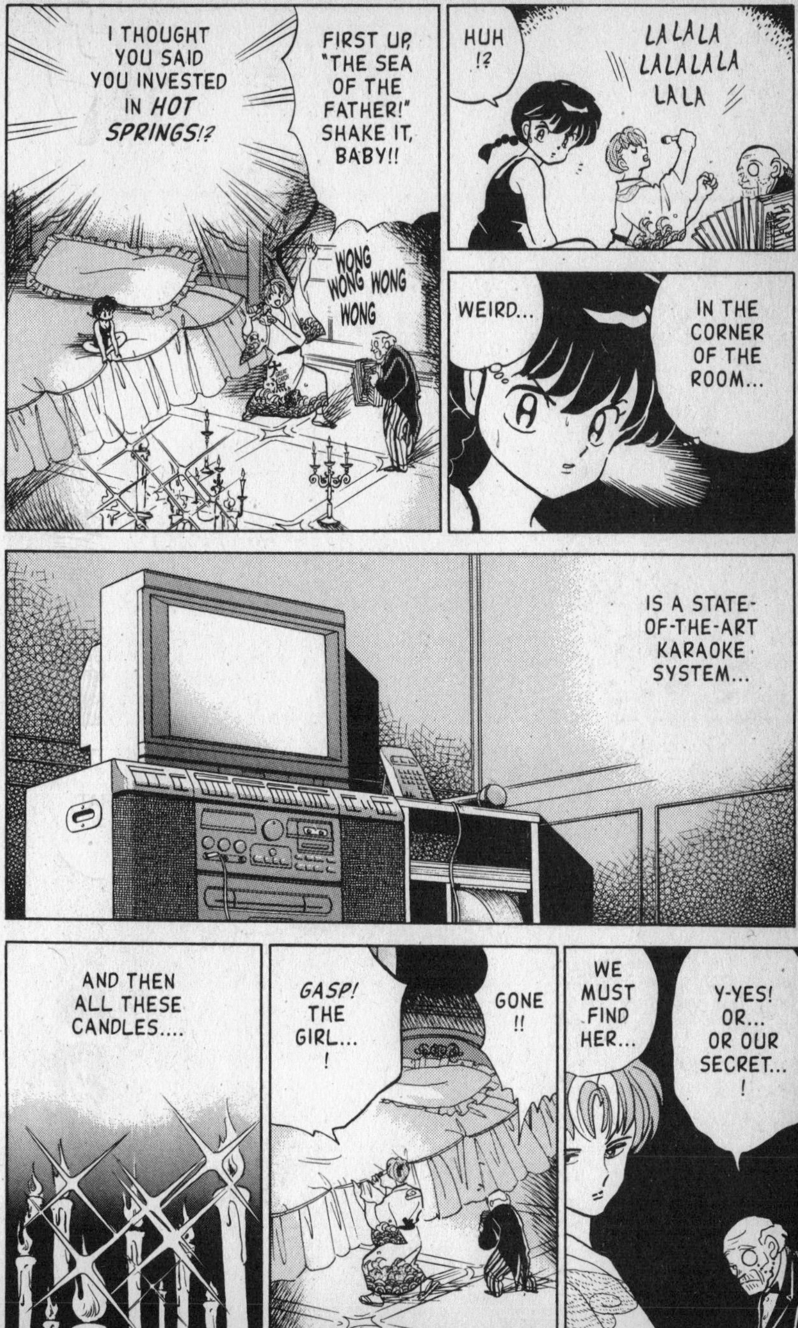
I THOUGHT YOU SAID YOU INVESTED IN *HOT SPRINGS!?*
FIRST UP, "THE SEA OF THE FATHER!" SHAKE IT, BABY!!
WONG WONG WONG WONG
HUH !?
LALALA LALALALA LALA
WEIRD...
IN THE CORNER OF THE ROOM...
IS A STATE-OF-THE-ART KARAOKE SYSTEM...
AND THEN ALL THESE CANDLES....
GASP! THE GIRL... !
GONE !!
WE MUST FIND HER...
Y-YES! OR... OR OUR SECRET... !

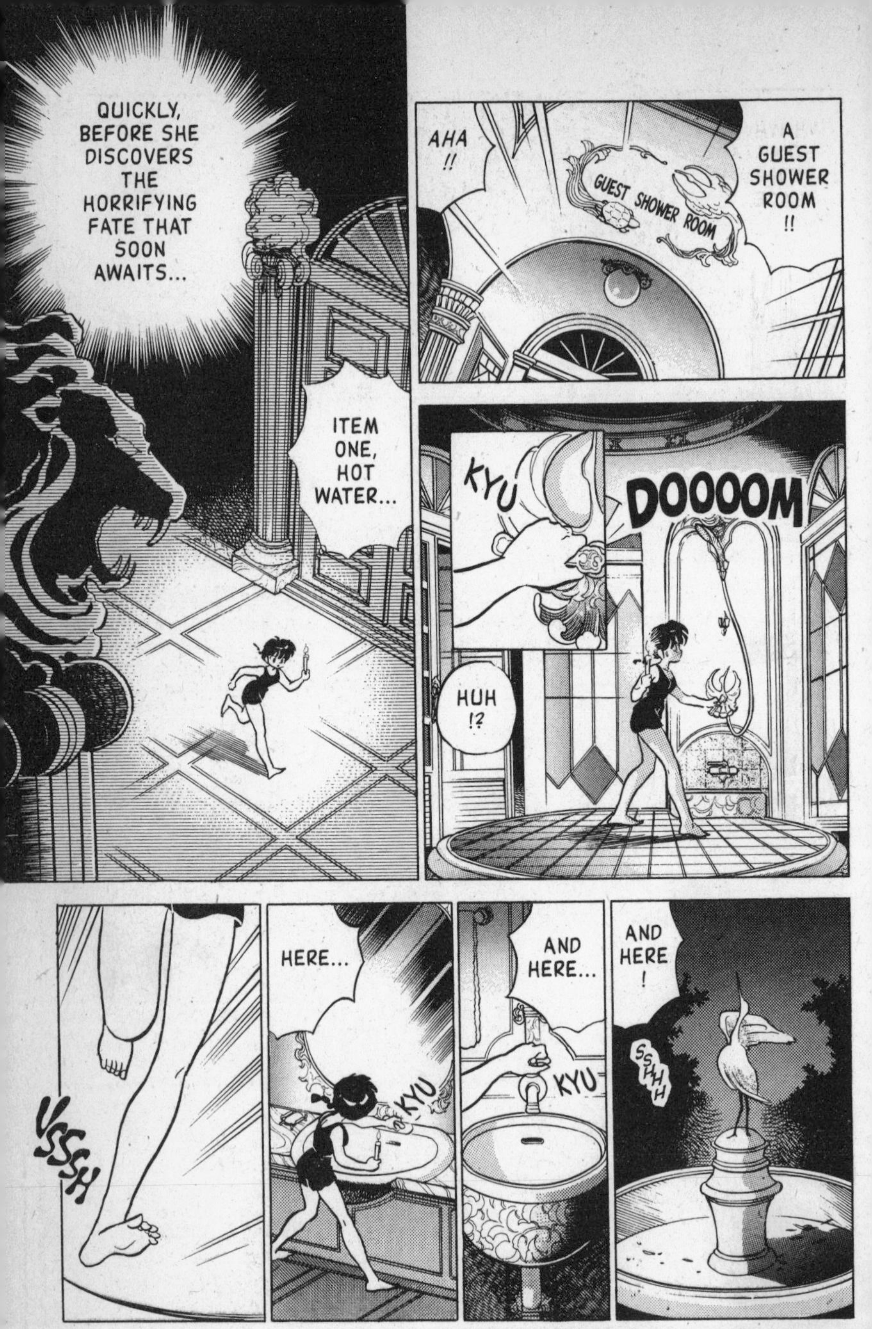
QUICKLY, BEFORE SHE DISCOVERS THE HORRIFYING FATE THAT SOON AWAITS...
ITEM ONE, HOT WATER...
AHA !!
GUEST SHOWER ROOM
A GUEST SHOWER ROOM !!
KYU
DOOOOM
HUH !?
VSSSH
HERE...
KYU
AND HERE...
KYU
AND HERE !
SSHHH

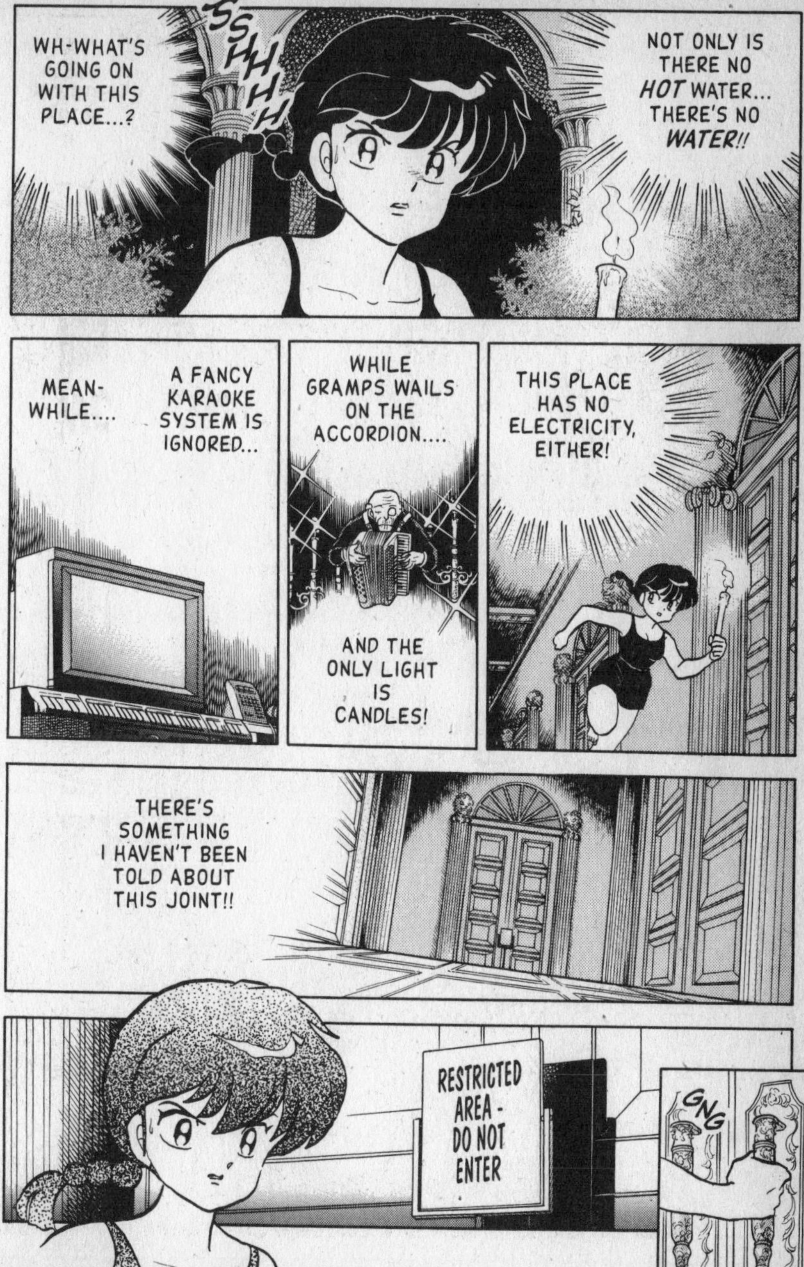
WH-WHAT'S GOING ON WITH THIS PLACE...?
SSHHHH
NOT ONLY IS THERE NO HOT WATER... THERE'S NO WATER!!
MEAN-WHILE....
A FANCY KARAOKE SYSTEM IS IGNORED...
WHILE GRAMPS WAILS ON THE ACCORDION....
AND THE ONLY LIGHT IS CANDLES!
THIS PLACE HAS NO ELECTRICITY, EITHER!
THERE'S SOMETHING I HAVEN'T BEEN TOLD ABOUT THIS JOINT!!
RESTRICTED AREA - DO NOT ENTER
GNG

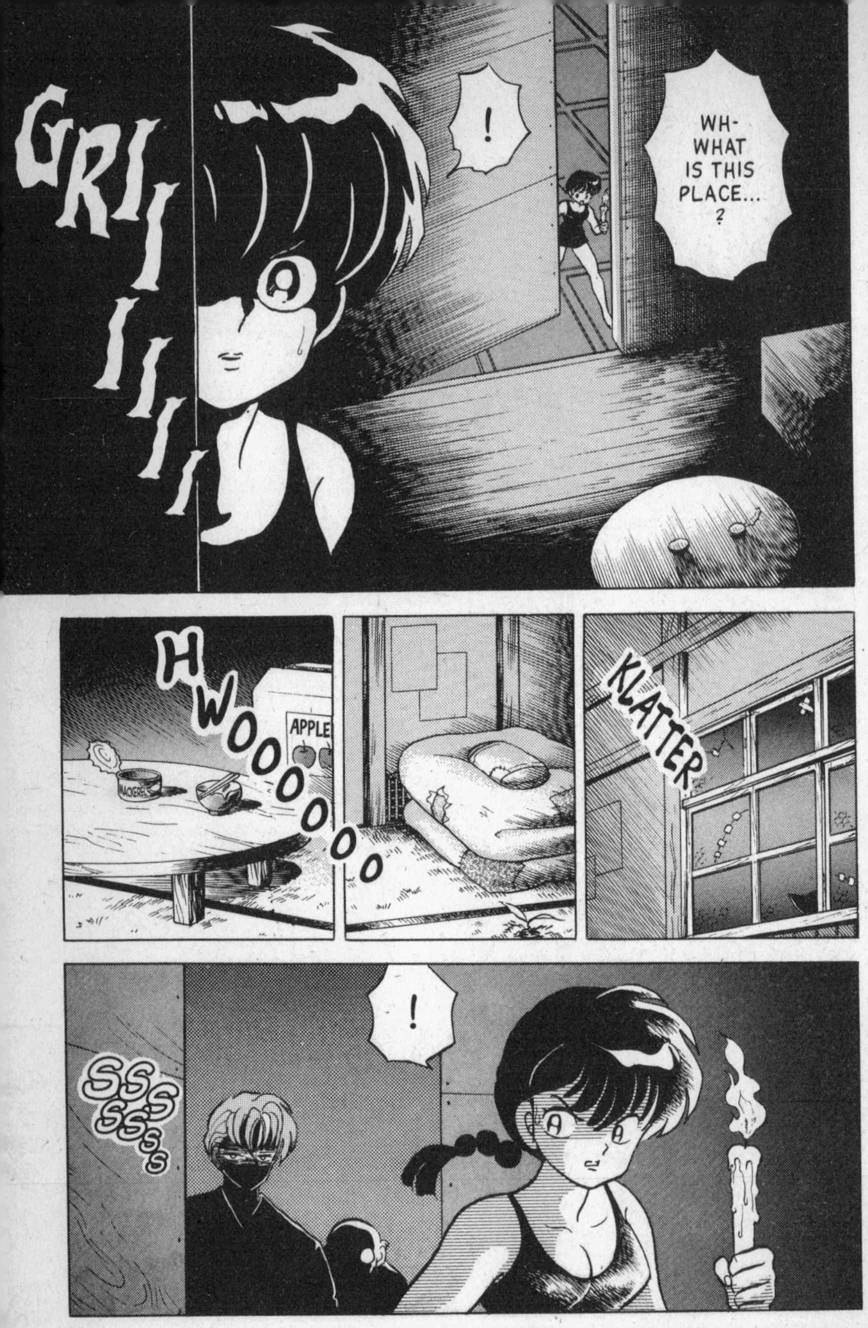
GRIIIIIII
!
WH-WHAT IS THIS PLACE...?
HWOOOOOOO
APPLE
MACKEREL
KLATTER
!
SSSSSSS

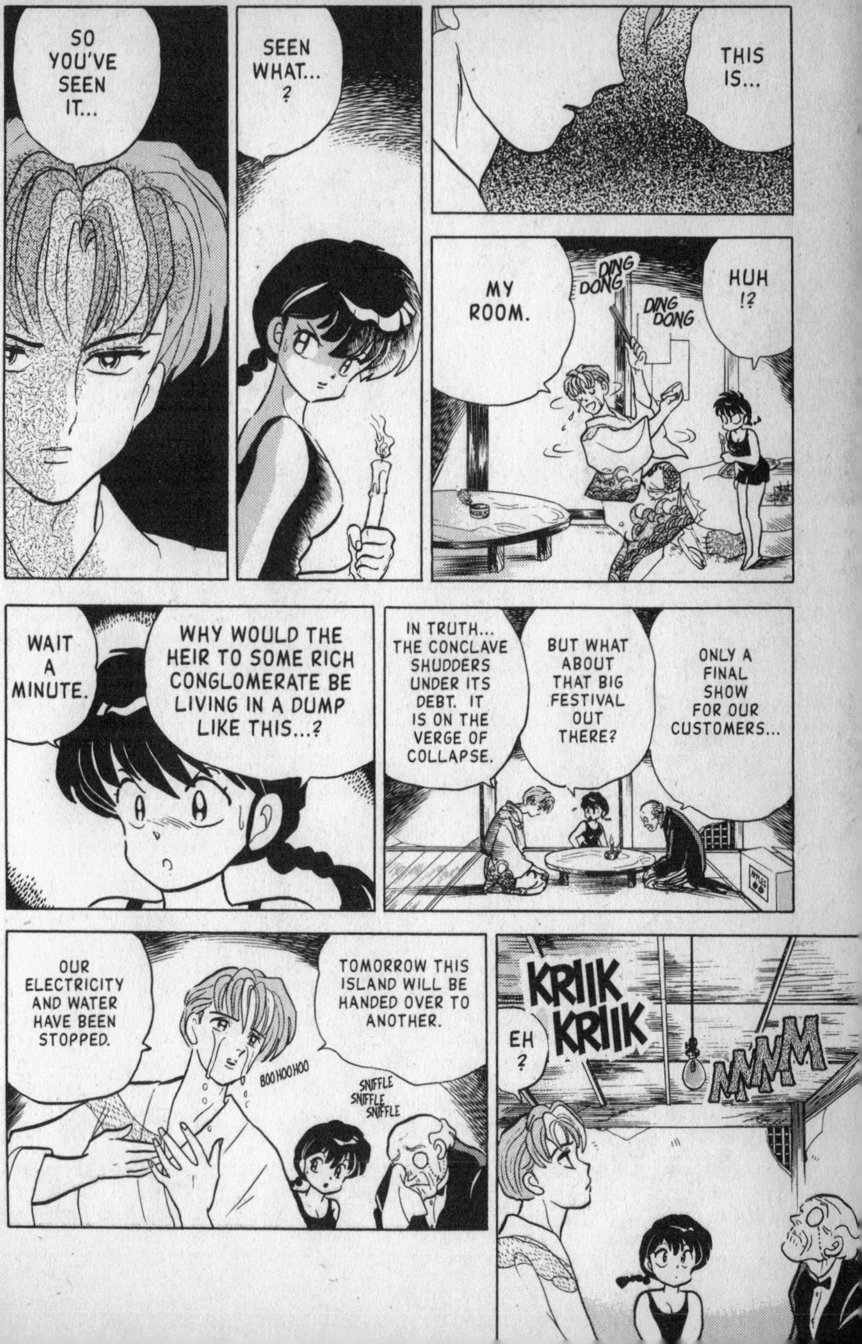
SO YOU'VE SEEN IT...
SEEN WHAT...?
THIS IS...
MY ROOM.
DING DONG
DING DONG
HUH!?
WAIT A MINUTE.
WHY WOULD THE HEIR TO SOME RICH CONGLOMERATE BE LIVING IN A DUMP LIKE THIS...?
IN TRUTH... THE CONCLAVE SHUDDERS UNDER ITS DEBT. IT IS ON THE VERGE OF COLLAPSE.
BUT WHAT ABOUT THAT BIG FESTIVAL OUT THERE?
ONLY A FINAL SHOW FOR OUR CUSTOMERS...
OUR ELECTRICITY AND WATER HAVE BEEN STOPPED.
TOMORROW THIS ISLAND WILL BE HANDED OVER TO ANOTHER.
BOO HOO HOO
SNIFFLE SNIFFLE SNIFFLE
KRIIK KRIIK
EH?
MMMM

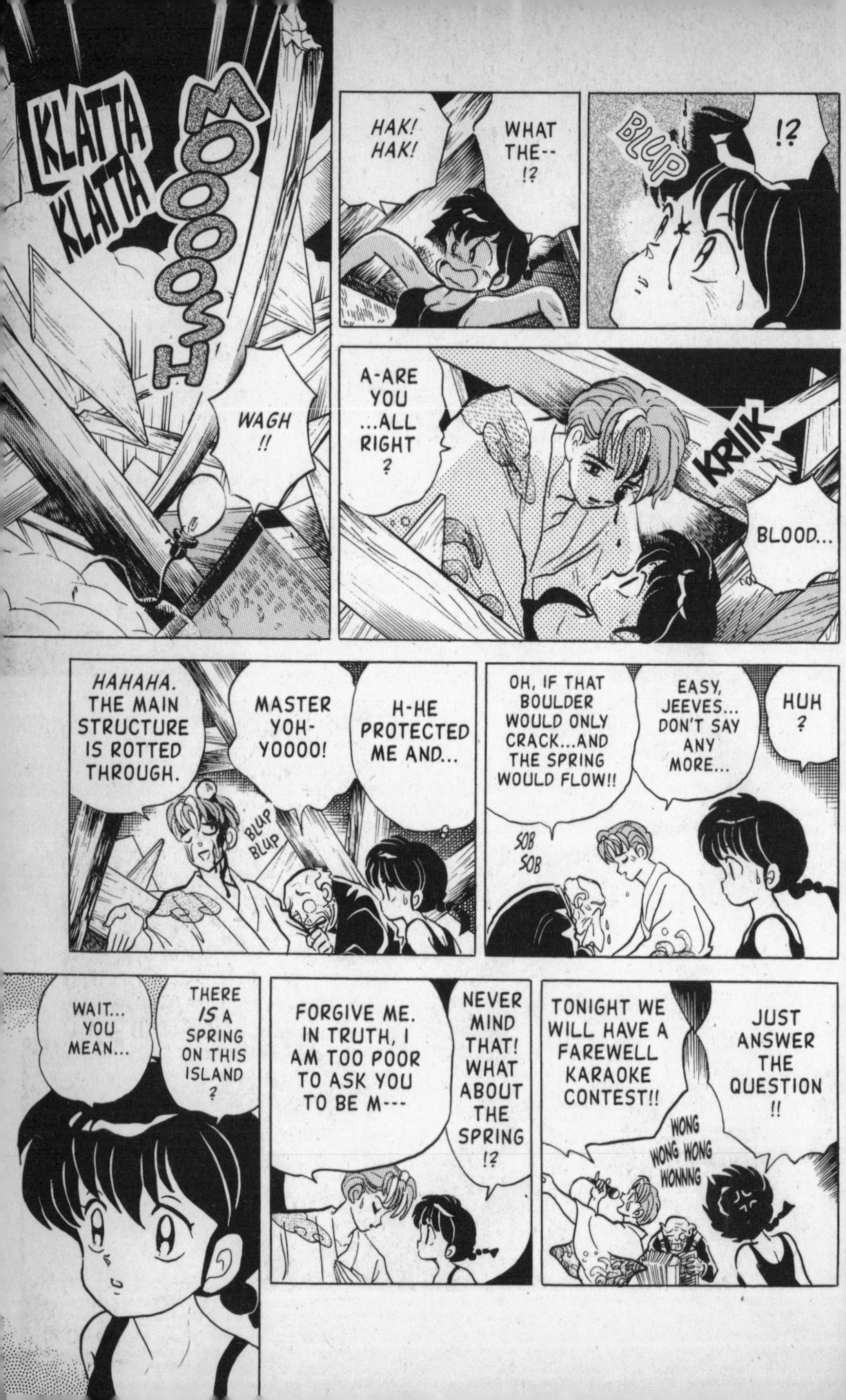
KLATTA KLATTA
MOOOOOSH
WAGH !!
HAK! HAK!
WHAT THE-- !?
BLUP
!?
A-ARE YOU ...ALL RIGHT ?
KRIIK
BLOOD...
HAHAHA. THE MAIN STRUCTURE IS ROTTED THROUGH.
MASTER YOH-YOOOO!
BLUP BLUP
H-HE PROTECTED ME AND...
OH, IF THAT BOULDER WOULD ONLY CRACK...AND THE SPRING WOULD FLOW!!
SOB SOB
EASY, JEEVES... DON'T SAY ANY MORE...
HUH ?
WAIT... YOU MEAN...
THERE *IS* A SPRING ON THIS ISLAND ?
FORGIVE ME. IN TRUTH, I AM TOO POOR TO ASK YOU TO BE M---
NEVER MIND THAT! WHAT ABOUT THE SPRING !?
TONIGHT WE WILL HAVE A FAREWELL KARAOKE CONTEST!!
WONG WONG WONG WONNNG
JUST ANSWER THE QUESTION !!

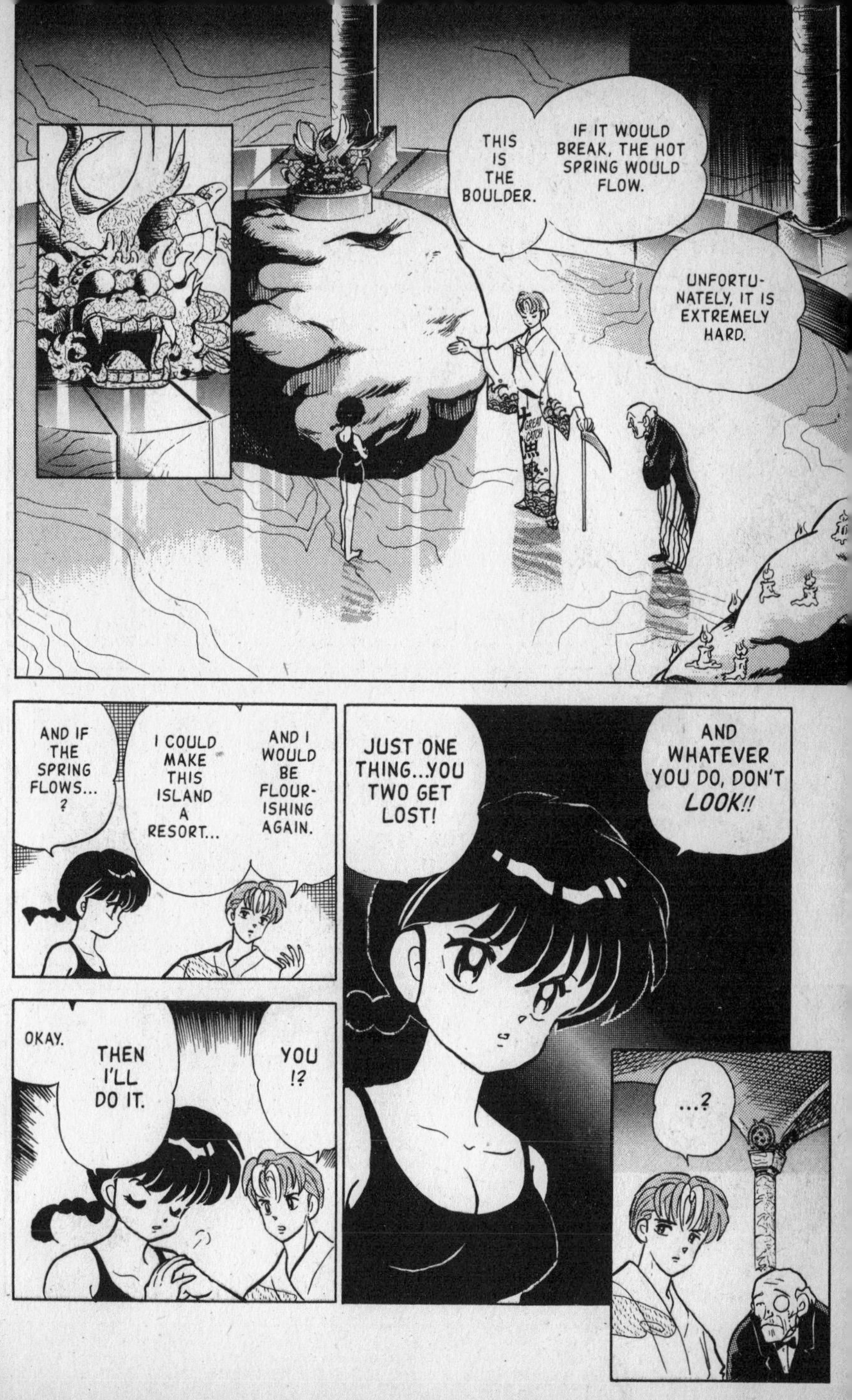
THIS IS THE BOULDER.
IF IT WOULD BREAK, THE HOT SPRING WOULD FLOW.
UNFORTUNATELY, IT IS EXTREMELY HARD.
GREAT CATCH
AND IF THE SPRING FLOWS...?
I COULD MAKE THIS ISLAND A RESORT...
AND I WOULD BE FLOURISHING AGAIN.
OKAY.
THEN I'LL DO IT.
YOU!?
JUST ONE THING...YOU TWO GET LOST!
AND WHATEVER YOU DO, DON'T *LOOK!!*
...?

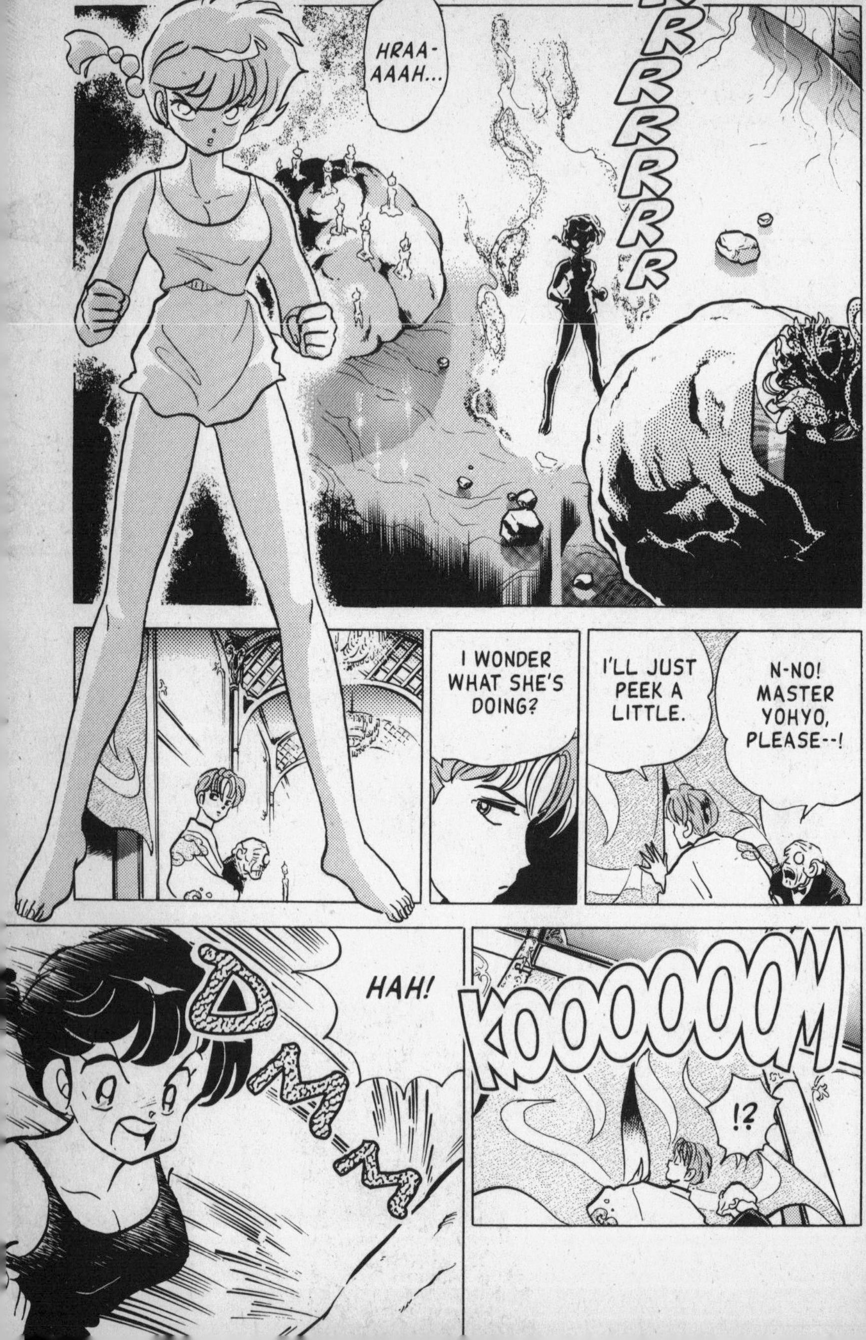
HRAA-AAAH...
RRRRRRR
I WONDER WHAT SHE'S DOING?
I'LL JUST PEEK A LITTLE.
N-NO! MASTER YOHYO, PLEASE--!
HAH!
KOOOOOOM
!?

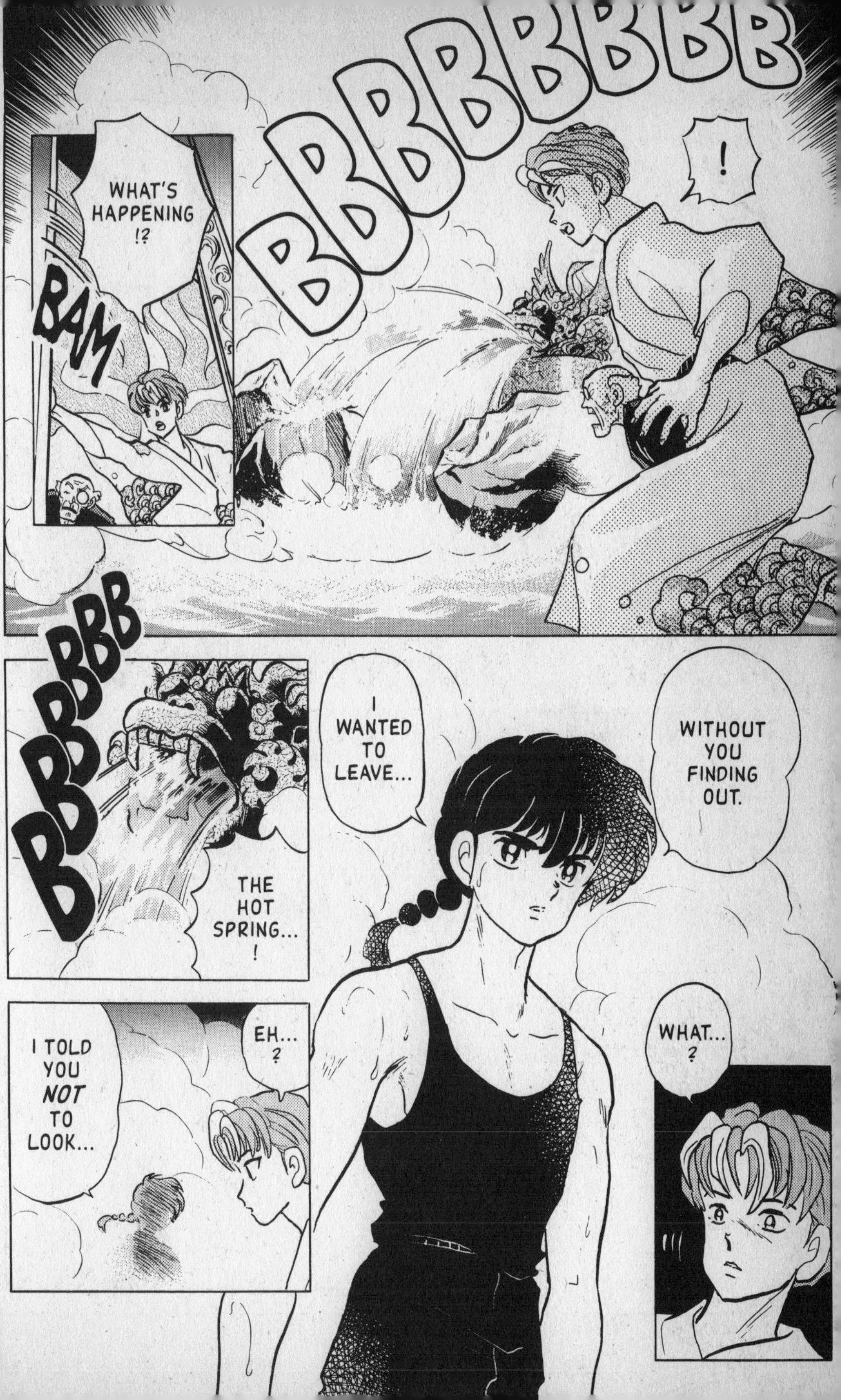
WHAT'S HAPPENING !?
BAM
BBBBBBBBB
!
BBBBBBB
THE HOT SPRING... !
I WANTED TO LEAVE...
WITHOUT YOU FINDING OUT.
I TOLD YOU *NOT* TO LOOK...
EH... ?
WHAT... ?

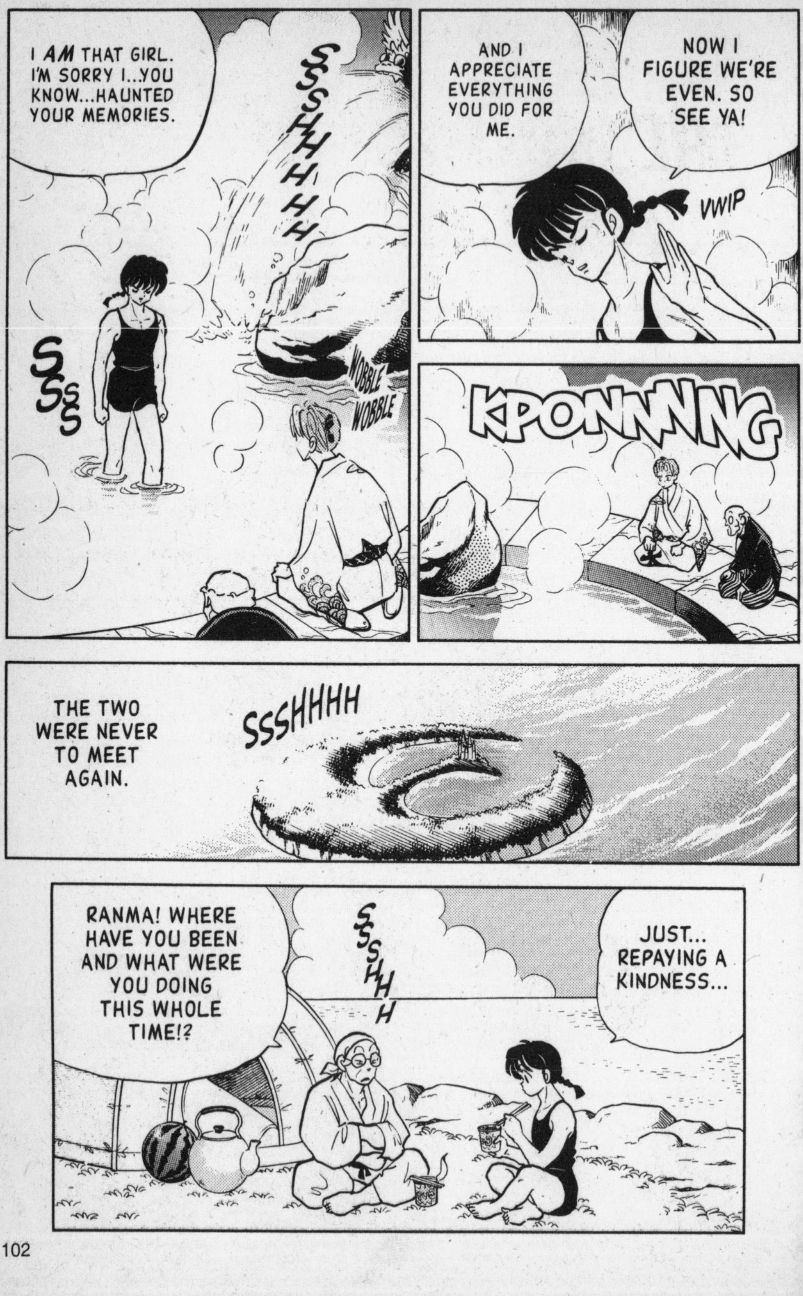
I AM THAT GIRL. I'M SORRY I...YOU KNOW...HAUNTED YOUR MEMORIES.
SSSHHHHHH
SSSS
WOBBLE WOBBLE
AND I APPRECIATE EVERYTHING YOU DID FOR ME.
NOW I FIGURE WE'RE EVEN. SO SEE YA!
VWIP
KPONNNNG
THE TWO WERE NEVER TO MEET AGAIN.
SSSHHHH
RANMA! WHERE HAVE YOU BEEN AND WHAT WERE YOU DOING THIS WHOLE TIME!?
SSSHHH
JUST... REPAYING A KINDNESS...

Part 7

THE VIOLENCE OF COOKING

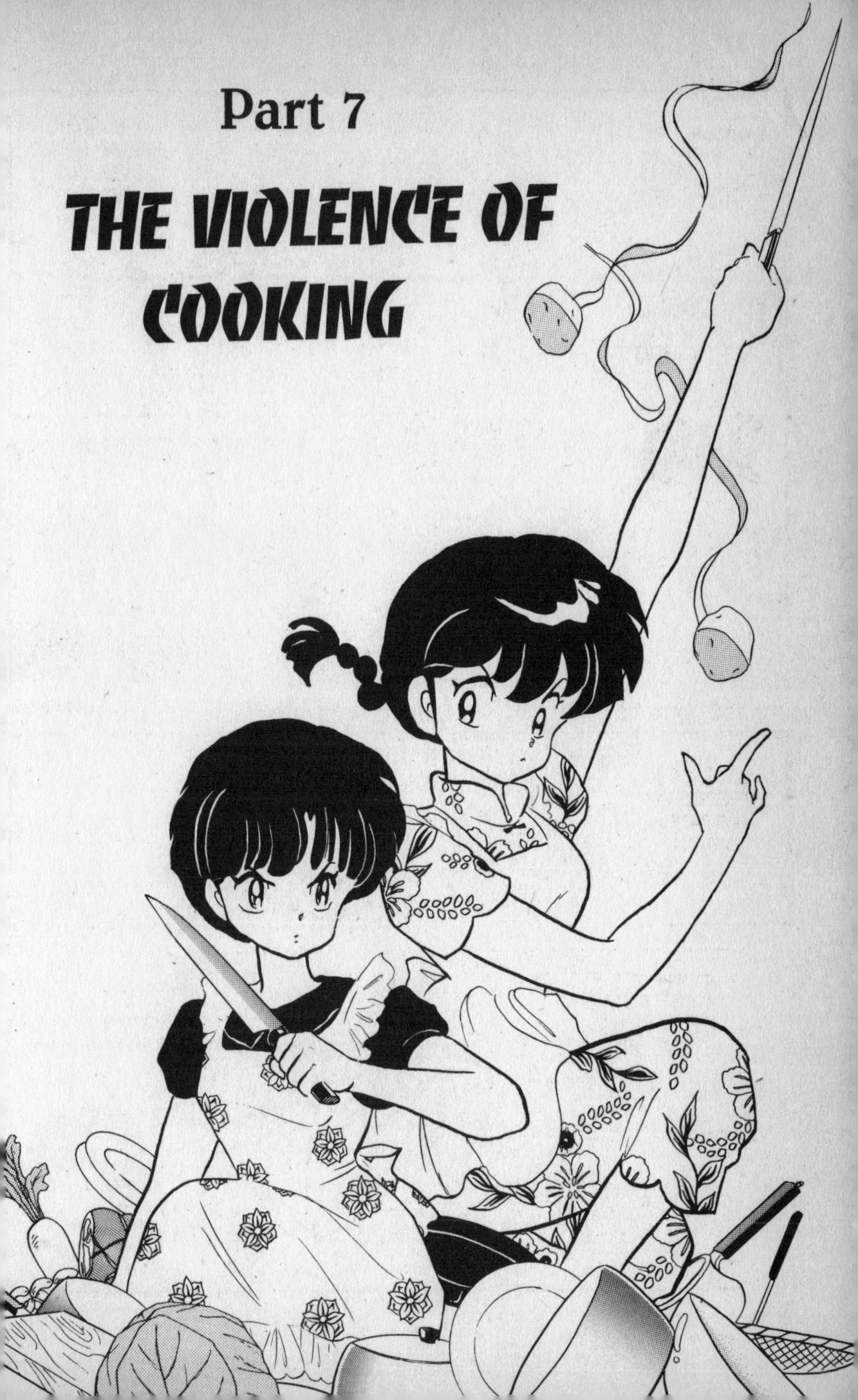

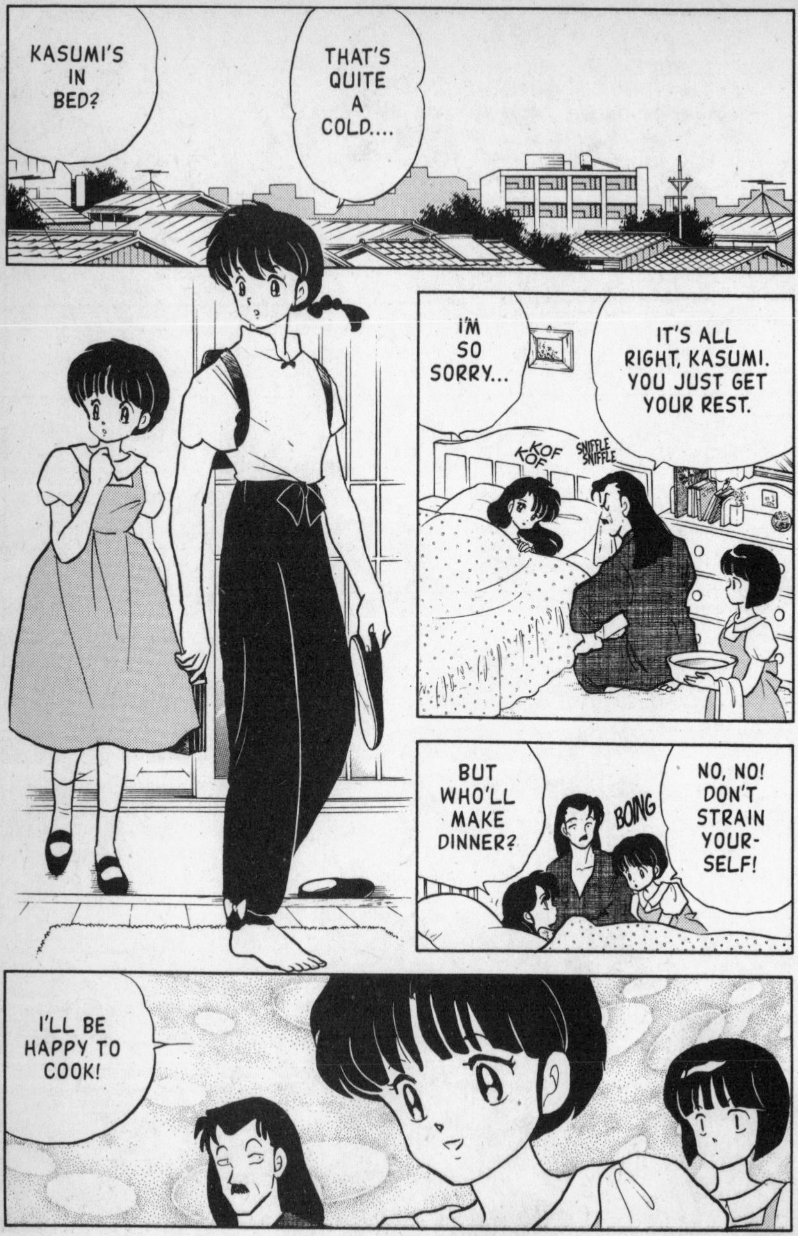
KASUMI'S IN BED?
THAT'S QUITE A COLD....
I'M SO SORRY...
KOF KOF
SNIFFLE SNIFFLE
IT'S ALL RIGHT, KASUMI. YOU JUST GET YOUR REST.
BUT WHO'LL MAKE DINNER?
BOING
NO, NO! DON'T STRAIN YOUR-SELF!
I'LL BE HAPPY TO COOK!

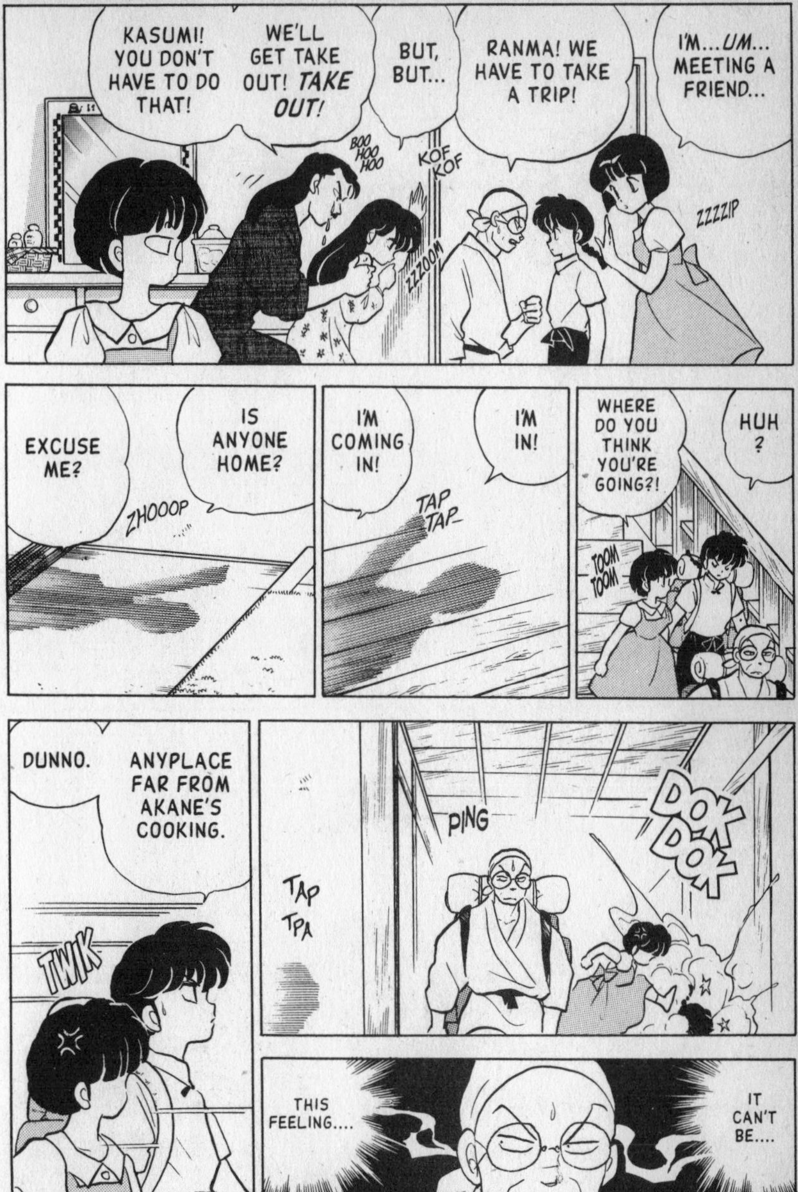
KASUMI! YOU DON'T HAVE TO DO THAT!
WE'LL GET TAKE OUT! TAKE OUT!
BOO HOO HOO
BUT, BUT...
KOF KOF
ZZZOOM
RANMA! WE HAVE TO TAKE A TRIP!
I'M...UM... MEETING A FRIEND...
ZZZZIP
EXCUSE ME?
IS ANYONE HOME?
ZHOOOP
I'M COMING IN!
I'M IN!
TAP TAP
WHERE DO YOU THINK YOU'RE GOING?!
HUH?
TOOM TOOM
DUNNO.
ANYPLACE FAR FROM AKANE'S COOKING.
TWIK
TAP TPA
PING
DOK DOK
THIS FEELING....
IT CAN'T BE....

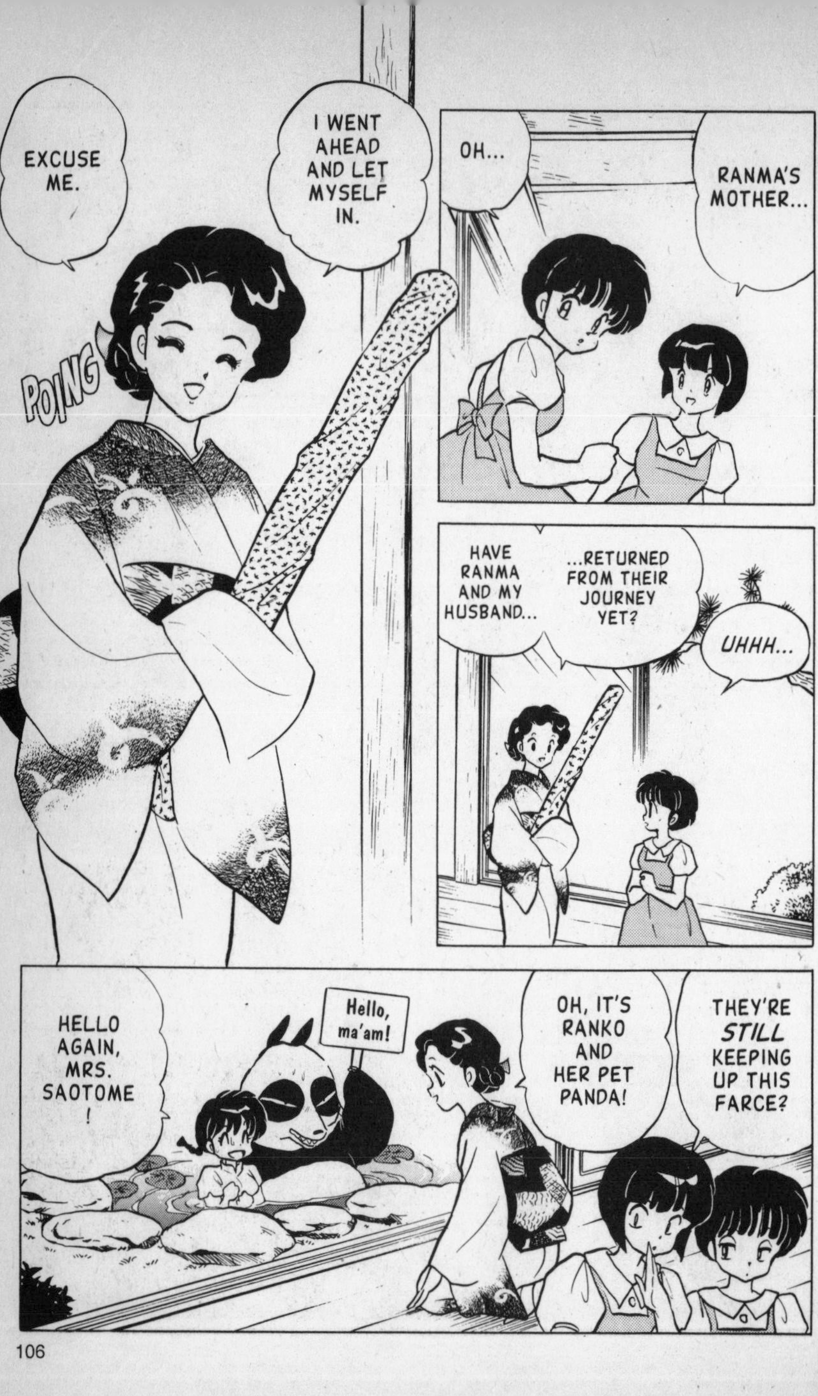
EXCUSE ME.
I WENT AHEAD AND LET MYSELF IN.
POING
OH...
RANMA'S MOTHER...
HAVE RANMA AND MY HUSBAND...
...RETURNED FROM THEIR JOURNEY YET?
UHHH...
HELLO AGAIN, MRS. SAOTOME!
Hello, ma'am!
OH, IT'S RANKO AND HER PET PANDA!
THEY'RE *STILL* KEEPING UP THIS FARCE?

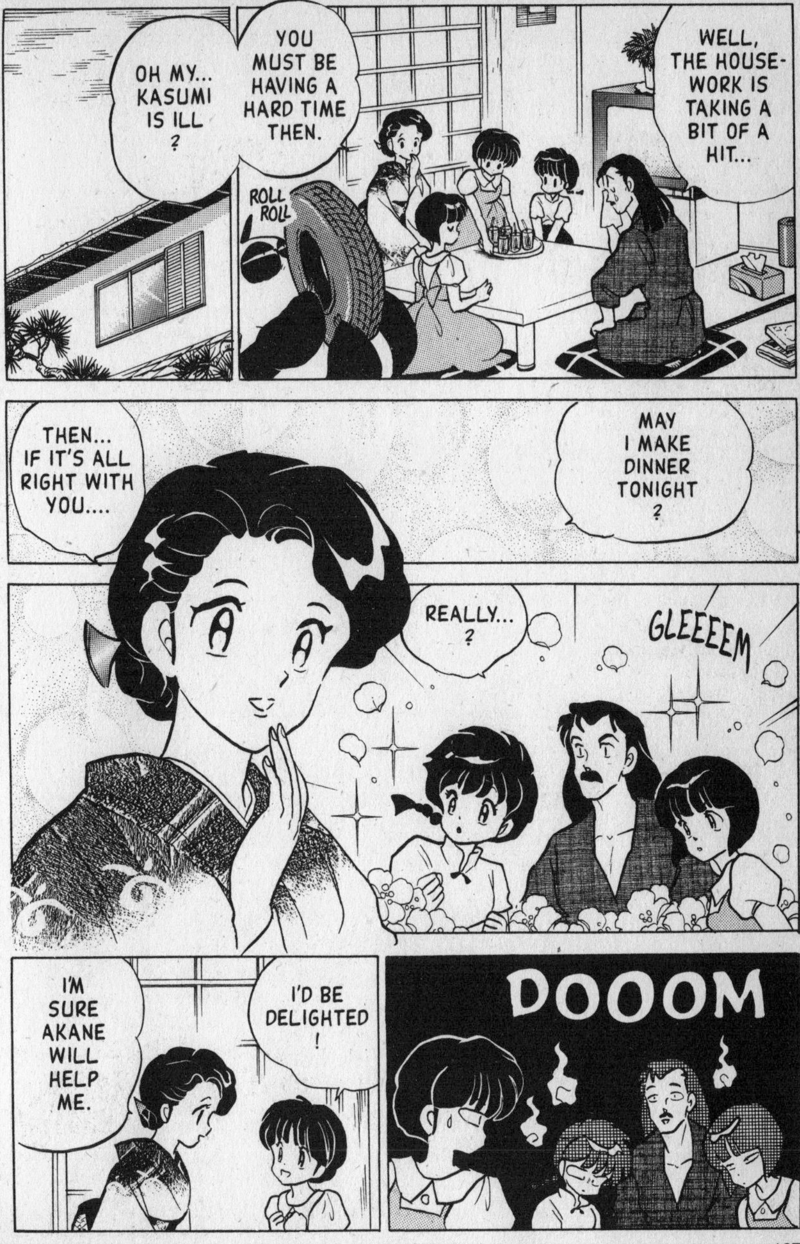
OH MY... KASUMI IS ILL?
YOU MUST BE HAVING A HARD TIME THEN.
ROLL ROLL
WELL, THE HOUSE-WORK IS TAKING A BIT OF A HIT...
THEN... IF IT'S ALL RIGHT WITH YOU....
MAY I MAKE DINNER TONIGHT?
REALLY...?
GLEEEEM
I'M SURE AKANE WILL HELP ME.
I'D BE DELIGHTED!
DOOOM

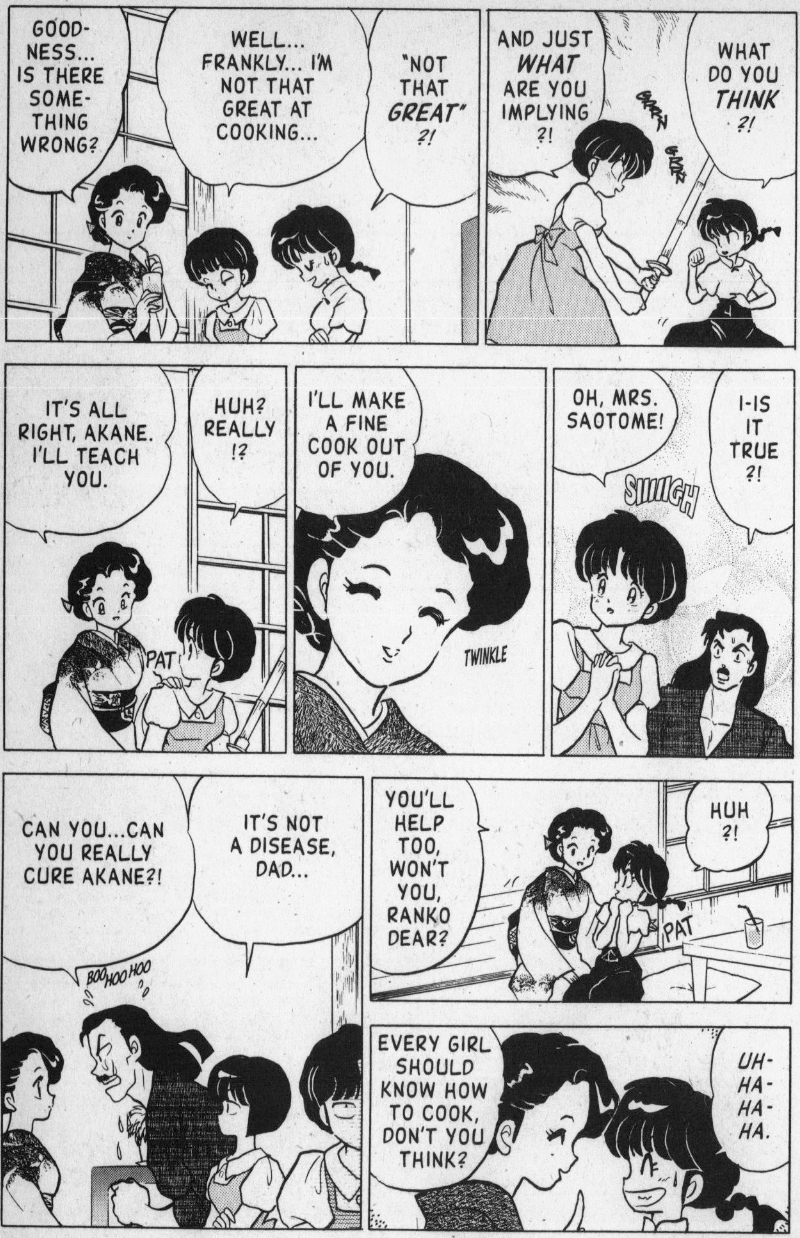
GOODNESS... IS THERE SOMETHING WRONG?
WELL... FRANKLY... I'M NOT THAT GREAT AT COOKING...
"NOT THAT *GREAT*"?!
AND JUST *WHAT* ARE YOU IMPLYING?!
WHAT DO YOU *THINK*?!
IT'S ALL RIGHT, AKANE. I'LL TEACH YOU.
HUH? REALLY!?
PAT
I'LL MAKE A FINE COOK OUT OF YOU.
TWINKLE
OH, MRS. SAOTOME!
SIIIIGH
I-IS IT TRUE?!
CAN YOU...CAN YOU REALLY CURE AKANE?!
IT'S NOT A DISEASE, DAD...
BOOHOOHOO
YOU'LL HELP TOO, WON'T YOU, RANKO DEAR?
HUH?!
PAT
EVERY GIRL SHOULD KNOW HOW TO COOK, DON'T YOU THINK?
UH-HA-HA-HA.

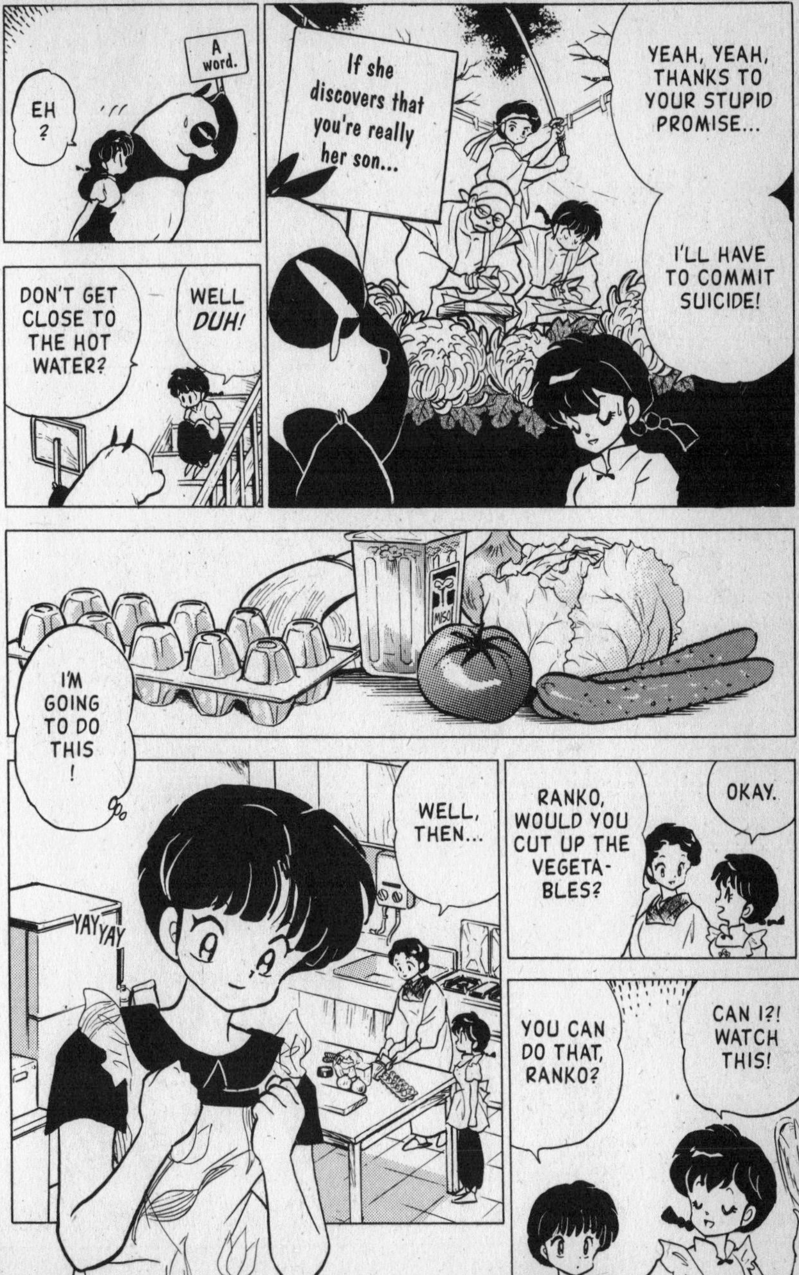
EH?
A word.
DON'T GET CLOSE TO THE HOT WATER?
WELL DUH!
If she discovers that you're really her son...
YEAH, YEAH, THANKS TO YOUR STUPID PROMISE...
I'LL HAVE TO COMMIT SUICIDE!
MISO
I'M GOING TO DO THIS!
WELL, THEN...
YAY YAY
RANKO, WOULD YOU CUT UP THE VEGETA-BLES?
OKAY.
YOU CAN DO THAT, RANKO?
CAN I?! WATCH THIS!
TWRLLLL

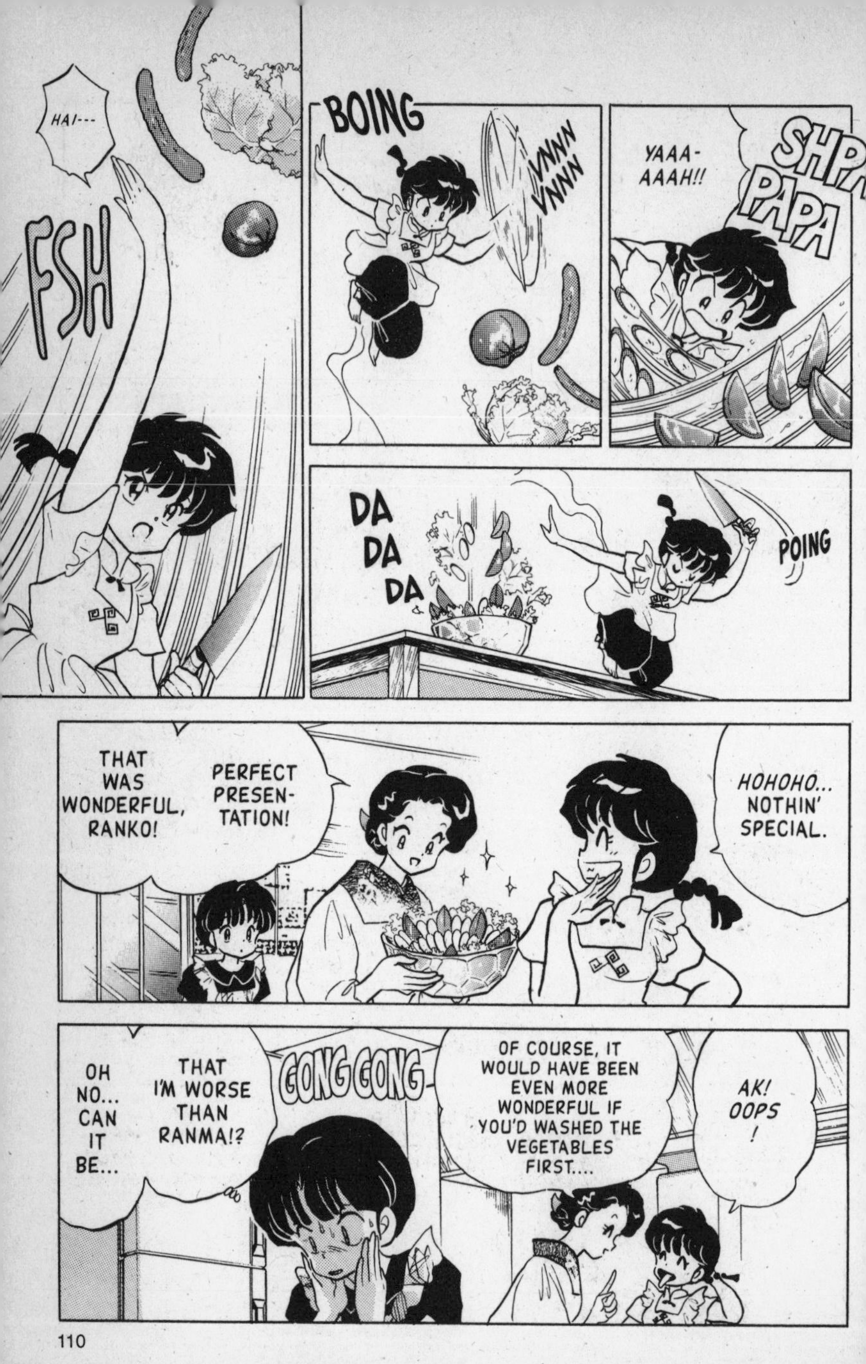
HAI---
FSH
BOING
VNNN VNNN
YAAA-AAAH!!
SHPA PAPA
DA DA DA
POING
THAT WAS WONDERFUL, RANKO!
PERFECT PRESEN-TATION!
HOHOHO... NOTHIN' SPECIAL.
OH NO... CAN IT BE...
THAT I'M WORSE THAN RANMA!?
GONG GONG
OF COURSE, IT WOULD HAVE BEEN EVEN MORE WONDERFUL IF YOU'D WASHED THE VEGETABLES FIRST....
AK! OOPS!

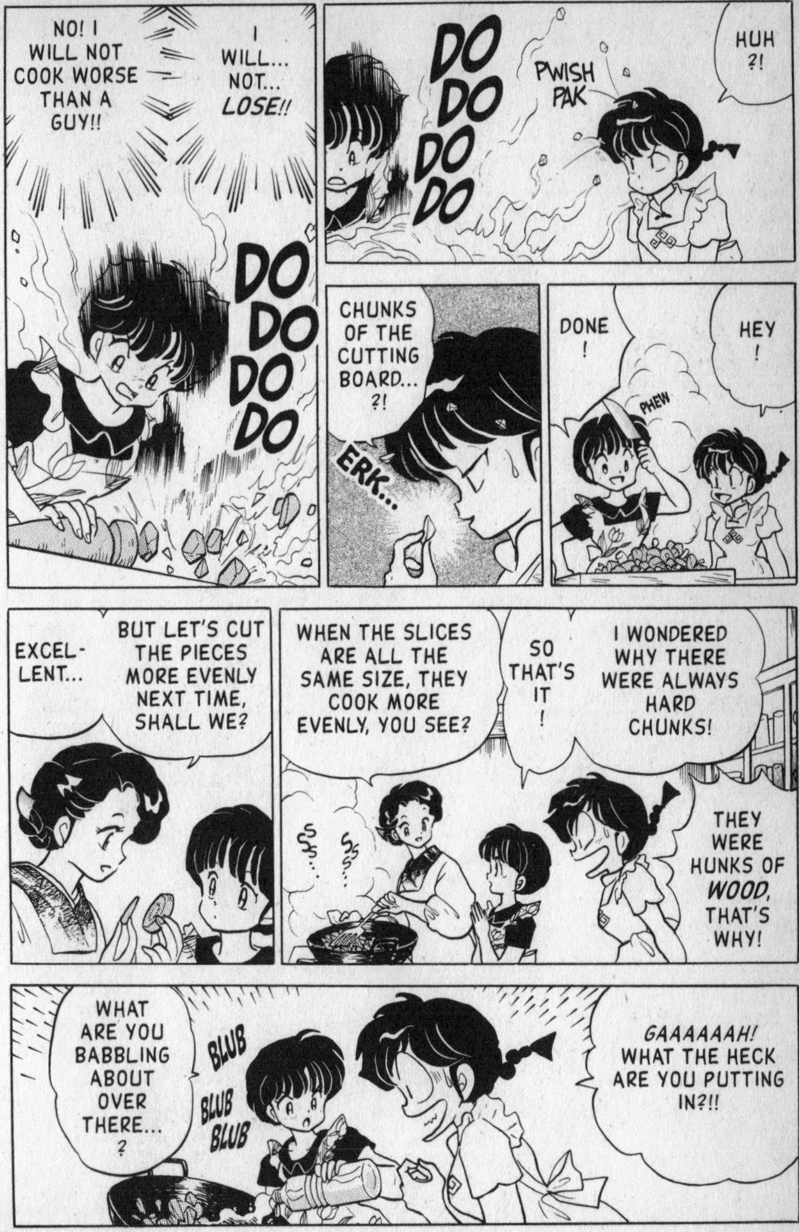
NO! I WILL NOT COOK WORSE THAN A GUY!!
I WILL... NOT... LOSE!!
DO DO DO DO
DO DO DO DO
PWISH PAK
HUH ?!
CHUNKS OF THE CUTTING BOARD... ?!
ERK...
DONE !
HEY !
PHEW
EXCEL-LENT...
BUT LET'S CUT THE PIECES MORE EVENLY NEXT TIME, SHALL WE?
WHEN THE SLICES ARE ALL THE SAME SIZE, THEY COOK MORE EVENLY, YOU SEE?
SO THAT'S IT !
I WONDERED WHY THERE WERE ALWAYS HARD CHUNKS!
THEY WERE HUNKS OF WOOD, THAT'S WHY!
WHAT ARE YOU BABBLING ABOUT OVER THERE... ?
BLUB BLUB BLUB
GAAAAAAH! WHAT THE HECK ARE YOU PUTTING IN?!!

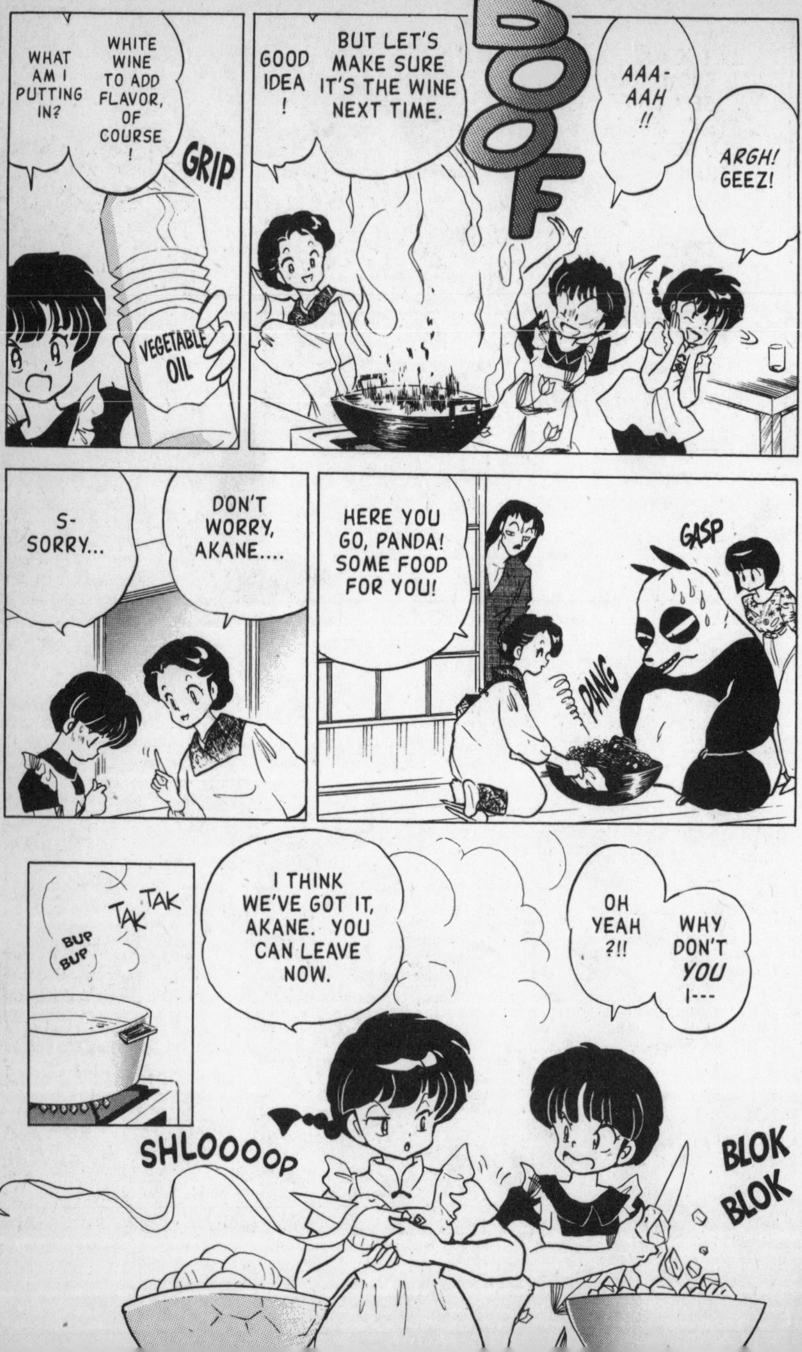
WHAT AM I PUTTING IN?
WHITE WINE TO ADD FLAVOR, OF COURSE!
GRIP
VEGETABLE OIL
GOOD IDEA!
BUT LET'S MAKE SURE IT'S THE WINE NEXT TIME.
BOOF
AAA-AAH!!
ARGH! GEEZ!
S-SORRY...
DON'T WORRY, AKANE....
HERE YOU GO, PANDA! SOME FOOD FOR YOU!
GASP
PANG
BUP BUP
TAK TAK
I THINK WE'VE GOT IT, AKANE. YOU CAN LEAVE NOW.
OH YEAH?!!
WHY DON'T *YOU* I---
SHLOOOOP
BLOK BLOK

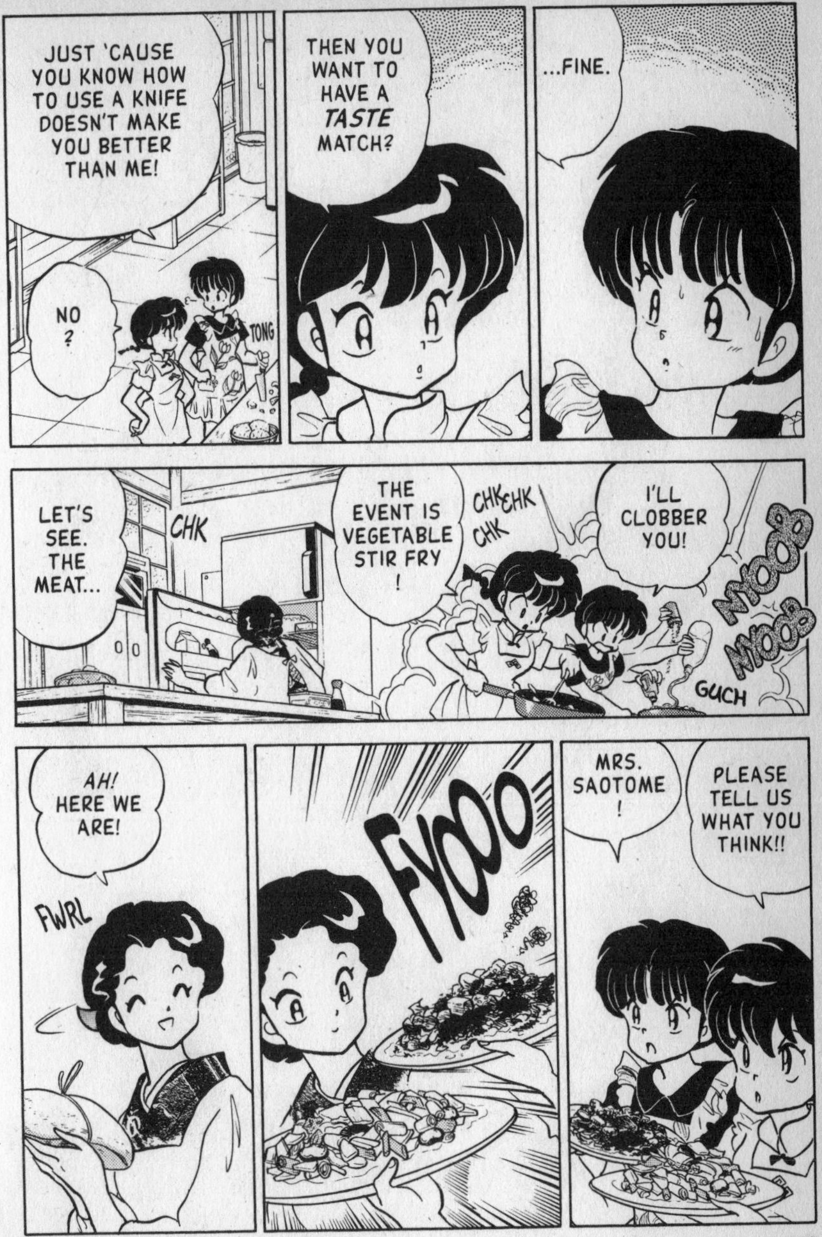
JUST 'CAUSE YOU KNOW HOW TO USE A KNIFE DOESN'T MAKE YOU BETTER THAN ME!
NO ?
TONG
THEN YOU WANT TO HAVE A *TASTE* MATCH?
...FINE.
LET'S SEE. THE MEAT...
CHK
THE EVENT IS VEGETABLE STIR FRY !
CHK CHK CHK
I'LL CLOBBER YOU!
MYOOB MYOOB
GUCH
AH! HERE WE ARE!
FWRL
FYOOO
MRS. SAOTOME !
PLEASE TELL US WHAT YOU THINK!!

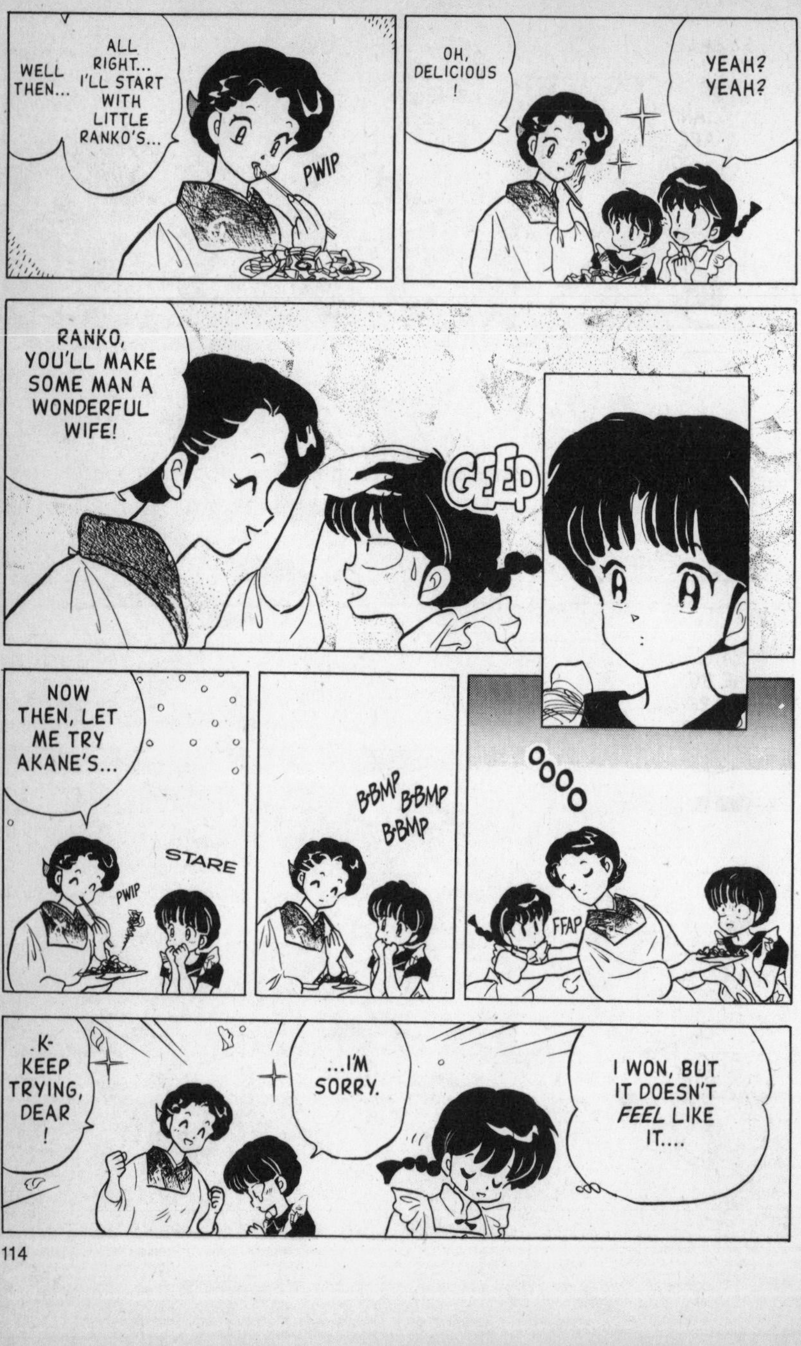
WELL THEN...
ALL RIGHT... I'LL START WITH LITTLE RANKO'S...
PWIP
OH, DELICIOUS !
YEAH? YEAH?
RANKO, YOU'LL MAKE SOME MAN A WONDERFUL WIFE!
GEEP
NOW THEN, LET ME TRY AKANE'S...
STARE
PWIP
B-BMP B-BMP B-BMP
OOOO
FFAP
.K-KEEP TRYING, DEAR !
...I'M SORRY.
I WON, BUT IT DOESN'T *FEEL* LIKE IT....

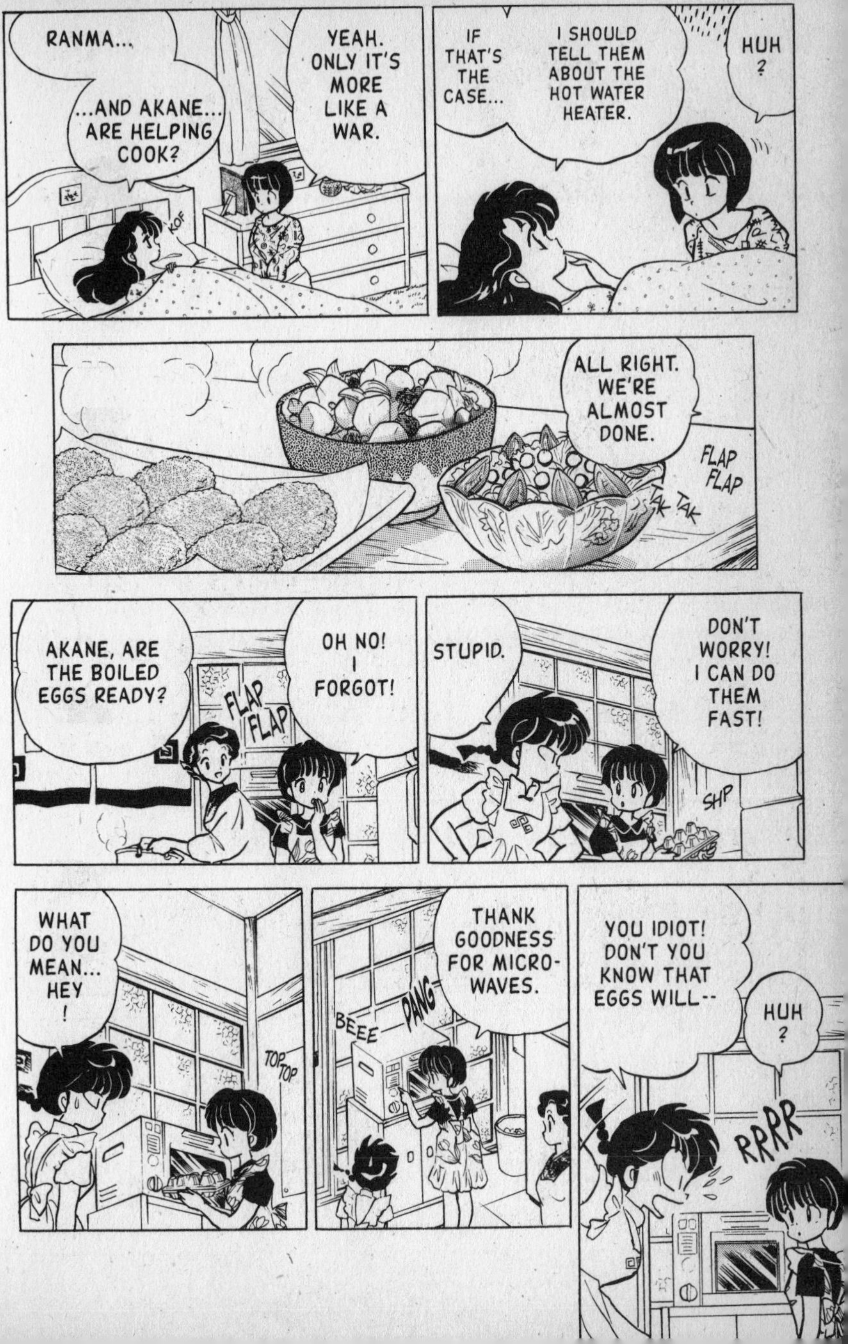
RANMA...
...AND AKANE... ARE HELPING COOK?
KOF
YEAH. ONLY IT'S MORE LIKE A WAR.
IF THAT'S THE CASE...
I SHOULD TELL THEM ABOUT THE HOT WATER HEATER.
HUH?
ALL RIGHT. WE'RE ALMOST DONE.
FLAP FLAP
TAK TAK
AKANE, ARE THE BOILED EGGS READY?
FLAP FLAP
OH NO! I FORGOT!
STUPID.
DON'T WORRY! I CAN DO THEM FAST!
SHP
WHAT DO YOU MEAN... HEY!
TOP TOP
BEEE
PANG
THANK GOODNESS FOR MICRO-WAVES.
YOU IDIOT! DON'T YOU KNOW THAT EGGS WILL--
HUH?
RRRR

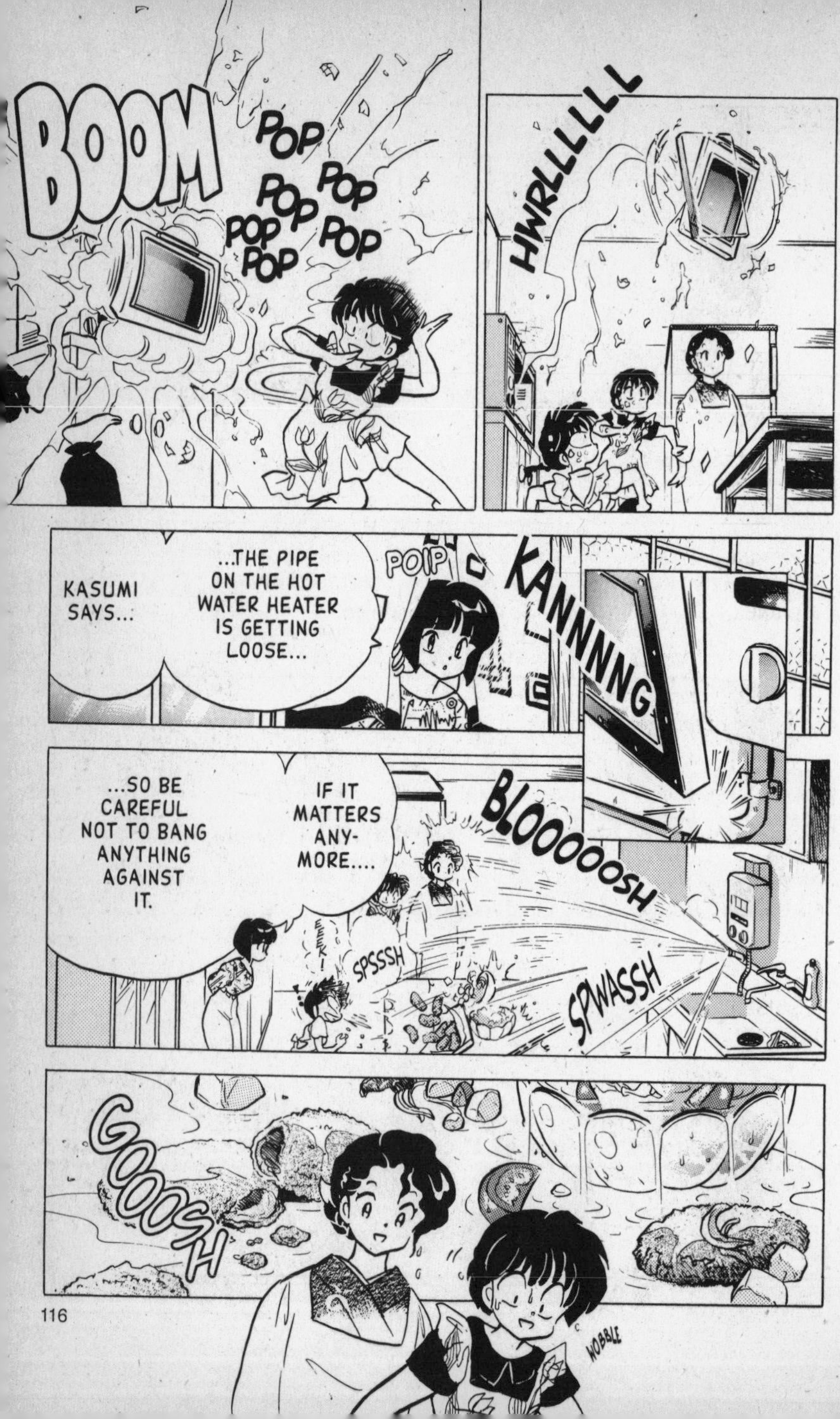
BOOM
POP POP POP POP POP POP
HWRLLLLLL
KASUMI SAYS...
...THE PIPE ON THE HOT WATER HEATER IS GETTING LOOSE...
POIP
KANNNNG
...SO BE CAREFUL NOT TO BANG ANYTHING AGAINST IT.
IF IT MATTERS ANY-MORE....
BLOOOOOOSH
EEK!
SPSSSH
SPWASSH
GOOOSH
WOBBLE

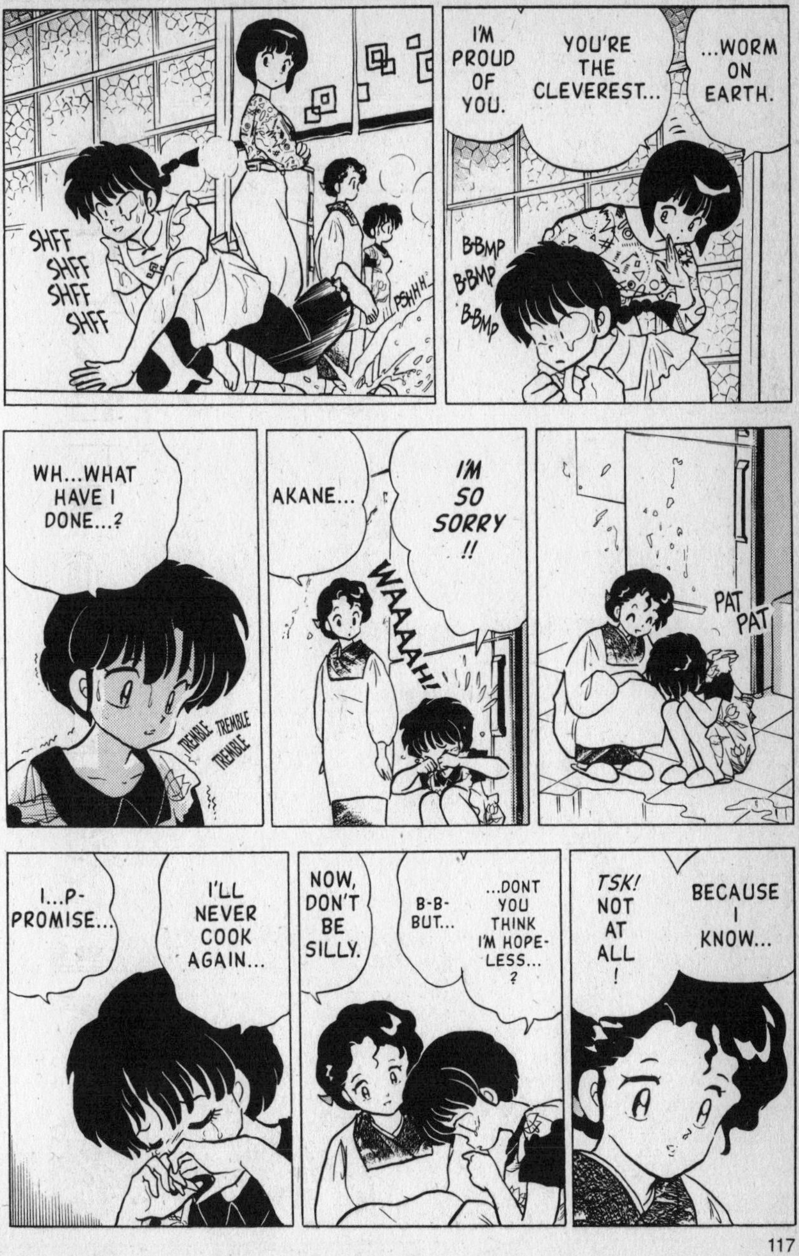
SHFF
SHFF
SHFF
SHFF
PSHHH...
I'M PROUD OF YOU.
YOU'RE THE CLEVEREST...
...WORM ON EARTH.
B-BMP
B-BMP
B-BMP
WH...WHAT HAVE I DONE...?
TREMBLE TREMBLE TREMBLE
AKANE...
I'M SO SORRY !!
WAAAAH!
PAT PAT
I...P-PROMISE...
I'LL NEVER COOK AGAIN...
NOW, DON'T BE SILLY.
B-B-BUT...
...DONT YOU THINK I'M HOPE-LESS...?
TSK! NOT AT ALL!
BECAUSE I KNOW...

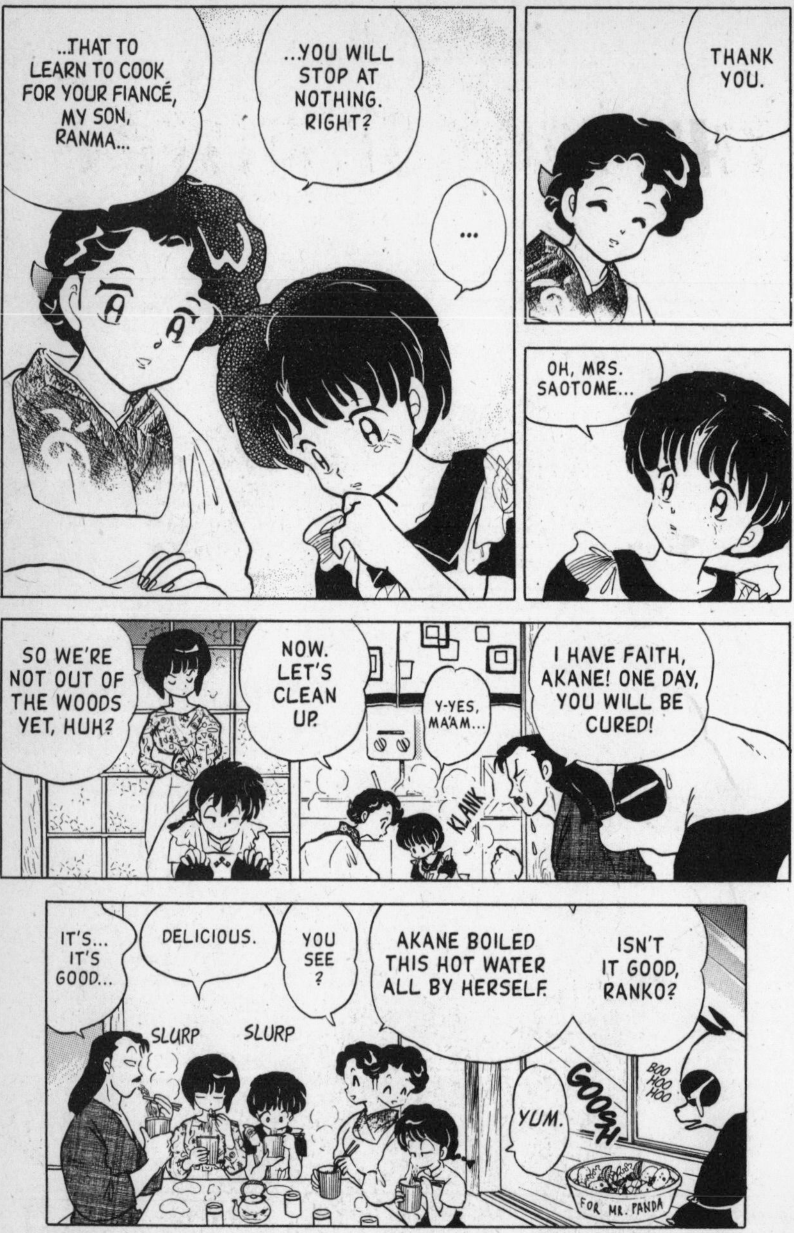
...THAT TO LEARN TO COOK FOR YOUR FIANCÉ, MY SON, RANMA...
...YOU WILL STOP AT NOTHING. RIGHT?
...
THANK YOU.
OH, MRS. SAOTOME...
SO WE'RE NOT OUT OF THE WOODS YET, HUH?
NOW. LET'S CLEAN UP.
Y-YES, MA'AM...
KLANK
I HAVE FAITH, AKANE! ONE DAY, YOU WILL BE CURED!
IT'S... IT'S GOOD...
DELICIOUS.
YOU SEE?
AKANE BOILED THIS HOT WATER ALL BY HERSELF.
ISN'T IT GOOD, RANKO?
SLURP
SLURP
YUM.
GOOSH
BOO HOO HOO
FOR MR. PANDA

Part 8

THE CARP OF MISERY

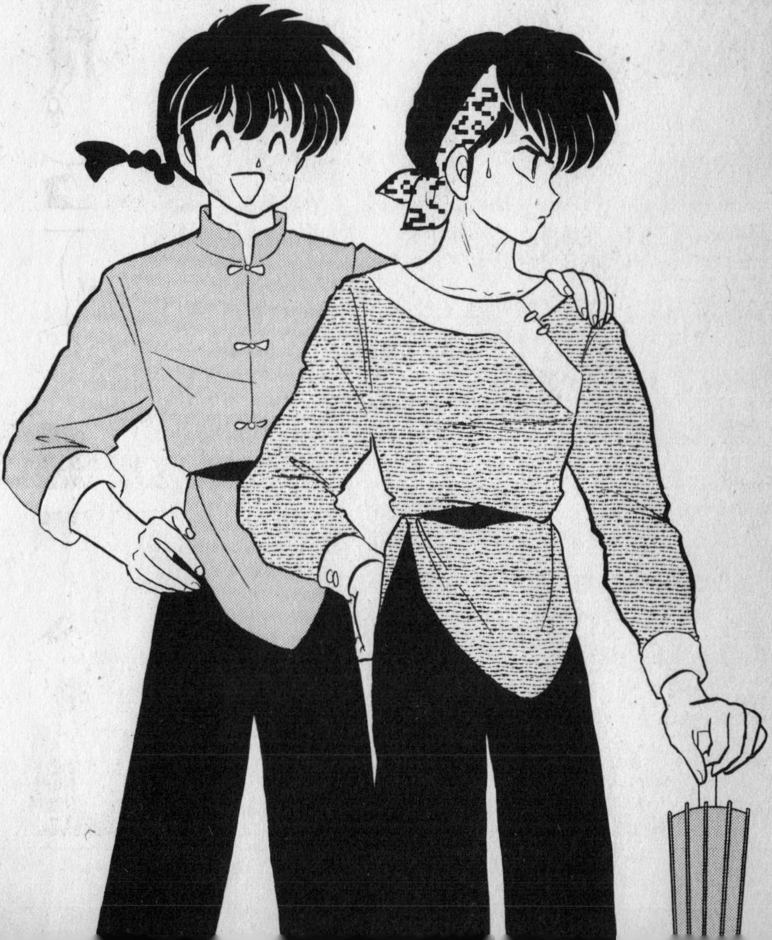

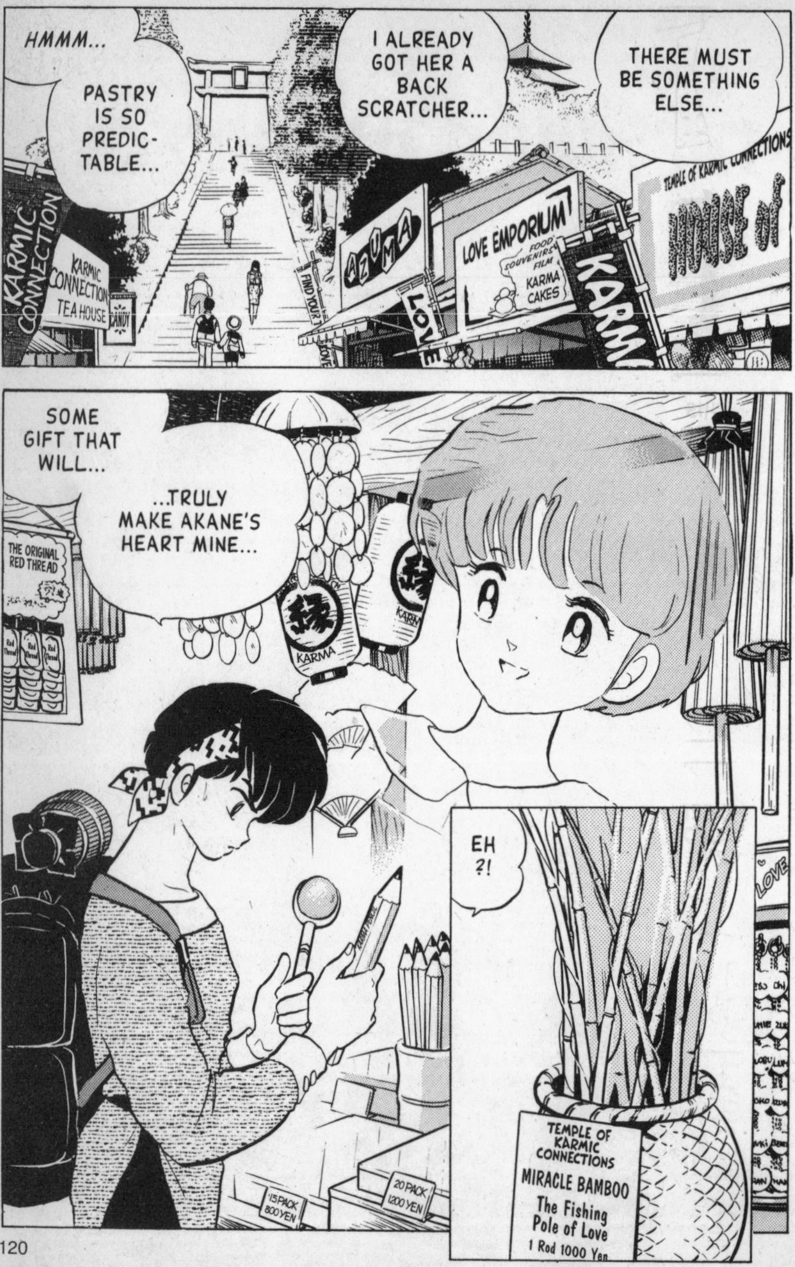
HMMM...
PASTRY IS SO PREDIC-TABLE...
I ALREADY GOT HER A BACK SCRATCHER...
THERE MUST BE SOMETHING ELSE...
KARMIC CONNECTION
KARMIC CONNECTION TEA HOUSE
CANDY
AZUMA
FIND YOUR
LOVE
LOVE EMPORIUM
FOOD SOUVENIRS FILM
KARMA CAKES
KARMA
TEMPLE OF KARMIC CONNECTIONS
HOUSE of
SOME GIFT THAT WILL...
...TRULY MAKE AKANE'S HEART MINE...
THE ORIGINAL RED THREAD
KARMA
EH ?!
LOVE
15 PACK 800 YEN
20 PACK 1200 YEN
TEMPLE OF KARMIC CONNECTIONS
MIRACLE BAMBOO
The Fishing Pole of Love
1 Rod 1000 Yen

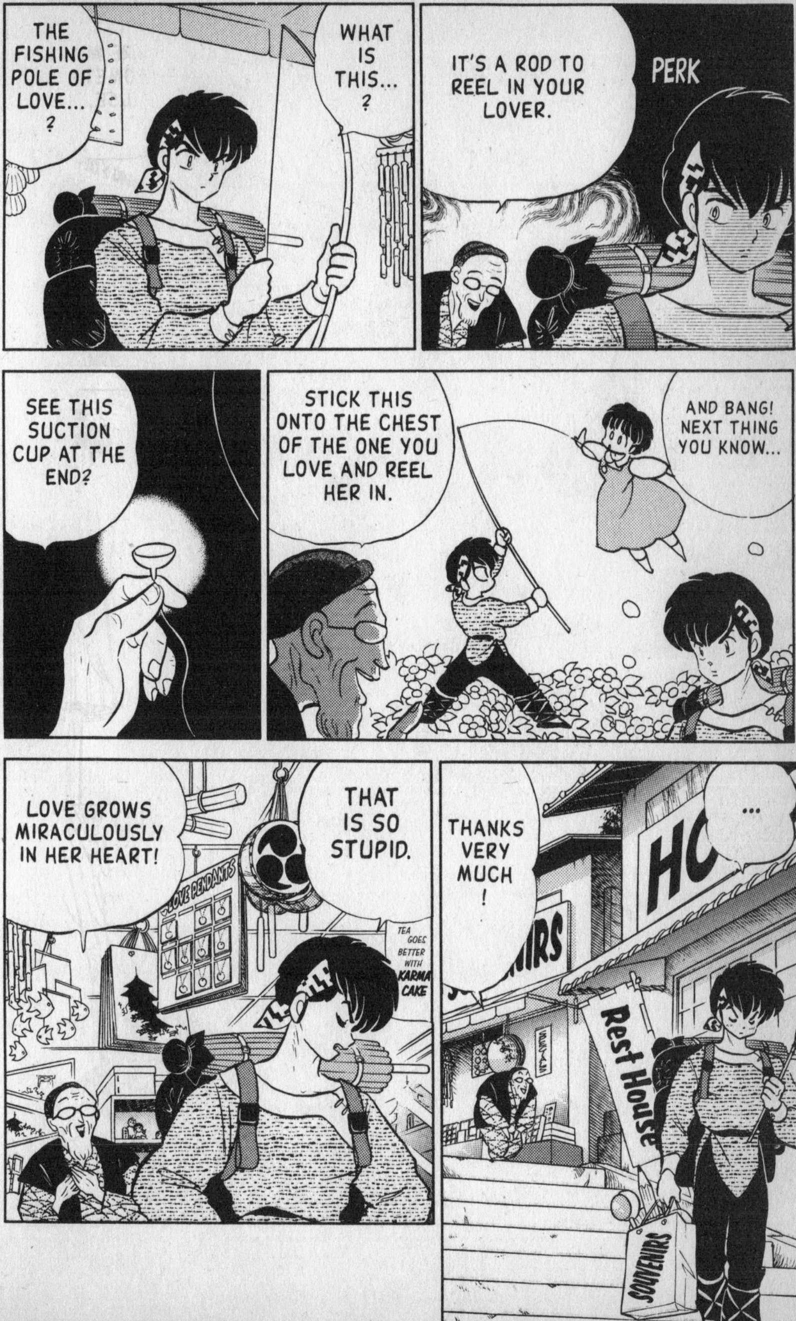

THE FISHING POLE OF LOVE...?
WHAT IS THIS...?
IT'S A ROD TO REEL IN YOUR LOVER.
PERK
SEE THIS SUCTION CUP AT THE END?
STICK THIS ONTO THE CHEST OF THE ONE YOU LOVE AND REEL HER IN.
AND BANG! NEXT THING YOU KNOW...
LOVE GROWS MIRACULOUSLY IN HER HEART!
LOVE PENDANTS
THAT IS SO STUPID.
TEA GOES BETTER WITH KARMA CAKE
THANKS VERY MUCH!
...
Rest House
SOUVENIRS

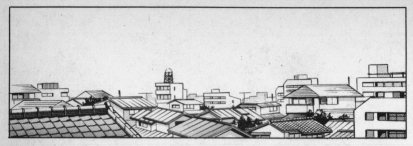

IT'S ALMOST TIME FOR AKANE TO GET OUT OF SCHOOL...

WHAT A WASTE. THIS IS ALL SO PATHETIC.

AS IF THIS JUNK COULD POSSIBLY WORK...

HWOOOO

UTTERLY PATHETIC...

I GIVE UP.

WHIRL

SEE YA LATER, AKANE!

BYE BYE!

B-BUMP

GASP! IT'S AKANE!

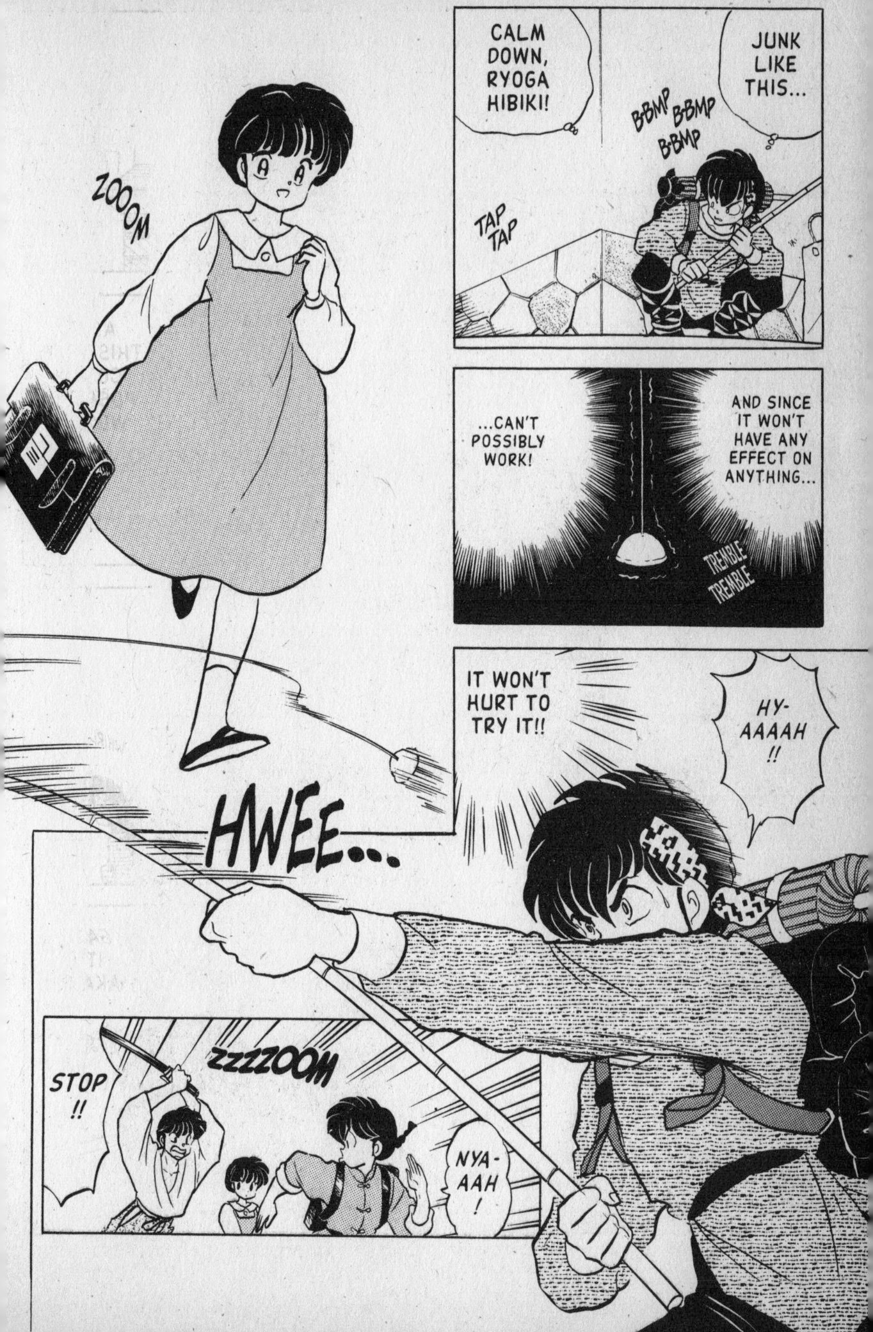
ZOOOM
CALM DOWN, RYOGA HIBIKI!
TAP TAP
JUNK LIKE THIS...
B-BMP B-BMP B-BMP
...CAN'T POSSIBLY WORK!
AND SINCE IT WON'T HAVE ANY EFFECT ON ANYTHING...
TREMBLE TREMBLE
IT WON'T HURT TO TRY IT!!
HY-AAAAH!!
HWEE...
STOP!!
ZZZZOOM
NYA-AAH!

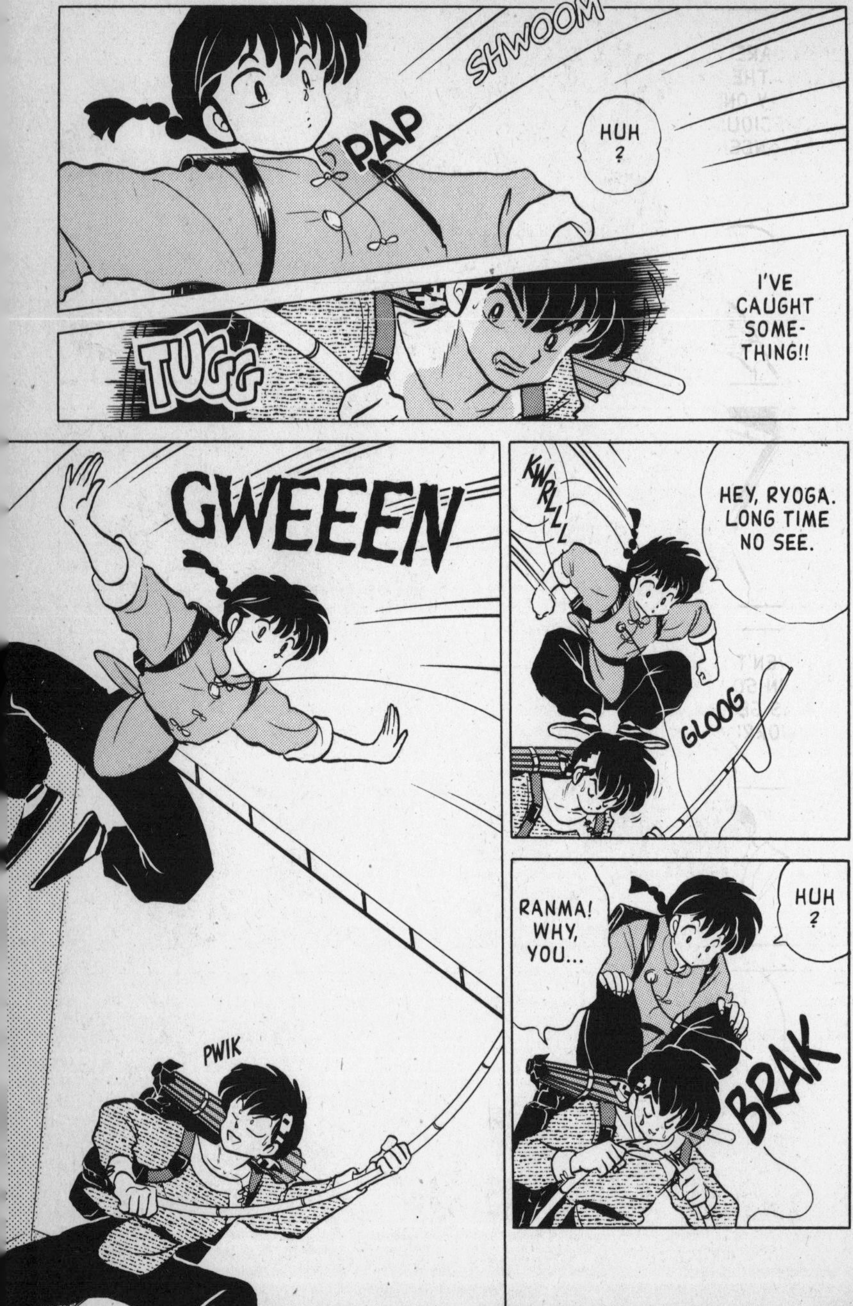
SHWOOM
PAP
HUH ?
TUGG
I'VE CAUGHT SOME-THING!!
GWEEEN
PWIK
KWRLLL
HEY, RYOGA. LONG TIME NO SEE.
GLOOG
RANMA! WHY, YOU...
HUH ?
BRAK

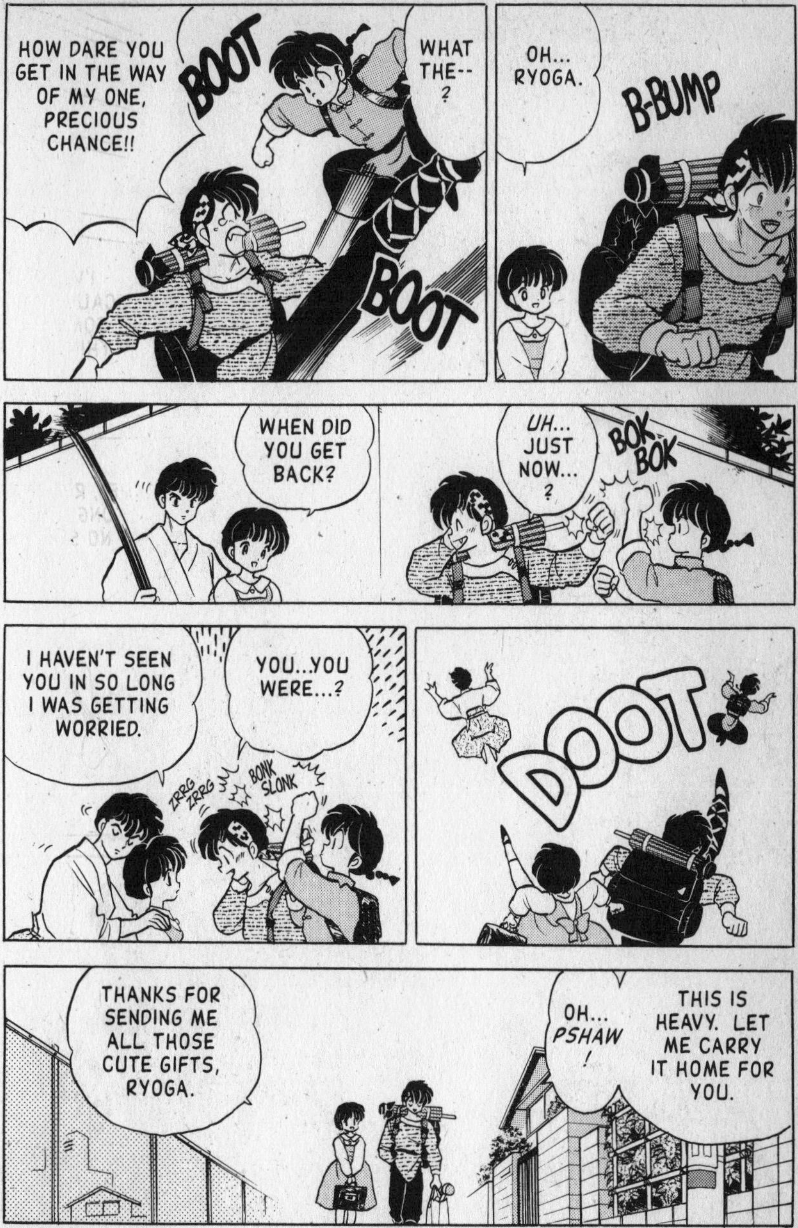
HOW DARE YOU GET IN THE WAY OF MY ONE, PRECIOUS CHANCE!!
BOOT
WHAT THE--?
BOOT
OH... RYOGA.
B-BUMP
WHEN DID YOU GET BACK?
UH... JUST NOW...?
BOK BOK
I HAVEN'T SEEN YOU IN SO LONG I WAS GETTING WORRIED.
YOU...YOU WERE...?
ZRRG ZRRG
BONK SLONK
DOOT
THANKS FOR SENDING ME ALL THOSE CUTE GIFTS, RYOGA.
OH... PSHAW!
THIS IS HEAVY. LET ME CARRY IT HOME FOR YOU.

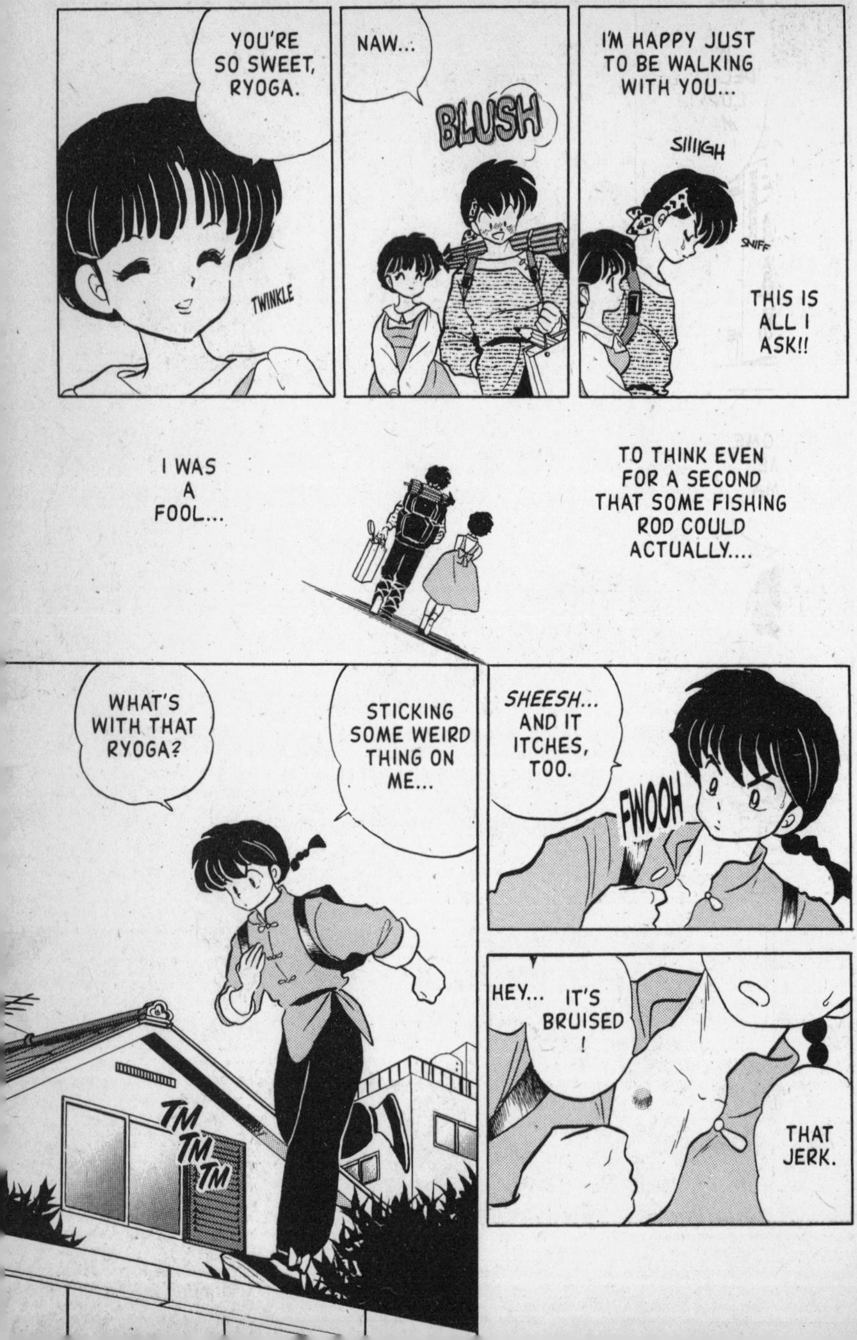
YOU'RE SO SWEET, RYOGA.
TWINKLE
NAW...
BLUSH
I'M HAPPY JUST TO BE WALKING WITH YOU...
SIIIIGH
SNIFF
THIS IS ALL I ASK!!
I WAS A FOOL...
TO THINK EVEN FOR A SECOND THAT SOME FISHING ROD COULD ACTUALLY....
WHAT'S WITH THAT RYOGA?
STICKING SOME WEIRD THING ON ME...
TM TM TM
SHEESH... AND IT ITCHES, TOO.
FWOOH
HEY...
IT'S BRUISED !
THAT JERK.

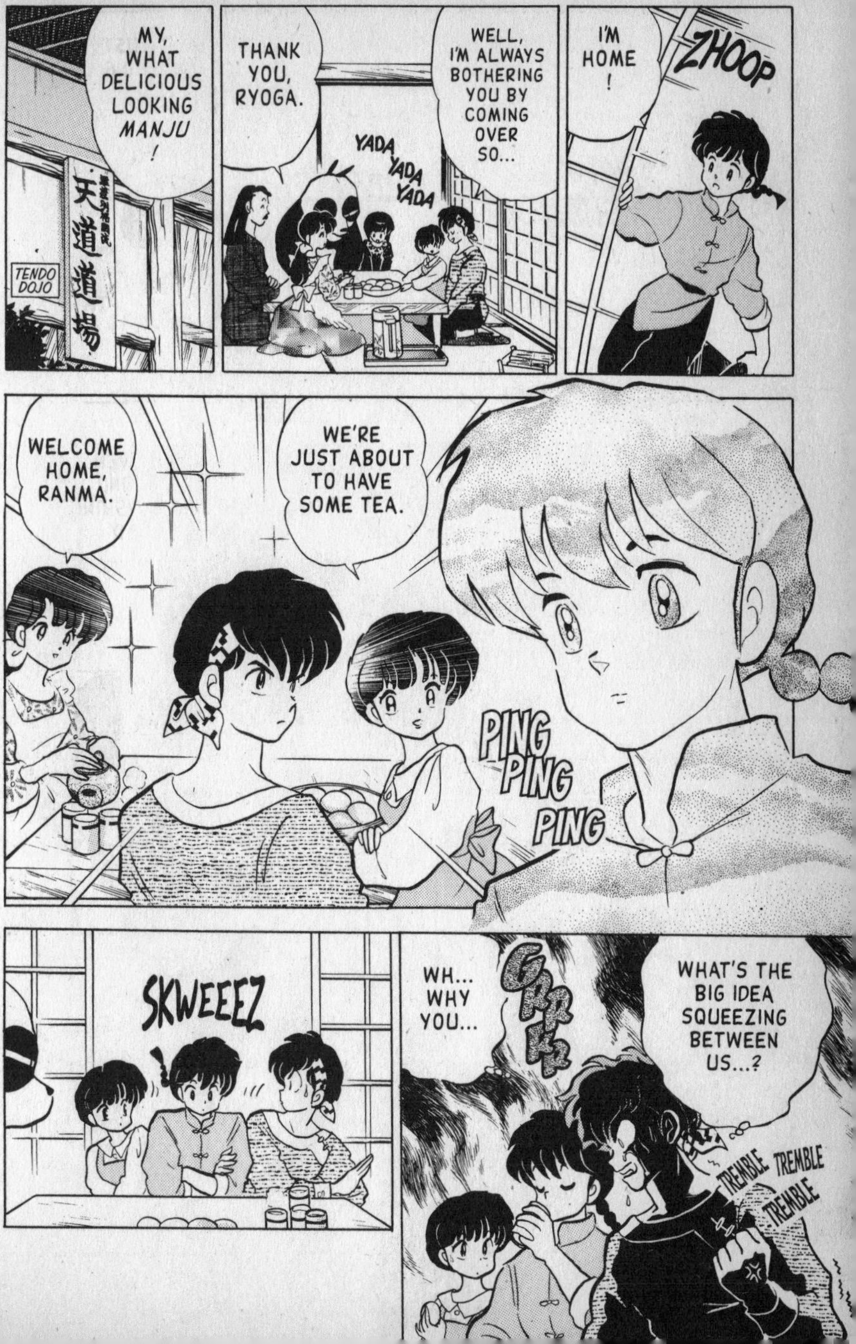
MY, WHAT DELICIOUS LOOKING MANJU!
TENDO DOJO
天道道場
THANK YOU, RYOGA.
YADA YADA YADA
WELL, I'M ALWAYS BOTHERING YOU BY COMING OVER SO...
I'M HOME!
ZHOOP
WELCOME HOME, RANMA.
WE'RE JUST ABOUT TO HAVE SOME TEA.
PING PING PING
SKWEEEZ
WH... WHY YOU...
GRRR
WHAT'S THE BIG IDEA SQUEEZING BETWEEN US...?
TREMBLE TREMBLE TREMBLE

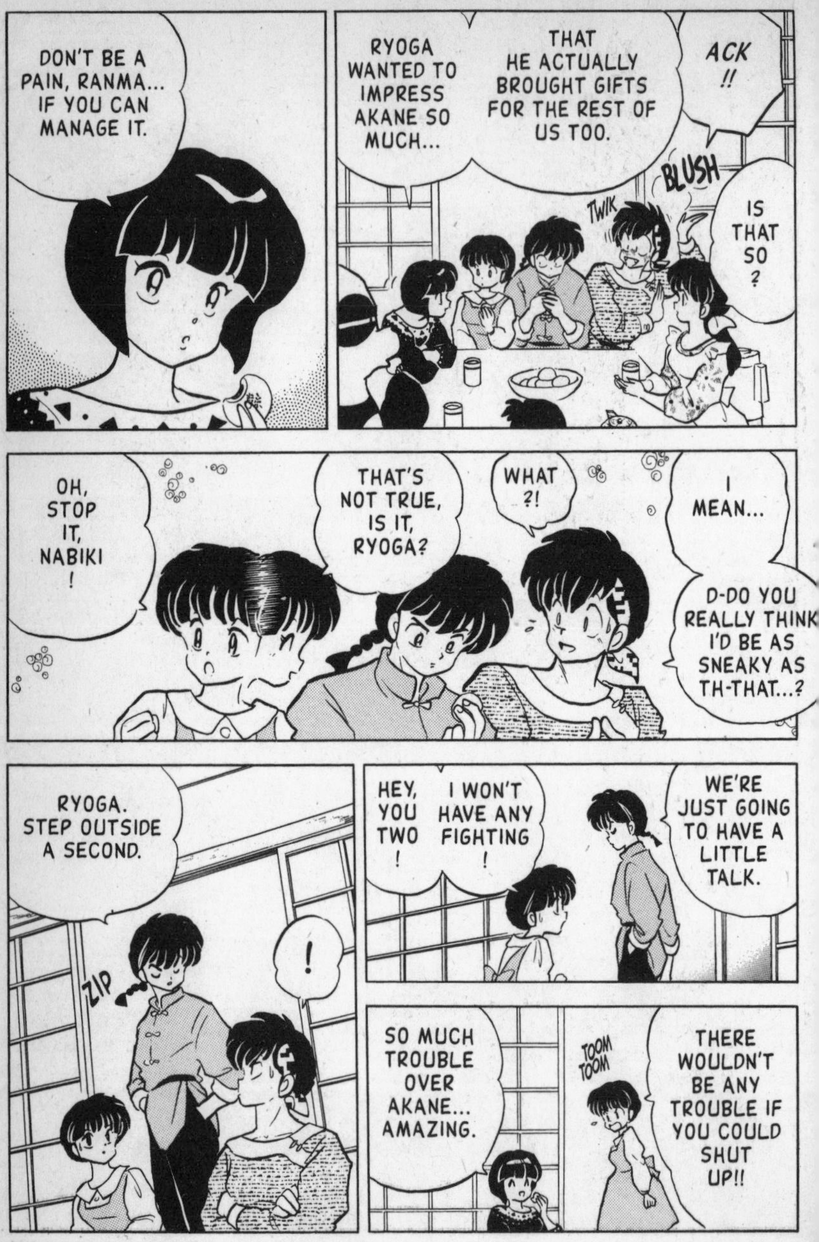
DON'T BE A PAIN, RANMA... IF YOU CAN MANAGE IT.
RYOGA WANTED TO IMPRESS AKANE SO MUCH...
THAT HE ACTUALLY BROUGHT GIFTS FOR THE REST OF US TOO.
ACK !!
TWIK
BLUSH
IS THAT SO ?
OH, STOP IT, NABIKI !
THAT'S NOT TRUE, IS IT, RYOGA?
WHAT ?!
I MEAN...
D-DO YOU REALLY THINK I'D BE AS SNEAKY AS TH-THAT...?
RYOGA. STEP OUTSIDE A SECOND.
ZIP
!
HEY, YOU TWO !
I WON'T HAVE ANY FIGHTING !
WE'RE JUST GOING TO HAVE A LITTLE TALK.
SO MUCH TROUBLE OVER AKANE... AMAZING.
TOOM TOOM
THERE WOULDN'T BE ANY TROUBLE IF YOU COULD SHUT UP!!

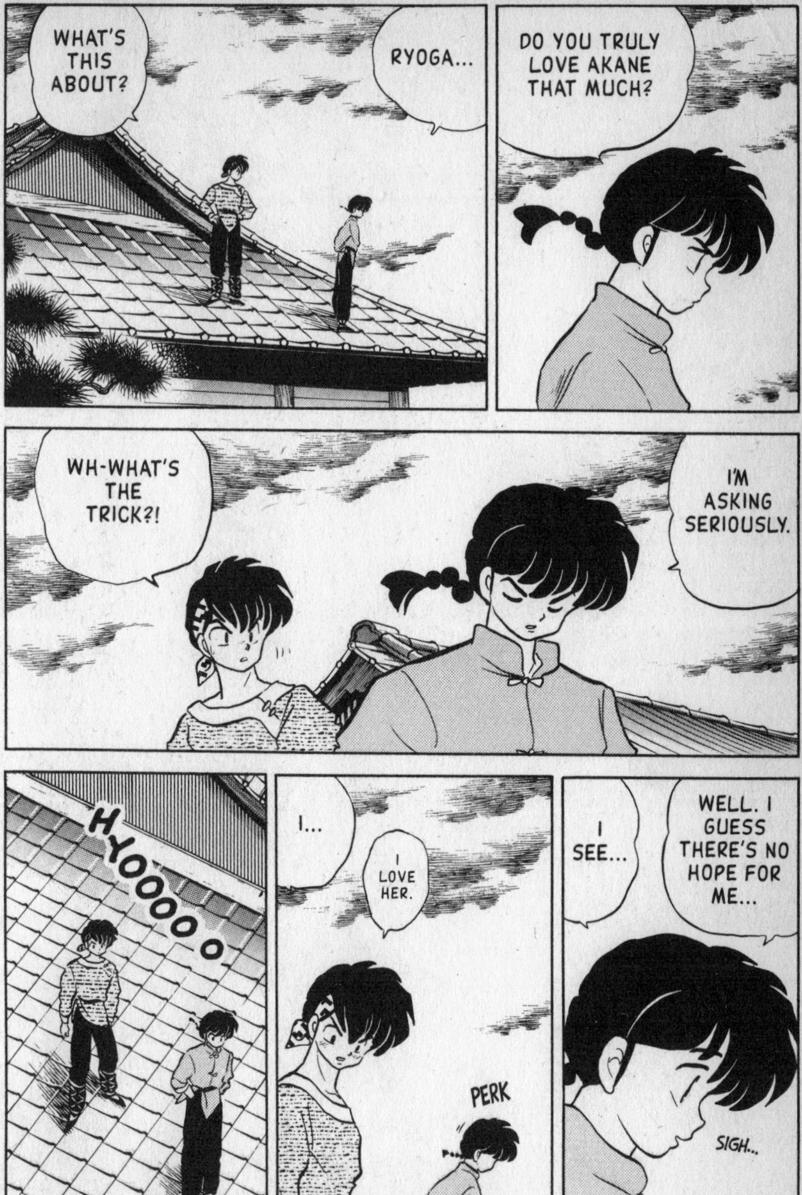
WHAT'S THIS ABOUT?
RYOGA...
DO YOU TRULY LOVE AKANE THAT MUCH?
WH-WHAT'S THE TRICK?!
I'M ASKING SERIOUSLY.
HYOOOO O
I...
I LOVE HER.
PERK
I SEE...
WELL. I GUESS THERE'S NO HOPE FOR ME...
SIGH...

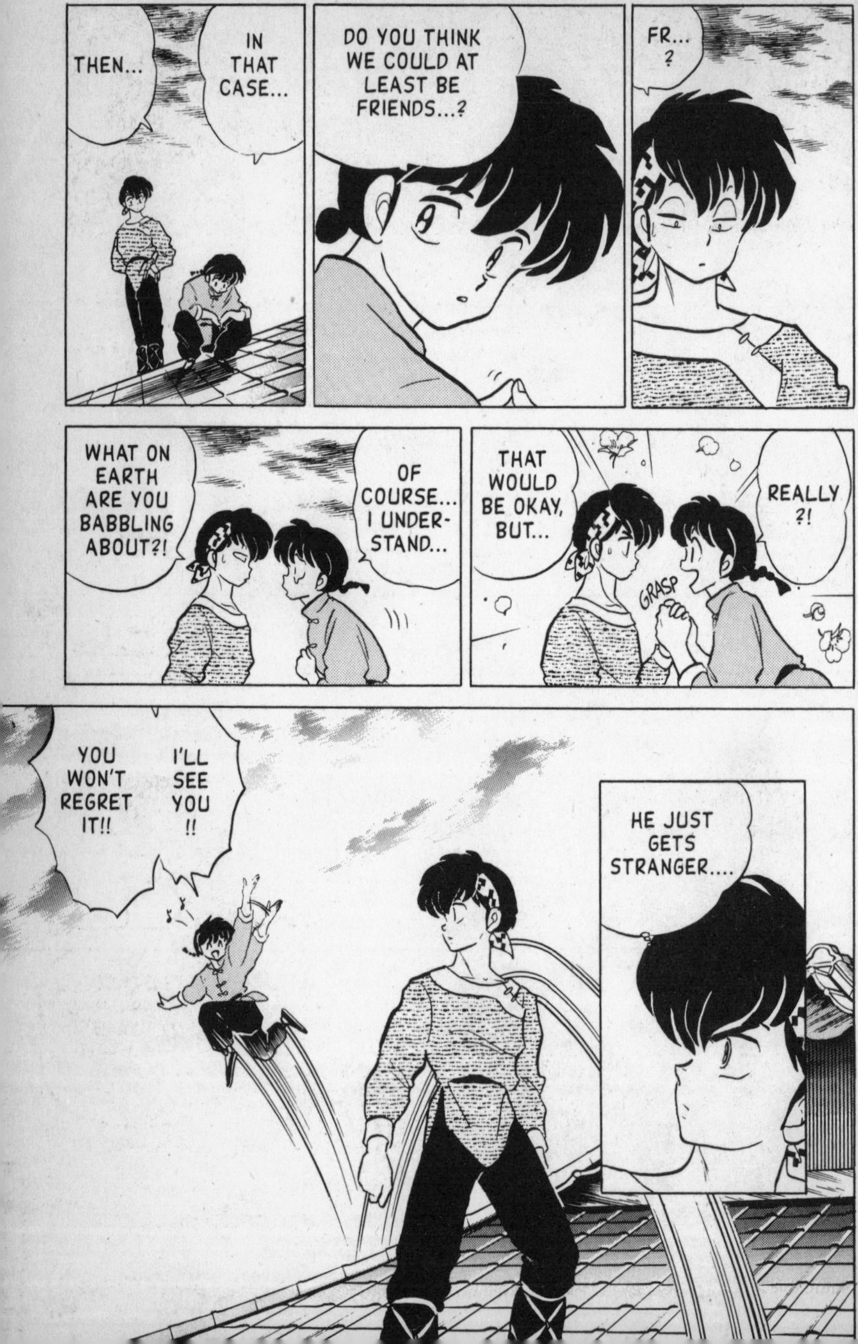
THEN...
IN THAT CASE...
DO YOU THINK WE COULD AT LEAST BE FRIENDS...?
FR...?
WHAT ON EARTH ARE YOU BABBLING ABOUT?!
OF COURSE... I UNDER-STAND...
THAT WOULD BE OKAY, BUT...
REALLY?!
GRASP
YOU WON'T REGRET IT!!
I'LL SEE YOU!!
HE JUST GETS STRANGER....

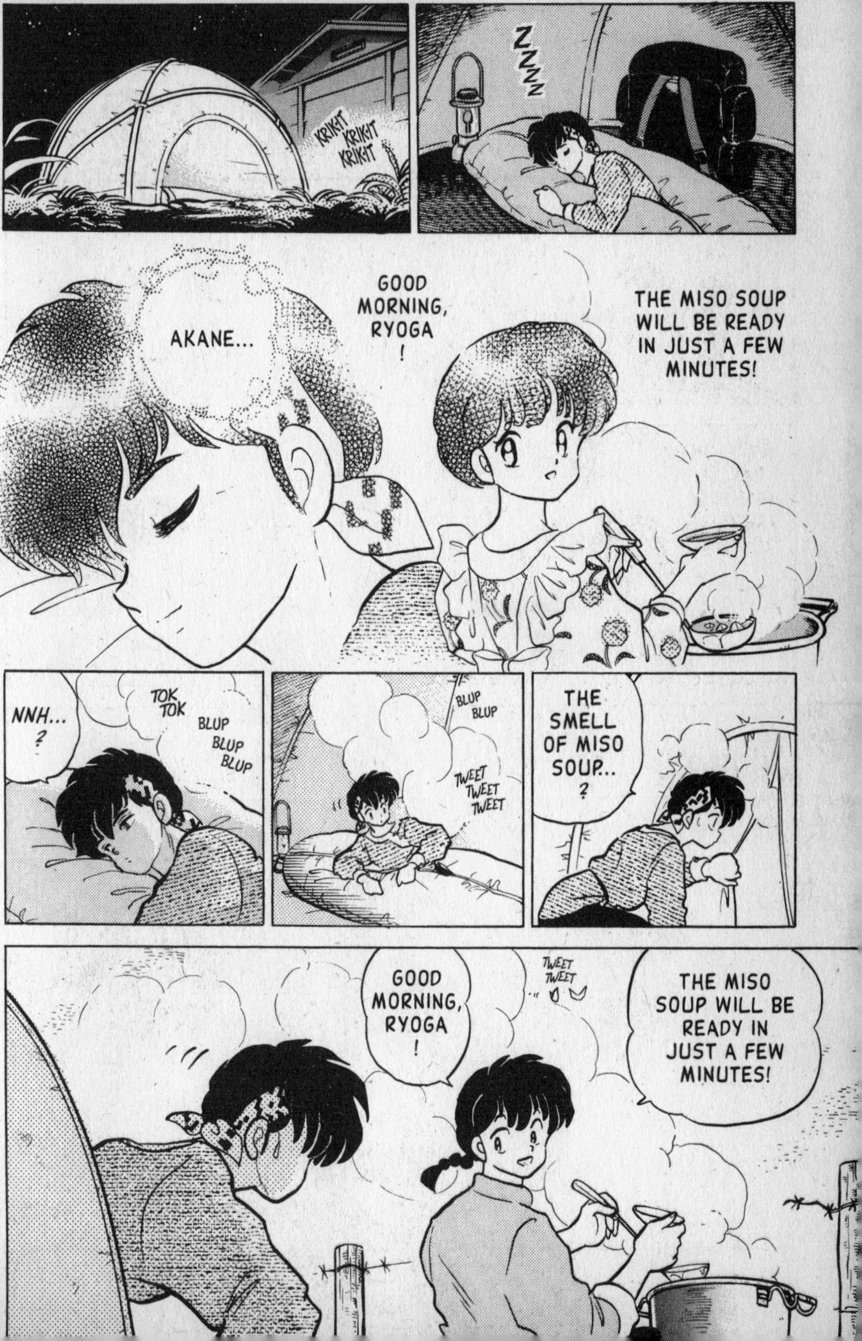
KRIK-IT KRIK-IT KRIK-IT
ZZZZ
AKANE...
GOOD MORNING, RYOGA!
THE MISO SOUP WILL BE READY IN JUST A FEW MINUTES!
NNH...?
TOK TOK
BLUP BLUP BLUP
BLUP BLUP
TWEET TWEET TWEET
THE SMELL OF MISO SOUP...?
GOOD MORNING, RYOGA!
TWEET TWEET
THE MISO SOUP WILL BE READY IN JUST A FEW MINUTES!

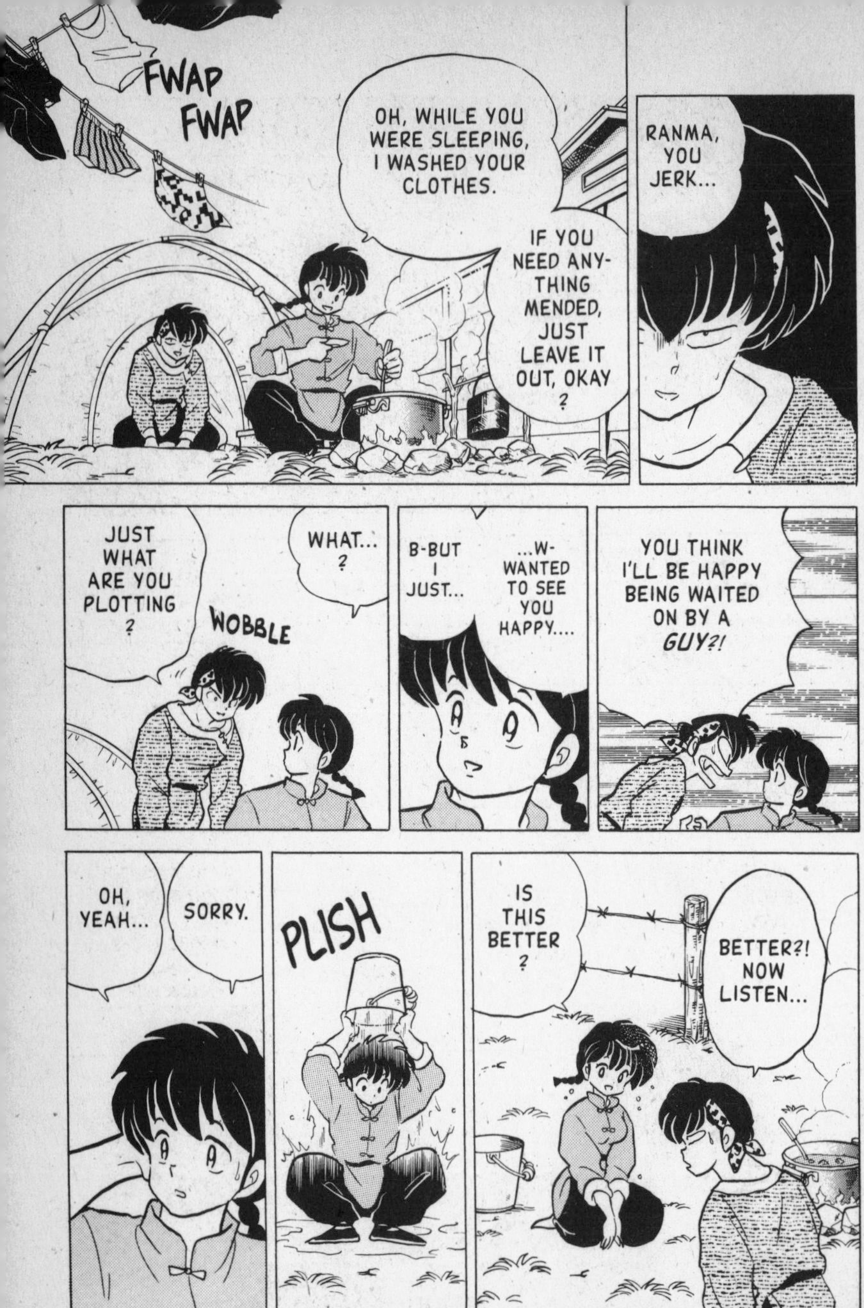
FWAP
FWAP
OH, WHILE YOU WERE SLEEPING, I WASHED YOUR CLOTHES.
IF YOU NEED ANYTHING MENDED, JUST LEAVE IT OUT, OKAY?
RANMA, YOU JERK...
JUST WHAT ARE YOU PLOTTING?
WHAT...?
WOBBLE
B-BUT I JUST...
...W-WANTED TO SEE YOU HAPPY....
YOU THINK I'LL BE HAPPY BEING WAITED ON BY A GUY?!
OH, YEAH...
SORRY.
PLISH
IS THIS BETTER?
BETTER?! NOW LISTEN...

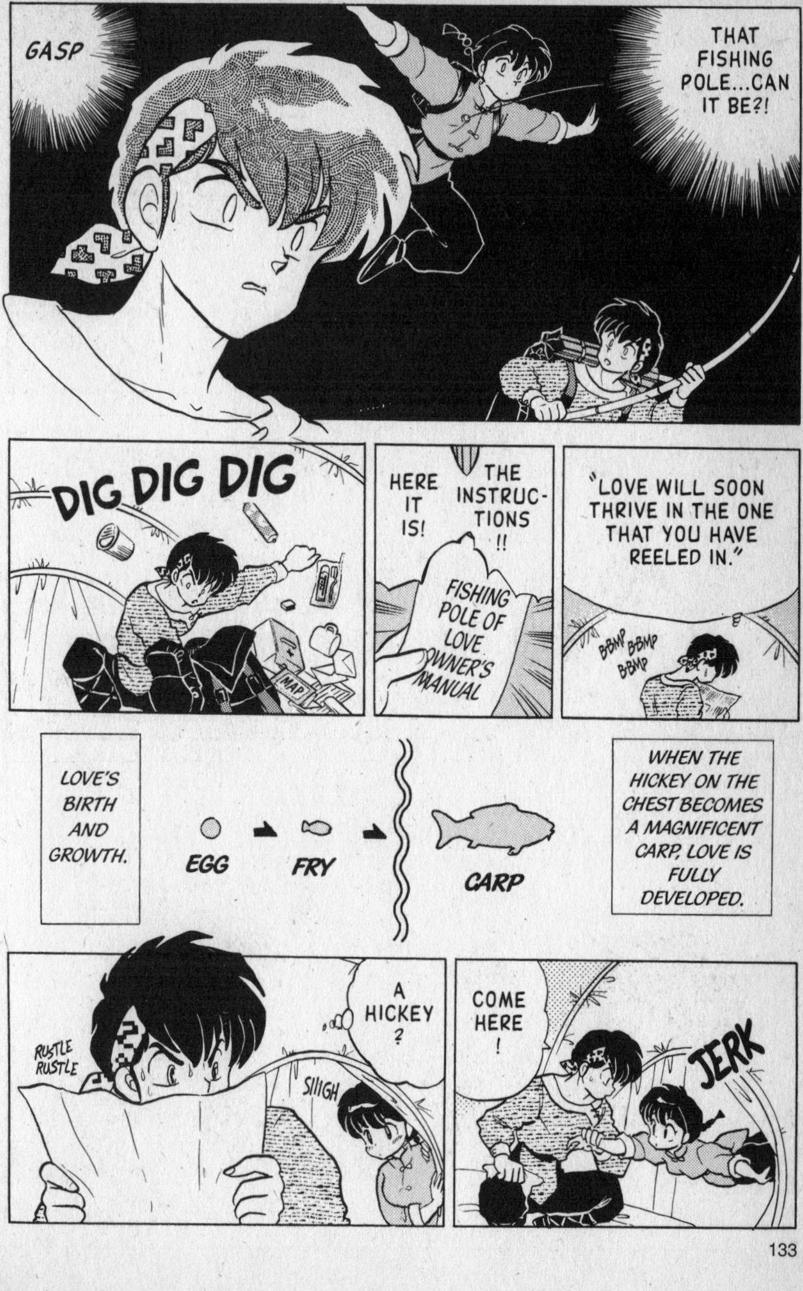
GASP
THAT FISHING POLE...CAN IT BE?!
DIG DIG DIG
MAP
HERE IT IS!
THE INSTRUCTIONS !!
FISHING POLE OF LOVE OWNER'S MANUAL
"LOVE WILL SOON THRIVE IN THE ONE THAT YOU HAVE REELED IN."
B-BMP B-BMP B-BMP
LOVE'S BIRTH AND GROWTH.
EGG
FRY
CARP
WHEN THE HICKEY ON THE CHEST BECOMES A MAGNIFICENT CARP, LOVE IS FULLY DEVELOPED.
RUSTLE RUSTLE
A HICKEY ?
SIIIGH
COME HERE !
JERK

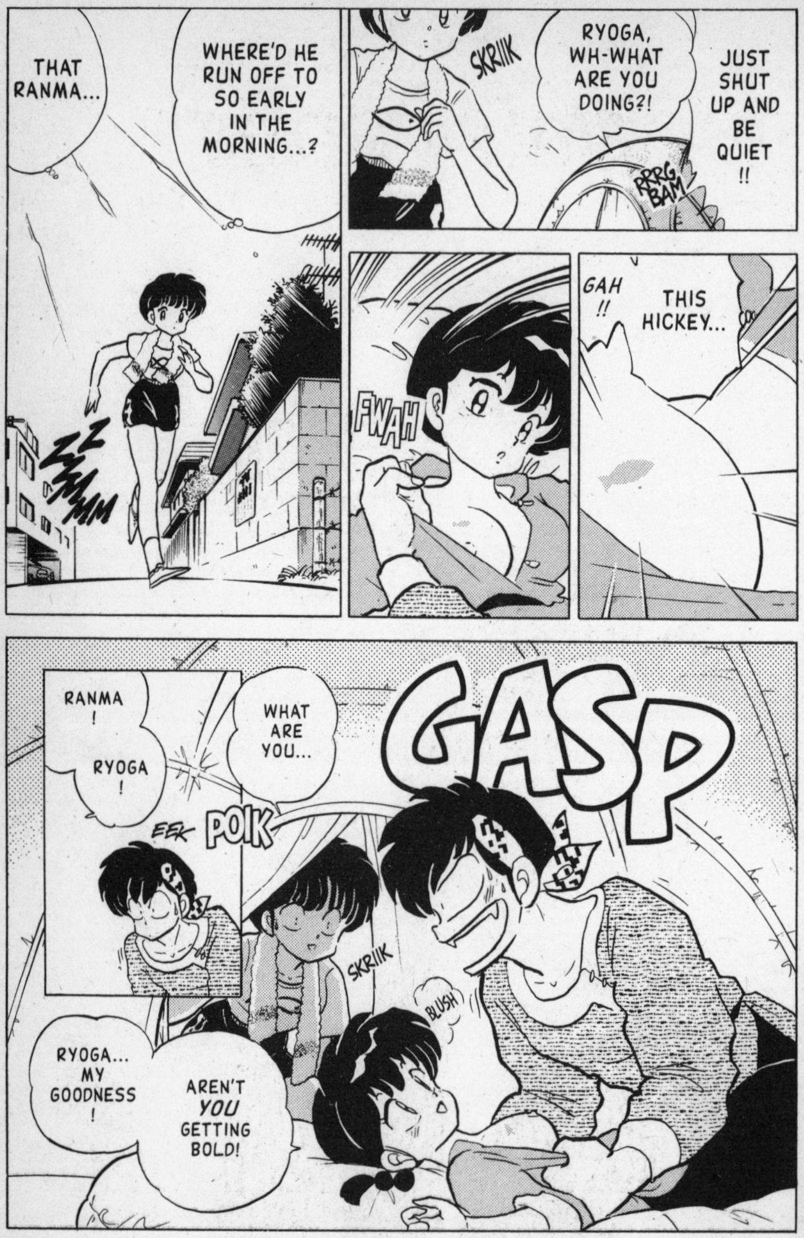
THAT RANMA...
WHERE'D HE RUN OFF TO SO EARLY IN THE MORNING...?
ZZZWMMM
SKRIIK
RYOGA, WH-WHAT ARE YOU DOING?!
JUST SHUT UP AND BE QUIET !!
RRRG BAM
FWAH
GAH !!
THIS HICKEY...
RANMA !
RYOGA !
WHAT ARE YOU...
EEK
POIK
GASP
SKRIIK
BLUSH
RYOGA... MY GOODNESS !
AREN'T *YOU* GETTING BOLD!

Part 9

CARPY DEUM

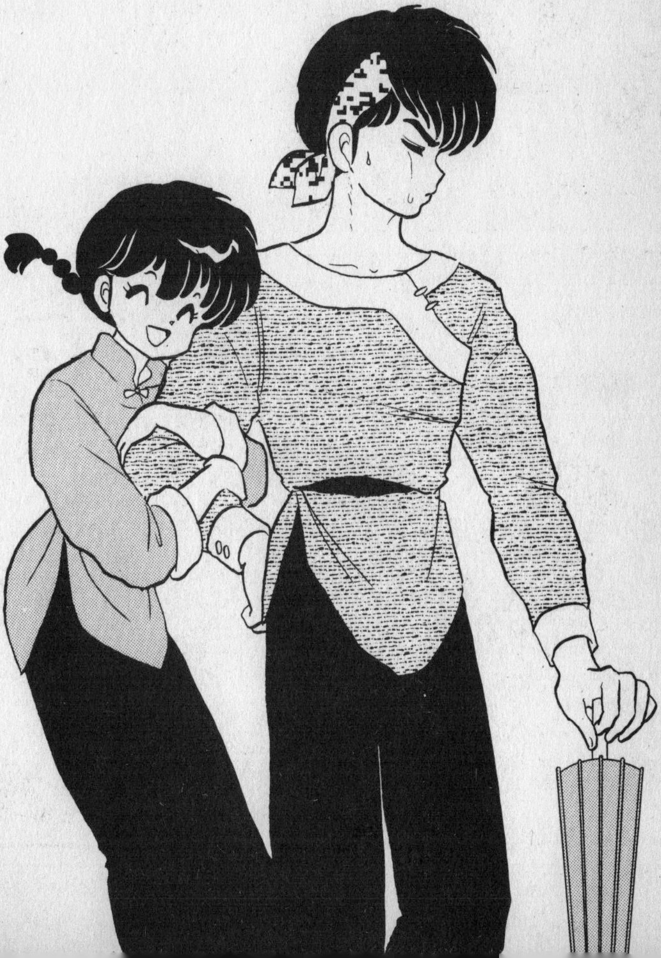

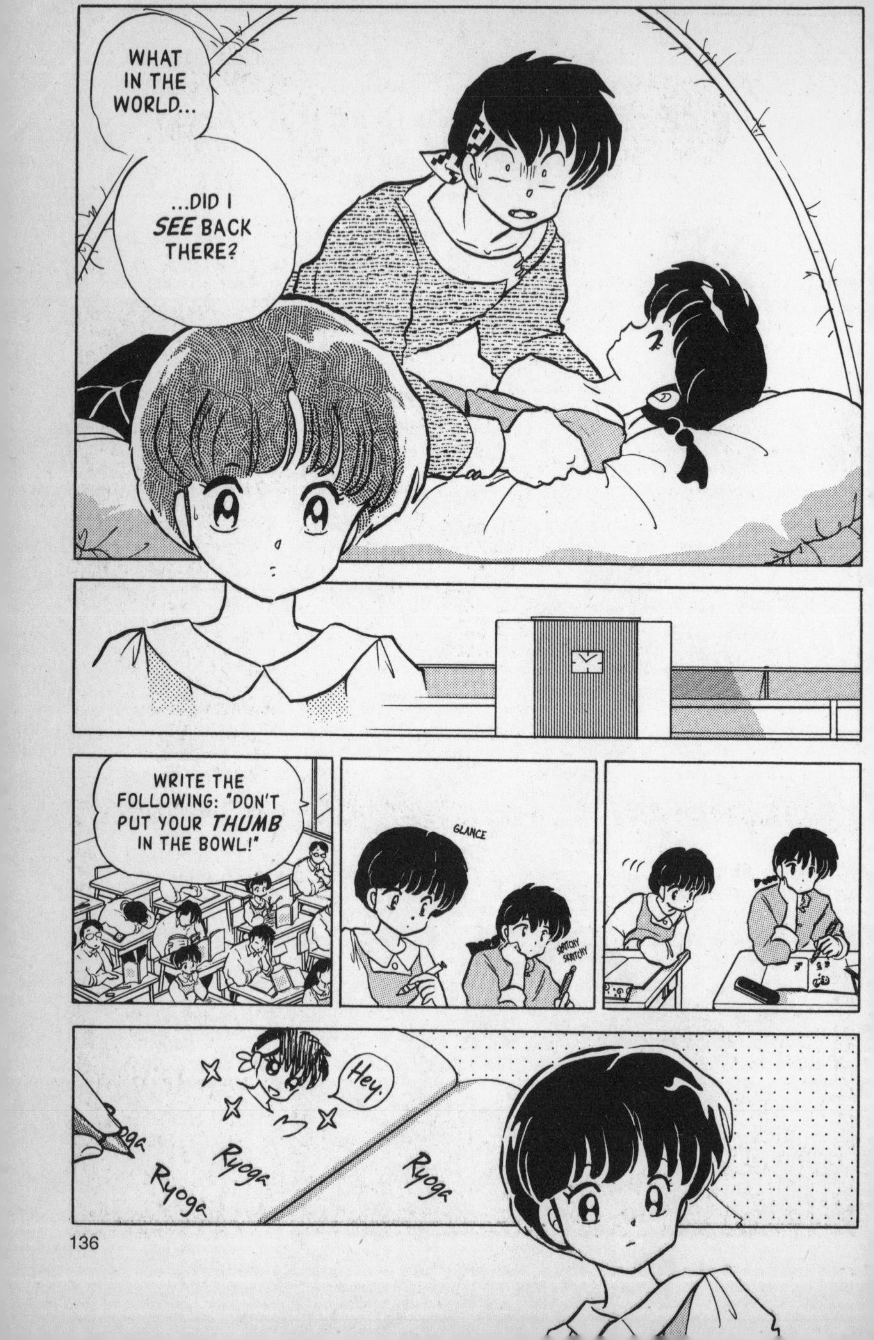
WHAT IN THE WORLD...
...DID I SEE BACK THERE?
WRITE THE FOLLOWING: "DON'T PUT YOUR THUMB IN THE BOWL!"
GLANCE
SCRATCHY SCRATCHY
Hey.
Ryoga
Ryoga
Ryoga
Ryoga

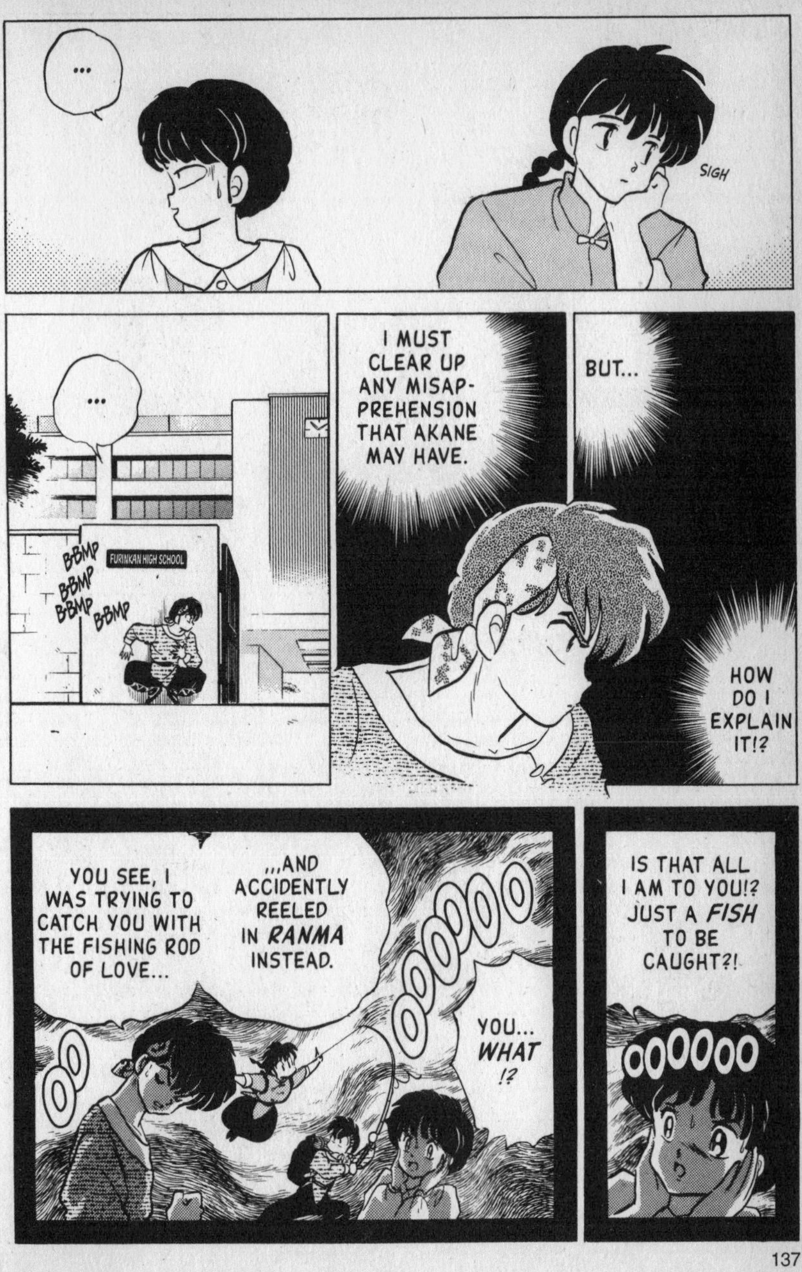
...
SIGH
...
FURINKAN HIGH SCHOOL
B-BMP B-BMP B-BMP B-BMP
I MUST CLEAR UP ANY MISAP-PREHENSION THAT AKANE MAY HAVE.
BUT...
HOW DO I EXPLAIN IT!?
YOU SEE, I WAS TRYING TO CATCH YOU WITH THE FISHING ROD OF LOVE...
...AND ACCIDENTLY REELED IN *RANMA* INSTEAD.
YOU... *WHAT* !?
IS THAT ALL I AM TO YOU!? JUST A *FISH* TO BE CAUGHT?!

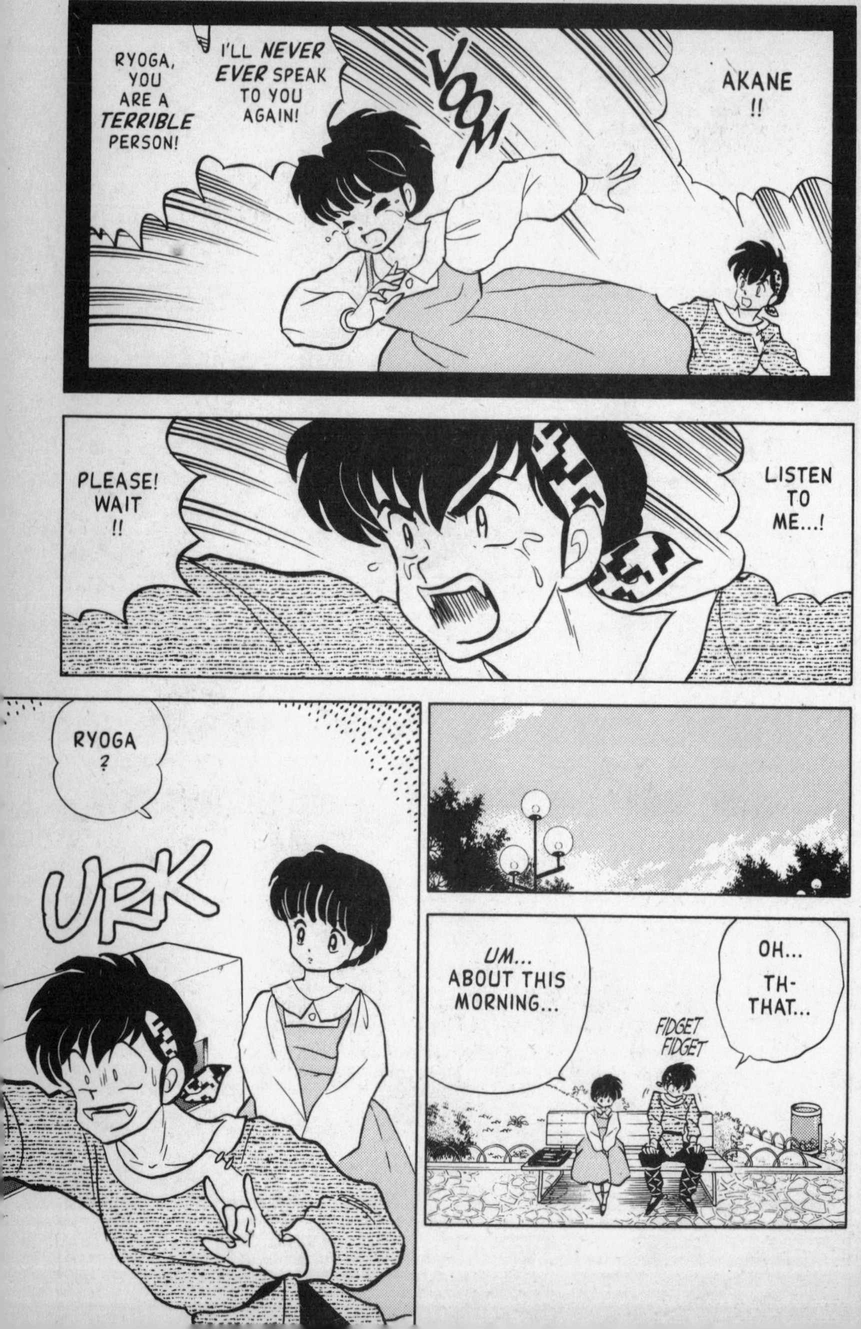
RYOGA, YOU ARE A *TERRIBLE* PERSON!
I'LL *NEVER EVER* SPEAK TO YOU AGAIN!
VOOM
AKANE !!
PLEASE! WAIT !!
LISTEN TO ME...!
RYOGA ?
URK
UM... ABOUT THIS MORNING...
FIDGET FIDGET
OH... TH-THAT...

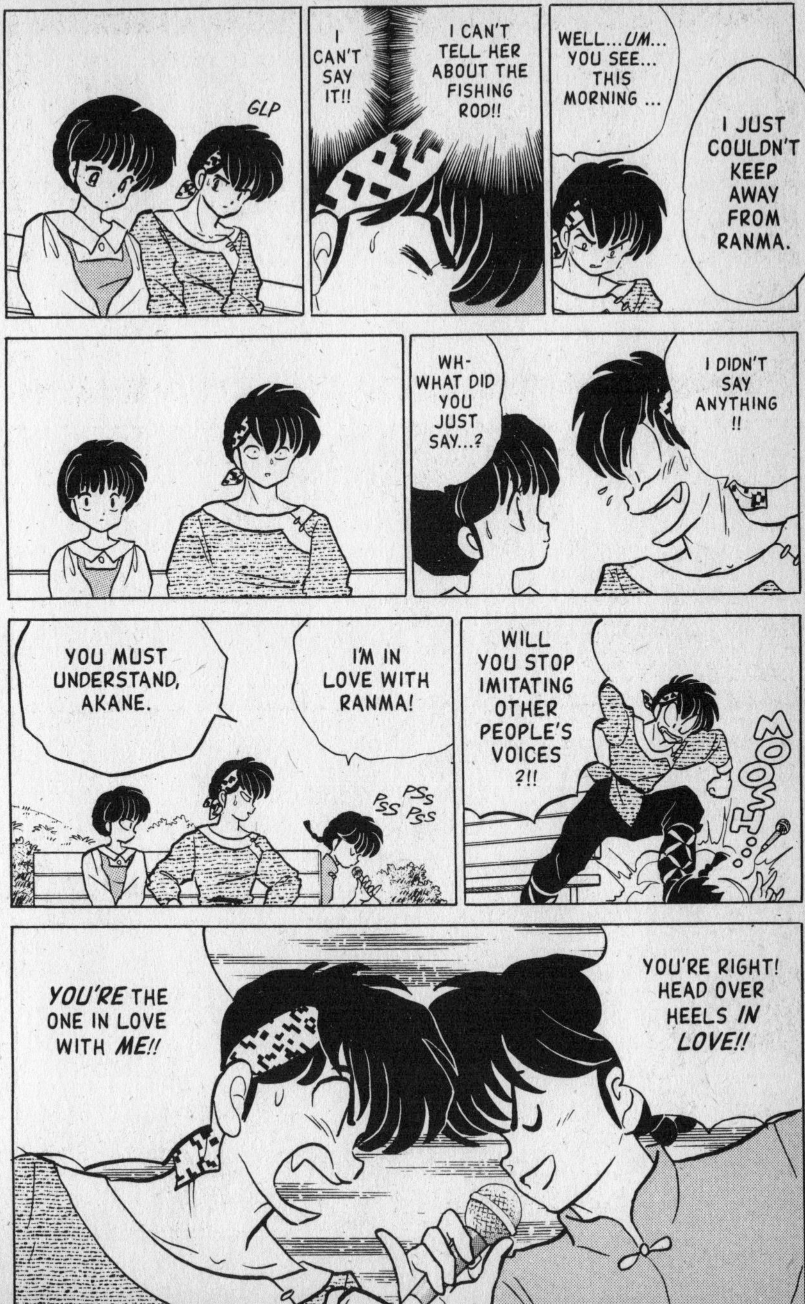
GLP
I CAN'T SAY IT!!
I CAN'T TELL HER ABOUT THE FISHING ROD!!
WELL...*UM*... YOU SEE... THIS MORNING ...
I JUST COULDN'T KEEP AWAY FROM RANMA.
WH- WHAT DID YOU JUST SAY...?
I DIDN'T SAY ANYTHING !!
YOU MUST UNDERSTAND, AKANE.
I'M IN LOVE WITH RANMA!
PSS PSS PSS
WILL YOU STOP IMITATING OTHER PEOPLE'S VOICES ?!!
WOOSH...
YOU'RE THE ONE IN LOVE WITH *ME*!!
YOU'RE RIGHT! HEAD OVER HEELS *IN LOVE*!!

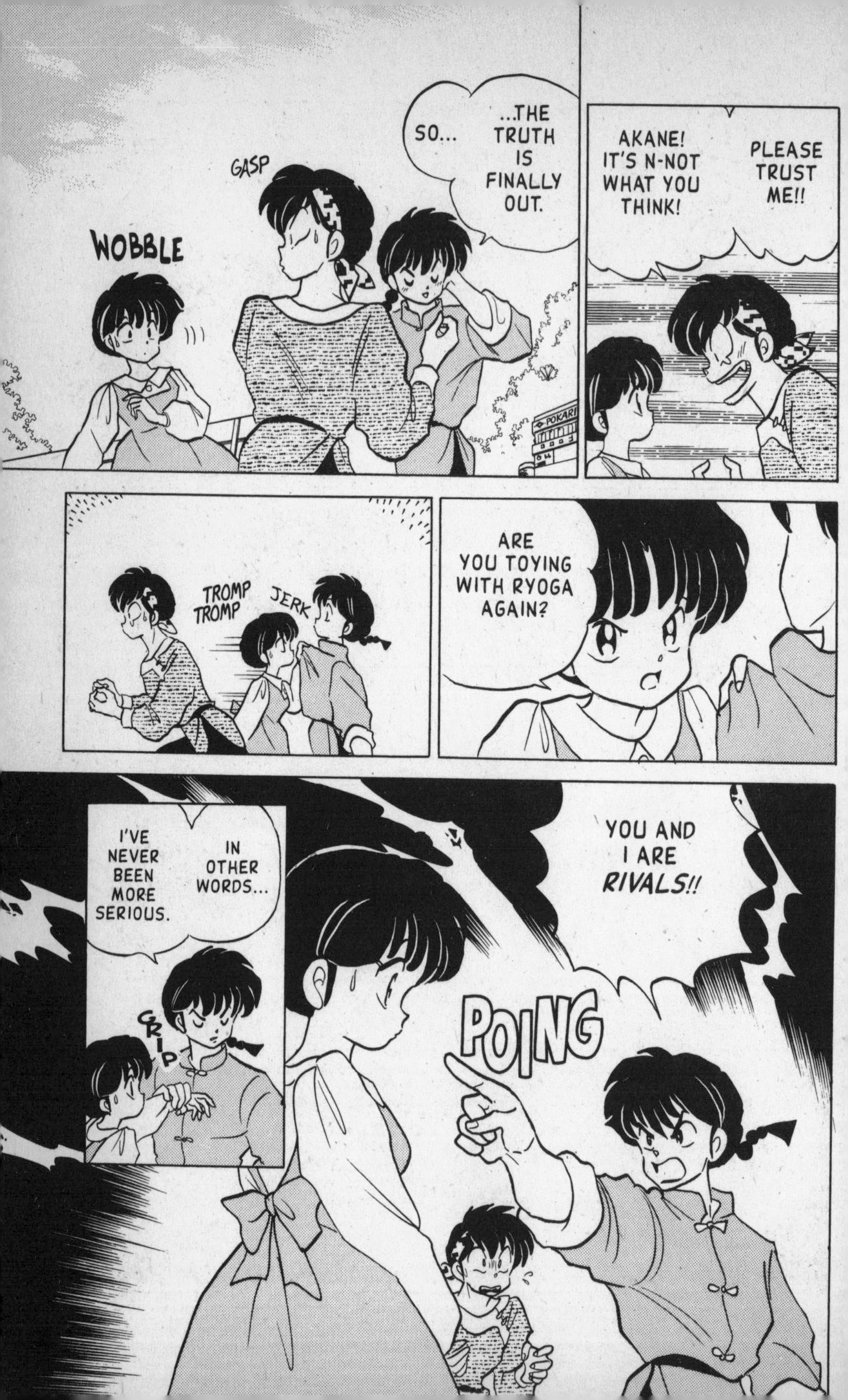
WOBBLE
GASP
SO...
...THE TRUTH IS FINALLY OUT.
AKANE! IT'S N-NOT WHAT YOU THINK!
PLEASE TRUST ME!!
TROMP TROMP
JERK
ARE YOU TOYING WITH RYOGA AGAIN?
IN OTHER WORDS...
I'VE NEVER BEEN MORE SERIOUS.
GRIP
YOU AND I ARE *RIVALS*!!
POING

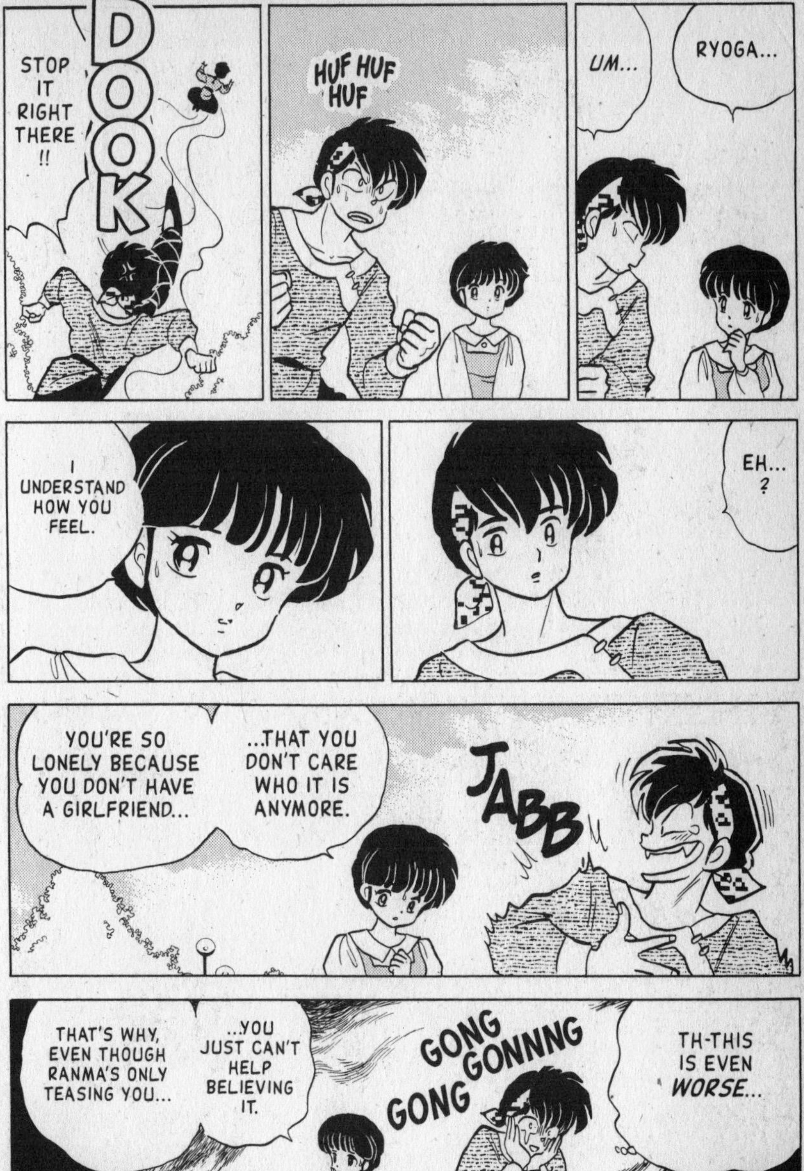

STOP IT RIGHT THERE !!
DOOK
HUF HUF HUF
UM...
RYOGA...
I UNDERSTAND HOW YOU FEEL.
EH...?
YOU'RE SO LONELY BECAUSE YOU DON'T HAVE A GIRLFRIEND...
...THAT YOU DON'T CARE WHO IT IS ANYMORE.
JABB
THAT'S WHY, EVEN THOUGH RANMA'S ONLY TEASING YOU...
...YOU JUST CAN'T HELP BELIEVING IT.
GONG GONG GONG GONNNG
TH-THIS IS EVEN *WORSE*...

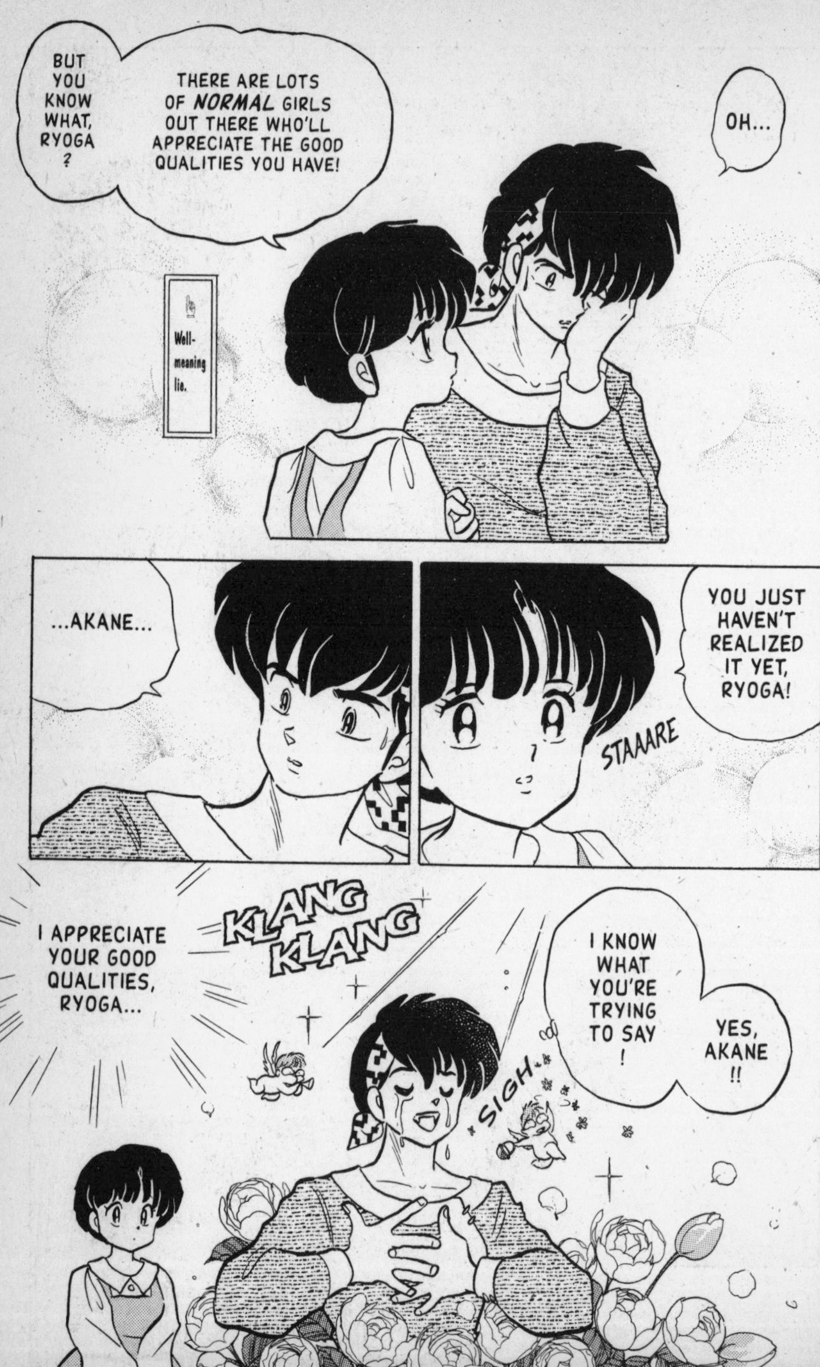
BUT YOU KNOW WHAT, RYOGA?
THERE ARE LOTS OF NORMAL GIRLS OUT THERE WHO'LL APPRECIATE THE GOOD QUALITIES YOU HAVE!
Well-meaning lie.
OH...
...AKANE...
YOU JUST HAVEN'T REALIZED IT YET, RYOGA!
STAAARE
I APPRECIATE YOUR GOOD QUALITIES, RYOGA...
KLANG KLANG
I KNOW WHAT YOU'RE TRYING TO SAY!
YES, AKANE!!
SIGH

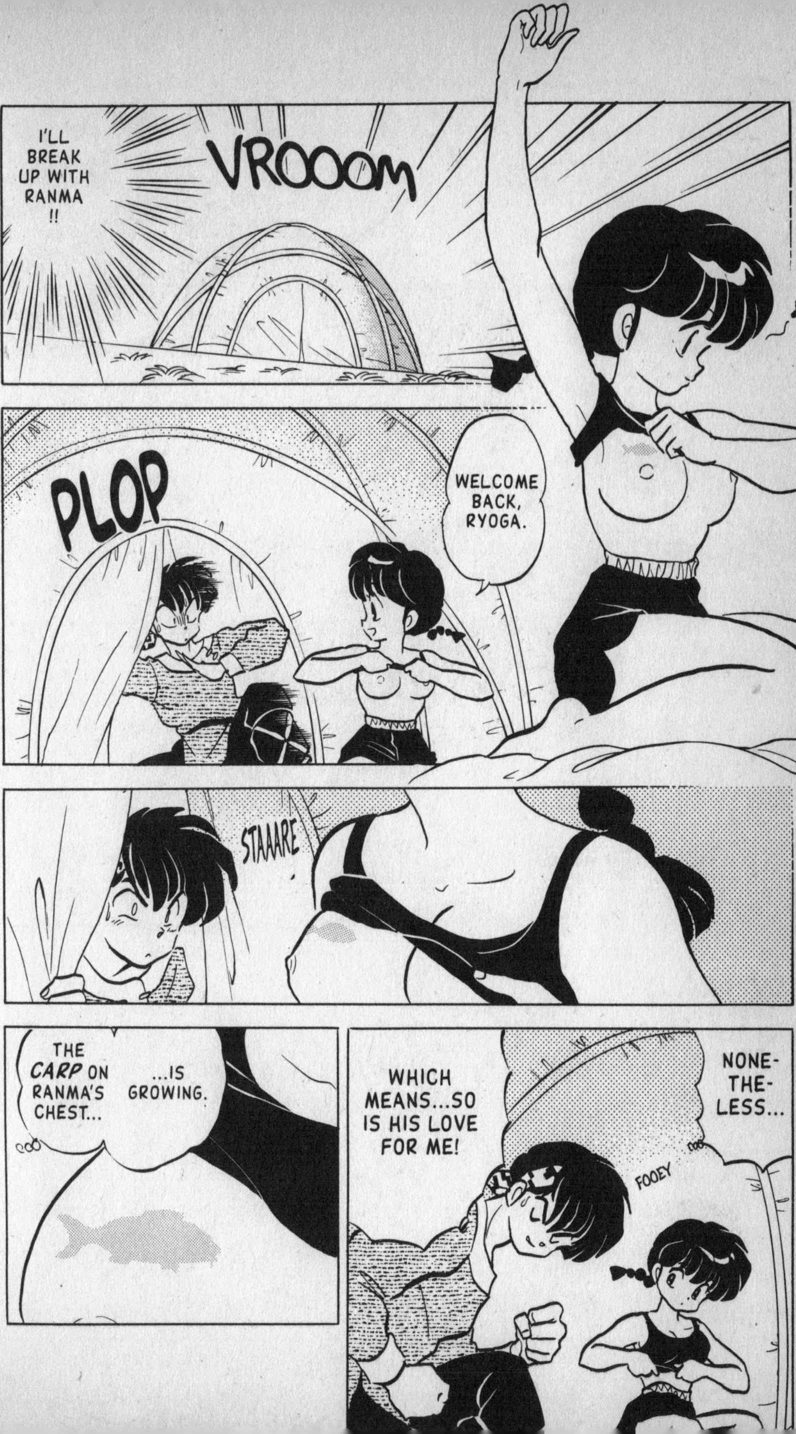
I'LL BREAK UP WITH RANMA !!
VROOOM
PLOP
WELCOME BACK, RYOGA.
STAAARE
THE CARP ON RANMA'S CHEST... ...IS GROWING.
WHICH MEANS...SO IS HIS LOVE FOR ME!
NONE-THE-LESS...
FOOEY

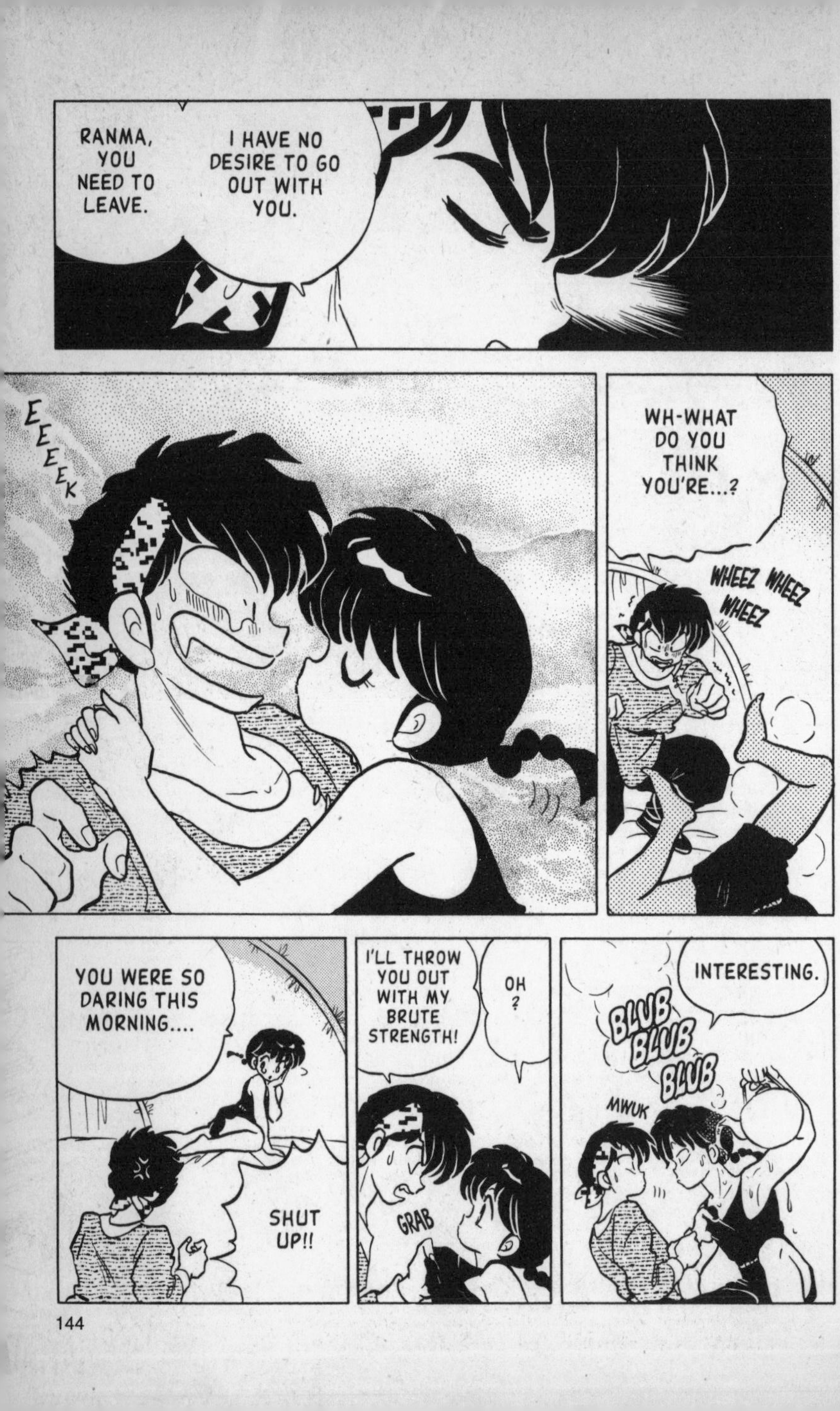
RANMA, YOU NEED TO LEAVE.
I HAVE NO DESIRE TO GO OUT WITH YOU.
EEEEEK
WH-WHAT DO YOU THINK YOU'RE...?
WHEEZ WHEEZ WHEEZ
YOU WERE SO DARING THIS MORNING....
SHUT UP!!
I'LL THROW YOU OUT WITH MY BRUTE STRENGTH!
OH?
GRAB
INTERESTING.
BLUB BLUB BLUB
MWUK

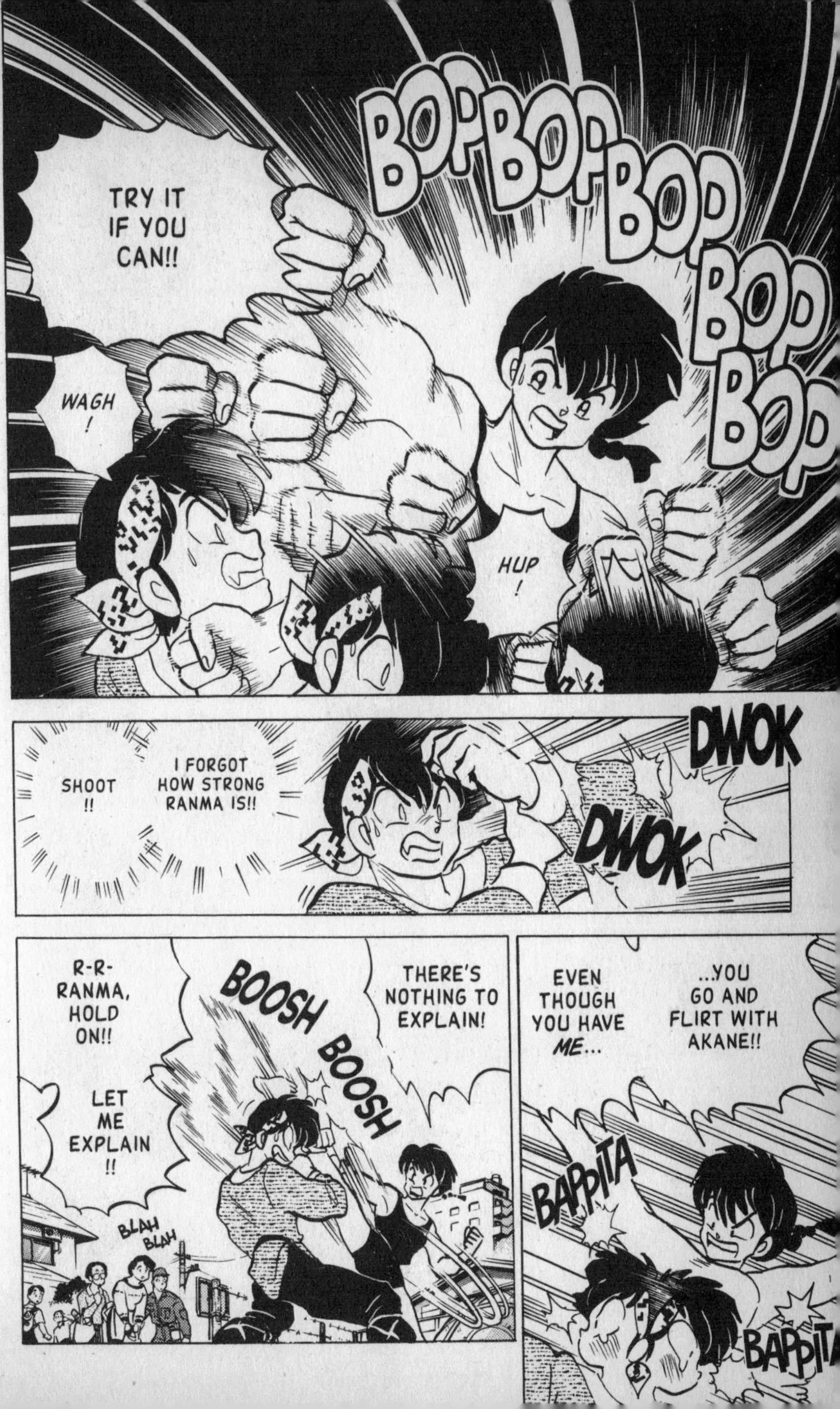
TRY IT IF YOU CAN!!
BOP BOP BOP BOP BOP
WAGH!
HUP!
SHOOT!!
I FORGOT HOW STRONG RANMA IS!!
DWOK
DWOK
R-R-RANMA, HOLD ON!!
LET ME EXPLAIN!!
BOOSH
BOOSH
THERE'S NOTHING TO EXPLAIN!
BLAH BLAH
EVEN THOUGH YOU HAVE *ME*...
...YOU GO AND FLIRT WITH AKANE!!
BAPPITA
BAPPITA

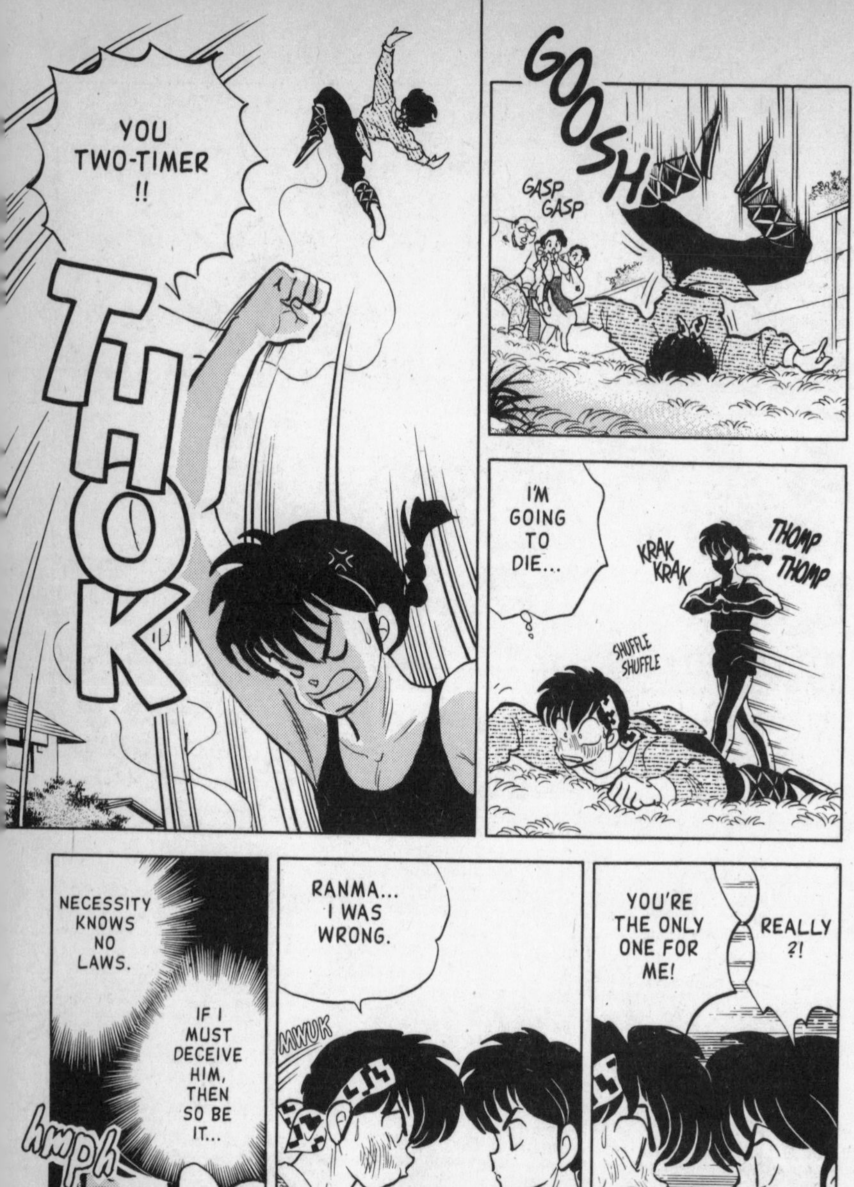
YOU TWO-TIMER !!
THOK
GOOSH
GASP GASP
I'M GOING TO DIE...
KRAK KRAK
THOMP THOMP
SHUFFLE SHUFFLE
NECESSITY KNOWS NO LAWS.
IF I MUST DECEIVE HIM, THEN SO BE IT...
hmph
RANMA... I WAS WRONG.
MWUK
GRIP
YOU'RE THE ONLY ONE FOR ME!
REALLY ?!

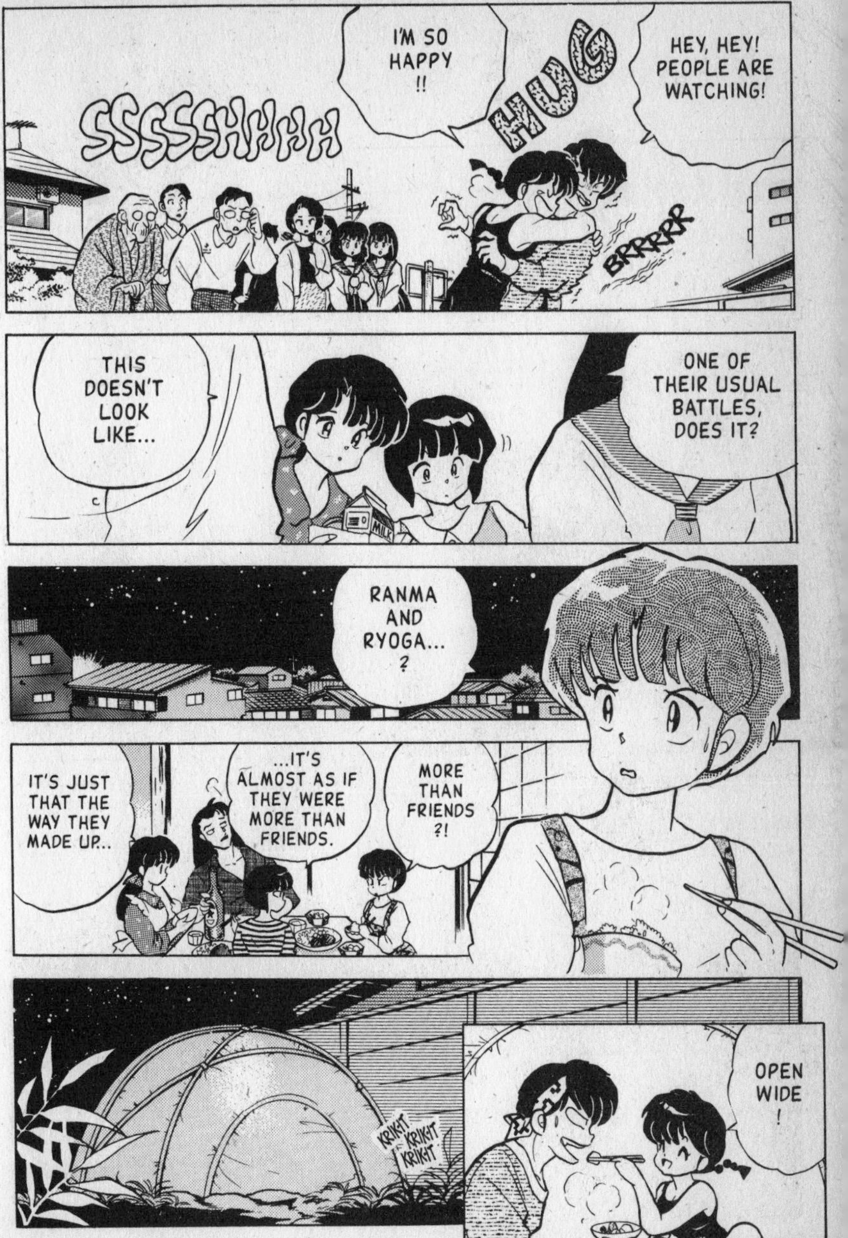
SSSSSHHHHH
I'M SO HAPPY !!
HUG
HEY, HEY! PEOPLE ARE WATCHING!
BRRRRR
THIS DOESN'T LOOK LIKE...
ONE OF THEIR USUAL BATTLES, DOES IT?
MILK
RANMA AND RYOGA...?
IT'S JUST THAT THE WAY THEY MADE UP...
...IT'S ALMOST AS IF THEY WERE MORE THAN FRIENDS.
MORE THAN FRIENDS ?!
KRIKIT KRIKIT KRIKIT
OPEN WIDE !

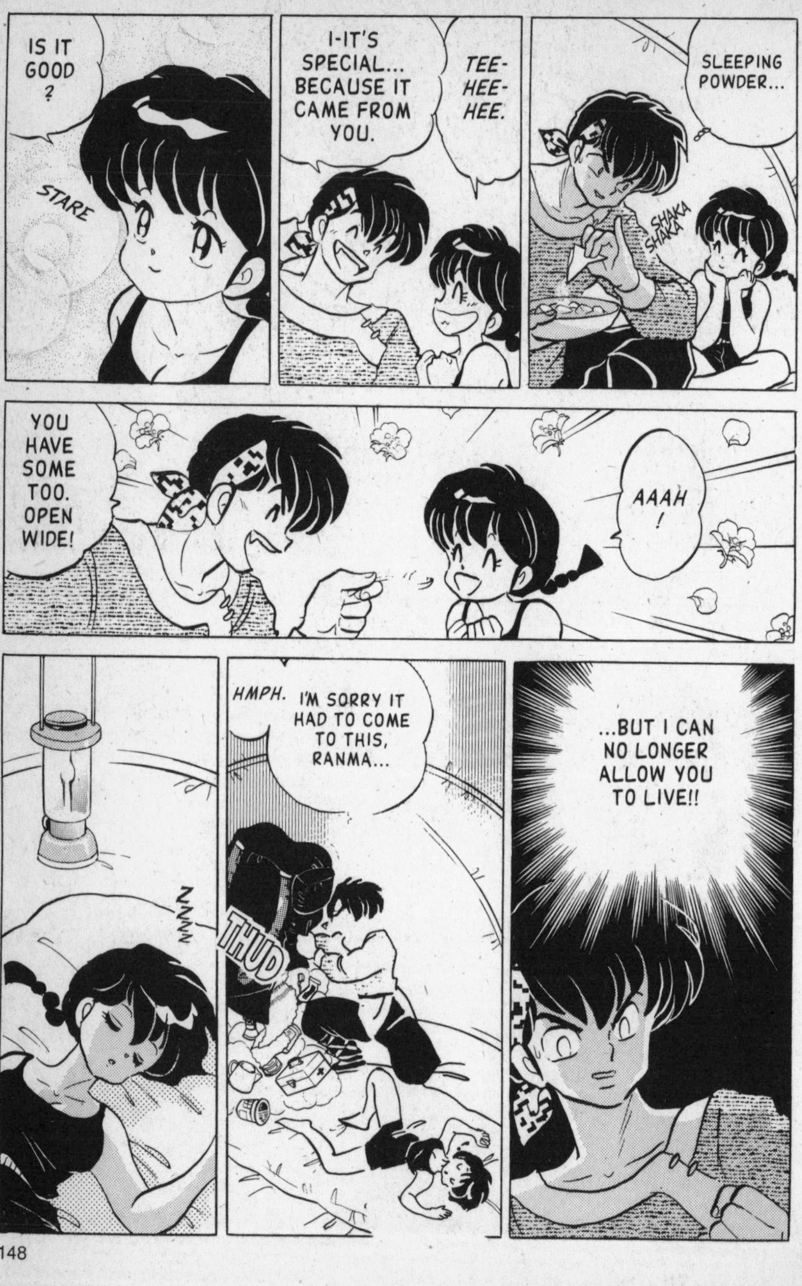
IS IT GOOD ?
STARE
I-IT'S SPECIAL... BECAUSE IT CAME FROM YOU.
TEE-HEE-HEE.
SLEEPING POWDER...
SHAKA SHAKA
YOU HAVE SOME TOO. OPEN WIDE!
AAAH !
ZZZZ
HMPH.
I'M SORRY IT HAD TO COME TO THIS, RANMA...
THUD
...BUT I CAN NO LONGER ALLOW YOU TO LIVE!!

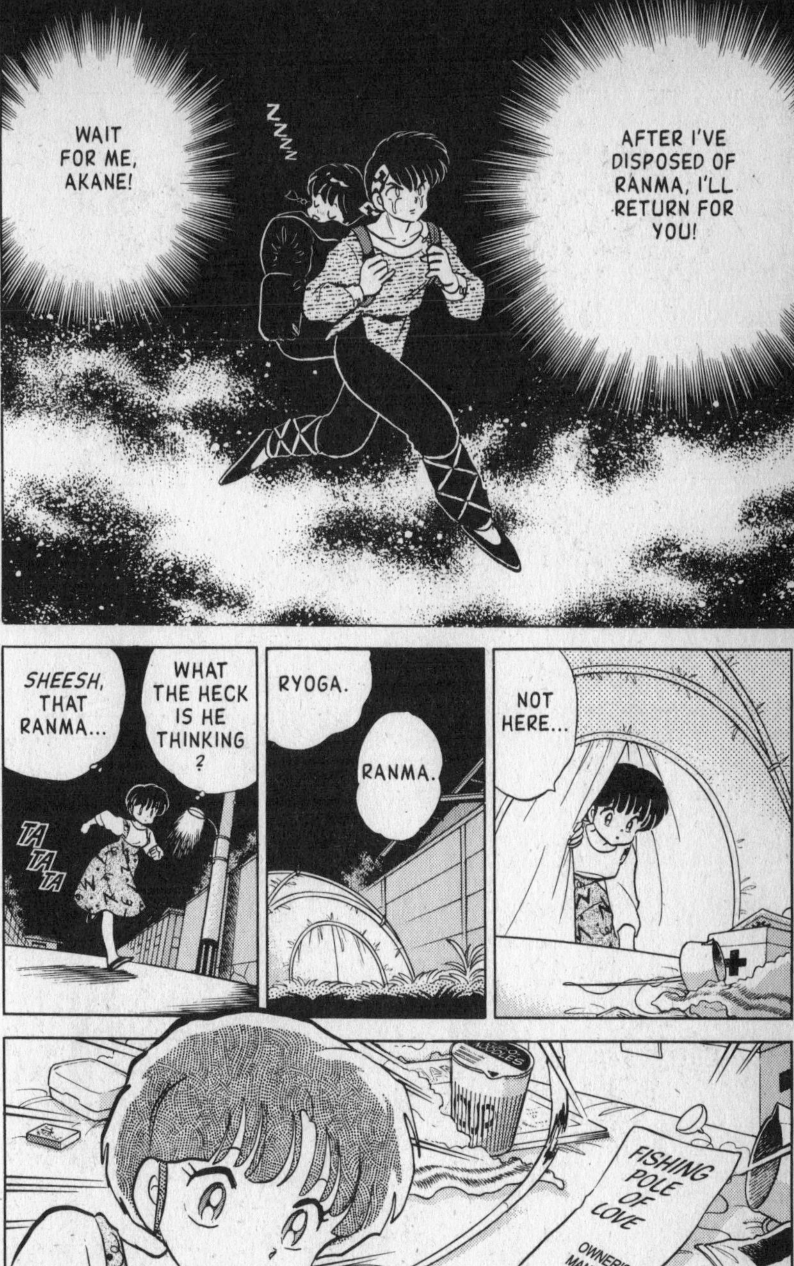
WAIT FOR ME, AKANE!
ZZZZ
AFTER I'VE DISPOSED OF RANMA, I'LL RETURN FOR YOU!
SHEESH, THAT RANMA...
WHAT THE HECK IS HE THINKING?
TA TA TA
RYOGA.
RANMA.
NOT HERE...
FISHING POLE OF LOVE
OWNER'S MANUAL

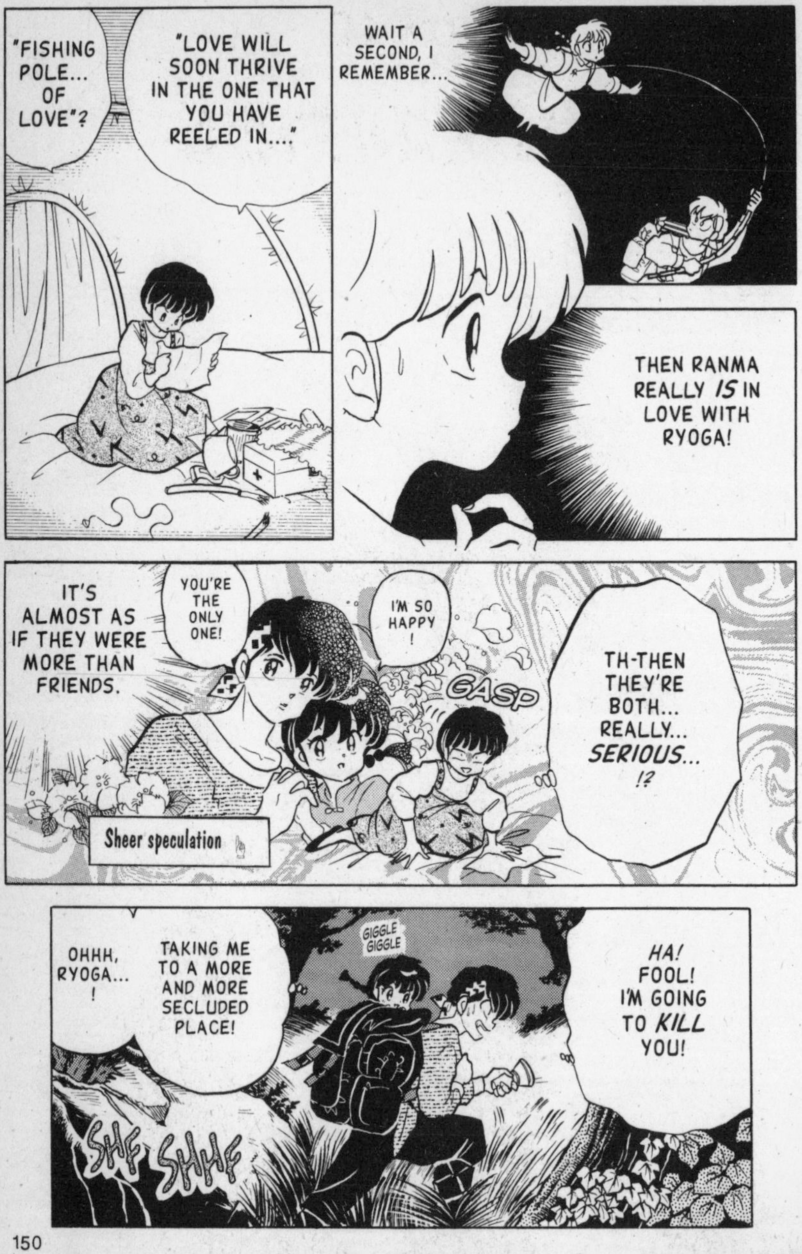
"FISHING POLE... OF LOVE"?
"LOVE WILL SOON THRIVE IN THE ONE THAT YOU HAVE REELED IN...."
WAIT A SECOND, I REMEMBER...
THEN RANMA REALLY *IS* IN LOVE WITH RYOGA!
IT'S ALMOST AS IF THEY WERE MORE THAN FRIENDS.
YOU'RE THE ONLY ONE!
I'M SO HAPPY!
GASP
TH-THEN THEY'RE BOTH... REALLY... *SERIOUS*...!?
Sheer speculation
OHHH, RYOGA...!
TAKING ME TO A MORE AND MORE SECLUDED PLACE!
GIGGLE GIGGLE
HA! FOOL! I'M GOING TO *KILL* YOU!
SHF SHHF

Part 10

QUIT CARPING

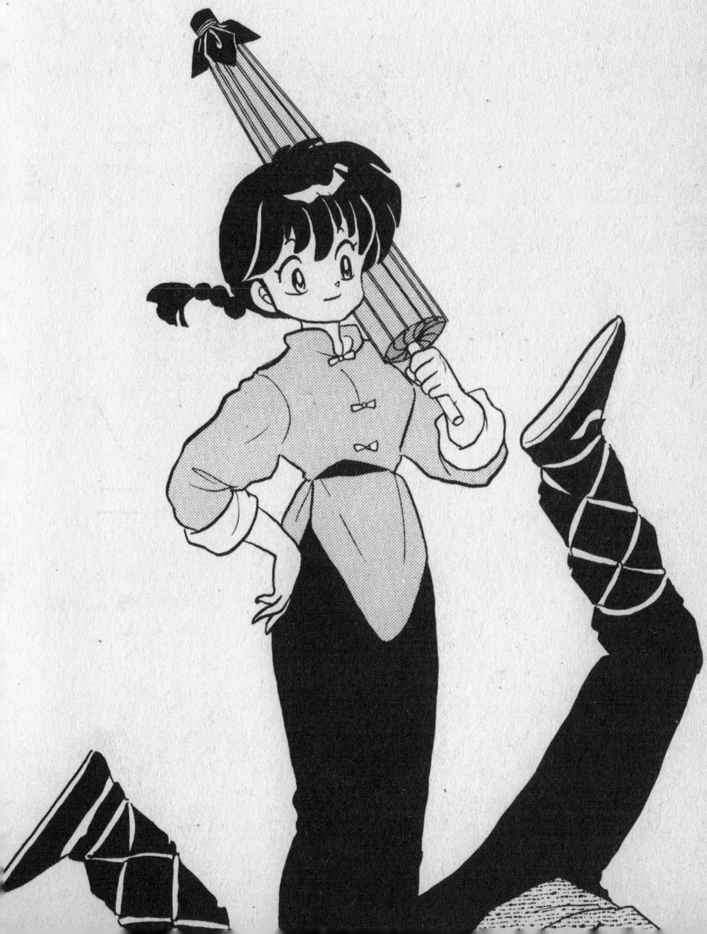

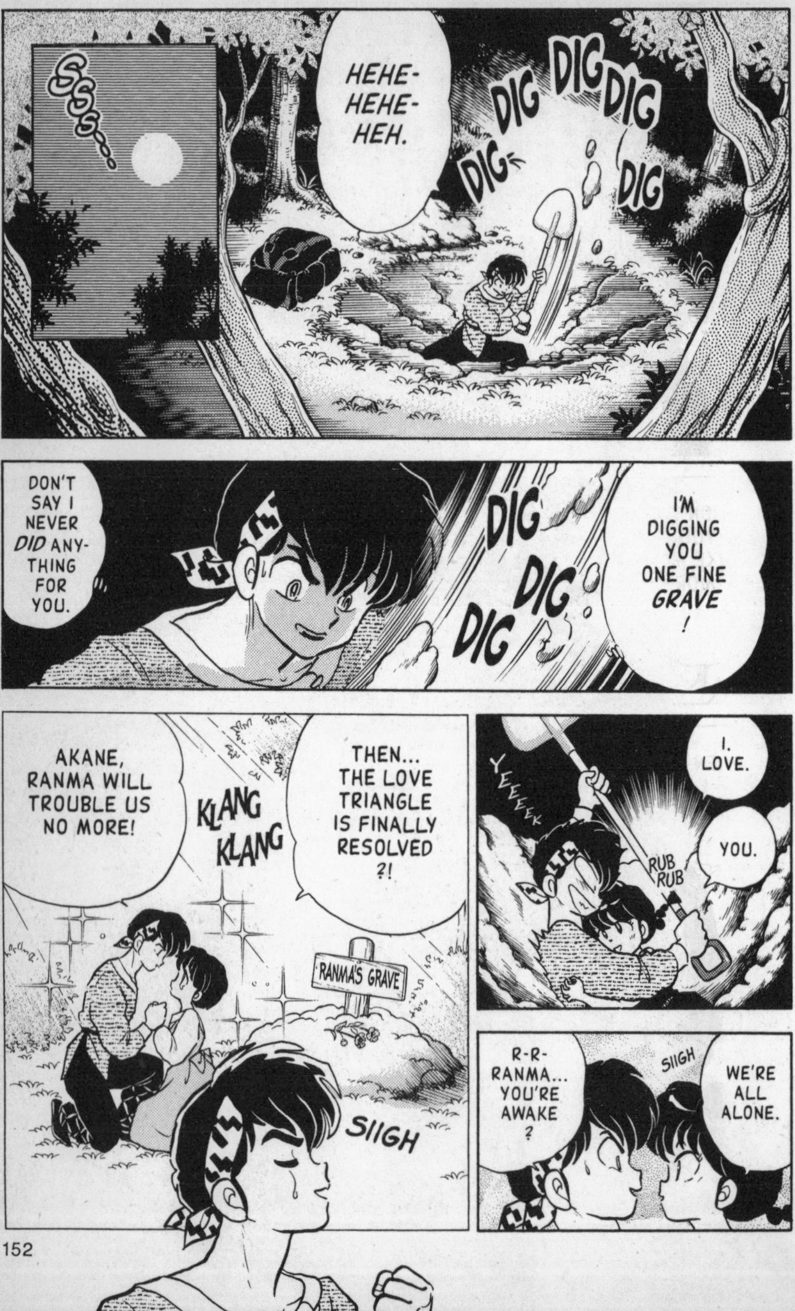
SSS...
HEHE-HEHE-HEH.
DIG DIG DIG DIG DIG DIG
DON'T SAY I NEVER *DID* ANYTHING FOR YOU.
DIG DIG DIG
I'M DIGGING YOU ONE FINE *GRAVE*!
AKANE, RANMA WILL TROUBLE US NO MORE!
KLANG KLANG
THEN... THE LOVE TRIANGLE IS FINALLY RESOLVED?!
RANMA'S GRAVE
SIIGH
YEEEEEK
I. LOVE.
RUB RUB
YOU.
R-R-RANMA... YOU'RE AWAKE?
SIIGH
WE'RE ALL ALONE.

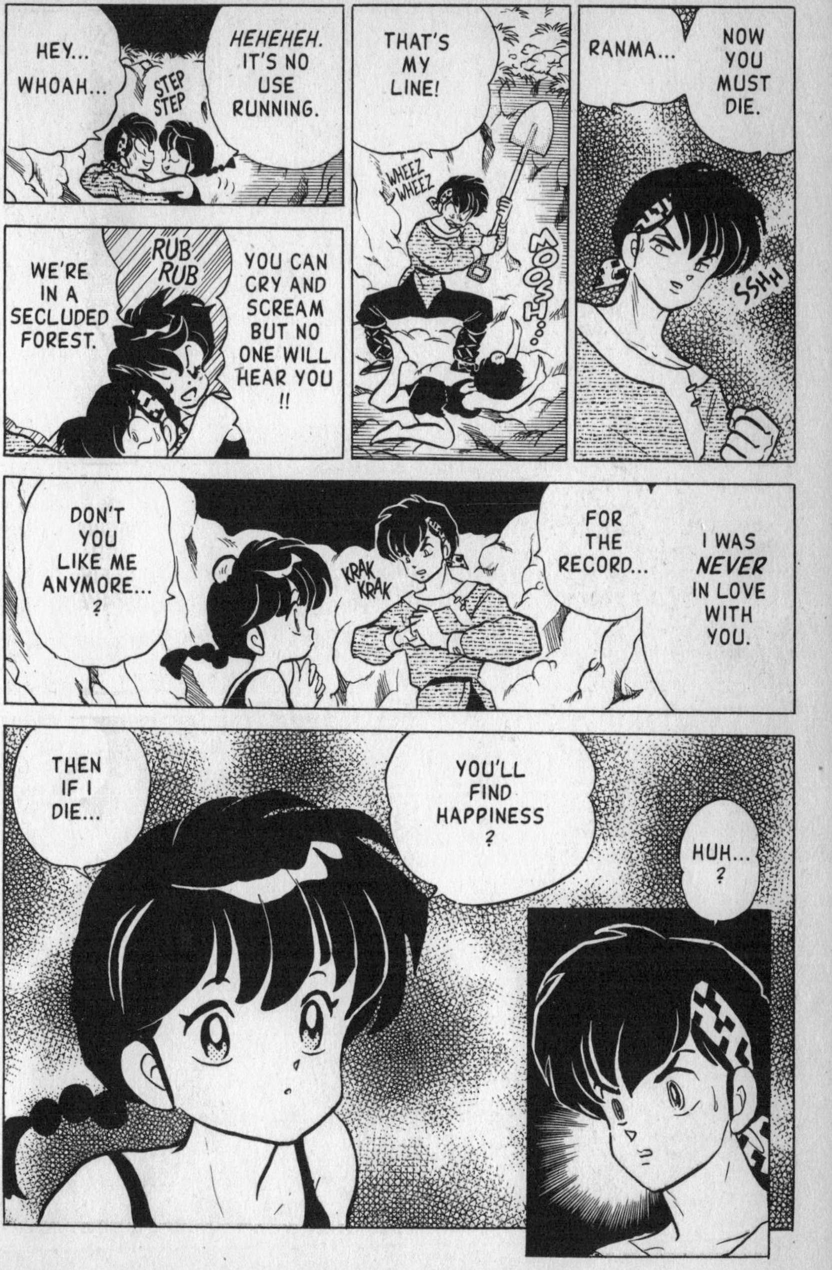
HEY... WHOAH...
STEP STEP
HEHEHEH. IT'S NO USE RUNNING.
WE'RE IN A SECLUDED FOREST.
RUB RUB
YOU CAN CRY AND SCREAM BUT NO ONE WILL HEAR YOU !!
THAT'S MY LINE!
WHEEZ WHEEZ
MOOSH...
RANMA...
NOW YOU MUST DIE.
SSHH
DON'T YOU LIKE ME ANYMORE...?
KRAK KRAK
FOR THE RECORD...
I WAS *NEVER* IN LOVE WITH YOU.
THEN IF I DIE...
YOU'LL FIND HAPPINESS?
HUH...?

IN THAT CASE...

DO IT QUICKLY!

R... RANMA...?

I'LL HAPPILY DIE FOR YOU.

SSSHHH

B-BMP B-BMP

B-BMP B-BMP B-BMP

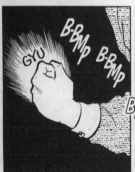

GYU B-BMP B-BMP B-BMP

WHSPA

B-BMP B-BMP

154

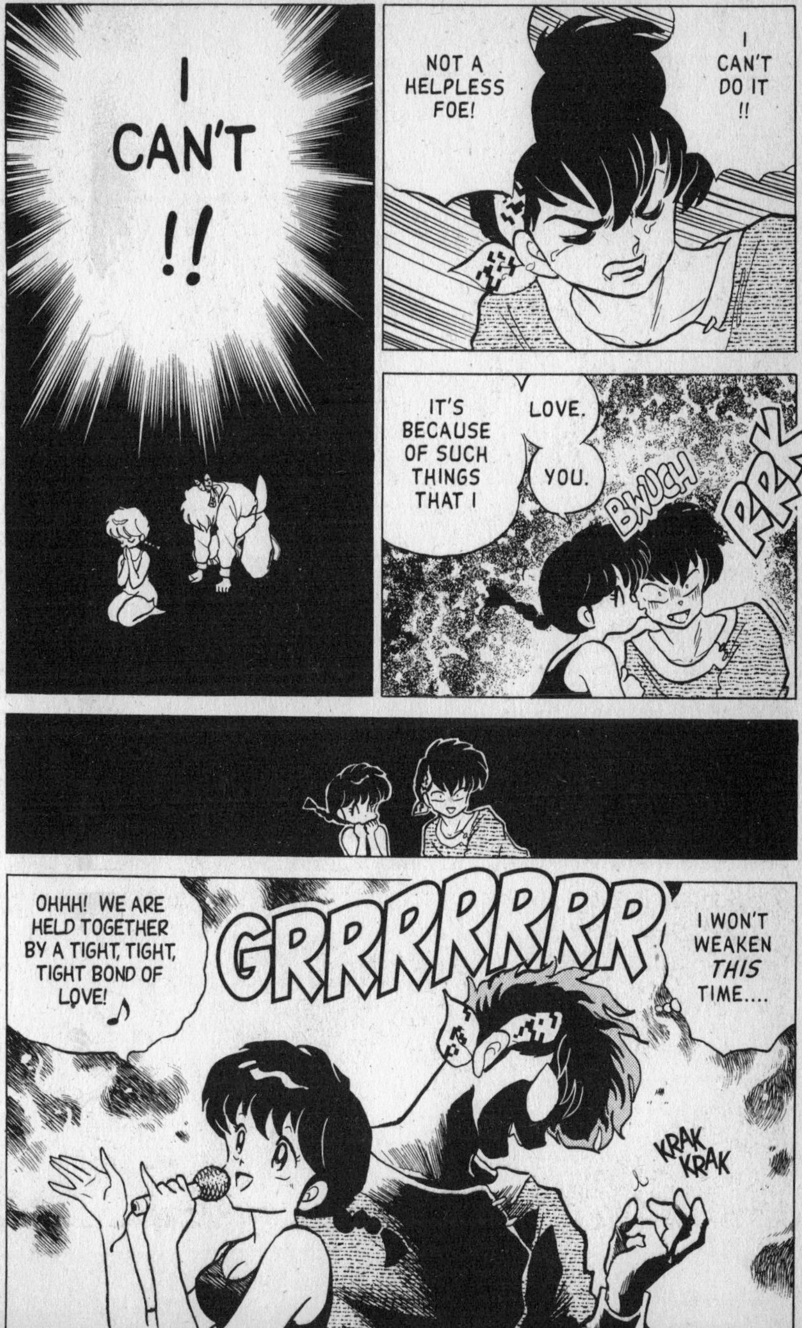
I CAN'T !!
NOT A HELPLESS FOE!
I CAN'T DO IT !!
IT'S BECAUSE OF SUCH THINGS THAT I
LOVE.
YOU.
BWUCH
RRK
OHHH! WE ARE HELD TOGETHER BY A TIGHT, TIGHT, TIGHT BOND OF LOVE! ♪
GRRRRRRR
I WON'T WEAKEN *THIS* TIME....
KRAK KRAK

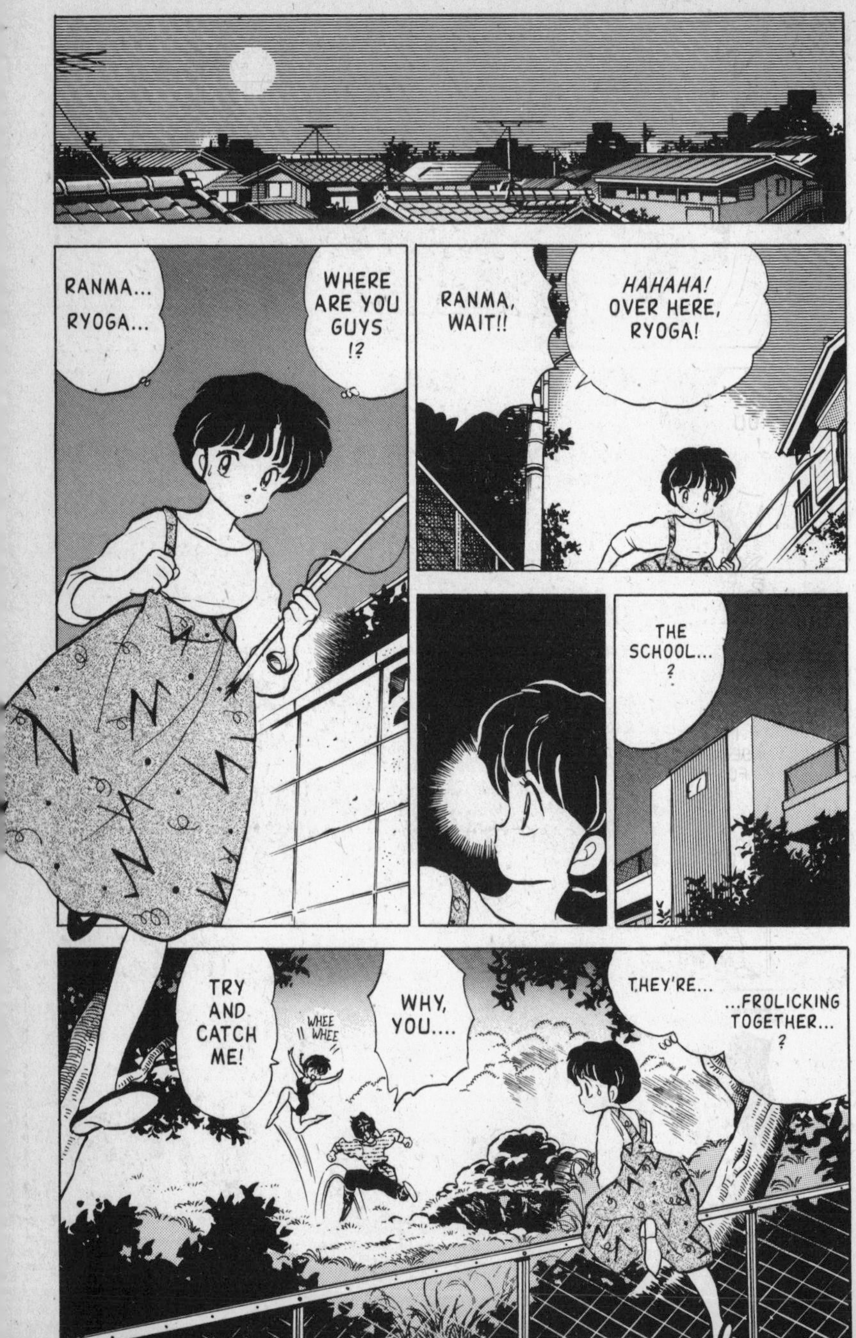
RANMA... RYOGA...
WHERE ARE YOU GUYS !?
RANMA, WAIT!!
HAHAHA! OVER HERE, RYOGA!
THE SCHOOL... ?
TRY AND CATCH ME!
WHEE WHEE
WHY, YOU....
THEY'RE...
...FROLICKING TOGETHER... ?

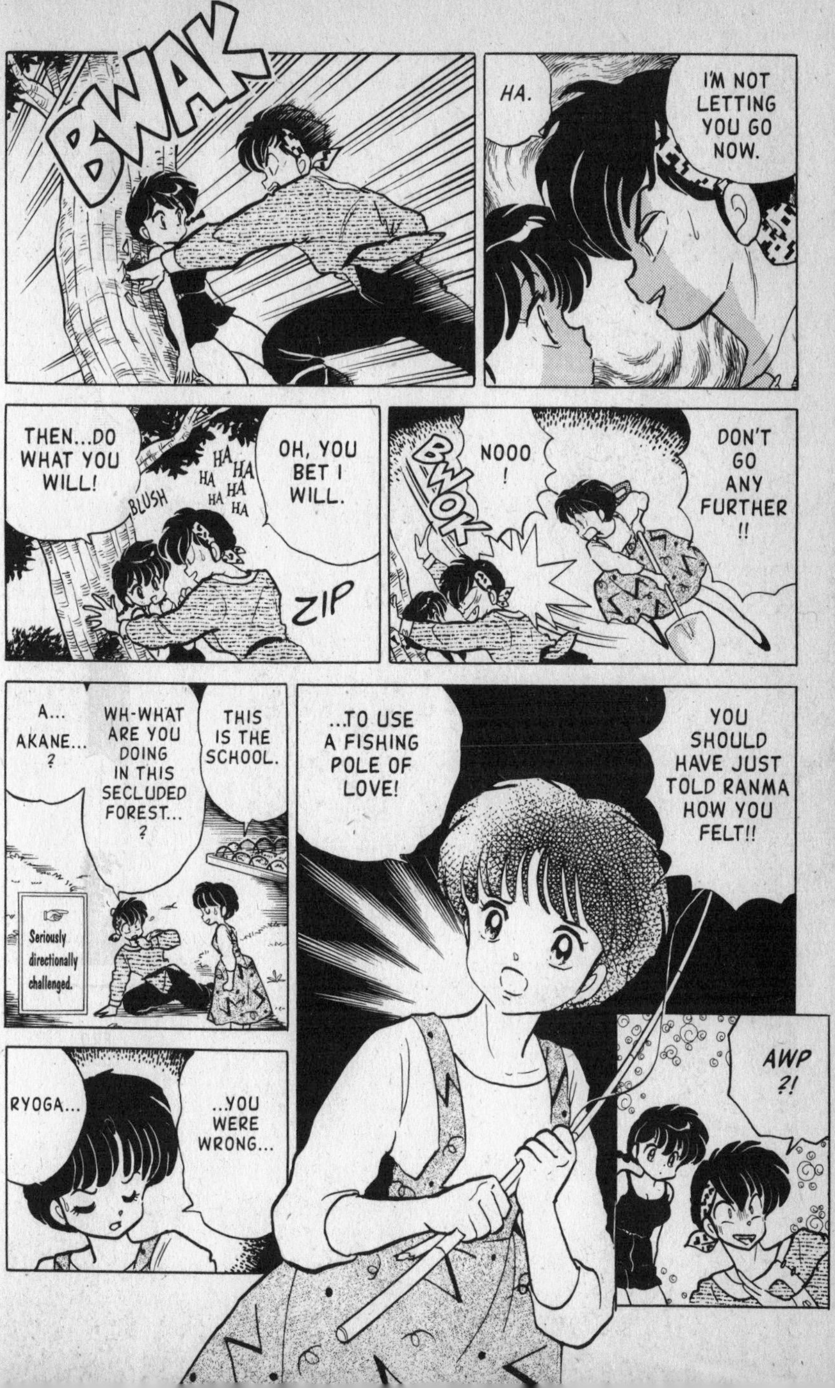
BWAK
HA.
I'M NOT LETTING YOU GO NOW.
THEN...DO WHAT YOU WILL!
BLUSH
HA HA HA HA HA HA HA
OH, YOU BET I WILL.
ZIP
BWOK
NOOO !
DON'T GO ANY FURTHER !!
A... AKANE... ?
WH-WHAT ARE YOU DOING IN THIS SECLUDED FOREST... ?
THIS IS THE SCHOOL.
Seriously directionally challenged.
...TO USE A FISHING POLE OF LOVE!
YOU SHOULD HAVE JUST TOLD RANMA HOW YOU FELT!!
RYOGA...
...YOU WERE WRONG...
AWP ?!

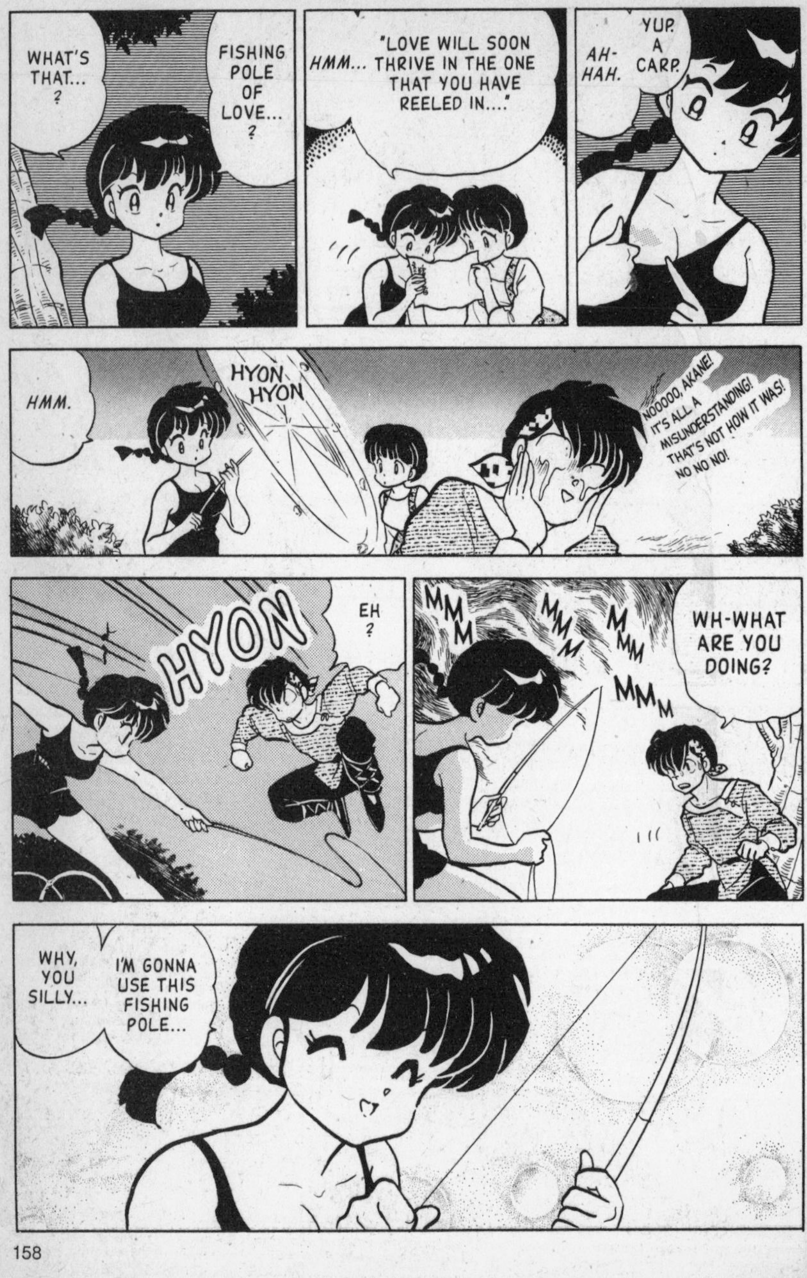

WHAT'S THAT... ?
FISHING POLE OF LOVE... ?
HMM...
"LOVE WILL SOON THRIVE IN THE ONE THAT YOU HAVE REELED IN...."
AH-HAH.
YUP. A CARP.
HMM.
HYON HYON
NOOOOO, AKANE! IT'S ALL A MISUNDERSTANDING! THAT'S NOT HOW IT WAS! NO NO NO!
HYON
EH ?
MMM MMM MMM MMM
WH-WHAT ARE YOU DOING?
WHY, YOU SILLY...
I'M GONNA USE THIS FISHING POLE...

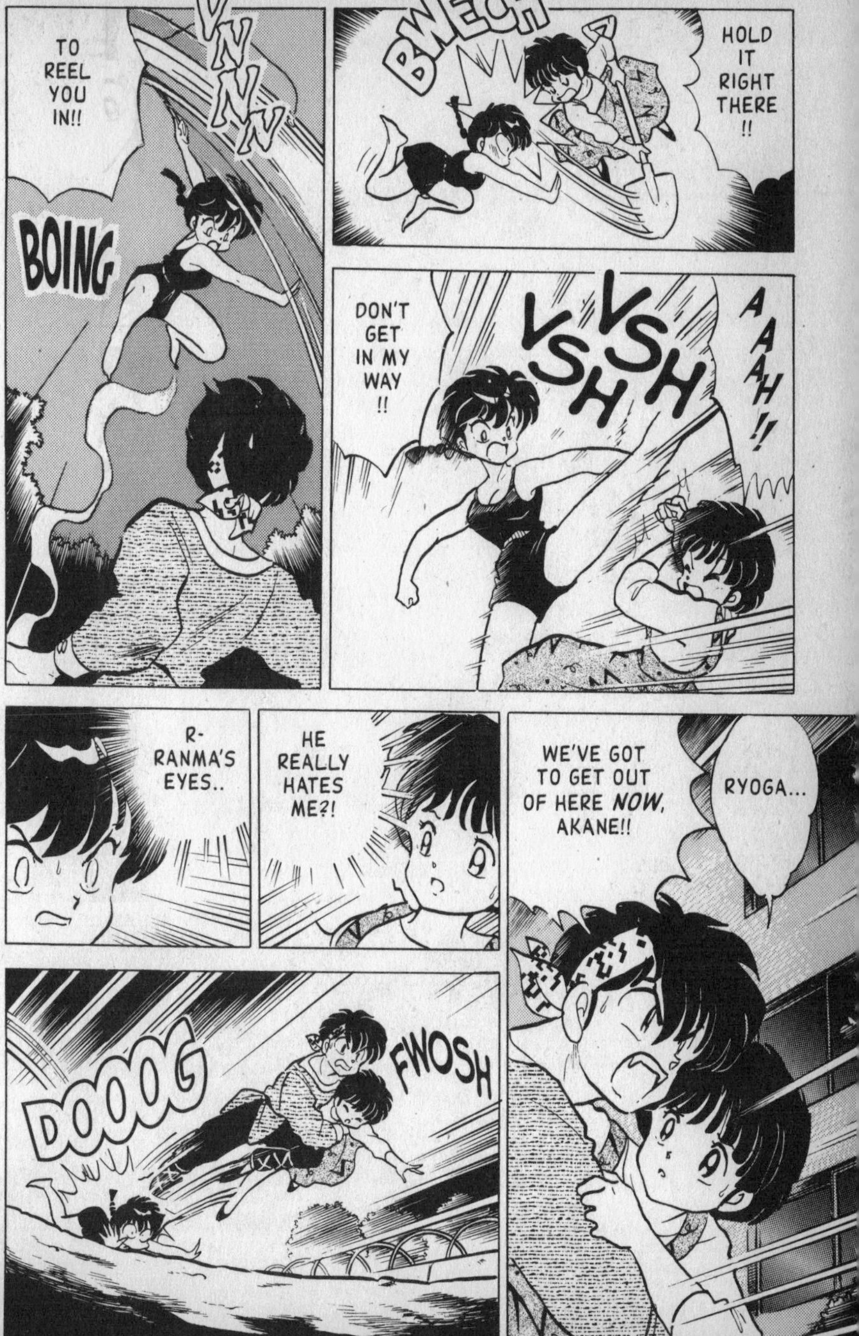
TO REEL YOU IN!!
VNNN
BOING
BWECH
HOLD IT RIGHT THERE!!
DON'T GET IN MY WAY!!
VSH
VSH
AAAH!!
R-RANMA'S EYES..
HE REALLY HATES ME?!
DOOOG
FWOSH
WE'VE GOT TO GET OUT OF HERE *NOW*, AKANE!!
RYOGA...

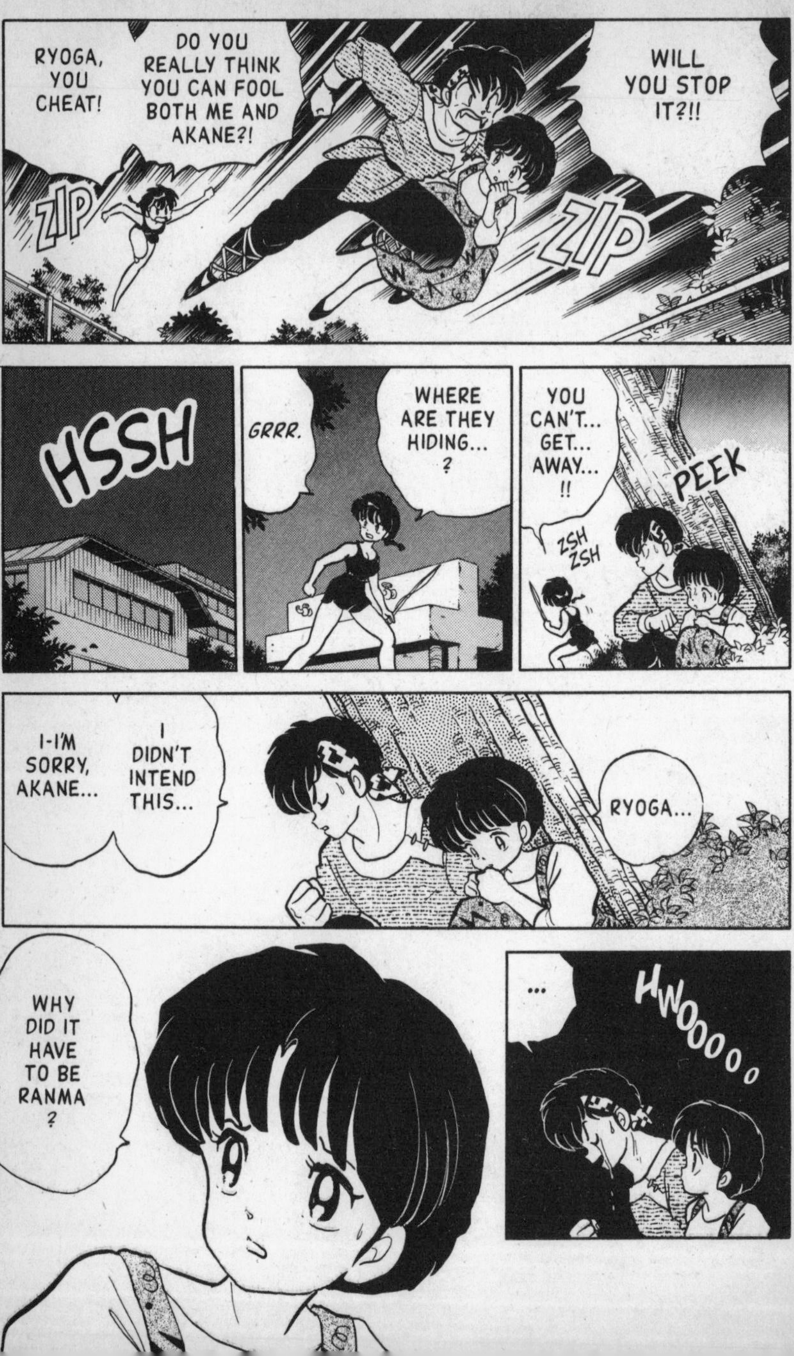
RYOGA, YOU CHEAT!
DO YOU REALLY THINK YOU CAN FOOL BOTH ME AND AKANE?!
ZIP
ZIP
WILL YOU STOP IT?!!
HSSH
GRRR.
WHERE ARE THEY HIDING...?
YOU CAN'T... GET... AWAY...!!
PEEK
ZSH ZSH
I-I'M SORRY, AKANE...
I DIDN'T INTEND THIS...
RYOGA...
WHY DID IT HAVE TO BE RANMA?
...
HWOOOOOO

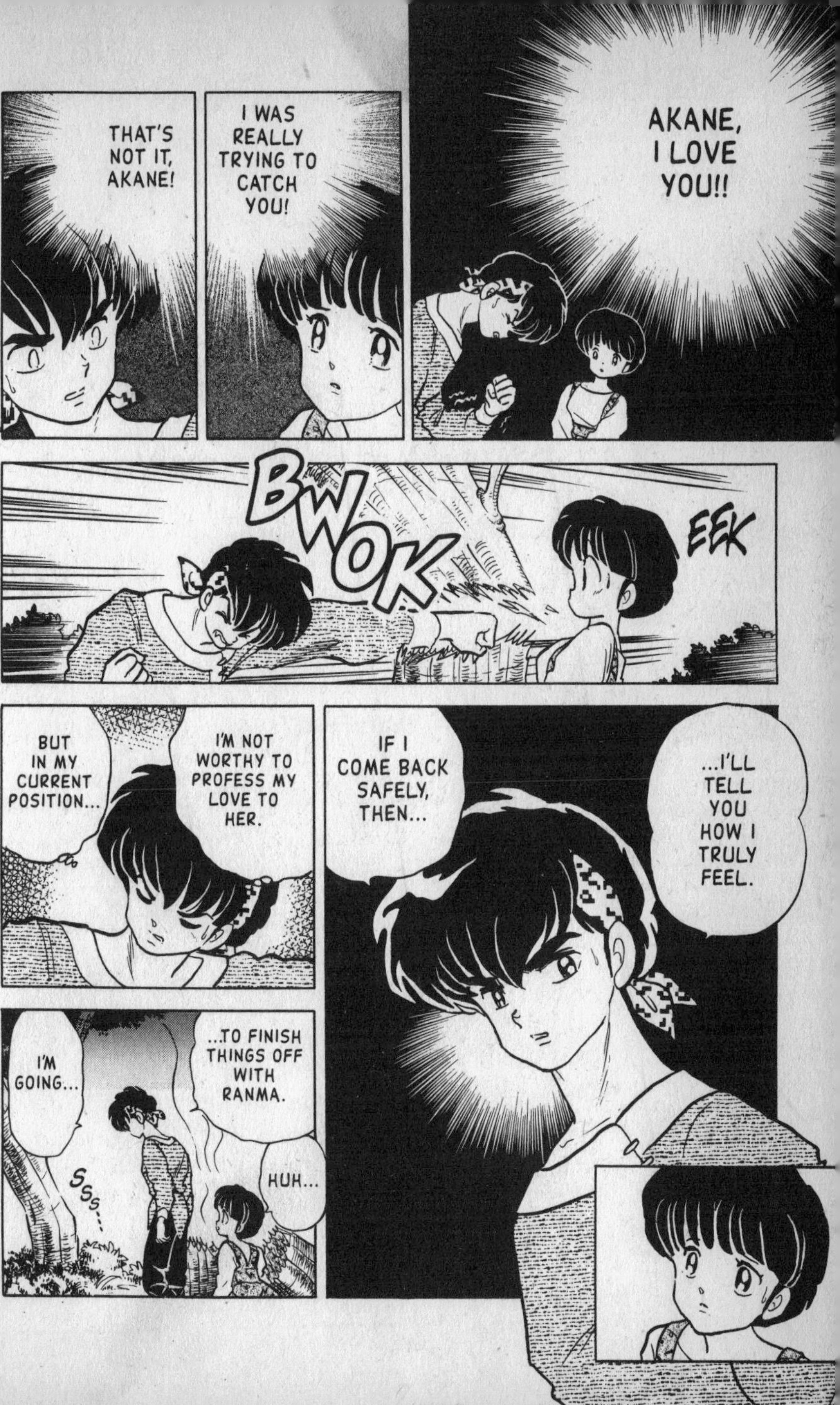
THAT'S NOT IT, AKANE!
I WAS REALLY TRYING TO CATCH YOU!
AKANE, I LOVE YOU!!
BWOK
EEK
BUT IN MY CURRENT POSITION...
I'M NOT WORTHY TO PROFESS MY LOVE TO HER.
I'M GOING...
...TO FINISH THINGS OFF WITH RANMA.
SSS...
HUH...
IF I COME BACK SAFELY, THEN...
...I'LL TELL YOU HOW I TRULY FEEL.

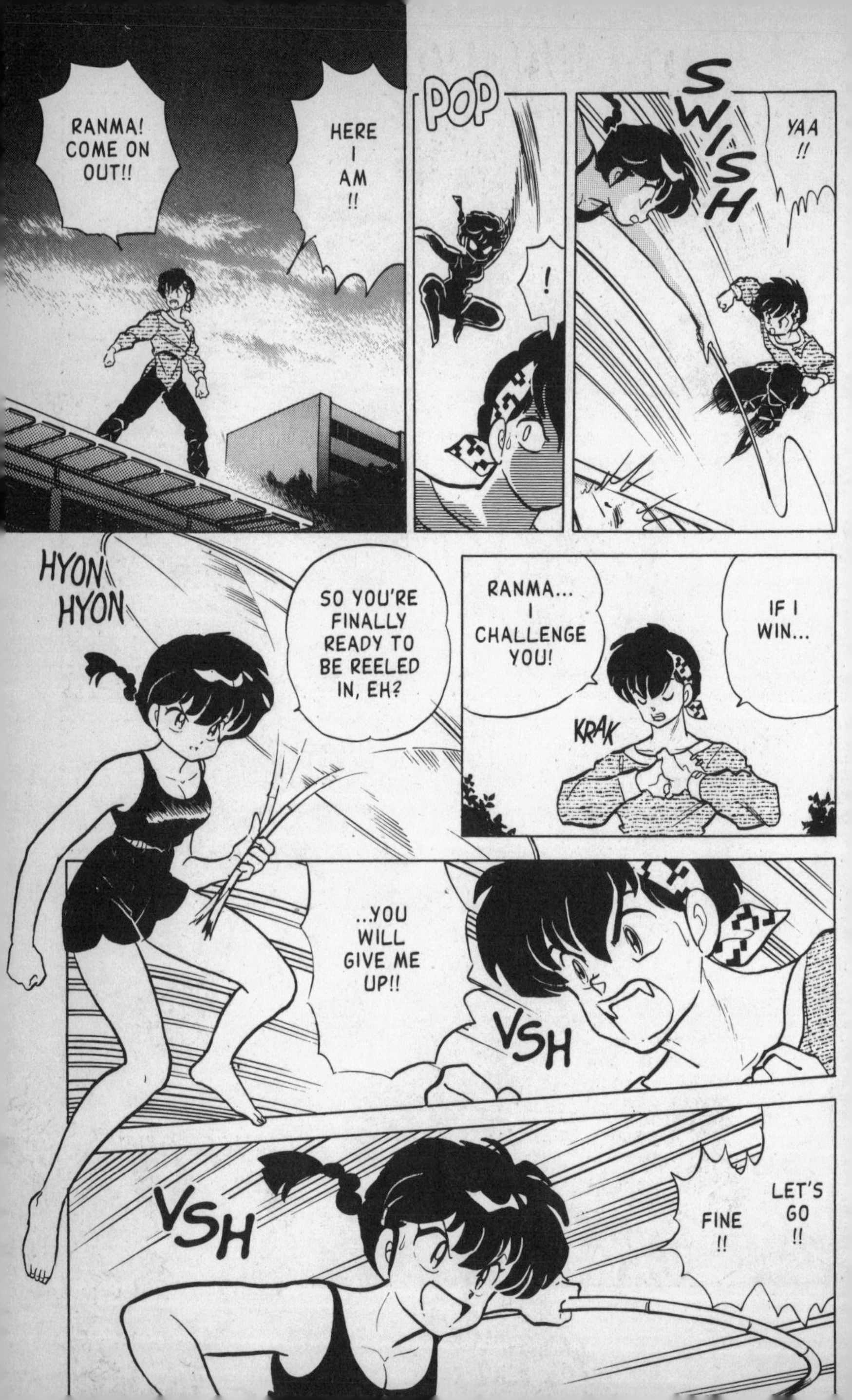
RANMA! COME ON OUT!!
HERE I AM !!
POP
!
SWISH
YAA !!
HYON HYON
SO YOU'RE FINALLY READY TO BE REELED IN, EH?
RANMA... I CHALLENGE YOU!
KRAK
IF I WIN...
...YOU WILL GIVE ME UP!!
VSH
VSH
FINE !!
LET'S GO !!

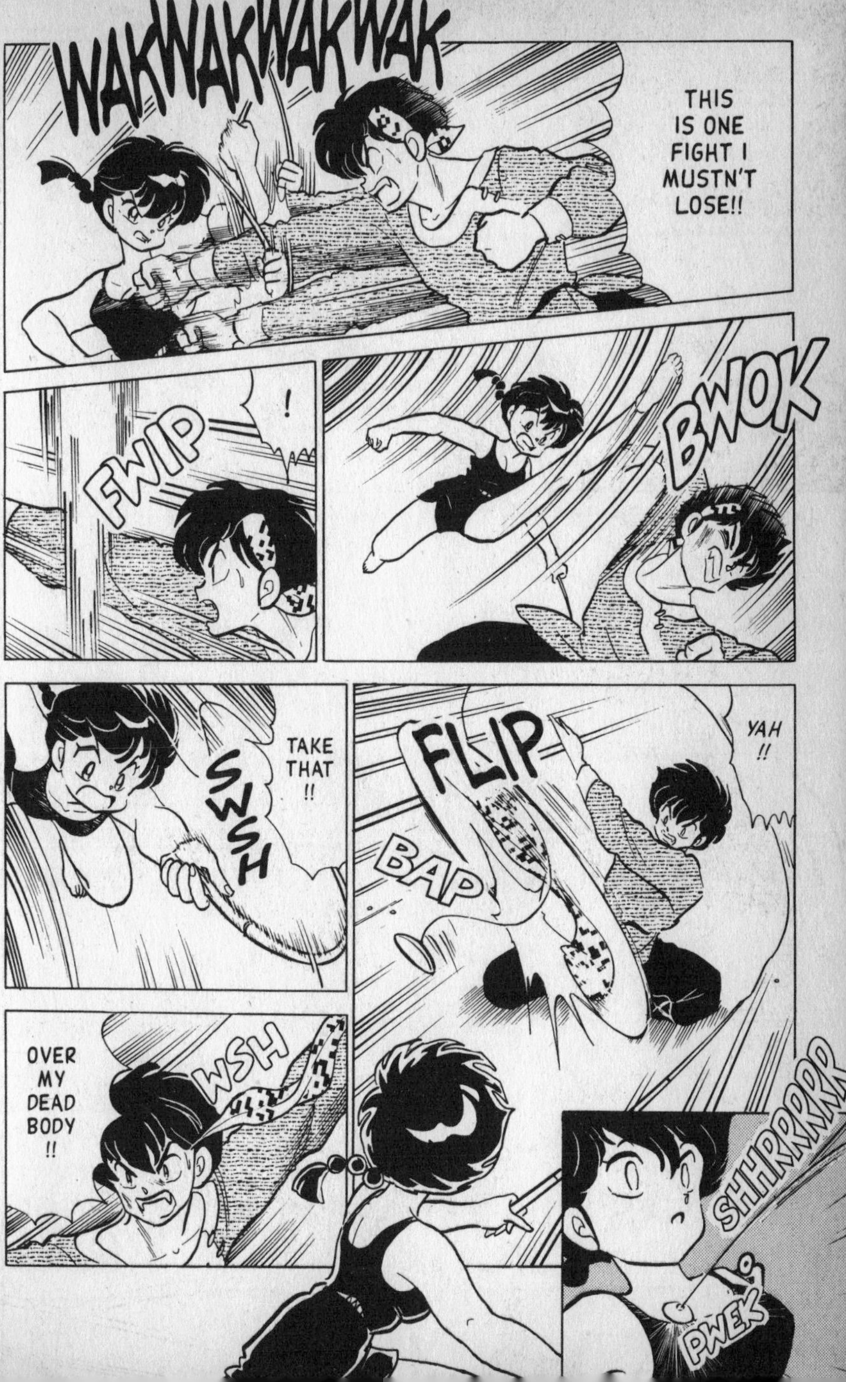
WAKWAKWAKWAKWAK
THIS IS ONE FIGHT I MUSTN'T LOSE!!
FWIP
!
BWOK
TAKE THAT !!
SWSH
FLIP
YAH !!
BAP
OVER MY DEAD BODY !!
WSH
SHHRRRRR
PWEK

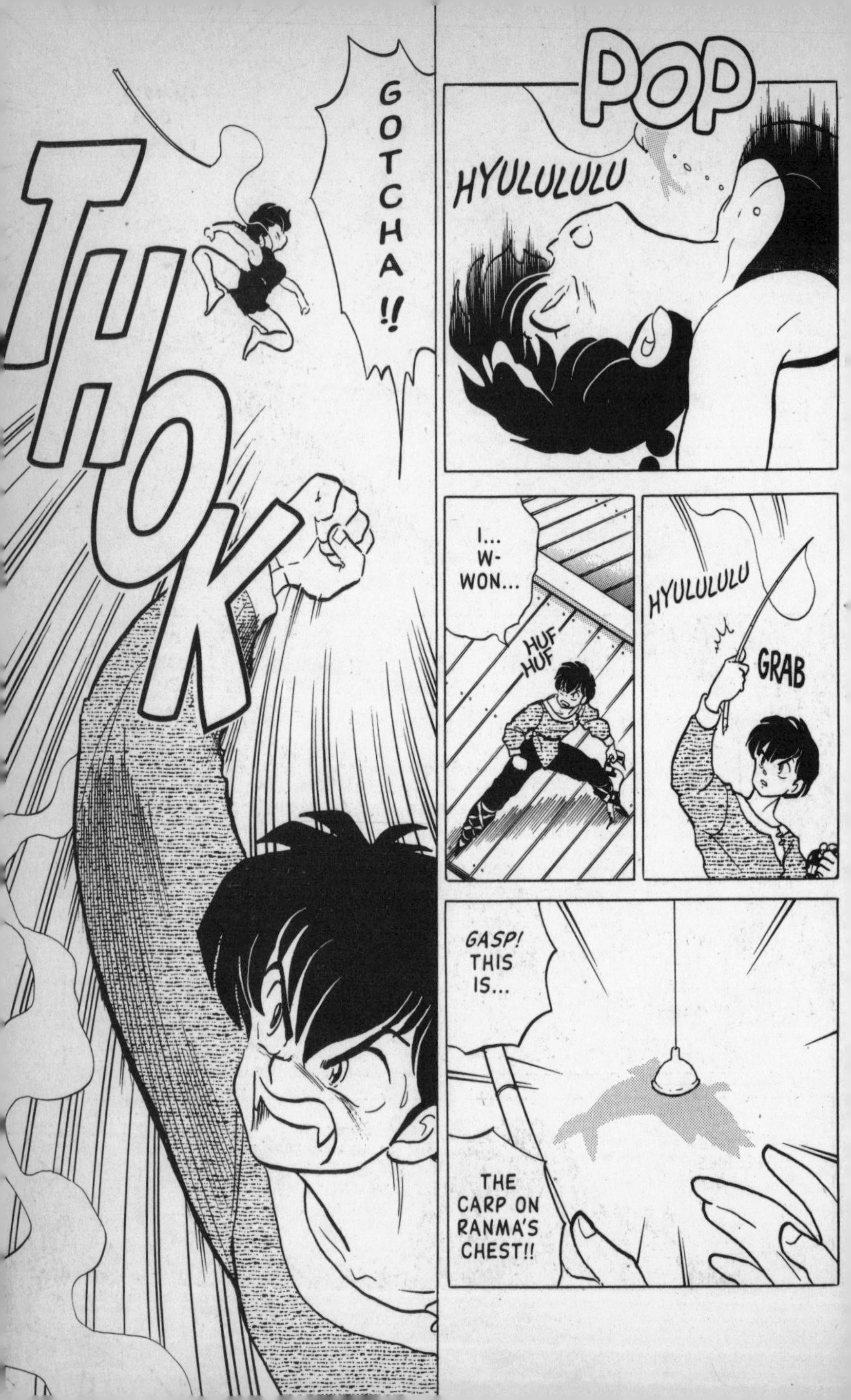
THOK
GOTCHA!!
POP
HYULULULU
I... W-WON...
HUF HUF
HYULULULU
GRAB
GASP! THIS IS...
THE CARP ON RANMA'S CHEST!!

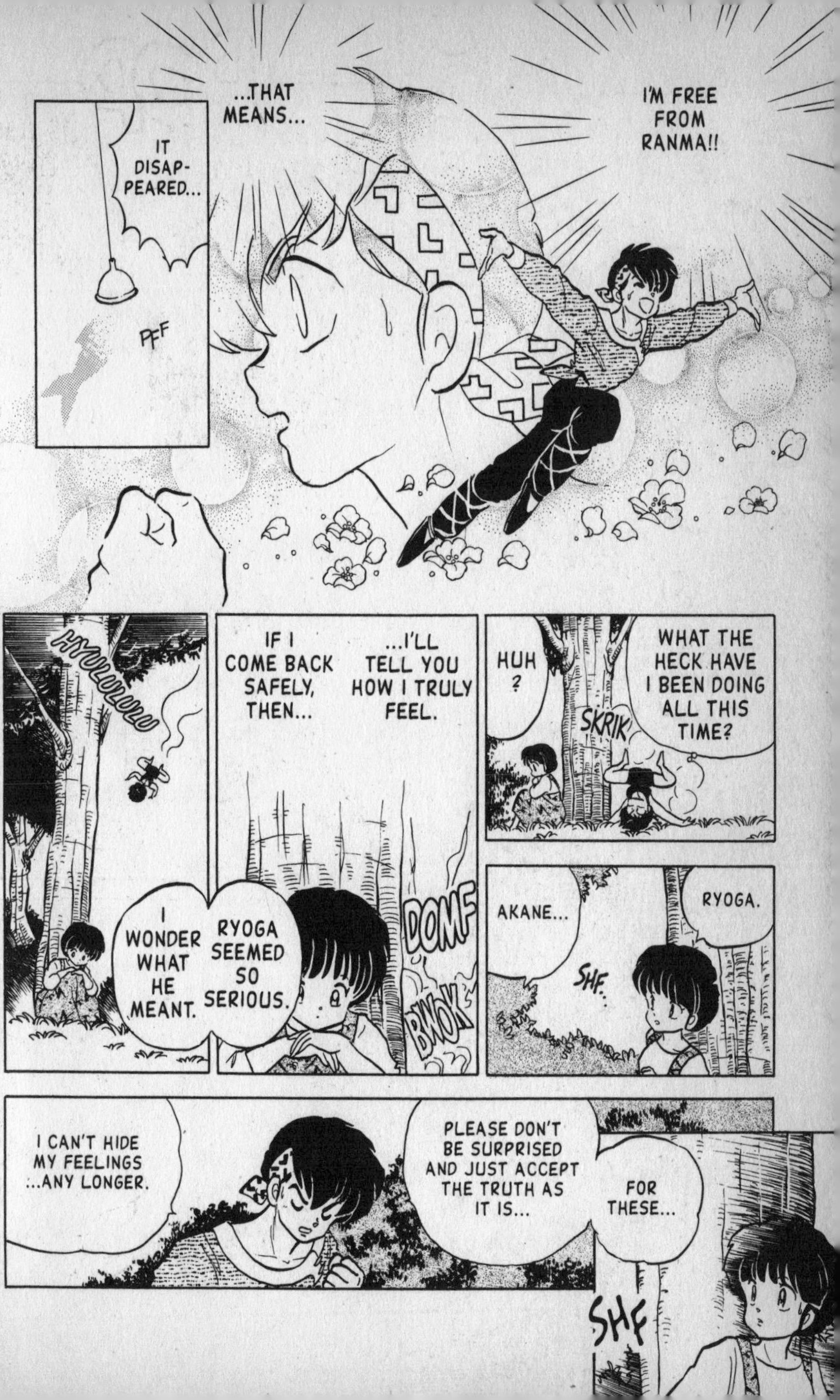
IT DISAPPEARED...
PFF
...THAT MEANS...
I'M FREE FROM RANMA!!
HYULULULU
I WONDER WHAT HE MEANT.
IF I COME BACK SAFELY, THEN...
...I'LL TELL YOU HOW I TRULY FEEL.
RYOGA SEEMED SO SERIOUS.
DOMF
BWOK
HUH?
WHAT THE HECK HAVE I BEEN DOING ALL THIS TIME?
SKRIK
AKANE...
RYOGA.
SHF...
I CAN'T HIDE MY FEELINGS ...ANY LONGER.
PLEASE DON'T BE SURPRISED AND JUST ACCEPT THE TRUTH AS IT IS...
FOR THESE...
SHF

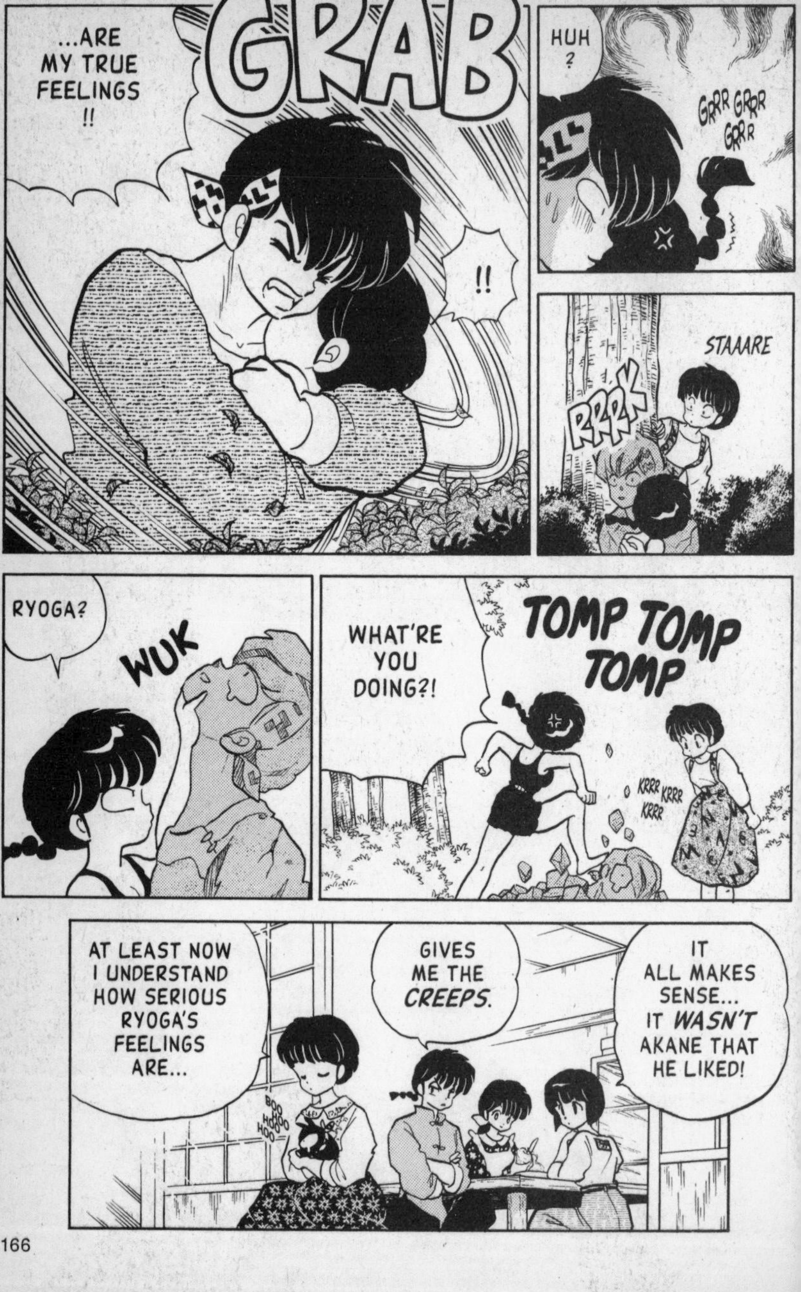
...ARE MY TRUE FEELINGS !!
GRAB
!!
HUH ?
GRRR GRRR GRRR
STAAARE
RRRK
RYOGA?
WUK
WHAT'RE YOU DOING?!
TOMP TOMP TOMP
KRRR KRRR KRRR
AT LEAST NOW I UNDERSTAND HOW SERIOUS RYOGA'S FEELINGS ARE...
BOO HOO HOO HOO
GIVES ME THE *CREEPS*.
IT ALL MAKES SENSE... IT *WASN'T* AKANE THAT HE LIKED!

Part 11

ONE-PUNCH

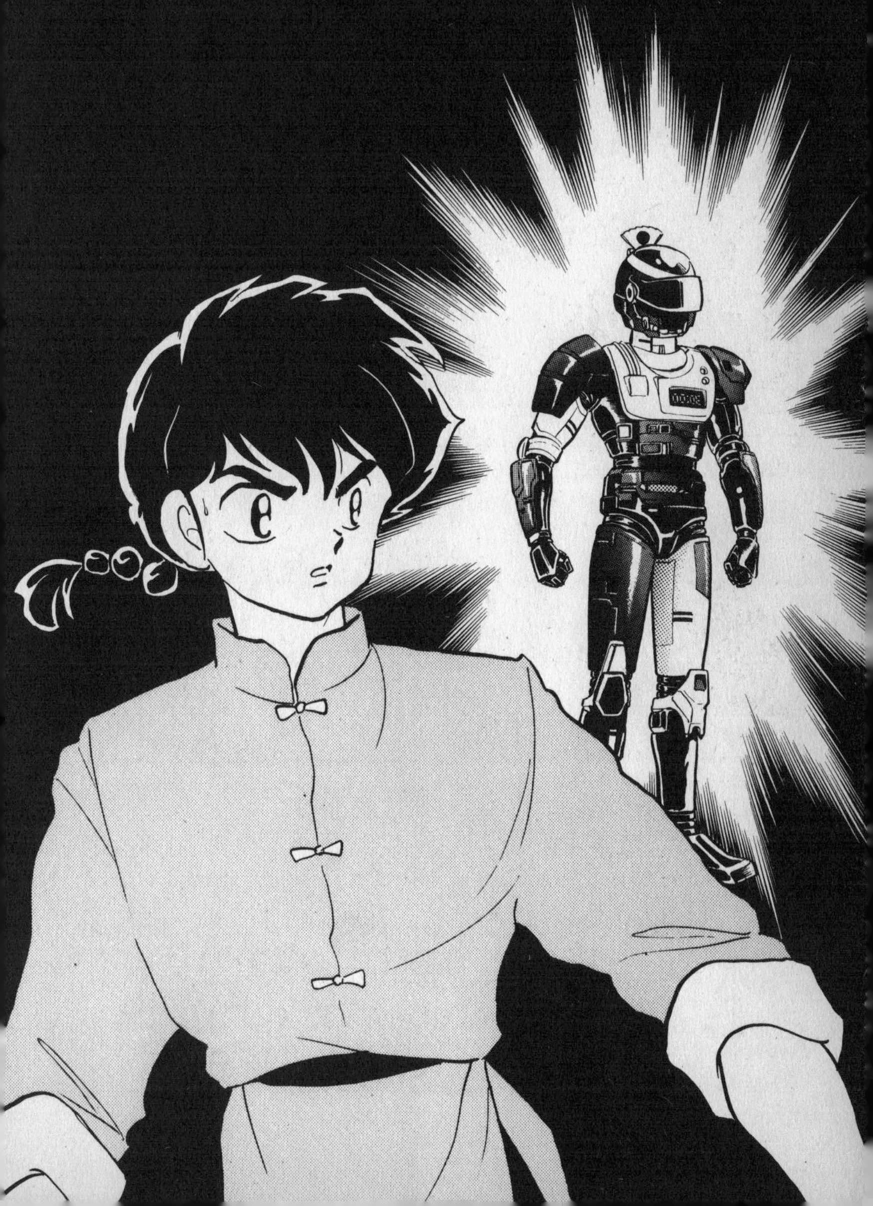

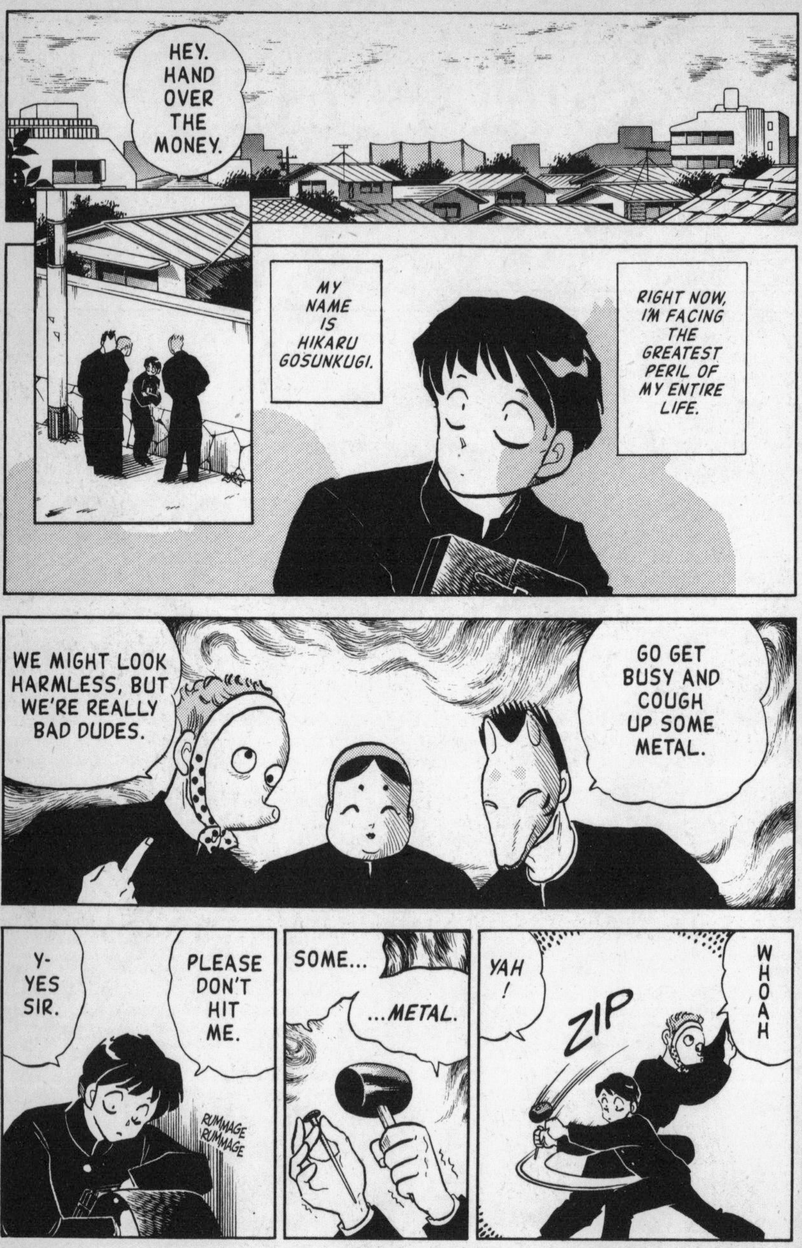
HEY. HAND OVER THE MONEY.
MY NAME IS HIKARU GOSUNKUGI.
RIGHT NOW, I'M FACING THE GREATEST PERIL OF MY ENTIRE LIFE.
WE MIGHT LOOK HARMLESS, BUT WE'RE REALLY BAD DUDES.
GO GET BUSY AND COUGH UP SOME METAL.
Y-YES SIR.
PLEASE DON'T HIT ME.
RUMMAGE RUMMAGE
SOME...
...METAL.
YAH!
ZIP
WHOAH

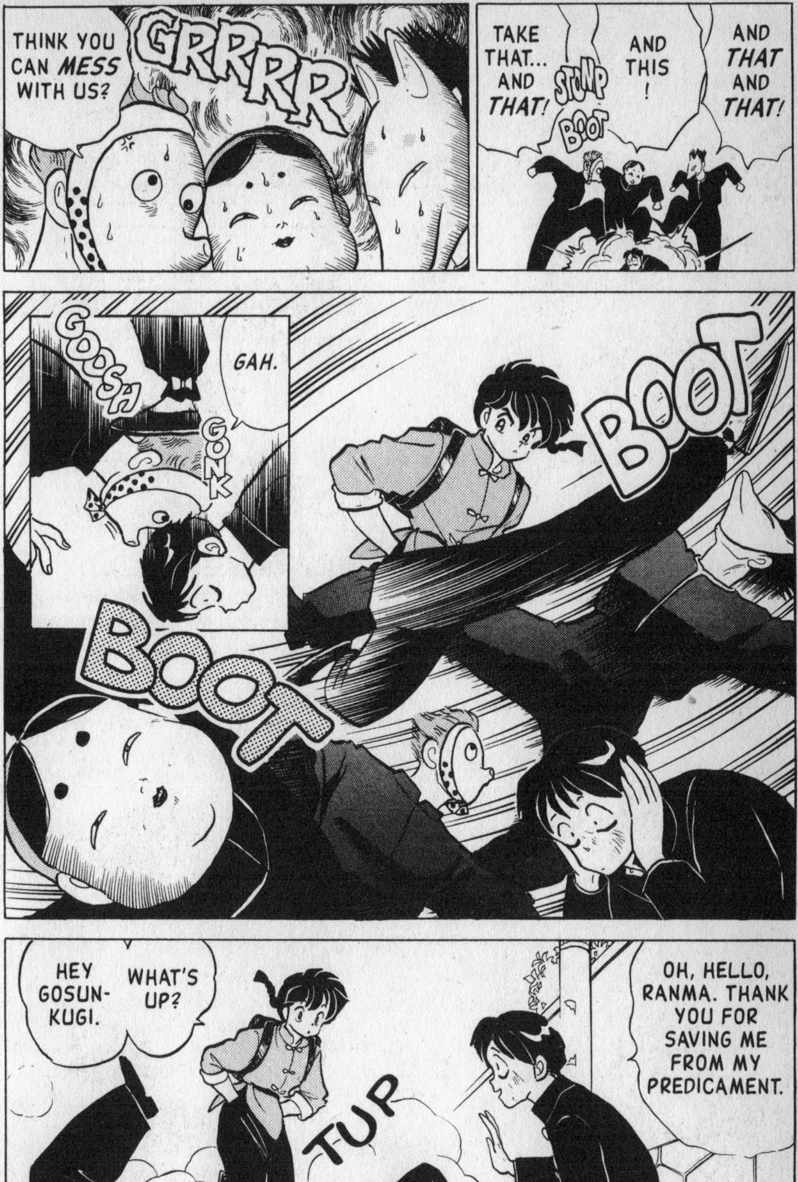
THINK YOU CAN *MESS* WITH US?
GRRRR
TAKE THAT... AND *THAT!*
STOMP
BOOT
AND THIS!
AND *THAT* AND *THAT!*
GOOSH
GAH.
GONK
BOOT
BOOT
HEY GOSUNKUGI.
WHAT'S UP?
TUP
OH, HELLO, RANMA. THANK YOU FOR SAVING ME FROM MY PREDICAMENT.

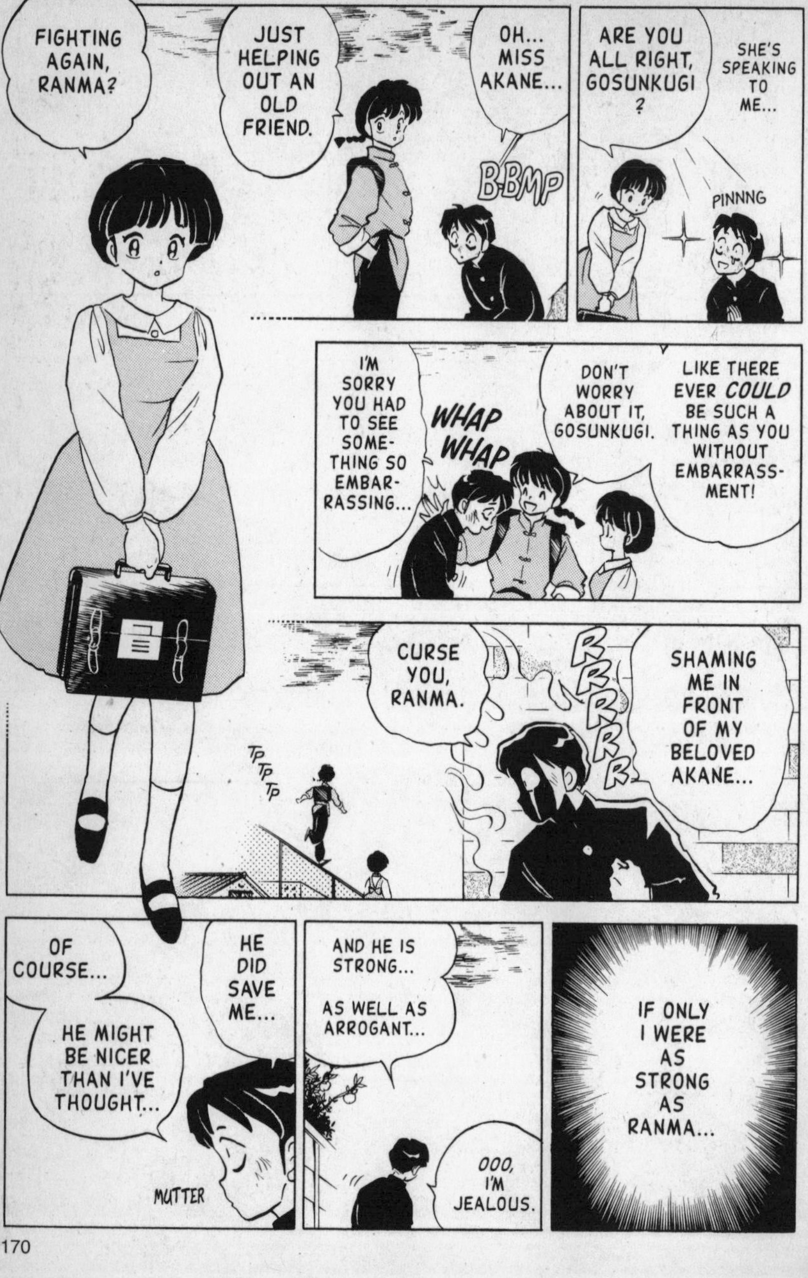

FIGHTING AGAIN, RANMA?
JUST HELPING OUT AN OLD FRIEND.
OH... MISS AKANE...
B-BMP
ARE YOU ALL RIGHT, GOSUNKUGI?
SHE'S SPEAKING TO ME...
PINNNG
I'M SORRY YOU HAD TO SEE SOME-THING SO EMBAR-RASSING...
WHAP WHAP
DON'T WORRY ABOUT IT, GOSUNKUGI.
LIKE THERE EVER *COULD* BE SUCH A THING AS YOU WITHOUT EMBARRASS-MENT!
TPTPTP
CURSE YOU, RANMA.
RRRRR
SHAMING ME IN FRONT OF MY BELOVED AKANE...
OF COURSE...
HE MIGHT BE NICER THAN I'VE THOUGHT...
HE DID SAVE ME...
MUTTER
AND HE IS STRONG...
AS WELL AS ARROGANT...
OOO, I'M JEALOUS.
IF ONLY I WERE AS STRONG AS RANMA...

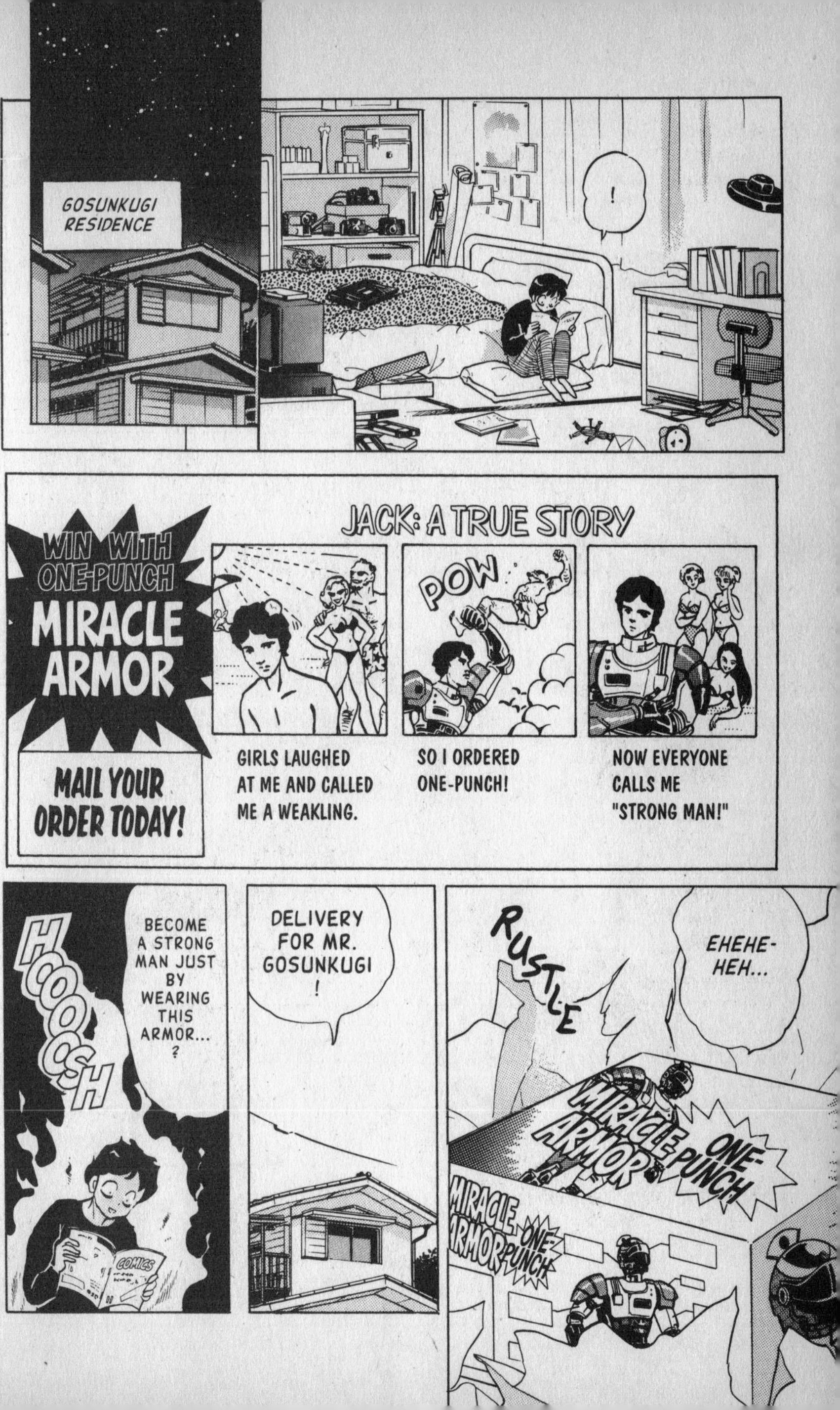
GOSUNKUGI RESIDENCE
!
JACK: A TRUE STORY
WIN WITH ONE-PUNCH
MIRACLE ARMOR
MAIL YOUR ORDER TODAY!
GIRLS LAUGHED AT ME AND CALLED ME A WEAKLING.
POW
SO I ORDERED ONE-PUNCH!
NOW EVERYONE CALLS ME "STRONG MAN!"
HOOOSH
BECOME A STRONG MAN JUST BY WEARING THIS ARMOR...?
COMICS
DELIVERY FOR MR. GOSUNKUGI!
RUSTLE
EHEHE-HEH...
MIRACLE ARMOR
ONE-PUNCH
MIRACLE ARMOR
ONE-PUNCH

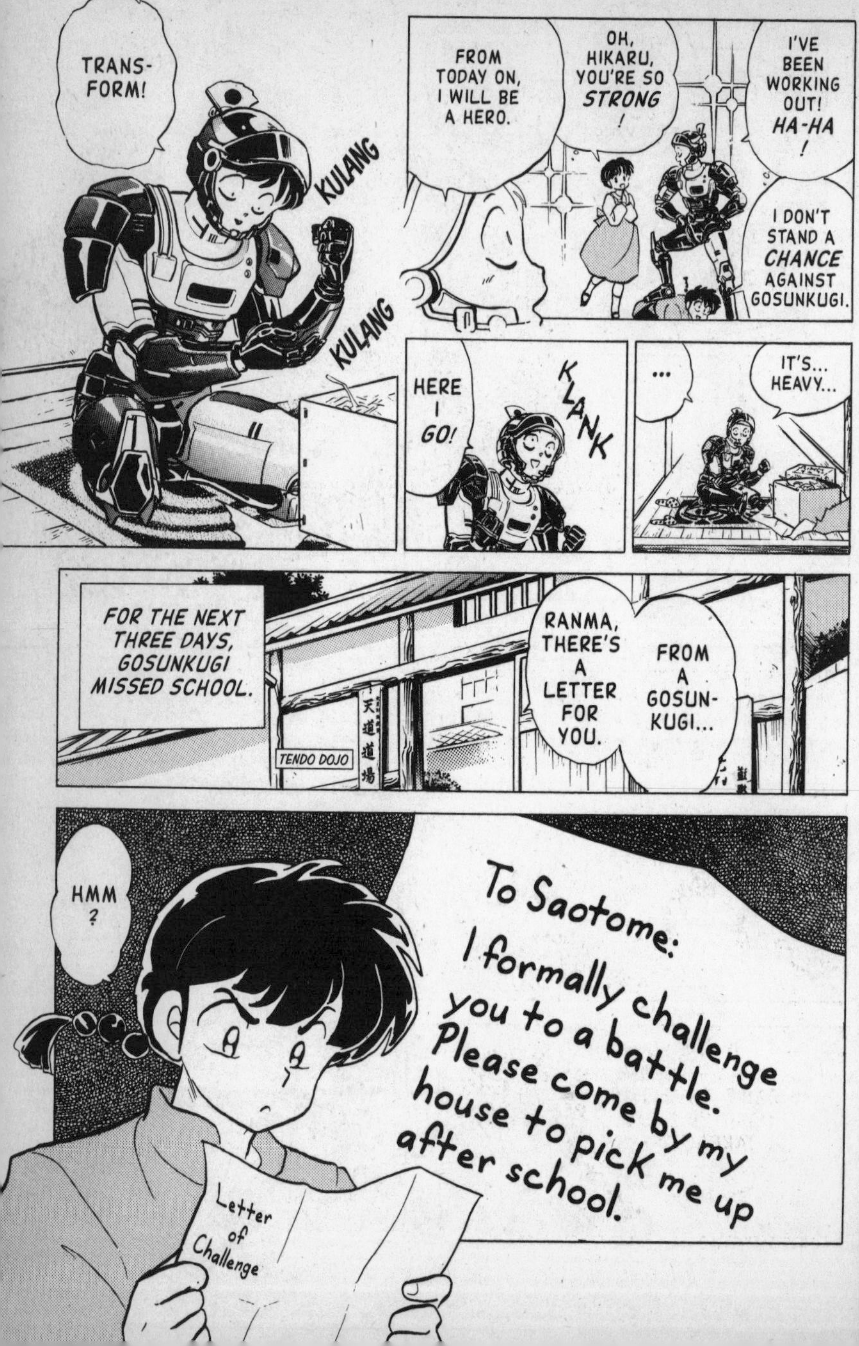
TRANS-FORM!
KULANG
KULANG
FROM TODAY ON, I WILL BE A HERO.
OH, HIKARU, YOU'RE SO STRONG!
I'VE BEEN WORKING OUT! HA-HA!
I DON'T STAND A CHANCE AGAINST GOSUNKUGI.
HERE I GO!
KLANK
...
IT'S... HEAVY...
FOR THE NEXT THREE DAYS, GOSUNKUGI MISSED SCHOOL.
TENDO DOJO
RANMA, THERE'S A LETTER FOR YOU.
FROM A GOSUN-KUGI...
HMM?
To Saotome:
I formally challenge you to a battle.
Please come by my house to pick me up after school.
Letter of Challenge

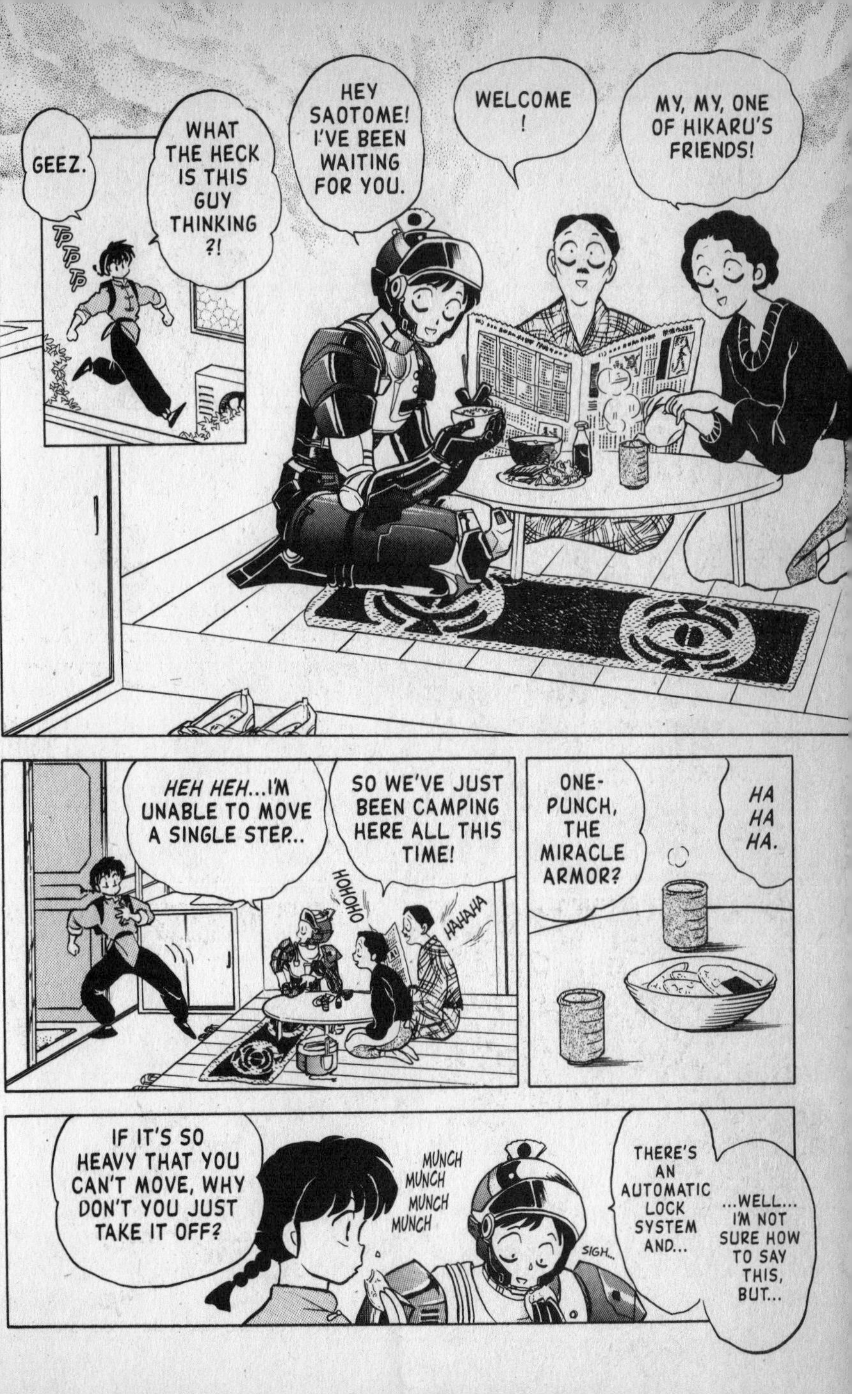
GEEZ.
TP TP TP
WHAT THE HECK IS THIS GUY THINKING?!
HEY SAOTOME! I'VE BEEN WAITING FOR YOU.
WELCOME!
MY, MY, ONE OF HIKARU'S FRIENDS!
HEH HEH...I'M UNABLE TO MOVE A SINGLE STEP...
SO WE'VE JUST BEEN CAMPING HERE ALL THIS TIME!
HOHOHO
HAHAHA
ONE-PUNCH, THE MIRACLE ARMOR?
HA HA HA.
IF IT'S SO HEAVY THAT YOU CAN'T MOVE, WHY DON'T YOU JUST TAKE IT OFF?
MUNCH MUNCH MUNCH MUNCH
SIGH...
THERE'S AN AUTOMATIC LOCK SYSTEM AND...
...WELL... I'M NOT SURE HOW TO SAY THIS, BUT...

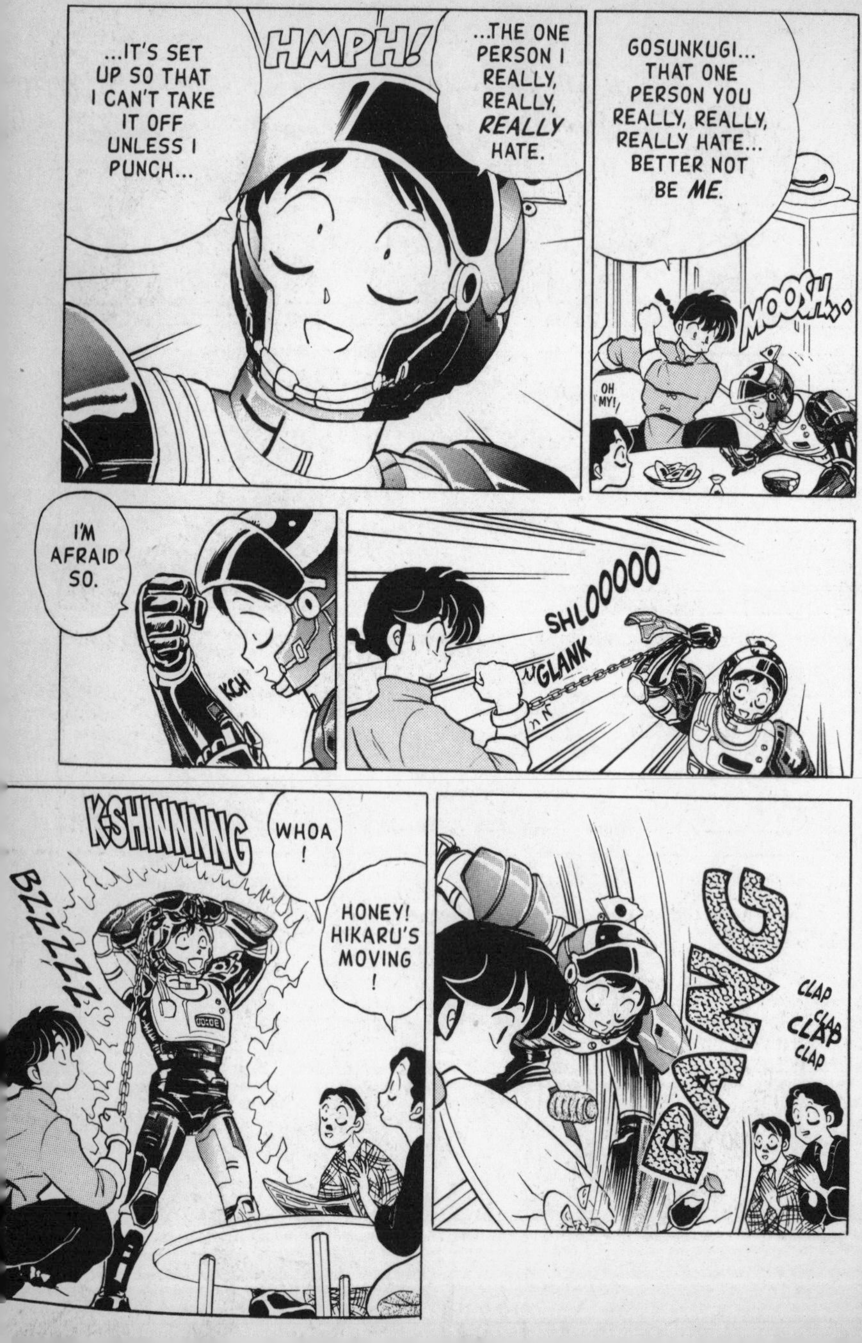
...IT'S SET UP SO THAT I CAN'T TAKE IT OFF UNLESS I PUNCH...
HMPH!
...THE ONE PERSON I REALLY, REALLY, REALLY HATE.
GOSUNKUGI... THAT ONE PERSON YOU REALLY, REALLY, REALLY HATE... BETTER NOT BE ME.
MOOSH...
OH MY!
I'M AFRAID SO.
KCH
SHLOOOOO
GLANK
K-SHINNNNG
WHOA!
BZZZZZ
HONEY! HIKARU'S MOVING!
BANG
CLAP
CLAP
CLAP
CLAP

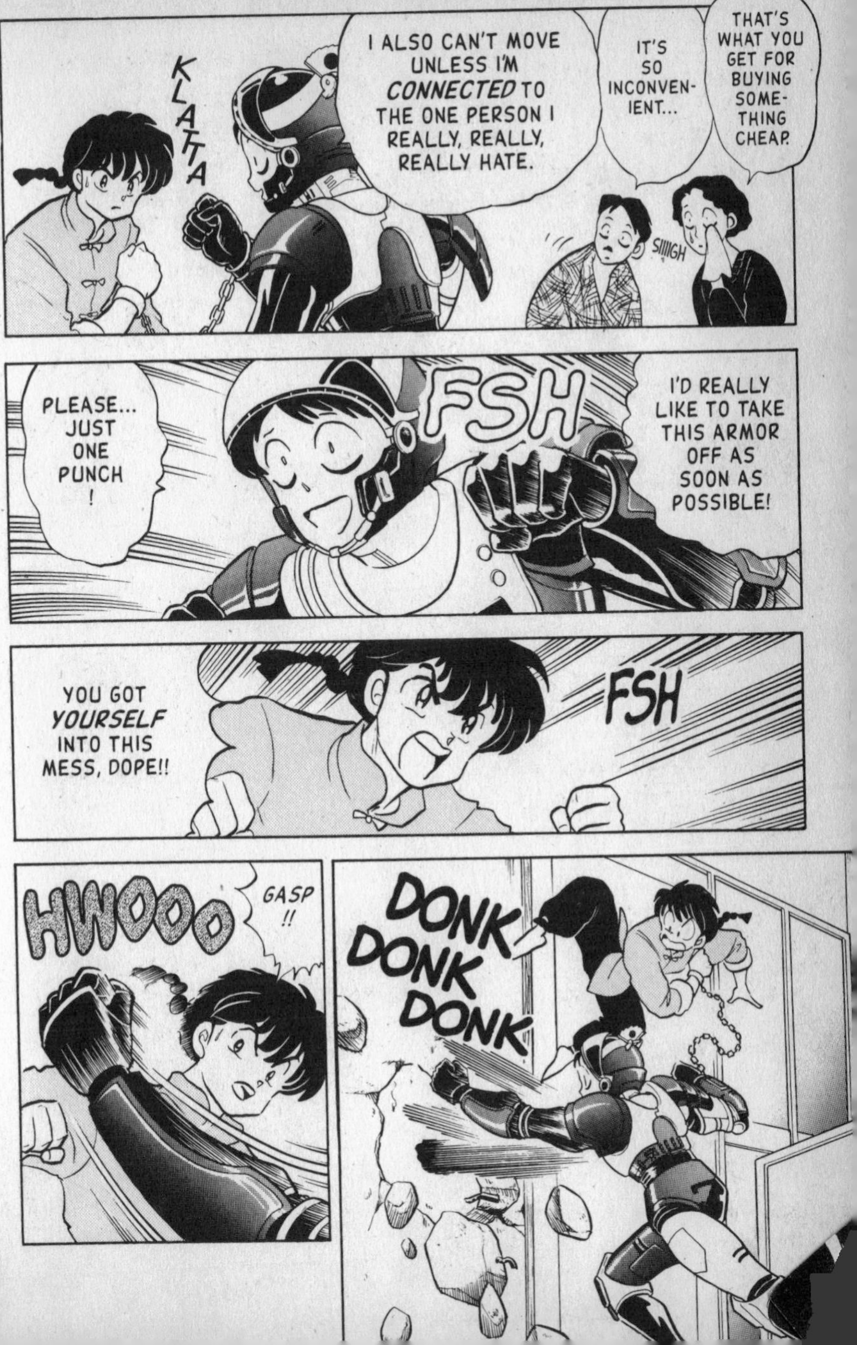
KLATTA
I ALSO CAN'T MOVE UNLESS I'M CONNECTED TO THE ONE PERSON I REALLY, REALLY, REALLY HATE.
IT'S SO INCONVENIENT...
THAT'S WHAT YOU GET FOR BUYING SOMETHING CHEAP.
SIIIGH
PLEASE... JUST ONE PUNCH!
FSH
I'D REALLY LIKE TO TAKE THIS ARMOR OFF AS SOON AS POSSIBLE!
YOU GOT YOURSELF INTO THIS MESS, DOPE!!
FSH
HWOOO
GASP!!
DONK DONK DONK DONK

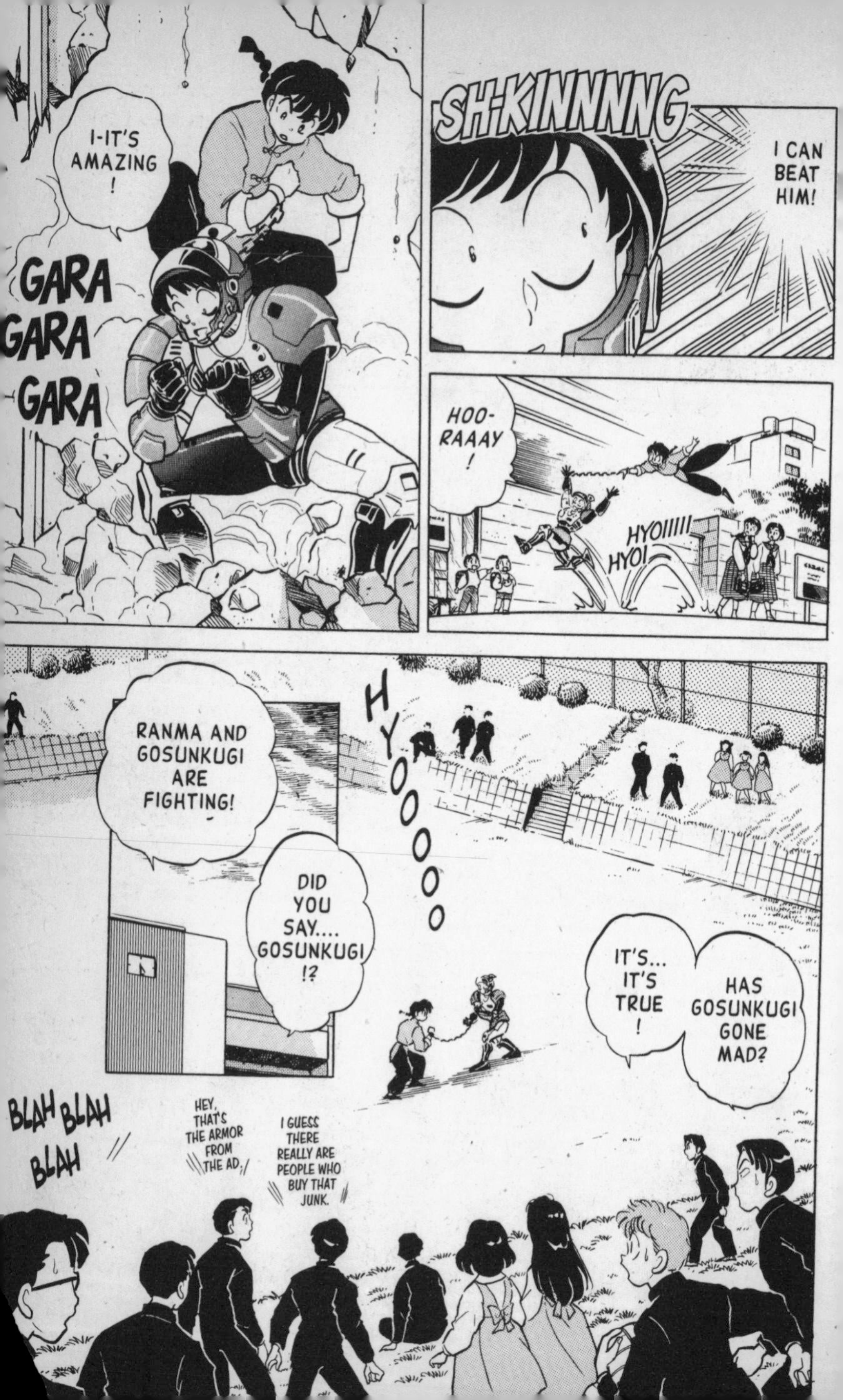
I-IT'S AMAZING!
GARA GARA GARA
SH-KINNNNG
I CAN BEAT HIM!
HOO-RAAAY!
HYOIIIII HYOI
RANMA AND GOSUNKUGI ARE FIGHTING!
DID YOU SAY.... GOSUNKUGI!?
HYOOOOOO
IT'S... IT'S TRUE!
HAS GOSUNKUGI GONE MAD?
BLAH BLAH BLAH
HEY, THAT'S THE ARMOR FROM THE AD.
I GUESS THERE REALLY ARE PEOPLE WHO BUY THAT JUNK.

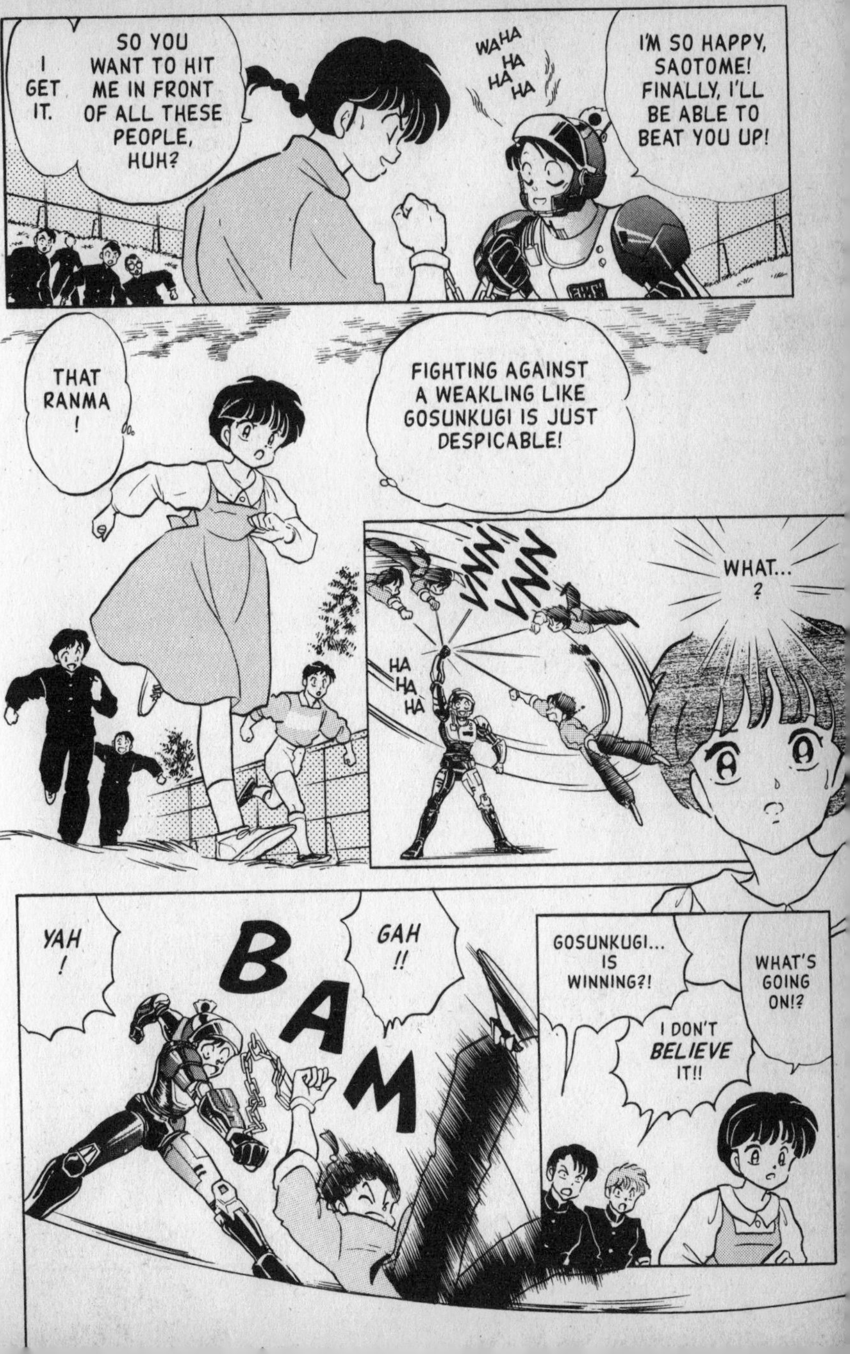
I GET IT.
SO YOU WANT TO HIT ME IN FRONT OF ALL THESE PEOPLE, HUH?
WAHA HA HA HA
I'M SO HAPPY, SAOTOME! FINALLY, I'LL BE ABLE TO BEAT YOU UP!
THAT RANMA!
FIGHTING AGAINST A WEAKLING LIKE GOSUNKUGI IS JUST DESPICABLE!
VNN VNN
HA HA HA
WHAT...?
YAH!
BAM
GAH!!
GOSUNKUGI... IS WINNING?!
WHAT'S GOING ON!?
I DON'T *BELIEVE* IT!!

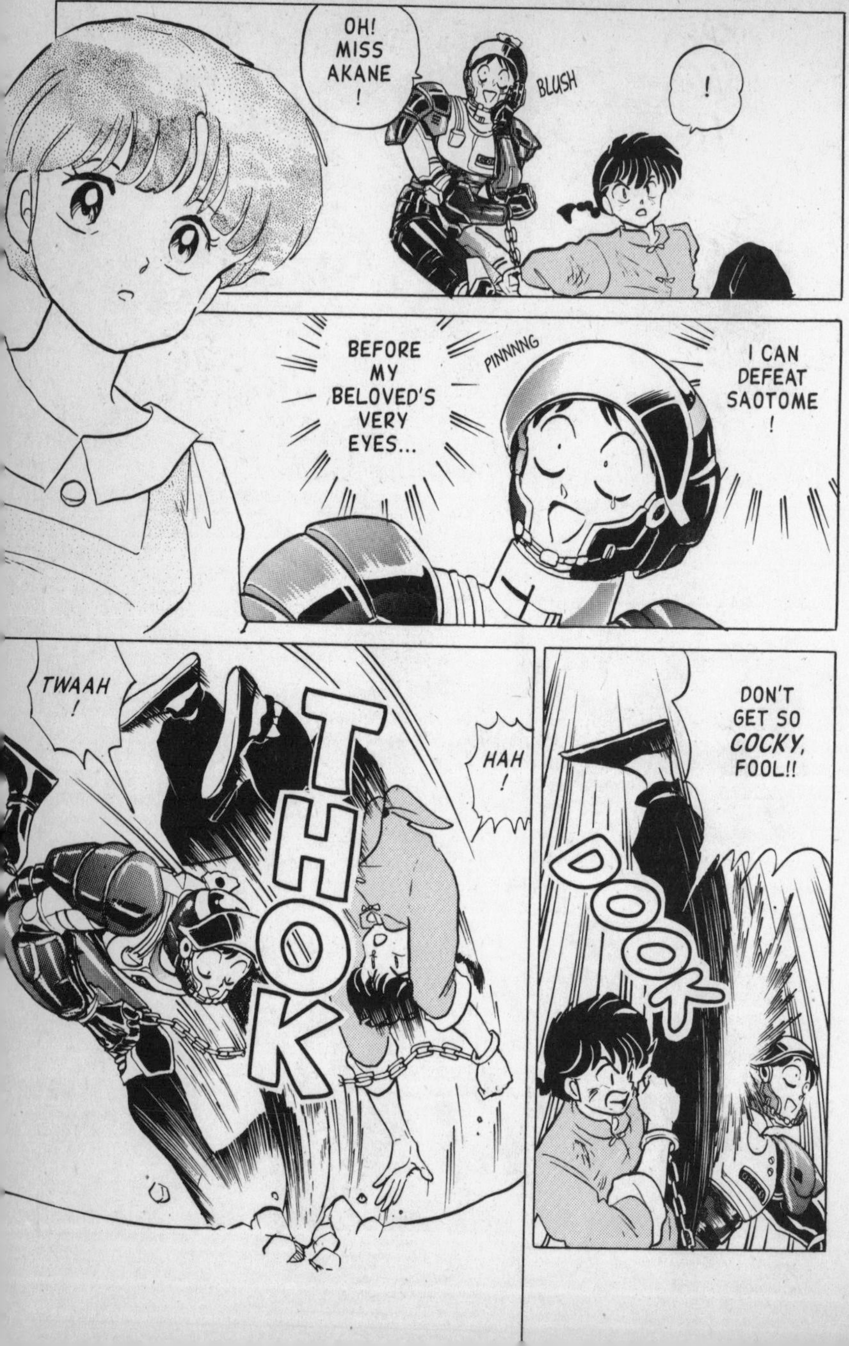
OH! MISS AKANE !
BLUSH
!
BEFORE MY BELOVED'S VERY EYES...
PINNNNG
I CAN DEFEAT SAOTOME !
TWAAH !
HAH !
THOK
DON'T GET SO COCKY, FOOL!!
DOOK

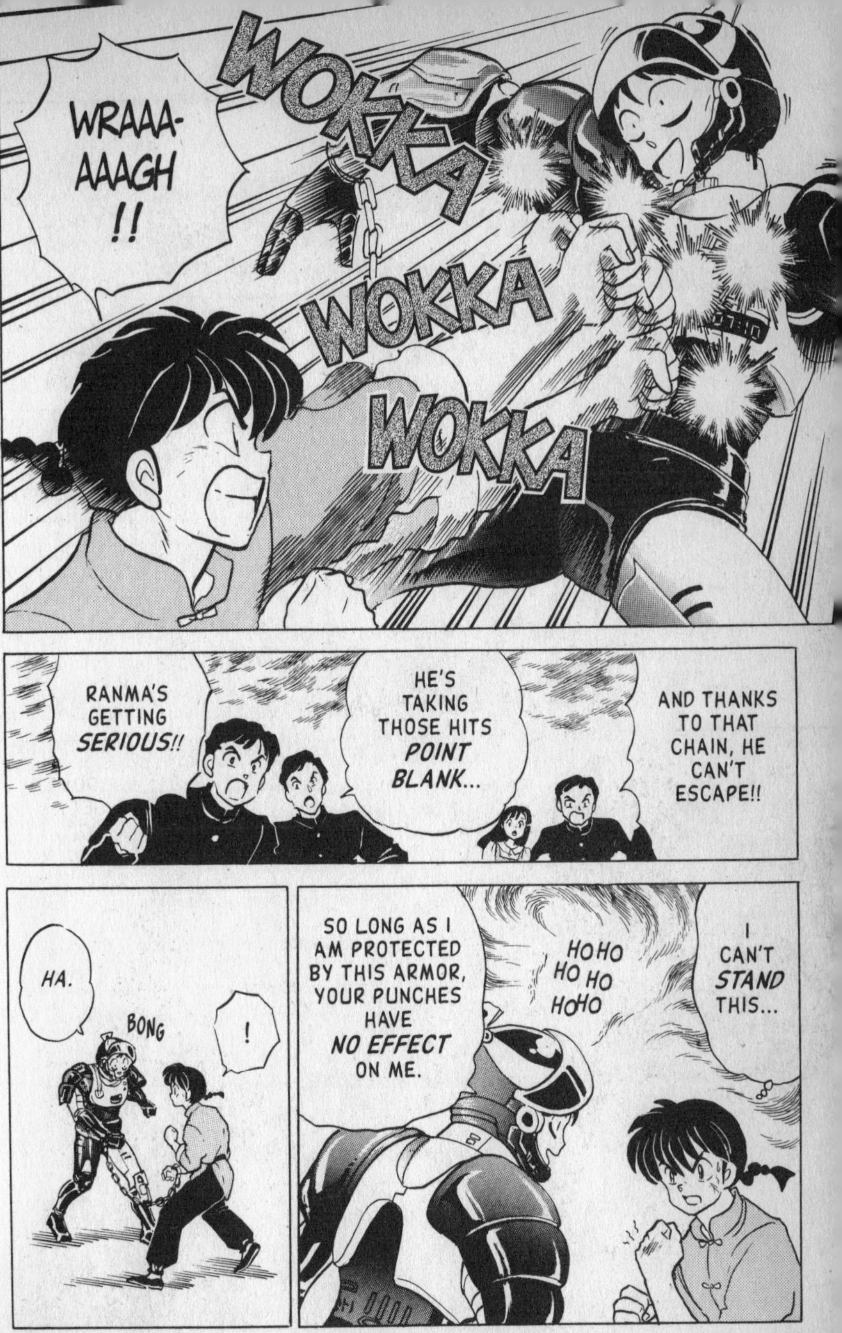
WRAAA-AAAGH!!
WOKKA
WOKKA
WOKKA
RANMA'S GETTING *SERIOUS*!!
HE'S TAKING THOSE HITS *POINT BLANK*...
AND THANKS TO THAT CHAIN, HE CAN'T ESCAPE!!
HA.
BONG
!
SO LONG AS I AM PROTECTED BY THIS ARMOR, YOUR PUNCHES HAVE *NO EFFECT* ON ME.
HOHO HO HO HOHO
I CAN'T *STAND* THIS...

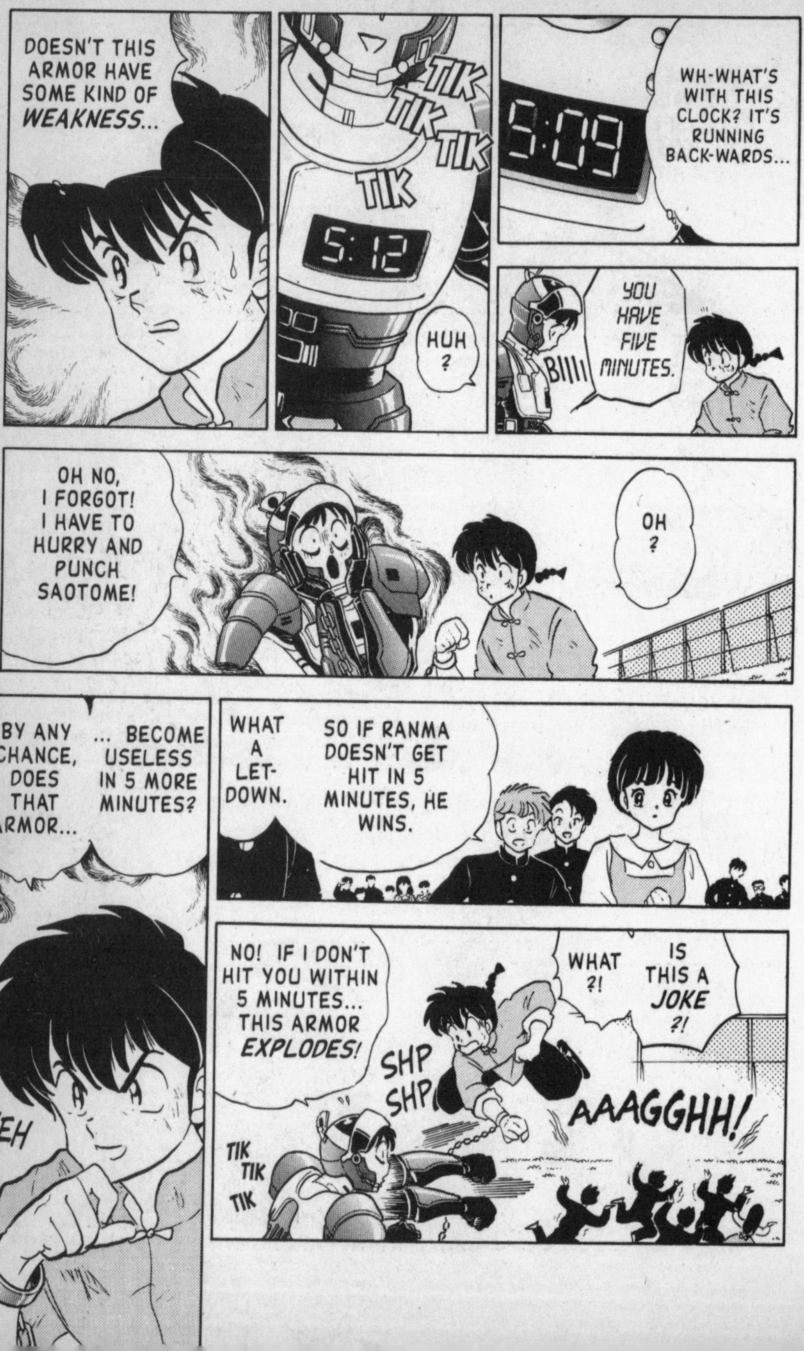
DOESN'T THIS ARMOR HAVE SOME KIND OF WEAKNESS...
TIK TIK TIK TIK
5:12
HUH ?
5:09
WH-WHAT'S WITH THIS CLOCK? IT'S RUNNING BACK-WARDS...
BIII
YOU HAVE FIVE MINUTES.
OH NO, I FORGOT! I HAVE TO HURRY AND PUNCH SAOTOME!
OH ?
BY ANY CHANCE, DOES THAT ARMOR...
... BECOME USELESS IN 5 MORE MINUTES?
WHAT A LET-DOWN.
SO IF RANMA DOESN'T GET HIT IN 5 MINUTES, HE WINS.
HEH
NO! IF I DON'T HIT YOU WITHIN 5 MINUTES... THIS ARMOR EXPLODES!
WHAT ?!
IS THIS A JOKE ?!
SHP SHP
AAAGGHH!
TIK TIK TIK

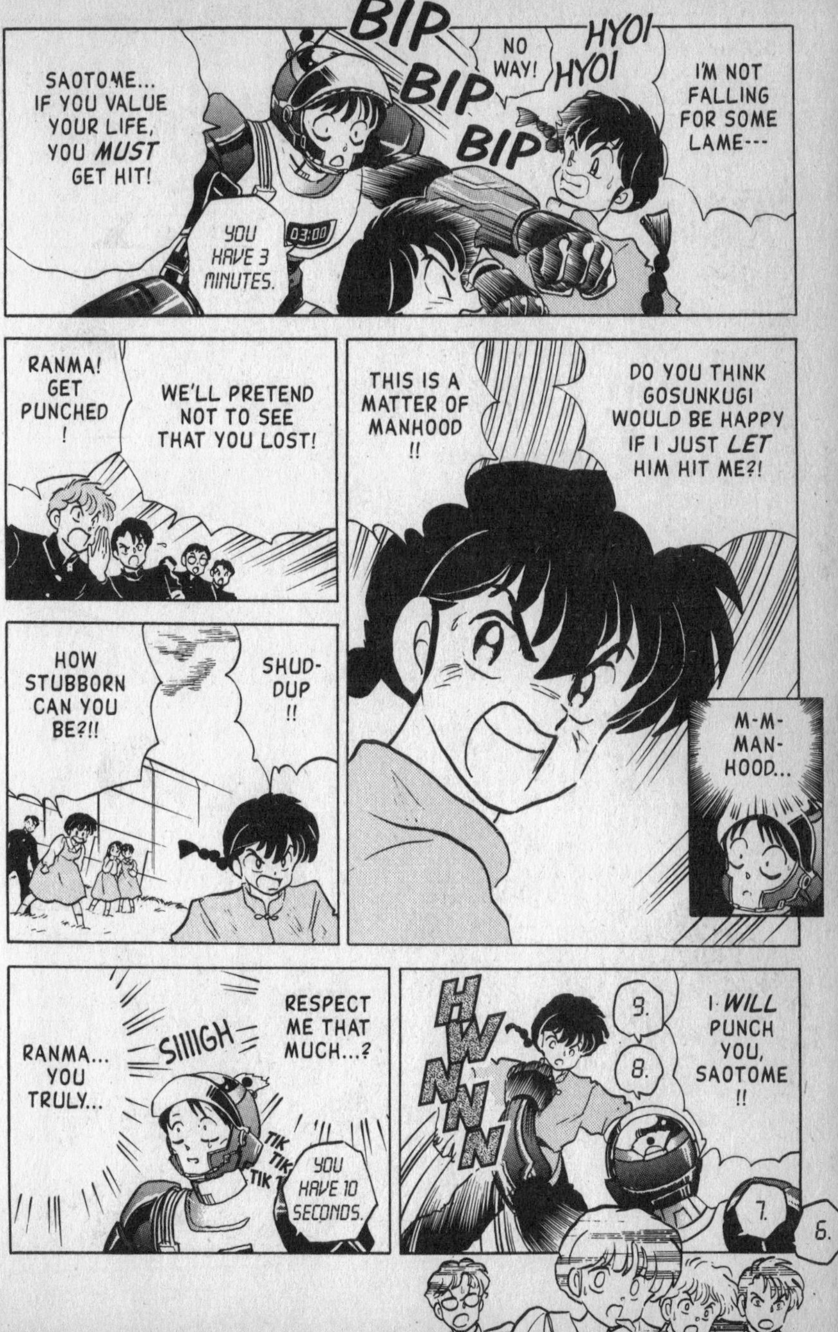
BIP BIP BIP
SAOTOME... IF YOU VALUE YOUR LIFE, YOU MUST GET HIT!
YOU HAVE 3 MINUTES.
03:00
NO WAY!
HYOI HYOI
I'M NOT FALLING FOR SOME LAME---
RANMA! GET PUNCHED!
WE'LL PRETEND NOT TO SEE THAT YOU LOST!
HOW STUBBORN CAN YOU BE?!!
SHUD-DUP!!
THIS IS A MATTER OF MANHOOD!!
DO YOU THINK GOSUNKUGI WOULD BE HAPPY IF I JUST LET HIM HIT ME?!
M-M-MAN-HOOD...
RANMA... YOU TRULY...
SIIIIGH
RESPECT ME THAT MUCH...?
TIK TIK TIK
YOU HAVE 10 SECONDS.
HWNNN
9.
8.
I WILL PUNCH YOU, SAOTOME!!
7.
6.

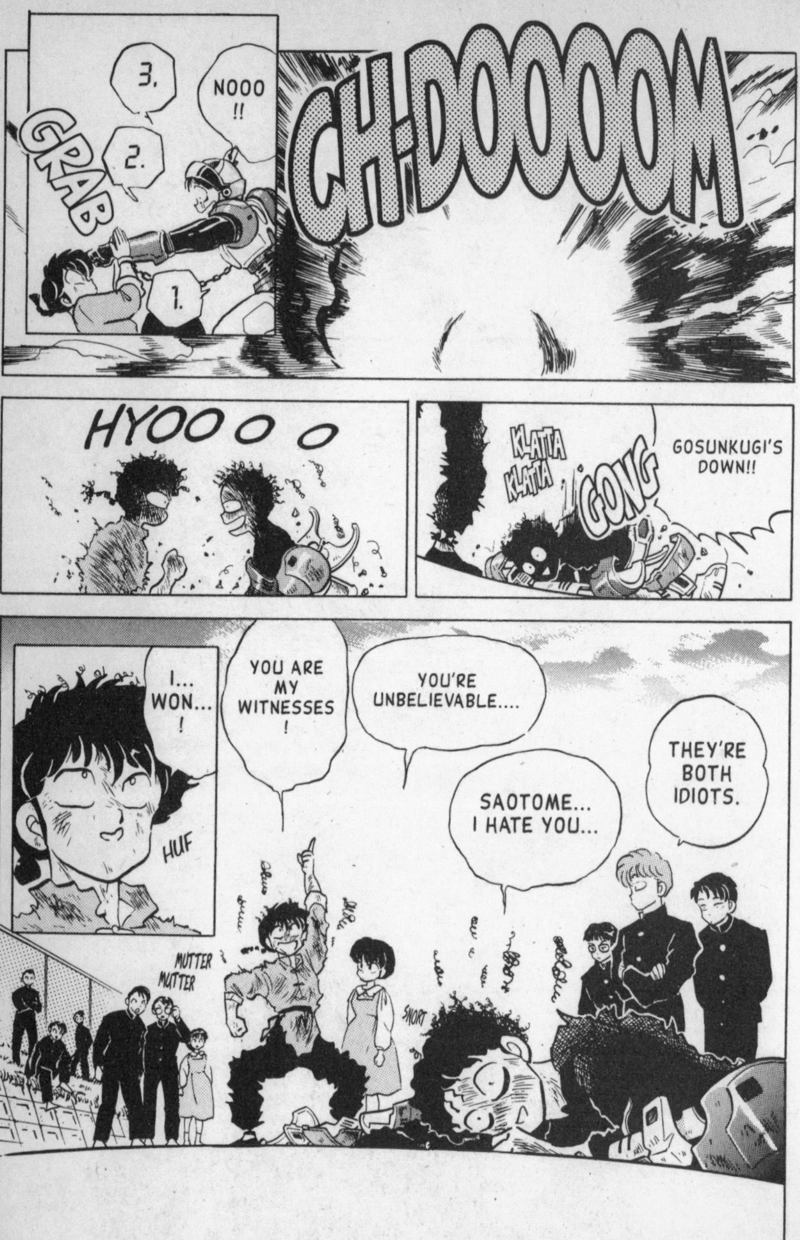
3.
NOOO !!
GRAB
2.
1.
CH-DOOOOOM
HYOO O O
KLATTA KLATTA
GONG
GOSUNKUGI'S DOWN!!
I... WON... !
HUF
YOU ARE MY WITNESSES !
YOU'RE UNBELIEVABLE....
SAOTOME... I HATE YOU...
THEY'RE BOTH IDIOTS.
MUTTER MUTTER
SNORT

About Rumiko Takahashi

Born in 1957 in Niigata, Japan, Rumiko Takahashi attended women's college in Tokyo, where she began studying comics with Kazuo Koike, author of CRYING FREEMAN. She later became an assistant to horror-manga artist Kazuo Umezu (OROCHI). In 1978, she won a prize in Shogakukan's annual "New Comic Artist Contest," and in that same year her boy-meets-alien comedy series URUSEI YATSURA began appearing in the weekly manga magazine SHÔNEN SUNDAY. This phenomenally successful series ran for nine years and sold over 22 million copies. Takahashi's later RANMA 1/2 series enjoyed even greater popularity.

Takahashi is considered by many to be one of the world's most popular manga artists. With the publication of Volume 34 of her RANMA 1/2 series in Japan, Takahashi's total sales passed one hundred million copies of her compiled works.

Takahashi's serial titles include URUSEI YATSURA, RANMA 1/2, ONE-POUND GOSPEL, MAISON IKKOKU and INUYASHA. Additionally, Takahashi has drawn many short stories which have been published in America under the title "Rumic Theater," and several install-ments of a saga known as her "Mermaid" series. Most of Takahashi's major stories have also been animated and are widely available in translation worldwide. INUYASHA is her most recent serial story, first published in SHÔNEN SUNDAY in 1996.

EDITOR'S RECOMMENDATIONS

If you enjoyed this volume of Ranma 1/2, then here is some more manga you might be interested in:

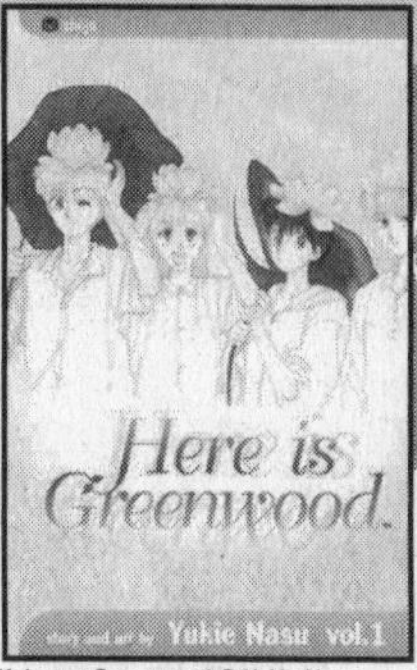

Here is Greenwood
story and art by Yukie Nasu vol.1

Koko wa Greenwood © Yukie Nasu
1986/HAKUSENSHA, Inc.

HERE IS GREENWOOD

Perhaps written for a slightly older audience than most of Rumiko Takahashi's work, Yukie Nasu's ***Here is Greenwood*** is exactly like ***Ranma 1/2***, except for the martial arts (none), the wacky hijinks (almost none), and the occasional depiction of the adult relationships among its students. Okay, aside from the fact that they both have male high school students in them, they have nothing in common. But they're both cool!

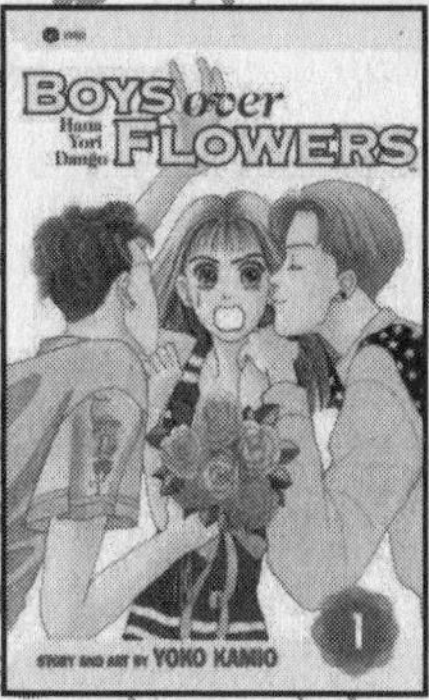

BOYS over FLOWERS
Hana Yori Dango
1
STORY AND ART BY YOKO KAMIO

HANA-YORI DANGO
© 1992 by Yoko Kamio/SHUEISHA Inc.

BOYS OVER FLOWERS (HANA YORI DANGO)

Another tale of high school life in Japan, ***Boys Over Flowers*** (or "HanaDan" to most of its fans) is not without its serious side, but overall tends to fall into the "rabu-kome" or "love-comedy" genre.

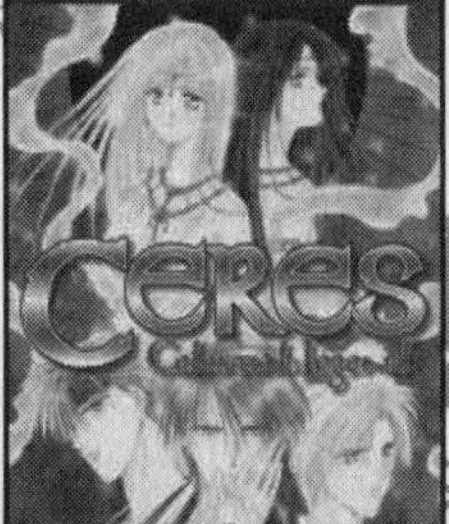

Ceres
story and art by YU WATASE
Vol. 1

© 1997 Yuu WATASE/Shogakukan Inc.

CERES: CELESTIAL LEGEND

Aya Mikage is a trendy Tokyo teen with not much else on her mind but fashion, karaoke, and boys. But a terrible family secret involving an ancient family "curse" is about to make things a lot more difficult.

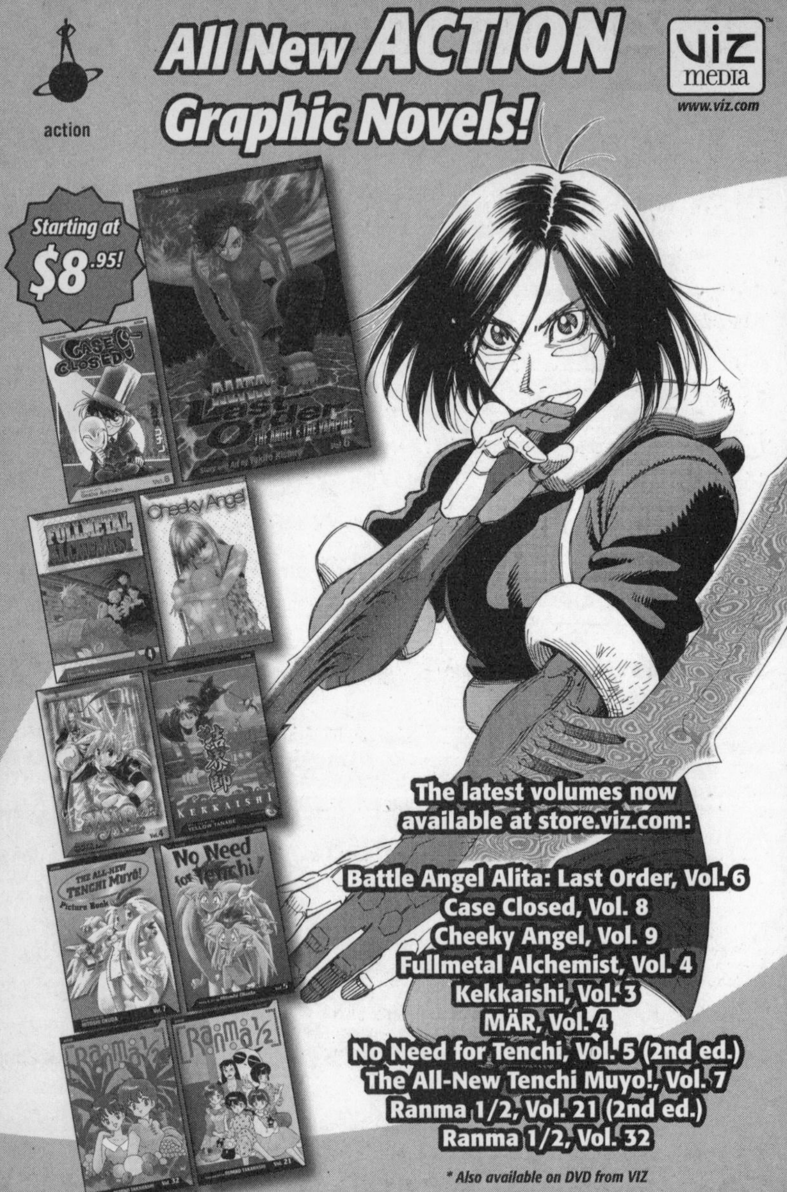
action
All New ACTION Graphic Novels!
VIZ media
www.viz.com
Starting at $8.95!
The latest volumes now available at store.viz.com:
Battle Angel Alita: Last Order, Vol. 6
Case Closed, Vol. 8
Cheeky Angel, Vol. 9
Fullmetal Alchemist, Vol. 4
Kekkaishi, Vol. 3
MÄR, Vol. 4
No Need for Tenchi, Vol. 5 (2nd ed.)
The All-New Tenchi Muyo!, Vol. 7
Ranma 1/2, Vol. 21 (2nd ed.)
Ranma 1/2, Vol. 32
* Also available on DVD from VIZ

LOVE MANGA? LET US KNOW!

☐ Please do NOT send me information about VIZ Media products, news and events, special offers, or other information.

☐ Please do NOT send me information from VIZ Media's trusted business partners.

Name: _____

Address: _____

City: _____ **State:** _____ **Zip:** _____

E-mail: _____

☐ **Male** ☐ **Female** **Date of Birth** (mm/dd/yyyy): ___/___/_____ (Under 13? Parental consent required)

What race/ethnicity do you consider yourself? (check all that apply)

☐ White/Caucasian ☐ Black/African American ☐ Hispanic/Latino

☐ Asian/Pacific Islander ☐ Native American/Alaskan Native ☐ Other: _____

What VIZ Media title(s) did you purchase? (indicate title(s) purchased) _____

_____

What other VIZ Media titles do you own? _____

_____

Reason for purchase: (check all that apply).

☐ Special offer ☐ Favorite title / author / artist / genre

☐ Gift ☐ Recommendation ☐ Collection

☐ Read excerpt in VIZ Media manga sampler ☐ Other _____

Where did you make your purchase? (please check one)

☐ Comic store ☐ Bookstore ☐ Grocery Store

☐ Convention ☐ Newsstand ☐ Video Game Store

☐ Online (site:_____) ☐ Other _____

How many manga titles have you purchased in the last year? How many were VIZ Media titles?
(please check one from each column)

MANGA
☐ None
☐ 1 – 4
☐ 5 – 10
☐ 11+

VIZ Media
☐ None
☐ 1 – 4
☐ 5 – 10
☐ 11+

How much influence do special promotions and gifts-with-purchase have on the titles you buy?
(please circle, with 5 being great influence and 1 being none)

1   2   3   4   5

Do you purchase every volume of your favorite series?
☐ Yes! Gotta have 'em as my own   ☐ No. Please explain: _____

What kind of manga storylines do you most enjoy? (check all that apply)

☐ Action / Adventure   ☐ Science Fiction   ☐ Horror
☐ Comedy   ☐ Romance (shojo)   ☐ Fantasy (shojo)
☐ Fighting   ☐ Sports   ☐ Historical
☐ Artistic / Alternative   ☐ Other _____

If you watch the anime or play a video or TCG game from a series, how likely are you to buy the manga? (please circle, with 5 being very likely and 1 being unlikely)

1   2   3   4   5

If unlikely, please explain: _____

Who are your favorite authors / artists? _____

_____

What titles would like you translated and sold in English? _____

_____

THANK YOU! Please send the completed form to:

NJW Research
42 Catharine Street
Poughkeepsie, NY 12601